Health Microinsurance

Implementing Universal Health Coverage in the Informal Sector

World Scientific Series in Health Investment and Financing

ISSN: 2591-7315

Series Editor: Alexander S. Preker *(Columbia University, USA and Health Investment & Financing Corp, USA)*

Most western developed countries offer universal access to healthcare through mechanisms that provide financial protection against its high cost, either through insurance or government subsidy programs.

In most middle- and low-income countries, financing is often at the center of reforms in the healthcare sector. Success or failure of these reforms can have major impact on the political survival of governments that get involved, and major implications for the dynamics of the healthcare industry and overall economy.

With this series, World Scientific will contribute knowledge about a policy area which is still poorly-understood. The series merges policy and practice, exploring the economic underpinnings of real trends in health investment and financing.

The series will appeal and be accessible to investors, the health insurance industry, healthcare actuaries, business schools with healthcare tracts, healthcare management programs, researchers, graduate students, policy makers and practitioners working in the health sector worldwide.

Vol. 4 *Health Microinsurance: Implementing Universal Health Coverage in the Informal Sector*
by David M. Dror

Vol. 3 *Financing the Education of Health Workers: Gaining A Competitive Edge*
by Alexander S. Preker, Hortenzia Beciu and Eric L. Keuffel

Vol. 2 *Financing Micro Health Insurance: Theory, Methods and Evidence*
by David M. Dror

Vol. 1 *Financing Universal Access to Healthcare: A Comparative Review of Landmark Legislative Health Reforms in the OECD*
by Alexander S. Preker

Forthcoming

Financing Universal Access to Healthcare: A Comparative Review of Incremental Health Insurance Reforms in the OECD
Alexander S. Preker

Capital Finance in the Health Industry: A User Manual for Investors and Companies
Alexander S. Preker and Les Funtleyder

Handbook on Health System Financing and Organization
Dov Chernichovsky

World Scientific Series in Health Investment and Financing – Vol. 4

Health Microinsurance

Implementing Universal Health Coverage in the Informal Sector

David M. Dror
Micro Insurance Academy, India

World Scientific

NEW JERSEY • LONDON • SINGAPORE • BEIJING • SHANGHAI • HONG KONG • TAIPEI • CHENNAI • TOKYO

Published by

World Scientific Publishing Co. Pte. Ltd.
5 Toh Tuck Link, Singapore 596224
USA office: 27 Warren Street, Suite 401-402, Hackensack, NJ 07601
UK office: 57 Shelton Street, Covent Garden, London WC2H 9HE

Library of Congress Cataloging-in-Publication Data
Names: Dror, David M., author.
Title: Health microinsurance : implementing universal health coverage in the informal sector / David M. Dror.
Other titles: World Scientific series in health investment and financing ; v. 4. 2591-7315
Description: New Jersey : World Scientific, [2020] | Series: World scientific series in health investment and financing, 2591-7315 ; vol 4 | Includes bibliographical references.
Identifiers: LCCN 2019047674 | ISBN 9789811208522
Subjects: MESH: Universal Health Insurance--organization & administration | Poverty | Informal Sector | Rural Population | Health Education
Classification: LCC RA412.3 | NLM W 100 | DDC 368.38/2--dc23
LC record available at https://lccn.loc.gov/2019047674

British Library Cataloguing-in-Publication Data
A catalogue record for this book is available from the British Library.

For any available supplementary material, please visit
https://www.worldscientific.com/worldscibooks/10.1142/11505#t=suppl

Desk Editors: Herbert Moses/Shreya Gopi

Typeset by Stallion Press
Email: enquiries@stallionpress.com

Foreword

Life is not easy for any of us. But what of that? We must have perseverance and above all, confidence in ourselves. We must believe that we are gifted for something and that this thing must be attained.

— Marie Curie

The world health leaders set a course toward universal healthcare for all through the Alma Ata Declaration in 1978, which called on governments to meet the needs of the populace. The WHO definition of health includes complete physical, mental, and social well-being. This visionary "everything to everyone" approach was quickly revisited by a group in Bellagio in 1979 to focus on selective health. However, how can a government achieve even a partial set of services to all when health spending is less than 4% of the gross domestic product, as is the case in most low-income countries? Thus, more than 40 years after Alma Ata we still struggle with workable answers to how the exchange of knowledge, the training, and mobilization of a health workforce, and the introduction of appropriate medications, technologies, and insurance systems — all part of healthcare — can be built on a shoestring? It is clear that more financial input is needed to fuel these efforts. In the open-ended interim, some 3 billion people lack healthcare coverage.

Dr. Dror and I met more than a decade ago while I was working on health systems and policy, based in Dhaka, Bangladesh. He was well established in his mission of building training and interventions from the Micro Insurance Academy in New Delhi.

In those early days in New Delhi over cups of tea, I perceived David as the guru on the mountain. A former ILO specialist, a practitioner with diplomatic rank, and a full professor, he left a typically comfortable scholarly life in Europe, to act on his insightful recognition that political support and more money, necessary as they are, might not be sufficient to deliver the desired results in the informal sector. In the substantial informal sector, argued David, the two leading strategies promoted by the West — mandating and subsidies — cannot be applied effectively, especially among those who have very little. Hence, he determined that communities in informal settings must be involved in the decision-making processes of what to cover and how much to pay for health insurance of the most impoverished families. To do so, they need "insurance education", the kind of awareness creation on the value of modern ways to help them understand health insurance that they never before practiced. They also need technical assistance to backstop their community's mutual aid in an environment where there is no supply of insurance and only very basic supply of health services.

David championed this approach, called "health microinsurance", to shed light on an area easily ignored by most mainstream development agencies. People at the base of the pyramid are not merely "the problem" but part of the solution when the health systems are people-centered, decentralized, and sensitive to the demand locally. He was committed to developing the business model and training to enable people in the informal sector to be not just involved in devising local solutions to health insurance needs but also to own those solutions, pay for them, and trust their system. David started the Micro Insurance Academy in New Delhi in 2007.

To be in his presence or hear his conversation, one could tell that David could not resist the call to translate his theories to action. He has been active mainly in India, where fewer than 15% of the people had any form of health insurance coverage at the time. He approached the task with infectious confidence and conviction and gave generously to those who were partners in like endeavors across South Asia and in the poorer regions of Africa.

The evolution of microinsurance is an incredible leap of faith, especially for those who may come from backgrounds that feature distrust of those collecting money only to disappear when the time comes to pay back from people's "rainy day" accounts. Trust-building is not a course taught in medical school, finance school, or public health school. Trust must be earned, and then it must be sustained. David Dror has walked the humble path of earning the trust of poor communities. He earns trust daily by walking the talk.

We worked together on a systematic review of factors affecting the uptake of community-based health insurance, which was funded by the Department for International Development (UKAID) because David knew that new methods had to be pioneered to understand the situation before jumping to proffering solutions. Later when I was based in faraway Jakarta, over Skype, I would plead with him to please take the time to write down the theories that drove him, the methods he applied in actions he was taking, and the results so that others could learn from him. Now David is writing these lessons for all of us, hoping that these insights can become more mainstream. The transition from top-down to bottom-up is still difficult for many to conceive and assimilate, especially those that have not done the kind of fieldwork that David has pioneered for many years. The Great Saint Mother Teresa, that other European immigrant who fulfilled her vocation serving the poorest in India, said, "We ourselves feel that what we are doing is just a drop in the ocean. However, the ocean would be less because of that missing drop."

May this book serve as the drop of knowledge that sends ripples to benefit all of humanity.

Tracey Pérez Koehlmoos, Ph.D., M.H.A.
Professor, F. Edward Hebert School of Medicine,
Uniformed Services, University of the Health Sciences,
Washington, DC
1 September 2019

About the Author

Dr. David M. Dror holds a Ph.D. (*summa cum laude*) from Université Claude Bernard Lyon 1, France and a D.B.A. degree (*magna cum laude*) in International Health Services. Dr. Dror has been Hon. Professor of health insurance at Erasmus University Rotterdam (2004–2014); Visiting Professor at CERDI/Université d'Auvergne, Clermont-Ferrand (2003–2010); and Associate Director of Research in Health Systems at Lyon-1 University/LASS, France (2002–2004). He established the *Micro Insurance Academy* (MIA) in New Delhi in 2007 and has been its Chairman ever since. Under his direction, MIA became the leading think tank on microinsurance and a significant provider of technical assistance toward implementation of microinsurance projects in the informal economy in many countries. MIA also provided insurance education and consultancy services in microinsurance. In 2010 and 2011, MIA received the "Educational Services Provider of the Year" award.

In 2009, the Asia Insurance Industry bestowed upon Prof. Dror the award of "Personality of the Year" for "groundbreaking research and study which has helped boost understanding of how the world's poorest communities can benefit from microinsurance." Prof. Dror published over 95 peer-reviewed publications and several books. He continued to generate such knowledge and encourage scholars and practitioners to publish their research, when he initiated the publication of a special issue on Microinsurance by *The Geneva Papers on Risk and Insurance* and served as the Guest Editor of the Special Issues in 2014, 2016, and 2019. In 2011 and 2014, Prof. Dror received the "Global Citizen Lifetime Achievement "Karmaveer Puraskaar" Award" for Social Justice and Citizen Action, from the Indian Confederation of NGOs.

From 1982 until 2003, Dr. Dror served as a Senior Social Security Specialist advising on the financing and implementation of social and health insurance systems in many developing countries in Africa and Asia within the International Labour Organization (UN-ILO). During the decade that followed, as a freelancer, Dr. Dror provided consultancy on health insurance and microinsurance in Kyrgyzstan, Uganda, South Africa, Ethiopia, Nigeria, Philippines, India, Sri Lanka, Nepal, Bangladesh, Vietnam, Cambodia, Indonesia, Kenya, Rwanda, Afghanistan, and Malawi.

This book, *Health Microinsurance: Implementing Universal Health Coverage in the Informal Sector* is Vol. 4 of the World Scientific Publications' series on *Financing and Investing in Health*. It is Dror's second book in this series of publications, following his volume entitled *Financing Micro Health Insurance: Theory, Methods, and Evidence* (Vol. 2 of this series). The first book addressed three issues. First, how to catalyze demand for health insurance and develop insurance literacy among the mostly illiterate and innumerate target population, using training programs to build an enabling consensus, allowing locals to create and administer such schemes. Second, developing simplified methods for risk assessment, which can help to underwrite risks, price the microhealth insurance schemes, and ensure proper implementation. The third issue is formulating a compelling business case which would make this health insurance affordable, financially sustainable, and "operationally scalable." This second book elaborates the implementation framework in the settings where demand-side considerations dominate the implementation context. The book takes the student through pre-implementation activities (notably collecting the necessary data for pricing and benefits-package design and estimating income generation from enrollees). It then details the role of key actors in the implementation process, the business process of microinsurance, the role of data collection and management. Finally, it guides practitioners and policymakers on the state of the art of impact evaluation activities by reference to metrics of performance, and environmental, social, and governance standards.

Acknowledgments

The content of this book comprises several chapters that have never been published before and others that are improved rewrites of earlier drafts that were used for training purposes, mainly in several locations in India during the years 2010–2017. The undersigned gratefully acknowledges the permission to publish (as Chapter 6) an article co-authored by Arpita Chakraborty, Atanu Majumdar and David M. Dror, which forms part of Ms. Chakraborti's Ph.D. thesis, supervised by Prof. Dr. Biswajit Dhar (Centre for Economic Studies and Planning, School of Social Sciences, Jawaharlal Nehru University, New Delhi). The undersigned also gratefully acknowledges Springer publications for issuing a license to reproduce (as Chapter 7) the article *Estimating Capital Requirements to Scale Health Microinsurance Serving Rural Poor Populations* published in July 2019 by *The Geneva Papers on Risk and Insurance — Issues and Practice*. The entire content draws on concepts and training material that were developed over a decade by the team of the Micro Insurance Academy (New Delhi) under the guidance and direction of the author of this book. During that decade, about 100 persons were team members at one time or the other, and it would be difficult to mention all names. However, some colleagues stood out for their creativity and industry. The author gratefully acknowledges the contributions of the following persons. Swapna Jambhekar (a homeopathic physician, a fellow of the Insurance Institute of India and holder of a master's degree in Hospital Administration from the Tata Institute of Social Sciences (TISS), Mumbai) was the Senior Training Specialist responsible for content creation and training communities on microinsurance for climate-related risks in health, livestock, and crop. She also led the documentation of the microinsurance business processes (Dror, DM and Jambhekar, S (Eds.) (2016) *Microinsurance Business Processes Handbook*, New Delhi, Micro Insurance Academy, January 2016, ISBN 978-81-909841-7-1, pp. xxii–144) and the training manual (Dror, DM and Jambhekar, S (2017) *Microinsurance Implementation Training Manual*, New Delhi, Micro Insurance Academy, March 2017, ISBN 978-81-909841-8-8, pp. xviii–113). Atanu Majumdar (holder of an M.Stat. degree in Statistics from the Indian Statistical Institute, with over 30 years of experience in data processing and management, particularly health data) led MIA's activities in data collection, interpretation, and synthesis, which resulted in several peer-reviewed articles and chapters in books on various microinsurance issues, notably Chapter 7 in this book. Sachin Hans (holds an M.Sc. degree in Applied Economics from the School of Social Sciences, Indira Gandhi National Open University and a degree in Mathematics (Honors) from Delhi University; presently with ICICI Lombard General Insurance Co. Ltd., Mumbai) provided support to conduct research, data mining, actuarial pricing, and MIA's data management system (which informed the performance of implementation). Arpita Chakraborty (M.Phil. in Economics and a Ph.D. candidate at the Jawaharlal Nehru University, New Delhi) was engaged in conducting a multi-year household survey and in analyzing the data and elaborating findings and insights that led to several peer-reviewed publications, notably the article that constitutes Chapter 6 here. Nihar Jangle (holds a doctorate (Dr. rer. nat.) in Mathematics from the Free University Berlin, plus postdoctoral studies in Germany and at Brown University, USA) works now at the German Society for International Cooperation (GIZ) in Germany) led a multi-year intervention on microinsurance solutions for climate-related risks covering health, crop, livestock, and natural catastrophes. This work experience led to several publications in peer-reviewed journals and other innovations in field implementation, notably the article reproduced as Chapter 7. Last but not least, Jacquiline Roberts Singh (M.Phil. in Economics from the Centre for Economic Studies and Planning, Jawaharlal Nehru University, New Delhi, and an actuarial consultant) organized MIA's Reinsurance School — a training workshop designed to introduce microinsurance practitioners to reinsurance concepts — and created content for the insurance education portal "MIA Online." Jacquiline also provided research and editorial assistance toward the production of this book.

If this book is a success, I thank all the contributors very much. And if it is not, I alone take responsibility for the naïve thought that it is possible to share, in book format, messages that our team synthesized from years of fieldwork. Gaining those insights involved countless field trips to remote villages and required back-and-forth translations between English and Hindi, Oriya, Marathi (and their many dialects). We hope to have shared the benefit of the experience without the hardships, time lost, and confounding situations.

Contents

Part 1

Introduction

Chapter 1

The Framework for Implementation of Microinsurance

LEARNING OBJECTIVES

Upon completion of this chapter, the reader should be able to:

- Understand the challenges to catalyzing demand for voluntary and contributory insurance
- Describe ways in which technology has increased the supply of microinsurance
- Explain how group dialog can help in converting dormant demand to solvent demand
- Describe the three fundamental social changes that are core to catalyzing demand for microinsurance
- Identify facilitators and barriers to implementing health microinsurance

Abstract

Catalyzing the demand has been a constant concern in the microinsurance space wherever enrollment has been voluntary and contributory. Here we learn about three significant effects of implementing health microinsurance (shifting from dormant demand to solvent demand; creating the framework at the community level for financial inclusion through insurance education, and establishing the financial institution at the community level that enables reshaping the mindset from dependent to dependable) that lie at the core of the implementation process.

Chapter Outline

Insurance is a comprehensive risk management financial instrument, which is based on the assumption that anything with a quantifiable value is worth protecting, by transferring the risk of loss or damage to someone else who agrees to pay compensation (*an insurer*) or directly to the owner (*self-insurance*). The act of accepting to insure (*insurance underwriting*) entails complex calculations of the fair price (*insurance pricing*) of the specific risk that would be transferred from the insured to the insurer. The *value proposition* of insurance is a clear statement that explains how the insurance contract (called *policy*) solves customers' problems or improves their situation by the quantified value of specific benefits payable to them.

Over the years, attention to the supply of microinsurance has increased, both through scientific and empirical research (Biener *et al.*, 2014) and through specific regulation (which India introduced first in 2005), with the additional support of novel technological applications. Technology has simplified or improved the production of insurance, e.g., by automating calculations at the stage of product design, using large datasets to improve the accuracy of estimates of risk probabilities, the pricing of premiums, faster loss assessment, and claims servicing. However, technology has not *per se* facilitated the creation of demand for insurance.

While there are several delivery models of microinsurance (described in Chapter 2), only one of these models is demand driven, and its implementation is particularly labor intensive due to the many activities to catalyze the demand side. Catalyzing the demand has been a constant concern in the microinsurance space wherever enrollment was voluntary and contributory. The three fundamental social changes that are core to this effort are components of lasting social maturity (Gudzovskaya, 2013), and thus more consequential than merely whether or not specific individuals bought insurance products in a particular year. The three social changes are described here.

SELF-TEST QUESTION

1. Give examples of ways in which technology has increased the supply of microinsurance.

Demand Redefined: From Dormant to Solvent Demand

Much of the economic literature posits that people buy insurance because they prefer a certain amount of wealth over an uncertain one with the equal expected value (Neumann and Morgenstern, 1944). The critical assumption is a preference for certainty. Hence, the expression *risk-averse* person. Economic theory takes that argument further by claiming that people agree to pay a premium to exchange uncertain wealth for a certain wealth; and as insurance offers that trade, the demand for insurance is explained as risk aversion. Tversky and Kahneman developed an alternative theory whereby people are *loss averse*, i.e., they prefer to avoid losses over their desire to make gains (Kahneman and Tversky, 1979). Loss aversion differs from risk aversion by considering previously experienced utility of monetary payoffs.

However, the framing of classical economic theories assumes that humans pursue their self-interested subjectively defined objectives individually (*homo oeconomicus*) (Zabieglik, 2002). We argue that in the settings of poverty and informality, humans pursue the objectives and priorities that are established by groups through iterative exchanges to establish consensus (Dror and Firth, 2014; Dror *et al.*, 2018). So, we challenge both the notion that the demand for health insurance is explained by individual decisions and the centrality of the proposition that insurance is offering a solution for risk aversion or loss aversion.

Consider, for starters, that most people in the informal sector might view the proposition of transacting with an insurance company as a problem rather than a solution. When the only thing people get in return for paying a premium is a conditional promise, without an effective mechanism to force insurance companies to keep their promise, the clients would consider insurance as a risk of loss because they fear that the insurer could use its financial and organizational superiority to renege on its promise. In the informal sector, most people cannot afford to pay for enforcing the contract. Thus, a clear financial cost replaces an unclear loss (which reflects the probability of the risk-generating event multiplied by the probability of insurer non-payment). The prevailing tendency would be *not* to buy insurance under such terms.

Moreover, insurance companies, whose objective is to generate profits, prefer to exercise considerable scrutiny in selecting the risks they underwrite and in pricing those risks. Therefore, insurers prefer individual policies over group policies that insure entire communities that they consider as *bad risk*. This two-sided reticence to insure has created a situation whereby most individuals and most risks are uninsured (*the protection gap*), and most demand for insurance is hidden, or *dormant*. Dormant demand describes the situation when consumers are unable to satisfy certain needs or preferences due to lack of money or information about the availability of suitable products.[1] Certain developed countries, recognizing the dormant nature of demand coupled with the overwhelming advantage of health insurance for the population (and for public finances), legislated that most individuals must buy health insurance (*individual mandate*). In parallel, governments oblige health insurance companies to supply a basic level of coverage, at government-approved premiums, which must be available to all individuals. Furthermore, certain governments enable resource-poor individuals to buy this coverage by paying them premium subsidies. These two basic strategies to achieve universal health insurance coverage (mandating and subsidies) have created a vast health insurance market in most developed countries.

Most low- and middle-income countries (LMICs) have not applied mandating and subsidies. The reasons are by-and-large related to the combined effect of three problems plaguing LMICs: governments' lack of information about their population (mostly in the informal sector); governments' inability to collect taxes; and the large share of resource-poor people in the population. Governments cannot monitor compliance with general mandating when they do not have accurate and complete population registers of the entire population. Also, LMIC governments cannot

---

[1] "Effective Demand | Economics | Fandom Powered by Wikia." Available at http://economics.wikia.com/wiki/Effective_Demand, N.p., n.d. Web. 03 March 2019. http://www.businessdictionary.com/definition/latent-demand.html.

afford to pay premium subsidies when their tax revenues are low and the estimated share of the poor in the population is high. Moreover, in many LMICs, private health insurance is expensive, and the price creates a *de facto* barrier to access for rural and resource-poor persons who cannot pay high premiums. Insurance companies intending to serve the rural and poor population would have to develop new products; those products could be unprofitable, which is a disincentive for insurers in a free market. Insurers would expand their business to settings of poverty and informality if obliged to do so, with the apparent risk that involuntarily outreach would yield flawed service. Finally, in some LMICs, governments prioritize a policy of providing health services rather than promoting individual responsibility for insuring healthcare risks.

While some development organizations and scholars press governments to become more proactive in reaching out to the informal sector and the poor by obliging insurance providers to cover the risks faced by these groups/communities (Dercon *et al.*, 2008), the counterargument is that there is no demand for health insurance in the informal sector (Ahuja and Johannes, 2004).

Thus, at present, most people in the informal sector of developing countries do not join health insurance, even though they pay for healthcare. The fundamental question is as follows: *Under what conditions would the four billion people in the informal sector of LMICs seek voluntary and contributory health insurance?* (Dror and Firth, 2014).

Insights from empirical studies help to reply this question. First, a recently published study (Dror *et al.*, 2018) stated that in the settings of poverty and informality, demand is catalyzed through a process of consensus building on perceptions of risk exposure, welfare gains from the insurance, and quality of local healthcare provision. These considerations are very different from an individual decision based on personal utility, a hypothesis that is the backbone of standard economic theory, and which was examined and rejected in this context. An earlier study (Dror *et al.*, 2014) examined in detail how groups prioritized the health risks that should be insured. This study concluded that more than price or the inclusion of a specific benefit type, the most potent motivator was the wish of group members to join a consensus, and the intention that many members should benefit (rather than winner-takes-all). The consensus among groups members (which can be weaker or stronger) improved with iterative rounds of discussions. Both the studies cited here upheld the notion that *demand for community-based health insurance (CBHI) relies on an engaging experience with others to validate the perceived priorities of the target group*. Such an engaging experience does not occur spontaneously, and it was necessary to create a catalytic intervention whose objective was harnessing group consensus and demand for health insurance. We conclude that in the informal sector, *the success in converting dormant demand to solvent demand depends on encouraging group dialog to validate priorities.* The same result cannot be achieved through a standard sales pitch to each person alone, which occurs, by definition, without the benefit of group dialog.

SELF-TEST QUESTIONS

1. What do we mean by dormant demand for insurance?
2. Most LMICs have not applied mandating and subsidies to achieve universal health insurance coverage. Discuss the reasons for avoiding this approach.
3. In the informal sector, the success in converting dormant demand to solvent demand depends on encouraging group dialog to validate priorities. Comment.

Financial Inclusion Through Insurance Education

In the informal sector, it is difficult to start a dialog on any topic dealing with *finance* or *insurance* because most people associate those topics with exclusion rather than with inclusion. *Inclusion begins by people's desire to be included* and a shared understanding of what this means. Shifting the paradigm from exclusion to inclusion requires that people first understand that *there is a benefit in inclusion and that the terms to avail of that benefit are reasonable.* Discussion, consensus building, and dialog must precede action, so that people understand the basic concepts, share a universe-of-discourse about the terminology, and reach cultural acceptance about the financial instrument before they decide to participate. Solvent demand can occur when the community of reference agrees that *insuring is what a responsible adult does*. Reaching this cultural acceptance requires insurance education and financial literacy. However, to this very day, there is no generalized recognition that it is necessary to impart insurance education to grassroots groups that is not a sales pitch. Neither governments nor the insurance industry has invested the resources in developing the necessary institutional support to impart insurance education on a large scale (different from insurance education for insurance professionals). We clarify that the narrow context of sales is not insurance education. The governments that wish to take action toward better financial inclusion would be well advised to start by enhancing financial/insurance education. Insurance companies that would like to capture new business by insuring informal sector populations should finance insurance education (but refrain from imparting it themselves, as their activities could be construed as marketing and lead to rejection). Ideally, insurance literacy should become part of the general primary education in the informal sector, so that children can repeat and reinforce the basic concepts at home. As for the adults, they are most likely to assimilate and accept insurance literacy when they obtain it in a group setting, together with peers from their location.

Reshaping the Mindset: From Dependent to Dependable

All countries have health systems. In the context of poverty and informality, the general health services (*horizontal system*) are often deficient, but there are several projects/programs (*vertical programs*) to deal with a specific condition, e.g., for HIV/AIDS control, tuberculosis control, malaria/vector-borne disease control, maternity. Vertical programs often deliver services free of charge, and in some cases even pay participants cash amounts for compliance. This long-standing practice has created a mentality of dependency on the government among many resource-poor persons. When a calamity occurs (e.g., due to an epidemic, floods, or drought), the population expects the government to provide help.

Moreover, common diseases that would not usually be considered as severe hardship can become a huge issue for a low-income family. The mentality that the family is frequently dependent on others is pervasive, particularly among women, who are tasked with caregiving but are often not given the material means they need to provide such care. Field evidence gained with CBHI has shown that women played leading roles in the administration, governance, and oversight of those schemes.[2,3] They reported that within those CBHI schemes, they have been, for the first time, able to decide on the care they obtain for themselves and other family members. They have reported high satisfaction with the transformation of their condition *from dependent to dependable*. This change, from having to rely on others to being relied upon, is probably the most potent *collateral benefit* of microinsurance. The intended advantage (of being compensated when health risks occur) delivers an unintended but definite advantage (that people can rely on themselves to deal with more situations than ever before, without having to wait for external intervention or for permission from others to take action).

The three significant effects of implementing health microinsurance (shifting from dormant demand to solvent demand; creating the framework at the community level for financial inclusion through insurance education; and establishing the financial institution at the community level that enables reshaping the mindset from dependent to dependable) are at the core of the implementation process.

SELF-TEST QUESTIONS

1. Suggest ways in which the government and insurance industry can develop the necessary institutional support to impart insurance education on a large scale.
2. Catalyzing the demand has been a constant concern in the microinsurance space wherever enrollment was voluntary and contributory. Describe the three fundamental social changes identified in this chapter, which are core to this effort.

---

[2]WHO: Investing in Rural Health Workers for the Economic Participation and Empowerment of Rural Women and Girls. Available at https://www.who.int/hrh/news/2018/rural-hw-economic-participation/en/ (accessed 25 April 2019).

[3]USAID/Health Finance & Governance Project: How Ethiopia is Empowering Women Through Community-Based Health Insurance. Available at https://www.hfgproject.org/ethiopia-empowering-women-community-based-health-insurance/ (accessed 25 April 2019).

Facilitators and Barriers to Implementing Health Microinsurance

Ever since the days when Kenneth Arrow (considered the father of health economics) analyzed the economic behavior of humans in the context of medical care and George A. Akerlof (together with A. Michael Spence and Joseph E. Stiglitz) got the 2001 Nobel Prize in economics *for their analyses (30 years earlier) of markets with asymmetric information*, there is a broad consensus that adverse selection (Akerlof, 1970), moral hazard (Kenneth, 1963), and free riding (Pasour, 1981) can endanger health insurance. All the three phenomena occur when the price of the insurance coverage is too low because it is assuming average exposure patterns, when in fact a specific insured person represents a higher risk that he/she does not disclose to the insurer. Thus, the insurer accepts to insure an adverse risk (hence the term *adverse selection*). Alternatively, when an insured person changes his/her behavior, e.g., takes great risks, without having to pay the higher cost of insuring such actions (*moral hazard*), insurers consider such changed behavior as bad-faith behavior and may refuse to pay unexpected payouts. Alternatively, insufficient information about the ownership or insufficient control on usage enables individuals to obtain the benefits of insurance without contributing to its cost (free rider problem).

Many publications deal with these three variants of insurance failure. Some refine the distinctions between the phenomena (Abbring, 2003). Others challenge the extent of their effect (Siegelman, 2003). Studies of adverse selection or moral hazard in the context of CBHI have also presented widely different conclusions. Some have claimed that such insurance aims to enable underserved groups to access healthcare services that were out of reach without the insurance, and therefore enhanced utilization in the context of health microinsurance is an indicator of success rather than of insurance failure (Dror *et al.*, 2005; De Allegri *et al.*, 2006). Other studies claim that the policy to promote the expansion of health microinsurance should make allowances for adverse selection at the design stage (Parmar *et al.*, 2014; Ahmed *et al.*, 2018). Other scholars pointed to significantly positive relationships between social capital of the CBHI in Nepal and willingness to join/willingness to pay. The bonding and bridging social capital effects lead to different relationships within the group vs. the willingness to cooperate with external funding sources (Ko, 2018).

In our context, the most relevant issue to consider is whether members of a mutual aid microinsurance scheme have the same opportunity and motivation as insured persons in a large health insurance plan to take advantage of others by disguising personal information on their riskiness from the insurance. The evidence suggests that health microinsurance creates a significantly lower and costlier opportunity to *game the system* compared to those in a large insurance plan. A recent systematic review of the literature (Fadlallah *et al.*, 2018) summarized several interrelated factors (at the individual, interpersonal, community, and systems levels) that facilitate the implementation, uptake, and sustainability of CBHI schemes. The individual factors include trust in the scheme and its managers; interpersonal factors include the enrollment of other family members and social solidarity. Community-level facilitators include community involvement in the sustainability of the scheme. Systems-level factors encompass governance, financial, and delivery arrangements. These factors highlight that the trust relations permeate the implementation. Conversely, all the three forms of insurance failure exist if the trust is breached, but not otherwise.

Moreover, such intricate trust relations work both ways, i.e., not only do members trust their peers and the scheme leadership, but they need to be trusted as well. As such schemes usually practice community rating, which impedes them from charging higher premiums from members who increase the overall risk pool, the alternative remedy of dealing with members who breach the trust of peers is for the peers to reject such individuals caught exercising adverse selection, moral hazard, or free riding. Stated simply, the risk of acting in bad faith in small groups in the informal sector is a sanction of excommunication. The temptation to obtain small gains is significantly dampened by the severity of a sanction if caught.

The Theoretical and Empirical Context for the Implementation of Microinsurance

This book hands implementers the practical information that they require to set up and operate microinsurance schemes at the grassroots level. Experience has shown, repeatedly, that implementers must be conversant with many topics. These include the following: how to deal with data collection and analysis for contextual risk assessment; knowing how to design suitable benefits packages; price the insurance; impart insurance education/literacy to illiterate and innumerate groups; train the staff to assume *key actor* functions; handle the management information system (MIS) so as to maintain reliable records of membership and financial transactions; and put in place the governance and oversight bodies that will gain the trust of the insured members that the administration is orderly, fair, transparent, and prompt. Practitioners have realized that *microinsurance is anything but micro knowledge.*

This book follows the first book published on health microinsurance in this series, entitled: *Financing Micro Health Insurance: Theory, Methods, and Evidence* (Dror, 2018). The first book contains the theoretical and methodological framing of microinsurance. This book, the second, is the practical guide that contains a specific reference to the various tasks and stages of implementation. This book contains the synthesis of hands-on experience over more than a decade of fieldwork (under the auspices of the Micro Insurance Academy, New Delhi). The experience was gained in low-income settings in several states of India, in some areas of Nepal, in Bangladesh, Cambodia, and several other countries in Asia and Africa. The section on the business process of microinsurance is a revised and updated version of our earlier publication on this topic (Dror and Jambhekar, 2016). The section on training is a reworked version of an earlier publication (Dror, 2017). The section on data science for microinsurance (including MIS) is published here for the first time. The chapter on monitoring and evaluation builds on earlier publications on performance indicators (Wipf and Garand, 2010) and expands the topic to also deal with impact evaluation. We include new research findings on improved projections of scheme income from premiums (in Chapter 6). Finally, Chapter 7 contains a first-of-its-kind model to enable implementers to estimate the capital they might require to launch a new microinsurance scheme. As grant funds are dwindling, implementers increasingly need to explore the option of attracting impact investors to lend the capital. The section in this book enables us to demonstrate how microinsurance schemes can repay with interest. Several Issue Briefs include examples of tools used in the process of implementation.

SELF-TEST QUESTION

1. Discuss the facilitators and barriers to implementing health microinsurance.

KEY TERMS

- **Dormant demand:** A situation when consumers are unable to satisfy specific needs or preferences due to lack of information about the availability of suitable products, or lack of money is called dormant demand.
- **Moral hazard:** It is a situation when an insured person changes his/her behavior, e.g., takes significant risks, without having to pay the higher cost of insuring such actions.
- **Group policy:** It is issued by the External Insurer wherein the policyholder is the community and the beneficiaries are the participants who enrolled for that particular cover.

Bibliography

Abbring, JH, Heckman, JJ, Chiappori, PA, and Pinquet, J (2003) Adverse Selection and Moral Hazard in Insurance: Can Dynamic Data Help to Distinguish. *Journal of the European Economic Association*, 1(23), 512–521.

Ahmed, S, Sarker, AR, Sultana, M, Chakrovorty, S, Hasan, Z Md, Mirelman, AJ, Khan, JAM (2018) Adverse Selection in Community Based Health Insurance among Informal Workers in Bangladesh: An EQ-5D Assessment. *International Journal of Environmental Research and Public Health*, 15(2), 242.

Ahuja, R and Jütting, J (2004) Are the Poor too Poor to Demand Health Insurance? New Delhi, Indian Council for Research on International Economic Relations, ICRIER Working Papers, Working Paper 118.

Akerlof, GA (1970) The Market for "Lemons": Quality Uncertainty and the Market Mechanism. *The Quarterly Journal of Economics*, 84(3), pp. 488–500.

Arrow, K (1963) Uncertainty and the Welfare Economics of Medical Care. *The American Economic Review*, 53(5), 941–973.

Biener, C, Eling, M, and Schmit JT (2014) Regulation in Microinsurance Markets: Principles, Practice, and Directions for Future Development. *World Development*, 58, 21–40.

De Allegri, M, Kouyaté, B, Becher, H, Gbangou, A, Pokhrel, S, Sanon, M, and Sauerborn, R (2006) Understanding Enrolment in Community Health Insurance in Sub-Saharan Africa: A Population-Based Case Control Study in Rural Burkina Faso. *Bulletin of the World Health Organization*. 84(11), 852–858.

Dercon, S, Bold, T, and Calvo, C (2008) Insurance for the Poor? In *Social Protection for the Poor and Poorest Barrientos*, ed. A Hulme, pp. 47–63. London: Palgrave Studies in Development.

Dror, DM, Soriano, E, Sarol, J, Azcuna, R, Lorenzo, M, and Koren, R (2005) Field-based Evidence of Enhanced Healthcare Utilization among Persons Insured by Micro Health Insurance Units in Philippines. *Health Policy*, 73(3), 263–271.

Dror, DM and Firth, LA (2014) The Demand for (Micro) Health Insurance in the Informal Sector. *The Geneva Papers on Risk and Insurance Issues and Practice*, 39(4), 693–711.

Dror, DM, Panda, P, May, C, Majumdar, A, and Koren, R (2014) 'One for All and All for One': Consensus-building within Communities in Rural India on their Health Microinsurance Package. *Risk Management and Healthcare Policy*, 7, 139–153.

Dror, DM and Jambhekar, S (Eds.) 2016 *Microinsurance Business Processes Handbook*. New Delhi: Micro Insurance Academy.

Dror, DM and Jambhekar, S (2017) Microinsurance Implementation Training Manual. New Delhi: Micro Insurance Academy.

Dror, DM (2018) *Financing Micro Health Insurance: Theory, Methods, and Evidence*. In *World Scientific Series in Health Investment and Financing*, ed. AS Preker, Vol. 2. Singapore: World Scientific Publishing.

Dror, DM, Chakraborty, A, and Majumdar, A (2018) The Effect of Consensus on Demand for Voluntary Micro Health Insurance in Rural India. *Risk Management and Healthcare Policy*, 11, 139–158.

Fadlallah *et al.* (2018) Barriers and Facilitators to Implementation, Uptake, and Sustainability of Community-Based Health Insurance Schemes in Low- and Middle-Income Countries: A Systematic Review. *International Journal for Equity in Health*, 17, 13.

Gudzovskaya, AA (2013) Inter- and Intrasubjective Factors of Social Maturity. Experience Longitudinal Study: Moscow. *National Psychological Journal*, 2(22), 105–113.

Kahneman, D and Tversky, A (1979) Prospect Theory: An Analysis of Decision under Risk. *Econometrica*, 47(2), 263–291.

Ko, H, Kim, H, Yoon, C, and Kim, C (2018) Social Capital as a Key Determinant of Willingness to Join Community-Based Health Insurance: A Household Survey in Nepal._*Public Health*, 160, 52–61.

Neumann, J and Morgenstern, O (1944) Theory of Games and Economic Behavior. Princeton, NJ. Available at https://archive.org/details/in.ernet.dli.2015.215284/page/n6 (accessed August 15, 2019).

Parmar, D, Souares, A, de Allegri, M, Savadogo, G, Sauerborn, R (2012): Adverse Selection in a Community-Based Health Insurance Scheme in Rural Africa: Implications for Introducing Targeted Subsidies. *BMC Health Services Research*, 28, 181.

Pasour, EC Jr (1981) The Free Rider as a Basis for Government Intervention. *Journal of Libertarian Studies*, 5(4), 453–464.

Siegelman, P (2003) Adverse Selection in Insurance Markets: An Exaggerated Threat. *Yale Law Journal*, 113, 1223–1281.

Wipf, J and Garand, D (2010) *Performance Indicators for Microinsurance: A Handbook for Microinsurance Practitioners*. 2nd ed. ADA/Luxembourg Dev Cooperation/BRS/Microinsurance Network. Available at https://microinsurancenetwork.org/sites/default/files/KPI_MI_Handbook_v2_EN_0.pdf (accessed August 15, 2019).

Zabieglik, S (2002) The Origins of the Term Homo Oeconomicus. *Economics And Values*, 1, 123–130.

Selected Websites

The following websites pertain to the content of this chapter:

- For more information on effective demand and latent demand, go to http://economics.wikia.com/wiki/Effective_Demand (accessed 3 March 2019). http://www.businessdictionary.com/definition/latent-demand.html.

Chapter 2

Health Microinsurance Models*

LEARNING OBJECTIVES

Upon completion of this chapter, the reader should be able to:

- Explain the basis for differentiating health microinsurance delivery models
- Describe the features and challenges of the four models discussed in the chapter
- Discuss the reasons for CBHI being best suited to deliver microinsurance

Abstract

The objective of this chapter is to describe the features and challenges of the primary health microinsurance delivery models and the factors contributing to the success of community-based health insurance (CBHI). The models are differentiated based on two dimensions: the main purpose of operating and the responsibility for the risk of losses. The chapter also emphasizes the factors that render CBHI as the best-suited model to deliver microinsurance.

*This chapter is based on the following three sources: Radermacher *et al.*, 2008; Dror, 2014; Dror and Piesse, 2014.

Chapter Outline

The use of the term *microinsurance* is still in flux. Since 1999, the term *microinsurance* has been used with much definitional disorder. According to the authors who published this term first (Dror and Jacquier, 1999), *micro* refers to *the level of society that takes the critical decisions* (micro means the local community, different from *meso*, i.e., regional scope, and *macro*, i.e., an entire country). Some people understand microinsurance to reflect *characteristics of the product* (low cost and low coverage). Others use microinsurance to refer to *the target population* (low-income people). This confusion has given rise to a profusion of specific terms, for example, community-based health insurance (CBHI), community-based health funds, health microinsurance (HMI), mutual health funds, mutual microinsurance, and others. The confusion about the terminology reflects the tensions between the models of insurance that claim to offer a best fit in bringing the vast uninsured population in the rural and informal sectors in low- and middle-income countries (LMICs) to formal risk management. However, while we describe four distinct models of delivery, in real life, it is possible to find the combination of several models, e.g., community-based insurance cooperating with commercial insurance (on package design and pricing that the insurance underwrites). Moreover, when schemes offer bundled packages covering several classes of risk (e.g., health, crop, and livestock, or life and health), they may retain certain risks and cede other risks to an insurance company. Thus, applying a simplified terminology should be viewed with some caution, as it may be misleading.

Suffice to say, we remain aware that in the setting of poverty and informality, we understand the main features of the four delivery models of insurance.

The following four main HMI models are recognized worldwide:

1. the partner–agent model;
2. the charitable insurance model;
3. the provider-driven model;
4. the CBHI also known as community-based mutual aid scheme.

In describing those four models, we draw attention to the following two dimensions that differentiate them:

1. the primary motivation for operating;
2. the responsibility to bear most of the risk of losses.

Partner–Agent Model

The descriptor of this model reflects the division of labor between an insurance company (*the partner*) and its distributional intermediary (*the agent*). A person can become insured only by dealing with both the partner and the agent under the partner–agent model. The agent deals with sales and product servicing, in return for a commission (usually set within the regulatory framework). In the microinsurance space, the role of the agent can be carried out either by a designated person or by an organization (e.g., an non-governmental organization (NGO), a microfinance institution, or any other organization with close contacts to the target group). The agent, empowered to manage all the contacts, carries no risk and is not empowered to design or price the insurance product. The partner (insurance company) carries the risk and retains responsibility for all the decisions affecting product manufacturing, sales, servicing, and maintenance of long-term sustainability. The partner is also the signatory of the contract with the insured.

Challenges of the model

(1) To who does the agent report?

(a) The agent reports first and foremost to his employer, the insurance company. The agent's role is to sell the insurance products that the insurance company has pre-designed and priced. Agents usually claim that they can leverage their better knowledge of (and ties with) the target market to sell successfully. However, the products that are offered by the insurer may not suit the needs of the clients or may be (considered) too expensive. Hence, the agent and his/her clients may be in conflicts of interest. Since the agent gets a commission only on sales, he/she must reach a compromise that satisfies the requirements of his employer as well as his clients. When agents cannot do so, they might prefer to concentrate their efforts elsewhere (e.g., sell in towns, rather than in rural areas). Agents may wish to advocate the desires and positions of their clients to the partner, but more often, they must communicate the insurance company's position. When the gap between the position of the insurance company and the clients is too big, the agents run the risk of losing the community's trust. This risk can occur both because of gaps in what the package should cover and because of disputes over claims.

(b) Agents can find themselves in the same conflicting situation when the insurance company increases the premium levels. Such adjustments to the premiums occur when the insurance company experiences a high claims ratio, and it is common for clients to mount stiff resistance to price hikes.

(2) The insurance company is usually interested in selling a pre-designed product (often a scaled-down version of a product that is already available in the formal sector). Selling existing products costs less in production and registration but could also introduce insufficient flexibility for the different clientele. When the agent can communicate the actual demand effectively, the insurer's actuaries could develop a product that meets that demand. From a structural viewpoint, the partner–agent model could facilitate the adaptation of products to the demand, and when this happens, the role of agents extends beyond merely selling, to becoming the agents of customization and flexibility.

(3) In the relationship that is typical to this model, clients have little incentive to provide (hidden) information about their, or their neighbor's, health status. Thus, the flow of information in both directions is incomplete and asymmetric. This information asymmetry constitutes an increased risk for insurance companies, commanding an expectation of additional revenues. This expectation translates into higher premiums and subsequently higher possibilities of moral hazard.

(4) When clients submit claims, they expect insurance companies to pay those claims. Insurers understandably wish to monitor claims, and

while there are tried-and-tested mechanisms to monitor claims, loading those costs on the premiums would render the insurance unaffordable for most low-income households. Hence, claims monitoring can lead to losing the entire market segment. There is an alternative solution, rarely applied in the informal sector at present, to create win–win incentives for the clients and the insurance company (e.g., through profit-sharing arrangements).

Charitable Insurance Model

A wide variety of institutions operate the charitable insurance model. These institutions share the following two essential features:

1. operating not-for-profit;
2. refraining from transferring the risk to the insured.

Charitable insurers can be owned or operated by NGOs or by associations (e.g., area-based, gender-based, faith-based, trade-based, or other), government-supported programs, or other well-meaning organizations. The motivation for establishing the insurance scheme is creating welfare gains for the target group, mainly in the form of increasing clients' access to healthcare. The health insurer bears the risk of losses. Charitable organizations usually agree to the relatively free provision of benefits, and product-servicing is also kept simple. Profits generated in some years are kept as reserves for future losses. The offering institution performs all activities of the business process, sometimes with the involvement of the target group. The distribution process is usually conducted through the organization's staff who also have other duties.

Challenges of the model

(1) The charitable model may at times place the priorities of donors or NGO management ahead of those of the clients. Notwithstanding good intentions, when clients perceive such priority-setting as paternalistic, the charitable provider and the clients may find themselves in a conflict of interest.

(2) Charitable organizations often rely on permanent external financing, which opens the door for less attention to ensuring that the insurance activities are operated on a sustainable basis. This situation could weaken the emphasis on imparting insurance literacy and practicing rigorous financial management.
(3) Charitable organizations attach great importance to understanding their clients' requirements but may be less well equipped to maintain actuarial pricing of the services.
(4) Maintenance of long-term sustainability is arguably a low priority of the charitable model.
    (a) Many charitable insurance schemes may find it difficult to reject claims, even those that are not entirely justified. The concern for the institution's reputation as a charitable body may prevail over the rigor that might require to reject a claim or deny service. Hence, the potential threat to achieving sustainability.
    (b) In some cases, charitable organizations may wish to promote social welfare beyond considerations of sustainability of the insurance scheme. When the operations unfold on the assumptions that deficit can occur, they are more likely to occur, requiring external subsidies.
(5) The charitable mission can at times also influence the business processes of insurance in a way that the organization would avoid collecting information on pre-existing conditions that are usually excluded from insurance coverage by other insurers.

SELF-TEST QUESTIONS

1. Discuss the information asymmetry inherent in the partner–agent model and its impact on the premium rate.
2. Comment on the following: Maintenance of long-term sustainability is arguably a low priority of the charitable model.
3. Discuss the challenges of the charitable model.
4. What are the two dimensions used in the chapter to differentiate the various microinsurance models? Would you suggest any other basis for differentiating these models?

Provider-Driven Model

Providers of care (e.g., hospitals, clinics, physician associations) may launch an insurance scheme. Those insured pay a premium to the healthcare provider in return for the right to consume health services (at reduced prices or) without fee-for-service billing. This model often limits the provision of healthcare services to the provider's dedicated facilities. The apparent reason is to capture a large volume of transactions in the dedicated facilities, which enable the provider to apply differential unit prices for the core insured population and for other customers. The healthcare provider can control all aspects of healthcare delivery by controlling the business process.

The provider benefits from this arrangement in several ways:

(1) It attracts a captive clientele to its facilities and services.
(2) The provider can select customers to its facility or restrict the access of the uninsured.
(3) The provider generates revenues from people, some of whom are unlikely to seek treatment, some of whom would have gone elsewhere, and some of whom might be able to get services for a lower price.

Challenges of the model

(1) Many provider-driven schemes restrict the clients' choice of healthcare provider (be it the choice of the facility or the free choice of the specific healthcare professional). Such schemes can significantly limit the benefits that can be obtained elsewhere than the dedicated facilities.
(2) In some such schemes, the internal payment to providers is based on capitation (a payment system in which an insurer or physician association pays a doctor or hospital a fixed amount per patient regardless of the time spent or complexity of the case). Such capitation payment can lead service providers to under-provide or compromise the quality of care.
(3) Most healthcare providers lack the administrative skills (and sometimes the financial capacity) to operate a health insurance scheme in a viable manner.

(4) There is a (potential) conflict of interest in product servicing. When healthcare providers bill their services on a fee-for-service basis, they can provide all the services they consider necessary. However, under the provider-driven model, the insurance has an incentive to restrict the services that the in-house providers can apply.
(5) Even though the model generates relatively good data about healthcare expenses, the products lack actuarial pricing.
(6) As the purchaser is also the provider of services, there is no competition on the price of services.

CBHI Model

Mutual aid societies, also known as community-based health insurance schemes or mutual health organizations, are voluntary, non-profit organizations that operate risk pooling of their members based on the ethics of mutual assistance and solidarity. These societies promote the principles of self-help, self-administration, and self-responsibility. Under this delivery model, the risk is borne by the insured collectively, who are both the owners of their scheme and its beneficiaries. This duality of role enables the members to benefit not only from payouts but also from the retained profits. As owners of these societies, members are actively involved in decision-making and in administering the application of those decisions and business rules. The CBHI is responsible for all aspects of product manufacturing, sales, servicing, and maintaining long-term stability. Such schemes have an incentive to *engage the members in insurance literacy*, which in turn enables the members to be more proactive in determining the scope of coverage and suitable contributions. The involvement of members in decisions and the administration promotes active empowerment (change in the mindset *from dependent to dependable*), satisfaction with the scheme and the protection it provides, and proactive adaptation of coverage to changing needs and priorities.

Challenges of the model

(1) Mutual aid schemes are rather informal bodies, in which personal relations and a regular flow of information among members play an essential role (*the gossip economy*). The free-flow of information

includes details about health issues, which would raise concerns about privacy in a more formal organization. As privacy cannot be guaranteed, some members who have *stigma diseases* may prefer not to claim benefits from the scheme to avoid social exclusion.

(2) The small group size of mutual schemes reduces the risk diversification and exposes them to a higher risk when covariate risk occurs. The solution is to open the way for the cession of risks to reinsurance or risk equalization mechanism. Unfortunately, for the time being, access of CBHI cannot readily transact with reinsurance providers.

(3) As mutual aid schemes grow, they must hire professional managers to fulfill the roles that members can assume when the scheme is small. The growth in membership brings about a weakening of the informal character of relations. Moreover, while insured members remain the owners of the scheme, they gradually find it challenging to keep abreast of activities and lose their sense of ownership. Managing a positive balance between professionalization and member involvement is a difficult challenge.

(4) Mutual aid organizations need external assistance, mainly at launch and in the early years, to obtain the specialist knowledge required to design and operate the insurance system. Such external specialist knowledge, which is also supportive of the mutual model, is hard to come by.

The Insurance Model that is the Focus of this Book

Health insurance penetration[1] and health insurance density[2] are so very low in most LMICs. This low insurance uptake implies that the fundamental question about enhancing insurance coverage is not merely about its supply (e.g., *what can insurance companies do better* or *what can healthcare providers do better*) but about the demand for insurance. The underlying question is as follows: *If the benefits of health insurance are positively provable, what are the conditions under which the 3 billion or so in the informal sector of LMICs would seek voluntary health insurance?*[3]

[1] Measured as the percentage of insurance premium to GDP.

[2] Calculated as the ratio of premium to population, or per capita premium, in a country.

[3] Dror, DM and Firth, LA (2014) The Demand for (Micro) Health Insurance in the Informal Sector. *The Geneva Papers on Risk and Insurance Issues and Practice*, 39(4), 693–711.

We stress *voluntary* insurance enrollment because almost all LMIC governments have refrained from imposing mandatory enrollment on their entire population. Of the various models presented here, the only one that is demand driven is the CBHI model. Hence, the focus of attention in this book is on implementing this model.

CBHI insurance plans must engage with target populations that — at the outset — cumulate several adverse conditions. They are unfamiliar with the process of insurance and have usually lived without it. Their limited educational background does not prepare them to evaluate the value proposition of an insurance policy. They are unable or unwilling to pay more than small amounts. They are very wary of paying in advance of service delivery, notably because of their concern that they are unable to enforce the contract. When dealing with dominant insurers, this concern about power disparity is very keen, and it is reinforced by the culture of distrusting anyone outside the immediate community.

The challenge for implementers is to demonstrate to such grassroots communities that the mutual aid model is based on an expansion of tried-and-tested notions of reciprocal relations for mutual aid among community members to overcome financial stress that each person cannot resolve alone.

SELF-TEST QUESTIONS

1. List the reasons for CBHI being best suited to deliver microinsurance successfully.
2. In the provider-driven model, the prices of provider services are usually based on capitation. What is capitation, and what are the repercussions of this pricing model?
3. Describe the benefits of involving CBHI members in insurance literacy, scheme decisions, and administration.
4. Describe the *dual role* played by each member of a CBHI scheme.
5. Why do mutual aid organizations need external assistance for their operations?
6. Of the various models presented here, CBHI is the only one that is demand driven. Explain why?

KEY TERMS

- **Capitation:** It is a payment system in which a provider (e.g., a doctor or hospital) receives a fixed amount per patient regardless of the time spent with the patient or the complexity of the case.
- **CBHI (Community-Based Health Insurance):** It is a mutual aid scheme owned and operated by the community members who have voluntarily enrolled and paid for the membership. CBHI schemes define the risks that they insure and the price of their coverage.
- **Claim:** It is a request by a participant for reimbursement of actual costs incurred due to an adverse event covered by the benefits package.

Bibliography

Dror, DM (2014) *Health Microinsurance Programs in Developing Countries.* In *Encyclopaedia of Health Economics*, ed. AJ Culye, Vol. 1, pp. 412–421. United States: Elsevier Science.

Dror, DM and Jacquier, C (1999) Micro-Insurance: Extending Health Insurance to the Excluded. *International Social Security Review* 52(1), 71–97.

Dror, DM and Firth, LA (2014) The Demand for (Micro) Health Insurance in the Informal Sector. *The Geneva Papers on Risk and Insurance Issues and Practice*, 39(4), 693–711.

Dror, DM and Piesse, D (2014) What is Microinsurance? In *A Practical Guide to Impact Assessments in Microinsurance*, eds. R Radermacher and K Roth, pp. 24–39. Luxemburg and New Delhi: Microinsurance Network and Micro Insurance Academy.

Radermacher, R, Dror, I, and Noble, G (2008) Challenges and Strategies to Extend Health Insurance to the Poor. In *Microinsurance Compendium*, ed. C Churchill, Chapter 2.1, pp. 66–93. Geneva: ILO.

Part 2

Pre-Implementation Activities

Chapter 3

Baseline Study and Its Purpose

LEARNING OBJECTIVES

Upon completion of this chapter, the reader should be able to:

- Define a baseline study and explain its objectives
- Elaborate the need for a baseline study before the launch of a microinsurance scheme
- Describe the methods used to collect data in a baseline study
- Understand the steps involved in planning and conducting a baseline study
- Discuss the type of information collected through a baseline study before the launch of a microinsurance scheme

Abstract

Understanding the local needs of a community lays the foundation for the launch of a microinsurance scheme. The baseline study must precede the operational processes of presenting different options of benefits packages to the community. This chapter discusses the relevance of a baseline study, its objectives, and the stages involved in planning and conducting the study.

Chapter Outline

The baseline study (or survey) is a structured (or systematic) gathering of data from various sources. The beginning of a project or intervention usually entails conducting a baseline study. In the microinsurance implementation model developed by the Micro Insurance Academy (please see *Annex 1 in the supplementary material for this chapter*), the baseline study sets the platform for launching a community-based health insurance scheme.

Before launching a health microinsurance scheme, it is necessary to address two crucial preliminary issues. First, every health microinsurance unit must assess the risks that people are facing in their specific context. Before the customers or the insurer can agree on the defined scope of insured risks (that are a partial set of the insurable risks), both parties must know their risk exposure. The first objective of a baseline survey is to collect data to estimate the frequency and severity of health-related issues (mainly illnesses and accidents), the local costs of treatment, and the availability of healthcare providers. This raises two related questions: Are the data elements available anywhere? Which methods serve best to process that data?

Notwithstanding the huge amount of information on the Internet, when the data required to set up a health microinsurance unit *in a specific location* are not readily available from secondary sources, it is necessary to conduct a baseline survey. The investigation employs qualitative and quantitative methods, including questionnaires, interviews, observations, and existing records, hence the description of such studies as *mixed methods*.

The quantitative methods are those that focus on expressing the information in *numbers*. The numbers can then serve as the raw material for analysis of the data, using mathematical or statistical techniques. In short, surveys (questionnaires) are usually quantitative.

The qualitative component of the collection of data assumes that people can describe events that occurred to them and that the broader contexts of peoples' lives explain social phenomena, behaviors, and choices. The data that qualitative methods collect tend to be *words*, in the form of transcripts; fieldwork notes of direct, unstructured interviewing; or ethnographic observations of real-life settings. Household (HH) survey questionnaires often include semi-structured interviews or the main questions that the interview should include. This format guides focus group discussions (FGDs). Qualitative questionnaires can also consist of structured interviews, e.g., key informant interviews (KIIs) or in-depth interviews (IDIs). Finally, observations are records of visits to health facilities.

That data are typically unstructured, which cannot be analyzed with statistical methods. However, combining quantitative and qualitative approaches can enhance research. Surveys (questionnaires) often contain both quantitative and qualitative questions. The quantitative questions might take the form of yes/no or rating scales (1–5), whereas the qualitative questions would present a box where people can write in their own words (*open question*).[1]

Reliance on secondary data sources presents the problem that secondary resources rarely allow access to raw data. Rather, secondary sources usually publish processed partial information, e.g., mean values. For our purpose, averages are insufficient information, as the calculation of premiums requires, besides mean values, also the mode and median values, and importantly, the distribution of costs (Dror, 2018, Chapter 8). The detailed information is the only way to decipher the significant differences in the patterns, frequencies, and costs of risks across geographic locations that average values given in national data do not reflect (Dror, 2007; Dror *et al.*, 2008, 2009). Therefore, it is necessary to estimate the specific risk exposure in a given location with information collected locally. The same also applies to many other data elements which one cannot usually obtain from secondary sources (that include reports of national statistics offices, medical centers, hospitals, or pharmacies).

Some information is necessary for comparative analysis of replies to different sections of the HH data collection questionnaire. Hence, it is necessary to devote the necessary time to think through the questions we seek to answer based on the information we plan to collect from the population. One way to facilitate the *learning curve* when preparing a baseline HH survey is to look at source material that other projects publish.

[1] Rlo: Qualitative and Quantitative Research Methods. Available at https://www.nottingham.ac.uk/nursing/sonet/rlos/ebp/qvq/page_four.html (accessed 24 March 2019).

The second objective of the baseline study is to set the reference point against which to measure the impact of insurance in the future. A baseline survey is a description of the circumstances in place before the development project is carried out. It provides the basis for subsequent assessment of how efficiently the project is being implemented and the eventual results achieved. Evaluation of the impact is now the standard practice of development projects. We devote Chapter 16 to a detailed discussion of impact evaluation.

Some authors refer to a baseline study as a *needs assessment study*. However, the two differ from each other in some subtle ways. The findings of needs assessments serve to validate that an intervention is necessary. The needs assessment can usually be completed with minimal time and cost. A baseline study should provide exhaustive information on many aspects needed for implementation. Its design must ensure its statistical validity. Finally, a baseline study can deliver the results of a needs assessment study, but the latter cannot fulfill the purpose of the former.

SELF-TEST QUESTIONS

1. Which are the two crucial issues that need to be resolved before the launch of a microinsurance scheme? How does a baseline study help in addressing these issues?
2. Differentiate between a baseline study and a needs assessment study.
3. What are the methods used to collect data in a baseline study? Why do you think different methods are adopted?
4. Why are secondary sources of data not very helpful in estimating the risk exposure of a given location?

Information Collected through Baseline Study in the Context of Microinsurance

Types and magnitudes of risks, e.g., frequency and severity of hospitalizations, and other types of risk that the microinsurance scheme proposes to insure are as follows:

- the local population's perceived priorities on the risks that insurance should cover;
- the local population's willingness to pay for the insurance;
- level of awareness and understanding of the principles of insurance;
- level of social capital and solidarity within the community;
- outlier/extreme risk patterns that the community should consider;
- access to services (again, specific to risks): A micro health insurance scheme must know the health-seeking preferences of people in the area of intervention, e.g., do they prefer public or private hospitals? Which clinics, labs, and imaging centers do they use?
- the socioeconomic and sociodemographic profile of the community;
- the disparities (gender, age, income, education, or any other parameter) in accessing services;
- the list of questions mentioned here is indicative, not exhaustive: Annex 1 provided in the supplementary material for this chapter gives an example of a baseline study *Questionnaire* that we developed and used. This example also includes the specifications of valid values for each question. When the correct answers are not specified within the questionnaire, the document is sometimes referred to as the *Codebook*. Many other examples can be accessed via the Internet. We stress that each project or study must define the information it aims to collect through its baseline questionnaire. As the baseline study is a one-off exercise, there is an advantage to design it in a way that it would collect all the information that is necessary for a more accurate design of the coverage contemplated.

Designing a Baseline Study (Grosh and Glewwe, 2000)

A baseline survey is usually a cross-sectional quantitative study, i.e., an observational study that records data from a representative subset of the target population at a specific point-in-time. The sample size is predetermined to ensure its statistical strength (or power). Often, the qualitative survey is complemented with qualitative data, collected through interviews (e.g., FGDs, KIIs, IDIs). Qualitative findings help explain or validate the quantitative findings. In specific cases, the baseline survey is part of a more elaborate or longer term experimental design (case–control, randomized control trials). The modern trend is to combine both techniques — quantitative and qualitative — to collect baseline data.

Deciding the sample size for the quantitative survey (also known as *power calculations*) determines the precision of the estimates and, thus, is very important for calculations of premiums. When the population is very small (a slum, a small village), it may be necessary/desirable to conduct a complete enumeration (census). More information on sampling is given in the Issue Brief dedicated to this topic attached to this chapter.

When resources are limited, there are simpler and cheaper ways to obtain at least some data. One way is to rely mainly on qualitative information. This option is the subject of Chapter 4.

Researchers have tried various qualitative techniques like illness mapping and risk priority mapping as alternatives to quantitative surveys and had got good results. One should always remember the critical differences between qualitative and quantitative studies. Qualitative studies (i) focus on one or two particular issues, (ii) involve small samples, and (iii) the findings are usually not generalizable beyond the geography where it was conducted.

On the other hand, a quantitative study (i) covers a range of issues and (ii) has a statistically valid sample size. Quality of data is better in qualitative studies because they probe in depth and sessions are facilitated by qualified researchers. Quantitative studies do not allow much scope for probing, and field investigators conducting interviews are not as expert as qualified researchers. While designing a baseline study, one has to remember to strike a balance between (i) the range and depth of issues and (ii) the quantity and quality of data (concerning sample size) depending on the resource and the availability of time.

Steps of Baseline Studies (Walonick, 2013)

There are several steps involved in planning and conducting baseline studies. It is recommended that implementers should give due weight to the following steps without any compromise:

- designing the study;
- quantitative and qualitative requirements;
- how much time, effort, and resources should be spent on each component;

- determining the sample size;
- deciding about the sampling process;
- preparing the tool;
- questionnaire for the quantitative component;
- various guidelines for the qualitative component;
- conducting field survey;
- training of the field surveyors;
- management of the field survey;
- ensuring data quality;
- data analysis;
- use of proper statistical techniques/statistical software;
- transcription and translation of the documentation of the qualitative sessions;
- triangulation of the findings from different sources.

SELF-TEST QUESTIONS

1. Enumerate the type of information collected through a baseline study before the launch of a microinsurance scheme.
2. What are the key differences between qualitative and quantitative studies?
3. What are the steps involved in planning and conducting a baseline study?
4. Discuss the factors that need to be kept in mind while designing a baseline study.
5. Qualitative surveys are often complemented with qualitative data collected through interviews. List the type of interviews used in such cases.

KEY TERMS

- **Baseline study (or survey):** It is a structured (or systematic) gathering of data from various sources. The beginning of a project or intervention usually entails conducting a baseline study.
- **Power calculations:** Deciding the sample size for the quantitative survey is called power calculations.

Issue Brief: Sampling

Sampling is a process used in statistical analysis in which a predetermined number of observations are taken from a larger population. Sampling is used when it is neither possible nor necessary to interview every person of a population within the exercise of data collection. Statistically speaking, a sample is a subset of the total population. The methodology used to sample from a larger population depends on the type of analysis being performed but may include simple random sampling or systematic sampling. The main concern in statistical sampling is that the sample obtained from the population must be representative of the same population. This can be accomplished by using randomized statistical sampling techniques. The word *random* means unbiased, and *random sample* means that every individual within the population has an equal probability of being included in the sample. This can be achieved when two primary issues are determined upfront:

(1) How many individuals should the sample include? (Sample size)
(2) How to draw that number randomly? (Randomization)

Sample Size

The size of the sample depends largely on how closely you want your results to match those of the entire population. The following two measures affect the accuracy of the data:

(1) the margin of error (or confidence intervals), which is the positive and negative deviation that the sampled respondents could be from the average opinion of the entire population;
(2) the confidence level, which is the degree of precision that the margin of error will be within the range set.

There are several online calculators of the sample size for defined population sizes, with a specific margin of error and confidence level [and additional calibration to take account of the fact that not every person asked to be sampled would agree (*response rate*)]. For example, https://www.checkmarket.com/sample-size-calculator/.

Drawing a Random Sample

Drawing a random sample (i.e., a sample representative of the population) is done by following several steps: (i) define the population (*the sampling frame*); (ii) choose the sample size; and (iii) draw the random numbers. This can be done in several ways as follows[2]:

Types of Random Sample

A random sample could be of two types: simple random sample with replacement (SRSWR) and simple random sample without replacement (SRSWOR). In SRSWR, an item or individual after being included in the sample is replaced in the population and the entire population constitutes the sampling frame in every draw. This, in other words, means that the same individual or item can be included in the sample more than once. In SRSWOR, the item or individual already selected is not replaced. Hence, it cannot reappear in the sample. This implies that in SRSWOR an item or individual cannot be selected multiple times. In reality, most of the samples are samples without replacement.

Sampling Mechanism

Ideally, one should create a sampling frame and draw a random sample using the frame. However, in reality, it is complicated and too expensive

---

[2](a) **Lottery method:** Write 1–100 on slips of paper, fold them to hide the number, mix it up, and keep it within a jar. Ask a person to pick three slips from the jar. Open the slips and see the numbers.

(b) **Excel function:** In MS Excel, you can use the RANDBETWEEN (x, y) function to draw a random number between x and y.

(c) **Currency notes:** The serial number of a currency note is like a random number. Though serial numbers are printed serially on the note, it is so widely circulated that the serial number of a note that lies in anybody's purse is a random number. If the sample size is less than 100, the first or last two digits of the currency note can be treated as a 2-digit random number. Fix 00 for 100. Similarly, if the sample size is less than or equal 1,000, one can use the first or last three digits as 3-digit random numbers. Fix 000 for 1000.

to create a sampling frame. It is next-to-impossible to get a list of all households (HHs) of a block or a district to be surveyed. However, still, there are many ways to draw a random sample.

Systematic sampling: It is a method of sampling where items are selected at equal intervals starting from a random point.

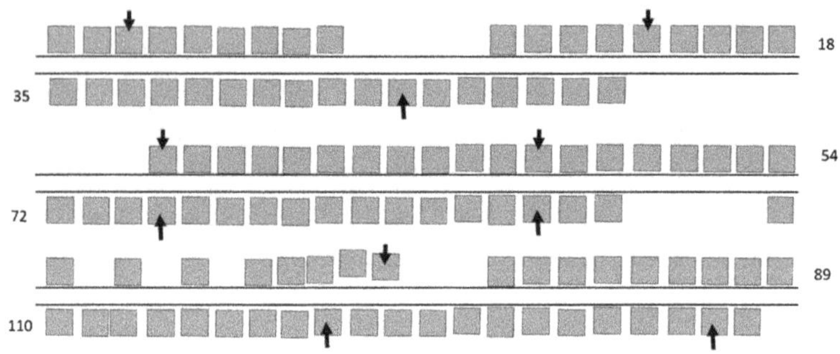

Suppose, you have to draw a random sample of 10 HHs from a village having 110 HHs. The houses are arranged in a more-or-less linear fashion as shown in the figure. This means you have to select one house from every 11 HHs. Draw a random number between 1 and 11. Say it is 3.

First select the third HH, start from any side. Then select the 11th HH starting from 3. This means you have selected 14th HH. Then select 11th HH starting from 14th. You have selected 14 + 11 = 25th household. Repeat the process, until you have selected the desired number of HHs in the sample. Note, that you did not prepare a sampling frame for sampling. You just started walking from one direction, covered the entire village, and selected every 11th HH starting from 3. The sample finally consists of the HHs with the following serial numbers: 3, 14, 25, 36, 47, 58, 69, 80, 91, and 102. This type of sampling is called systematic sampling.

Cluster Sampling: In cluster sampling, the total population is divided into small equal-size clusters. One has to draw a random sample of clusters first, and all items or individuals of the selected clusters are included in the sample.

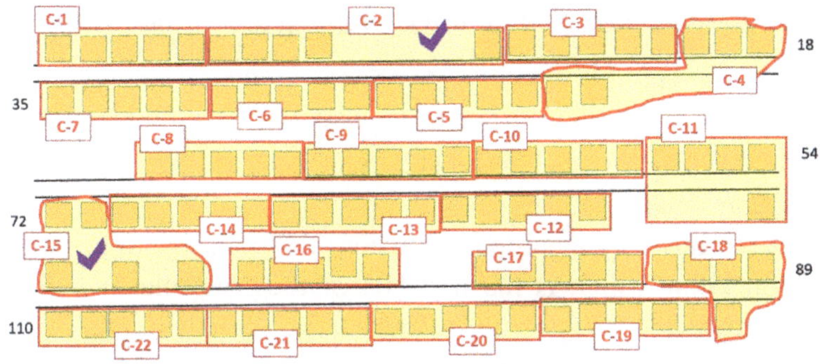

Let us draw a sample of size 10 from the population referred to in the previous example. We divide the HHs into many clusters. Each cluster is of size 5. There are 22 clusters. 22 × 5 = 110. Number the clusters from 1, 2, 3, …, 22. To draw 10 HHs at random, we have to select 2 clusters (2 × 5 = 10). We have selected two random numbers between 1 and 11. Say, they are 2 and 15. The sample contains all HHs of the clusters 2 and 15. This is cluster sampling.

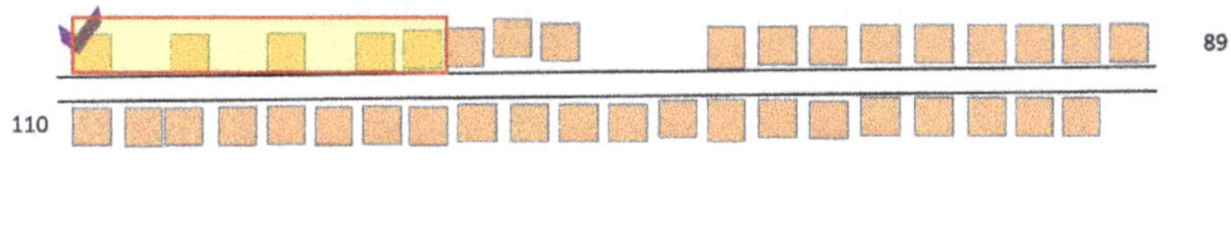

In reality, such clusters are not literally formed. If you have to select two clusters, go in two different directions and start from any two points (chosen at random, i.e., without any bias). Survey five consecutive HHs from the starting points. If the sample size is 25, choose the five starting points far away from each other (preferably in five different directions) and then survey five consecutive HHs from the starting points.

Points to remember about cluster sampling are as follows:

- In cluster samplings, you include all HHs of the selected cluster in the sample. This means you reach the first HH of the cluster and then survey five consecutive HHs. This is why cluster sampling is logistically convenient.
- However, reaching a particular cluster does not seem to be easy. How do you know which is the first HH of the 15th cluster without the sampling frame?
- Note that there is no such rule that clusters have to be formed only with consecutive HHs. Clusters may be formed by grouping the HHs in any manner — the only prerequisite is that no HH should belong to more than one cluster. See, we have rearranged the clusters 4, 11, and 18 differently and it is perfectly okay. This makes one of the most convenient features of cluster sampling.
- In reality, such clusters are not formed. If you have to select two clusters, go in two different directions and start from any two points (chosen at random, i.e., without any bias). Survey five consecutive HHs from the starting points. If the sample size is 25, choose the five starting points far away from each other (preferably in five different directions) and then survey five consecutive HHs from the starting points.
- Cluster size should be small (five is the right size). If you have to draw a sample of 20, then choose 4 clusters of size 5 each, rather than, 2 clusters of size 10 each.
- Clusters (I mean starting points of each selected cluster) should be located as far away from each other as possible.
- Cluster sampling is statistically less efficient sampling. Wherever possible, one should try to get a sampling frame. However, in reality, cluster sampling is done for most of the surveys because of its logistical convenience.

Note that if the clusters are of size 1, then cluster sampling is equivalent to SRSWOR.

PPS Sampling: A PPS sampling is a method of drawing sample where the probability of an item or individual being selected in the sample is proportional to its size.

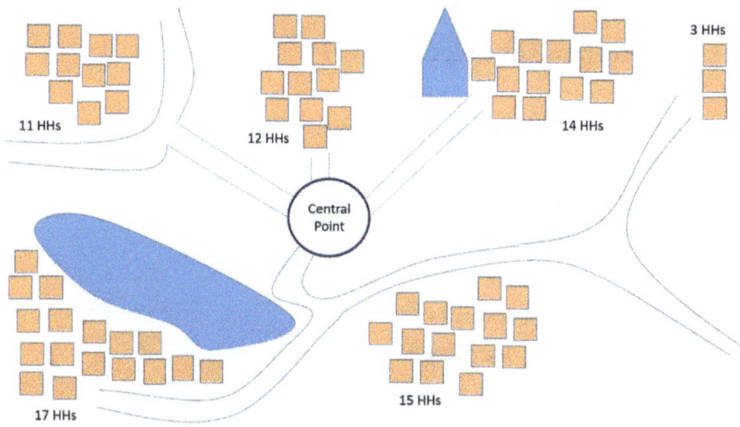

To understand PPS sampling, we consider the example of the village as in the given figure. The village consists of six localities with a varied number of HHs. We select two localities in the sample in such a way that *the localities with the higher number of HHs get an advantage with higher chances of being included in the sample*. This does not mean that only localities with a higher number of HHs are selected in the sample or the localities with a smaller number of HHs are never selected in the sample. We create the drawing algorithm in such a way that every locality has a chance — proportional to its size — of being selected. Actual selection depends on the random number or result of the random experiment (lottery).

Note that, this sample of two localities is *not a random sample as per our definition*. This is because each locality has a different probability of being included in the sample. This type of sampling is also required at times. We show you two ways (algorithms) to draw a PPS sample.

Distribution of HHs in the Village

Locality	Size = Number of HHs	Cumulative Number of HHs
A	10	10
B	12	22
C	14	36
D	3	39
E	16	55
F	15	70
Total	70	

Sampling Mechanism (Algorithm) 1

Step 1

We will draw a random number (r) between 1 and 70.

If $1 \leq r \leq 10$, select locality A.
If $10 < r \leq 22$, select locality B.
If $22 < r \leq 36$, select locality C.
If $36 < r \leq 39$, select locality D.
If $39 < r \leq 55$, select locality E.
If $55 < r \leq 70$, select locality F.

Step 2

Our First draw [excel function: =randbetween(1,70)] gives 42, **we select locality E**.

Repeat the process of Step 1.
Our Second draw [excel function: =randbetween(1,70)] gives 12, **we select locality B**.

Sampling Mechanism (Algorithm) 2

Step 1

Calculate: 70 (= total size) ÷ 2 (=sample size for the clusters) = 35.

Step 2

Draw a random number (r_1) between 1 and 35 [excel function = randbetween (1, 35)].

If $1 \leq r_1 \leq 10$, select locality A.
If $10 < r_1 \leq 22$, select locality B.
If $22 < r_1 \leq 35$, select locality C.

Step 3

Then compute $r_2 = r_1 + 35$.

If $36 \leq r_2 \leq 36$, i.e., $r_2 = 36$.
select locality *c*.
If $36 < r_2 \leq 39$, select locality D.
If $39 < r_2 \leq 55$, select locality E.

If $55 < r_2 \leq 70$, select locality F.

The first draw gives us $r_1 = 34$. We select C. $r_2 = r_1 + 35 = 69$. We select F.

Two-stage sampling: Now that we know cluster sampling and PPS sampling, we are in a position to draw a random sample from this village. Suppose we have to draw a sample of size 15 from this village which has 70 HHs in total spread over six localities.

Distribution of HHs in the Village

Locality	Size = Number of HHs	Cumulative Number of HHs
A	10	10
B	12	22
C + D	17	39
E	16	55
F	15	70
Total	70	

Total sample size = 15, we draw 3 clusters of 5 HHs each.

Step 1. Draw 3 localities from the village using PPS.
Random numbers drawn are as follows:
38 → select C + D. (We combine D with C as D has less than 5 HHs.)
27 → Reject as it again selects C + D.
49 → Select E.
22 → Select B.
So we have selected (C + D) combined, E and B.

Step 2. Select one cluster of 5 HHs from every locality. Go to any point in a selected locality and survey 5 consecutive HHs. Repeat the process for all three selected localities.

We have done the sampling in two stages — first selecting the localities using PPS and then selecting individual HHs in each selected locality using cluster sampling. This is why it is called two-stage sampling.

Now there is a question. Is the final sample a random sample? Stated otherwise, did every HH in the village have an equal chance of being included in the sample? Let us see.

Locality	Size = Number of HHs	The Probability that this Locality is Selected in the First Stage (PPS)	Say an HH h belongs to this Locality (as Mentioned in Each Row). Conditional Probability that h is Selected at the Second Stage (Cluster Sampling) Given that the Locality It belongs to has Already been Selected at the First Stage	Unconditional Probability that h is Selected in the Sample
A	10	10/70	${}^{9}C_4 \div {}^{10}C_5 = 5/10$	10/70 × 5/10 = 5/70
B	12	12/70	${}^{11}C_4 \div {}^{12}C_5 = 5/12$	12/70 × 5/12 = 5/70
C + D	17	17/70	${}^{16}C_4 \div {}^{17}C_5 = 5/17$	17/70 × 5/17 = 5/70
E	16	16/70	${}^{15}C_4 \div {}^{16}C_5 = 5/16$	16/70 × 5/16 = 5/70
F	15	15/70	${}^{14}C_4 \div {}^{15}C_5 = 5/15$	15/70 × 5/15 = 5/70
Total	70			

An HH (h) may belong to any of the localities. However, the probabilities of being included in the sample are all equal.

Multistage sampling: A sample can be drawn in more than two stages as well. Then it is called multistage sampling.

Suppose that you have to survey a sample of 900 individuals from a block called M Rampur. This block is located in Kalahandi district of Odisha (India). The purpose is to get an idea about the rate of hospitalization in the district. Note that we have to draw individuals (*not* HHs). We can think every HH as a cluster of individuals. Assume every HH has five members. (It is not perfect, but serves to simplify the explanation at this stage.)

Step 1. Calculating Primary Details			
900	Total Sample (of Individuals)		
5	Individuals per cluster	*Why is five the optimum size of the cluster?*	
180	Clusters (HHs) to be sampled	*An HH may be treated as a cluster of individuals.*	Cluster sampling
15	Clusters (HHs)/village	*Why? We employ a team of three people. Each can survey five HHs in one day. The team spends one day in each village.*	
12	Villages to be sampled		PPS sampling
3	Villages/panchayat	*Why? This is the minimum number of villages in a panchayat. If we plan to take four or more villages from every panchayat and the panchayat with three villages is selected, then it is a problem.*	
4	Panchayats to be sampled		PPS sampling

Step 2 Get Sizes of the Panchayats (Populations) of M Rampur Block (Source: Census)				**Step 3** Selecting four Panchayats using PPS Sampling (First Stage Sampling)		
Name of the Panchayat	Number of Villages	# HHs	Population	Cumulative Population	Selection of Panchayats	Random Numbers
M Rampur	7	2,693	8,466	8,466	Selected (3)	28,263
Panda Kamal	3	808	2,706	11,172		12,771
Salepali	6	700	2,766	13,938	Selected (2)	27,414 (Reject)
Madanpur	5	644	3,068	17,006		6,837
Alatara	3	646	2,301	19,307		999 (Reject)
Gochhadeogoan	20	1,588	6,924	26,231	Selected (4)	11,657 (Reject)
Damkarlakhunta	13	807	3,887	30,118	Selected (1)	21,274
Nunpur	9	926	4,266	34,384		
Bamak (Aenlapali)	6	904	3,242	37,626		
Saidalanga	5	992	3,432	41,058		
Muding	7	1,251	4,870	45,928		
# GPs = 11	84	11,959	45,928			

Step 4 Get Information about the Villages of Panchayat M Rampur			**Step 5** Choose three Villages using PPS Sampling (Second Stage Sampling)		
Village	HHs	Population	Cumulative Population	Selection of Village	Random Numbers
M Rampur	1,781	6,908	6,908	Selected (1)	2,825
Goudkela	58	207	7,115		5,476 (Reject)
Harischandrapur	82	321	7,436	Selected (3)	4,238 (Reject)
Jakabahali	50	198	7,634		8,099
G Karlakhunta	93	316	7,950		2,791 (Reject)
Motoganda	88	370	8,320	Selected (2)	5,218 (Reject)
Burat	541	146	8,466		8,138 (Reject)
					6,595 (Reject) 7,278

Step 6 Get Information about the Villages of Panchayat Salepali			**Step 7** Choose 3 Villages using PPS Sampling (Second Stage Sampling)		
Village	HHs	Population	Cumulative Population	Selection of Village	Random Numbers
Salepali	116	428	428	Selected (3)	970
Dutta	188	619	1,047	Selected (1)	1,754
Jhaliagobha	114	364	1,411		88
Kachharpali	51	306	1,717		
Karnimal	60	194	1,911	Selected (2)	
Maskadandi	171	855	2,766		

Step 8 Get Information about the Villages of Panchayat Damkarlakhunta			**Step 9** Choose three Villages using PPS Sampling (Second Stage Sampling)		
Village	HHs	Population	Cumulative Population	Selection of Village	Random Numbers
Dumerguda	146	820	820	Selected (3)	3,041

Kandegoan	55	390	1,210	Selected (2)	858
Pajibahali	29	145	1,355		760
Borebhata	85	425	1,780		
Jharandunguri	35	93	1,873		
Kusmel	35	136	2,009		
Phatamunda	64	229	2,238		
Podelkuna	87	326	2,564		
Dullen	32	128	2,692		
Penjikupa	38	190	2,882		
Ulimunda	37	185	3,067	Selected (1)	
Masarlpada	18	90	3,157		
Damkarlakhunta	146	730	3,887		

Block	Four Panchayats Selected (First Stage — PPS)	12 Villages Selected (Second Stage — PPS)	Selection of HHs from Villages (Third Stage — Cluster Sampling)
M Rampur	M Rampur	M Rampur	Three surveyors go in three different directions. Each selects 5 HHs (or more, so that, at least 25 individuals are covered) *located far apart from each other.*
		Harischandrapur	
		Motoganda	
	Salepali	Salepali	
		Dutta	
		Karnimal	
	Gochhadeogoan	Talkuna	
		Gochh'degoan	
		Belur	
	Damkarlakhunta	Dumerguda	
		Kandegoan	
		Ulimunda	

Let us do the sampling in one village. The same process is repeated for all 12 villages selected in the Second stage of sampling.

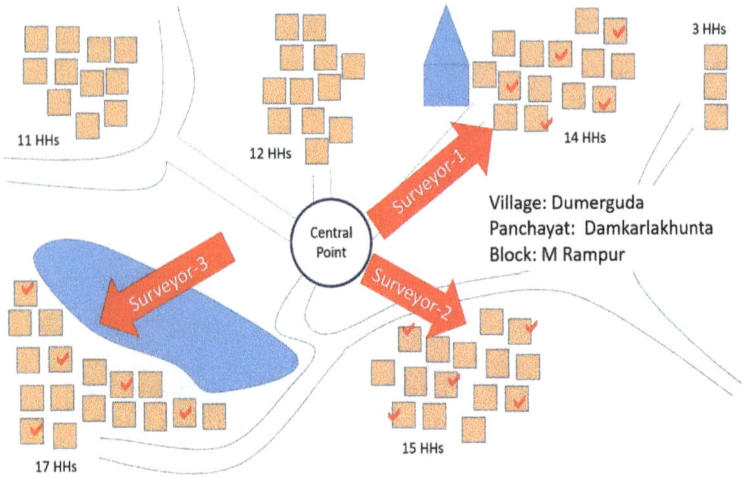

Stratified Random Sample: Stratified random sampling is an exceptional kind of sampling where the population is divided into several non-overlapping (mutually exclusive) groups. Each group is called a stratum. All groups together are called strata.

Examples: Suppose we are interested in measuring the level of insurance awareness among four groups of adult populations of an area, *viz.* (i) working in the government sector, (ii) working in private sectors, (iii) working in the informal sector, and (iv) non-working. We are interested in measuring the level in four groups *separately* and *also in all four groups combined* (basically implies the total population).

Total Population		
Sector	Size	Proportion
Government sector	500	5%
Private sector	1,000	10%
Informal sector	6,000	60%
Non-working	2,500	25%

Take an independent sample from each sector.
Let us take 200 samples from each sector.

So, in the combined sample, you have 200 people working in the government sector, 200 people working in the private sector, 200 people working in the informal sector, and 200 people who are not working.

Question: Does the combined sample represent the total population?

Answer: No. Proportions of different sectors in the combined sample do not match with their actual proportions in the total population. So if you want to get an idea about the level of insurance awareness in the total population from the combined sample, it does not portray the correct picture.

Remember our definition of a random sample. Each member of the population has an equal probability of being included in the sample. This condition is violated here. Here the probabilities are as follows:

Government sector: 200/500 = 2/5, private sector: 200/1,000 = 1/5,

Informal sector: 200/6,000 = 1/30, non-working: 200/2500 = 2/25.

In other words, the sample from each stratum is a random sample for the corresponding stratum, but the combined sample is not a random sample for the total population.

Then, what is the way out?

There are three ways out.

Way out 1: Sample size from each stratum should be proportional to their actual proportions in the total population. This implies that the sample sizes from various sectors might be as follows:

If government sector = 200, then private sector = 400, informal sector = 2,400 and non-working = 1000. Total sample size = 200 + 400 + 2400 + 1000 = 4000.

Check the probabilities now:

Government sector: 200/500=2/5, private sector: 400/1,000=2/5,

Informal sector: 2,400/6,000 =2/5, non-working: 1,000/2,500 = 2/5.

This is called proportional allocation. However, note that to calculate the proportional sample size, you have to have prior knowledge of the actual proportions of different strata in the total population, which is often not the case.

Way out 2: If the sample size from each stratum is not proportional to the population size, for all calculations involving the combined sample, you have to multiply the estimate for each stratum with the suitable corresponding weights to get the estimate for the total population.

These weights are inverses of the probabilities being included in the combined sample.

For example, if your sample size is 200 from each stratum, we know that the probabilities are as under:

Government sector: 200/500=2/5, private sector: 200/1000 = 1/5,

Informal sector: 200/6000 =1/30, non-working: 200/2500 = 2/25.

Hence, the corresponding weights are as follows: government sector: 5/2, private sector: 5/1, informal sector: 30/1, non-working: 25/2. Observe that the proportions of the weights are the same as the population proportion of the corresponding stratum.

$$5/2 : 5/1 : 30/1 : 25/2 = 5:10:60:25.$$

In this case too, you have to have prior knowledge of the actual proportions of different strata in the total population, which is often not the case.

Way out 3: If it is not possible to do proportional allocation and population proportions are unknown, then treat the strata and the total population separately. This means the following: take a suitable sample from each stratum, which gives stratumwise estimates, and take another sample (in this particular example, a fifth sample) from the entire population using a suitable sampling mechanism explained earlier.

Not to confuse, if we apply PPS sampling in the process, the sizes used for PPS sampling are not the sizes of the strata. If we know the sizes of the strata beforehand, then a separate sample representing the total population is not necessary. Instead, we use weights.

In PPS, we work with the sizes of the geographic segmentation. Strata usually refer to non-geographic segmentations. Like, gender strata: male, female; education strata: illiterate, primary, secondary, undergraduate, postgraduate, etc.; income strata: poor, middle income, high income.

Some Key Issues Regarding Sampling

• *The more the merrier. The bigger the sample, the better.*

Better means a more precise estimate (or a better idea about the population). However, a larger sample means higher cost and handling many management issues which may infuse errors in the estimate. This error is called a non-sampling error. If you have a team of five, you can supervise them better. If you deploy a team of 500, you do not know whether each person works with equal sincerity.

• *Remember: no data is better than wrong data.*

Always try to get a *random* sample.

Remember the definition — each member of the population should get an equal chance to be included in the sample. Sometimes it may not be possible to apply proper scientific mechanism (e.g., lottery, random numbers, excel) to ensure randomness. However, no way should your sample be influenced by *convenience*. Often, we exclude remote areas because of logistical inconvenience. This is wrong.

This is why cluster sampling is not a very efficient sampling. To compensate for efficiency loss in cluster sampling, you need to increase the sample size. This is known as *design effect*. Design effect = 2 means that you must take a sample double in size of what was initially recommended by a statistician.

Take expert help to calculate the sample size. This has not been discussed here. If no such help is readily available, then decide about the sample size based on the resources (= money) available for the survey and the extent you can manage. Remember, the accuracy of an estimate does not increase proportionally with the sample size.

The best sampling procedure when no information about the population is available is SRSWOR. *Without replacement* means the same member of the population should not be repeated in the sample. Remember we rejected some random numbers because they referred to the same members already selected.

Wherever possible use the sampling frame. If you have a sampling frame, you can apply SRSWOR. The originally recommended sample size need not be altered due to the design effect. This is cost-effective.

The sample should be as spread as possible in the population without compromising with the randomness. In our earlier example of drawing a sample from M Rampur block, if the list of villages is available for the entire block, we should choose the random villages from the list without choosing the panchayats first.

Annexes

The annexes for this chapter are available online as supplementary material at https://www.worldscientific.com/worldscibooks/10.1142/11505#t=suppl.

Bibliography

Dror, DM (2018) *Financing Micro Health Insurance: Theory, Methods, and Evidence*. In *World Scientific Series in Health Investment and Financing*, ed. AS Preker, Vol. 2. Singapore: World Scientific Publishing.

Dror, DM (2007) Why "One-Size-Fits-All" Health Insurance Products Are Unsuitable for Low-Income Persons in the Informal Economy in India. *Asian Economic Review*, 49(1), 47–56.

Dror, DM, Van Putten, O, and Koren, R (2008) Cost of Illness: Evidence from a Study in Five Resource-Poor Locations in India. *Indian Journal of Medical Research*, 127, 347–361.

Dror, DM, van Putten-Rademaker, O, and Koren, R (2009) Incidence of Illness among Resource-Poor Households: Evidence from Five Locations in India. *Indian Journal of Medical Research*, 130, 146–154.

A comprehensive, albeit a bit dated, source is Grosh, M and Glewwe, P (Eds.) (2000) *Designing Household Survey Questionnaires for Developing Countries: Lessons from 15 Years of the Living Standards Measurement Study*, Vol. 1. Washington, D.C.: The World Bank. Available at http://documents.worldbank.org/curated/en/452741468778781879/Volume-One.

A useful Questionnaire Research Flow Chart is published in Walonick, DS (2013) *Survival Statistics*. Bloomington: StatPac, Inc.

Selected Websites

The following websites pertain to the content of this chapter:

- For more information on Qualitative and Quantitative Research Methods, go to https://www.nottingham.ac.uk/nursing/sonet/rlos/ebp/qvq/page_four.html (accessed 24 March 2019).
- For more information on sample size calculators, go to https://www.checkmarket.com/sample-size-calculator/ (accessed 13 April 2019).

Chapter 4

Substitutes to Baseline Surveys

LEARNING OBJECTIVES

Upon completion of this chapter, the reader should be able to:

- Discuss the constraints in conducting a household survey
- Identify the information that helps in optimizing data collection for benefits package design and pricing
- Understand how the illness mapping method can act as a substitute for household surveys
- Explain the method adopted to test the effectiveness of the illness mapping method

Abstract

This chapter seeks to propose an efficient alternative to household surveys (HHSs) for obtaining data needed to launch a community-based health insurance scheme. We discuss the three essential pieces of information that are used for the design of the benefits package and its pricing. These are morbidity and utilization patterns, the average cost of care locally, and the distribution of that cost. The methods available to source these data without conducting a full HHS are elaborated.

Chapter Outline

Future innovations notwithstanding, the two most common ways of obtaining the data needed to launch a (micro)insurance operation are either reliance on secondary data (e.g., national statistical reports) or conducting household surveys (HHSs). Using national statistical reports is quite risky because the national average values of the utilization of healthcare and the costs of such utilization are, in all likelihood, inaccurate representations of the correct values that apply in a remote, rural, or resource-poor community. Simply put, knowing the average value is insufficient information to calculate accurate premiums or launch a microinsurance scheme.[1] The alternative solution, conducting an HHS to obtain local data, is very costly and time consuming. It takes time to prepare a survey; it requires a large team to go from house to house to interview the respondents; and more time to clean, organize, and analyze the high amount of data collected to reach the stage that the data are exploitable for premium calculations. The high cost makes it necessary first to raise funds, and it is difficult to estimate the time needed to succeed to raise funds. A process that is so slow to unfold creates adverse effects among the target community that loses trust in the process and interest in the insurance solution. In Annex 1 provided in the supplementary material for

[1] "The (t)error of averages." When carrying out large HHSs, as governments do, there is a tendency to publish many findings as average values. Averages are useful because they summarize a large amount of data into a single value. However, average values obscure the variability around this single value within the original data, and the more heterogeneous the groups of samples, the less reflective the average value is of the true situation. The use of mean values is subject to three errors. First, when the data series has outliers, the average of that series might be skewed in the direction of the outliers. In such situations, the median value, which is less impacted by outliers, might be useful. Second, it is a statistical error to apply the average of many data points to a single point and assume it to be true (see Why Averages Are Often Wrong — Towards Data Science, https://towardsdatascience.com/why-averages-are-often-wrong-1ff08e409a5b (accessed 25 March 2019). Applying the average to individual scenarios is erroneous regardless of the distribution of the data series, and the probability that an average value accurately describes any one data point drops as the data distribution approaches the tails of the curve. Third, it is common for people to think of "average" as "typical." However, there are many exceptions to "typical" in human behavior, economic choices, and priority setting.

this chapter, we explain in more detail the weighty constraints to conducting an HHS.

> **SELF-TEST QUESTION**
>
> 1. Discuss the various constraints associated with conducting a baseline survey.

We submit that operating microinsurance needs a faster and cheaper method to obtain the essential data. The optimal solution we seek should enable implementers of health microinsurance to source data locally while having the reasonable assurance that the cheaper and faster method is robust statistically and that data quality is comparable to data sources through an HHS.

The first step in optimizing data collection is to limit the exploration only to the data components that are used for the design of the benefits package and its pricing. The three essential pieces of information are morbidity and utilization patterns; the average cost of care locally; and the distribution of that cost.

The following sections contain an explanation of how each of the three data elements can be sourced without conducting a full HHS.

Sourcing data on morbidity and healthcare utilization patterns

The objective is to elicit estimates of morbidity and healthcare utilization from "Experts" in the target community (village representatives carefully selected for their social skills and knowledge about neighboring households).

There is ample scientific literature on methods to obtain and verify information from several experts (sometimes referred to as "the expert group") even without convening groups of many experts, which may be impossible (methods called "non-interactive group methods"). Two of the better known methods are the Delphi[2] method and the nominal group

[2] Developed in 1950s by RAND (https://www.rand.org/topics/delphi-method.html), also called Estimate–Talk–Estimate.

technique (Delbecq and Van de Ven, 1971). However, these methods deliver reliable results only after several iterations, which require more time. As we set out to obtain results within weeks rather than months and considering the target population that is not very suited to follow the strict rules of these two techniques, we planned to conduct qualitative research with group interaction. Focus group discussions (FGDs) is an interactive method. The challenge, however, was to alter the standard process that unfolds in FGDs so that we would enhance the accuracy of the estimates of morbidity and utilization obtained by discussions with the experts. We wanted to reinforce the FGDs by applying a modified version of the two robust methods mentioned above within the FGD technique, i.e., within an interactive group method. The result has been a novel method, developed by our research team in 2012, which we called the *Illness Mapping* (IM) method (Dror, 2018, Chapter 7). The IM is an interactive method that applies certain elements initially conceived for non-interactive methods (based on the Delphi and nominal group technique methods).

Annex 2 provided in the supplementary material for this chapter contains the research tools to apply IM. The FGD tool is a guideline for the facilitator(s) on how to conduct the discussions in such a manner that estimates would be reviewed by the participating experts several times until the consensus reflects the wisdom of the group. The interactions between facilitator and experts are essential to bridge literacy constraints and to reach consensus.

When we developed the IM method, we also tested it by comparison to those obtained in the same locations and period through an HHS. The households were selected randomly. For the IM, small group discussions were held in the villages with men and women who, while marginally literate and numerate, were experts in the details of their village communities.[3] In the HHS,[4] respondents were asked separately about illness episodes in their household during the month preceding the survey.

The classification of the illnesses mentioned (initially into four categories: acute, chronic, accidents, and undefined) was converted into three "benefit types": the prevalence of illness for *acute and chronic illnesses,*

---

[3] The IM were conducted with 18 women's and 17 men's groups.

[4] The HHS was conducted in 50 villages with 1,000 randomly selected households (6,656 individuals).

the incidence of *hospitalizations*, and the incidence of *deliveries* (especially hospital deliveries).

The results of the comparison were as follows:

The overall prevalence of illness (IM: 25.9% ± 3.6; HHS: 31.4%) — good agreement;

Prevalence of acute illnesses (IM: 76.9%; HHS: 69.2%) — good agreement;

Prevalence of chronic illnesses (IM: 20.1%; HHS: 16.6%) — good agreement;

Incidence of deliveries (IM: 3.9% ± 0.4; HHS: 3.9%) — very good agreement;

Hospital deliveries (IM: 61.0% ± 5.4; HHS: 51.4%) — good agreement;

Hospitalizations (IM: 1.1% ± 0.4; HHS: 2.6%) — significant difference.

Source: Dror (2018), p. 191.

The results of the IM exercise seem very useful for estimating utilization patterns of prevalence of illnesses that usually require outpatient services. Considering that most health microinsurance schemes provide coverage of those services and only rarely cover hospitalizations, we conclude that the IM method is sufficient for the needs of microinsurance operations.

SELF-TEST QUESTIONS

1. Do you think that the classification of illnesses into three "benefit types" to assess the robustness of the IM method was prudent? Why?
2. Summarize the findings on comparing the results of the IM method with the HHS results. Do you see any limitations of such a comparison?

Sourcing the average cost of care locally

The cost of care can be obtained in the same way as the data morbidity and utilization of FGDs. When all the expert opinions on the cost of care per benefit type are in hand, we were able to calculate the average cost per benefit type, which was used for premium calculations.

Sourcing the distribution of the local cost of care

We are interested in the distribution of healthcare costs because, even though everybody spends something on healthcare, in a group or population, a small portion of the people spends a substantial percentage of total health spending (only very few people spend very much money). Moreover, individuals' utilization of health services varies from year to year throughout their lifetimes. Therefore, average health spending would not be very instructive, as, in reality, it is rare that any particular person spends precisely the average amount. For health insurance, knowing the distribution of costs is essential for two purposes: first, to predict the expected costs for the insurance based on the distribution of those costs in the population; second, to establish *thresholds* (below which costs are not reimbursed) or *caps* (above which costs are not payable by the insurance).

We obtained data on healthcare expenditure (hospitalization and tests) from 11 baseline HHSs conducted between 2008 and 2010 in several rural locations (9 in India and 2 in Nepal) to compare the empirical distribution to the distribution obtained through a computer simulation of the health costs. The shape of the distributions was very similar in all 11 locations for both benefits, and this could be represented by a model based on a lognormal distribution. This fit to the lognormal distribution was remarkable as there was a considerable variation in the incidence/prevalence of illness, utilization of healthcare, and the mean cost of the two benefits across the 11 locations. A detailed write-up of that analysis has been published elsewhere (Dror, 2018, Chapter 8). We are not aware of any other study of the distribution of healthcare costs in microinsurance. Hence, we assume that the lognormal distribution suitably reflects the spread of healthcare costs in health microinsurance. The only information that is required to fix thresholds and caps (as part of package design) is the average cost of each benefit type that is included in the benefits package.

SELF-TEST QUESTIONS

1. Discuss the three pieces of information that help in optimizing data collection for the design of the benefits package and its pricing.
2. Why is it important to know the distribution of healthcare costs?

KEY TERMS

- **Illness Mapping:** It is an interactive method of sourcing data on morbidity and healthcare utilization patterns without conducting an HHS.
- **Threshold:** The maximum amount payable by the participant before entitlement to any payout from community-based health insurance is the threshold.
- **Cap:** The maximum amount payable by the insurance is called the cap.
- **Respondents' fatigue:** A phenomenon that occurs when survey participants become tired of the survey task, and the quality of the data they provide begins to deteriorate.[5]

Annexes

The annexes for this chapter are available online as supplementary material at https://www.worldscientific.com/worldscibooks/10.1142/11505#t=suppl.

Bibliography

Delbecq, AL and Van de Ven, AH (1971) A Group Process Model for Problem Identification and Program Planning. *Journal of Applied Behavioral Science*, 7, 466–491.

Dror, DM (2018) *Financing Micro Health Insurance: Theory, Methods, and Evidence*. In World Scientific Series in Health Investment and Financing, ed. AS Preker, Vol. 2. Singapore: World Scientific Publishing.

[5] http://methods.sagepub.com/reference/encyclopedia-of-survey-research-methods/n480.xml (accessed 26 April 2019).

Selected Websites

The following websites pertain to the content of this chapter:

- To understand why it is erroneous to publish household survey findings as average values, go to "Why Averages Are Often Wrong — Towards Data Science" https://towardsdatascience.com/why-averages-are-often-wrong-1ff08e409a5b (accessed 25 March 2019).
- For more information on the Delphi method, go to https://www.rand.org/topics/delphi-method.html (accessed 10 April 2019).

Chapter 5

Pricing of Microinsurance or Rate Making

LEARNING OBJECTIVES

Upon completion of this chapter, the reader should be able to:

- Understand the challenges inherent in the pricing of microinsurance schemes
- Differentiate between risk rating, community rating, and experience rating
- Explain the calculation for estimating the contribution per capita required to run the scheme
- Describe the "condition parameters" applied to health benefits packages
- Design a hypothetical benefits package with condition parameters
- Understand the modeling of annual payout per individual for a benefit type and the aggregated contribution
- Explain the estimation of per capita contribution for wage loss compensation
- Identify and estimate cost-generating health events to calculate the premium per person

Abstract

In commercial insurance, it is common practice to charge each individual the premium that reflects that person's estimated contribution to the risk pool. However, in microinsurance, community rating is applied, whereby every participant pays the same premium, irrespective of age, gender, health status, or claims history. This methodology is challenging in terms of pricing the package and maintaining an equilibrium between high-risk and low-risk individuals. The reality in microinsurance practice is that *the price determines the package*, rather than the other way around. This chapter provides a detailed guideline on context-dependent pricing.

Chapter Outline

The logic underlying the pricing of any good or service is that the price should reflect its value. On the assumption that the value of the good or service (the product) determines its price, many producers of goods and services admit that the clients can choose the product they wish to consume, but do not admit discussions over its price. Increasingly, the suppliers even decide when to offer price discounts and the volume of such discounts. Such pricing practices entail opacity about the assigned value of the various price components and thus often are irrelevant in health microinsurance even though they are standard practice in insurance. Recalling that microinsurance is relevant mainly in the settings of poverty, rurality, and informality, we remind that the population in each location knows to begin with *whether they can avail of a specific service* and at what price (based mainly on *how much other persons pay* for the same service). Experience has shown that in each location people have a heuristic (rule-of-thumb) evaluation of what they agree to pay for a given product, which reflects the local perception of the *quality* of the specific service provider. Therefore, in microinsurance practice, the basic logic underlying pricing is that *context is king*. Beyond the constant concern about the availability of data, there is the more profound challenge of the considerable disparity in the quantity, quality, and diversity of available services across different locations. That gap in the supply poses a general challenge to any claim that the same "fact-based" fair price could apply everywhere. The reality in microinsurance practice is that *the price determines the package*, rather than the other way around. This chapter provides a detailed guideline on context-dependent pricing. Readers may find an elaborate discussion of the way conventional pricing practices in insurance may influence microinsurance elsewhere (Biener, 2013).

Definitions

Price and premium

In the insurance business, often there is a definition of a unit of liability. For example, in life insurance, the unit may be $1,000 (or ₹1,000, or any other currency). For each such unit of liability, there is a *price* (aka *rate*). The price is the cost of that risk, i.e., the likelihood of payment for losses.

In addition to the insurance rate, there are other expenses (e.g., sales expenses (aka acquisition costs), claims processing costs, and profit) which are added. They are called *Loadings*. Sometimes the different components are identified separately, e.g., operational loadings and profit loading.

The *pure premium* is obtained by multiplying the price (or the rate) per unit of liability by the number of units insured. The *gross premium* is the pure premium plus the loadings.

Risk rating

Insurance exploits the gap between individual risk and the risk of a large "risk pool" composed of many individuals. The statistical probability of a "risk pool" to incur cost-generating events decreases as the size of the pool increases and as it becomes more heterogeneous. Also, the average amount of damage may also go down. Thus, the average risk of the pool is lower than the average risk of its components. The common practice of commercial insurance is to charge each individual the premium that reflects that person's estimated contribution to the risk pool. The insurer calculates the premium payable by a potential policyholder based on various factors such as the risk of a claim and the value of any such claims occurring to people of the same age and gender, in the same profession, or living in the same region as the insured person. Risk rating is the practice of charging each person the premium reflecting that person's probability (aka frequency) of a risk multiplied by that person's amount of damage (aka severity), rather than the (lower) average cost of the risk pool in which the person participates, due to a lower frequency or a lower severity, or both.

Community rating

Community rating is a method whereby everyone participating in a specific community is assessed as contributing the same risk to the pool as every other member of that community. This business rule means that when the overall risk of the pool (or the community) is allocated evenly across all participants, everybody pays the same premium, regardless of age, gender, health status, or claims history. When the insurer applies community rating, it evaluates the risk factors of the entire population, rather than those of any one person separately. A community-rated system creates a form of risk equalization between all the members of the community.

Experience rating

Experience rating (or Experience Modification Factor) is a method to adjust the premiums based on the health history of those covered. This rule means that two groups which start with an identical community-rated premium may in subsequent years pay different premiums for the same package as a result of the amount of losses one community experiences compared to the amount of loss that the other community experienced.

Loss-generating events: Health risks are not uniform across places and social groups. People are more likely to join a community-based health insurance (CBHI) when it covers the risks to which they are most exposed. Consider the following example. A person suffering from tuberculosis (TB) consulted her physician, who prescribed some medicines, a chest X-ray, and a few blood tests. The patient's condition worsened; she was diagnosed as suffering from TB. She had to be hospitalized. This illness episode entailed costs for hired transport to the hospital, hospitalized once, had to consult doctors five times, bought medicine five times, and had blood tests and X-rays twice each. This example describes a *single episode* of illness. An *episode* is the span of treatments a person receives simultaneously or consecutively in the course of a single illness or associated illnesses. This example was composed of 16 events of six types, namely hospitalization (1), consultations (5), medicines (5), lab tests (2), X-rays (2), and transportation (1). Events are categorized by "benefit types" that are specified as part of the "benefits package"; examples include hospitalization, lab tests, etc., and the only events that matter are those that generate costs for the household. Under CBHI, risks are defined as *events,* not as episodes.

The magnitude of risks: Two dimensions measure a risk associated with events of a particular benefit type: (1) *frequency of occurrence* and (2) *severity of a loss.* The frequency of occurrence measures how often such an event happens, and severity measures its impact in terms of loss incurred. Hospitalization usually has a low frequency of occurrence and high severity. An Outpatient Department (OPD) visit has a high frequency of occurrence and low severity.

Frequency of occurrence can be characterized by an *average number of loss-generating health events per person per year* (PPPY) in the community. Severity is characterized by the *average loss per event.* Table 5.1 shows how the frequency of occurrence and severity of loss are estimated from the distribution of events and losses from individual events.

Risk Appraisal

Critical appraisal of the risks involves estimating the contribution required to cover the risks borne by the CBHI. This process ultimately leads to the design of a set of benefits packages from which the community finally selects one through the Choosing Healthplans All Together (CHAT) exercise.

Benefits package: A *benefits package* is a *combination of benefit types* (e.g., hospitalization, lab test, imaging, transport) with limitations and qualifications applying to each type, together with its *price.* Limitations

Table 5.1 Loss-Generating Health Events (average number PPPY)

Participant in CBHI / Occurrence	Loss per occurrence for various types of health events: Hospitalization			Consultation and medicine			Lab			Imaging		
	1	2	3	1	2	3	1	2	3	1	2	3
1	20,000	—	—	—	—	—	—	—	—	—	—	—
2	—	—	—	65	—	—	500	200	—	—	—	—
3	—	—	—	—	—	—	—	—	—	—	—	—
4	—	—	—	275	—	—	400	—	—	800	—	—
5	—	—	—	370	—	—	500	—	—	—	—	—
6	—	—	—	222	—	—	—	—	—	200	100	—
7	8,000	—	—	22	—	—	—	—	—	—	—	—
8	—	—	—	116	—	—	—	—	—	—	—	—
9	—	—	—	352	—	—	—	—	—	—	—	—
10	—	—	—	292	—	—	—	—	—	—	—	—
11	—	—	—	22	—	444	—	—	—	—	—	—
12	—	—	—	103	159	357	—	—	—	1,200	—	—
13	—	—	—	62	271	356	—	—	—	—	—	—
14	—	—	—	26	43	393	—	—	—	—	—	—
15	—	—	—	59	—	—	—	—	—	—	—	—
16	—	—	—	184	—	—	—	—	—	—	—	—
17	—	—	—	—	—	—	—	—	—	—	—	—
18	—	—	—	269	—	—	—	—	—	—	—	—
19	—	—	—	86	63	—	—	—	—	—	—	—
20	—	—	—	252	31	—	—	—	—	—	—	—
Total number of events (*A*)			2			25			4			4
Community size (*B*)			20			20			20			20
Average occurrence (*C*) = (*A*)/(*B*)			0.1			1.25			0.2			0.2
Total loss (*D*)			28,000			4,450			1,600			2,300
Average loss per event (Severity) (*E*) = (*D*)/(*A*)			14,000			178			400			575

Note: Figures are hypothetical, in local currency.

SELF-TEST QUESTIONS

1. Briefly discuss the challenges faced by microinsurance schemes in pricing their products.
2. How is the price of insurance defined in terms of a unit of liability?
3. Explain what "risk rating" is. How is community rating different from risk rating, and how does it help the community members?
4. Explain what "experience rating" is. What bearing does it have on the CBHI in future years?
5. Do you think experience rating would be acceptable to the community members? Why/why not?
6. In a CBHI, risks are defined as *events*, not as episodes. With the help of an example, differentiate between a health episode and an event.
7. Explain the two dimensions used to measure the magnitude of a risk.

and qualifications are the condition/parameters that are applied to determine the actual payouts due, based on the participant's actual losses. An occurrence that generates loss but no cost (such as a wage loss) can also be included as a benefit type.

Condition parameters: The specific conditions (threshold, copayment, event cap, and annual individual/family cap) are specified in the benefits package, next to the appropriate benefit type covered. A *threshold* is the amount payable by the participant before the CBHI pays a benefit for the specific benefit type. The threshold amount is deducted from the total loss to determine the claim value. A participant who incurred a loss below the threshold is not entitled to payouts from the CBHI, and payouts are due for losses beyond the threshold. Stated differently, the *threshold* is the self-insured part of the total loss. A *copayment* is the percentage of total claims borne by each participant. Like a threshold, a copayment is also deducted from the total loss to determine the claim value. Thresholds and copayments have a similar impact on the claim value. The threshold is expressed in terms of absolute value, whereas copayment is expressed as a percentage. It is possible that either threshold or copayment could limit a given benefit type, or even by both conditions.

Event cap is the maximum amount payable per event claimed. *Annual individual/family cap* is the maximum amount payable for a specific benefit type for the entire policy period to an individual or a family. Some CBHIs apply an annual cap to each participant separately; others apply an annual cap to a group of individuals tied by family links.

Payouts for claims of wage loss benefit type are determined differently: the benefit is payable only after a waiting period (defined by a minimum number of days' stay in the hospital) is capped by a predetermined maximum amount of compensation per day and a maximum number of days. Example: wage loss benefit is payable to participants who are hospitalized three or more days (the threshold), for up to nine days' stay in the hospital (day cap), and the payout is a lump sum of ₹100 per day (amount cap).

Certain benefit types are defined in terms of a lump sum. This practice may be the preferred way when it is difficult to ascertain the actual loss (e.g., transportation costs) or when adherence to a reasonable, usual, and customary tariff is advantageous (e.g., antenatal care and maternity-related benefit). Table 5.2 shows an example of a benefits package.

Estimating the contribution per capita requires considering several conditions. First, a CBHI usually starts with zero reserves, so it cannot be assumed that it can use surpluses from previous years. Second, it cannot count on subsidy income from any source to complement its contributions. Third, the total premium income may fluctuate depending on how many community members enroll for the new policy period. While one objective is to keep contributions low and affordable, another objective is to ensure that the CBHI can always pay all benefits due. If contributions

Table 5.2 A Typical Health Benefits Package

Benefits	Condition parameters
Hospitalization	Threshold = 0, Event Cap = 5,000, Annual Family Cap = 20,000
Lab test	Threshold = 0, Event Cap = 200, Annual Family Cap = 2,000
Imaging	Threshold = 0, Event Cap = 200, Annual Family Cap = 2,000
Transportation	Flat rate 200 for hospitalization (Fixed Rate Compensation)
Wage loss (local currency)	From third day to ninth day of inpatient care @ 100 per day

Note: Figures are hypothetical, in local currency.

are too low, the CBHI is at risk of default; and if contributions are too high, people might not be willing or able to pay. Hence, contributions must be calculated by applying a solid mathematical basis and cannot be fixed arbitrarily, should not be too low or too high, and should consider a reasonable contribution compliance rate of the participants. The contributions are expressed PPPY.

Per capita contribution PPPY has two additive components: (1) risk cost and (2) operating cost of day-to-day administration and management of the scheme. The *risk cost* is the sum of the *pure risk contribution*, which is the expected total claim payout PPPY (the long-term average payout PPPY converge against this value), plus the *risk loading*, which is supposed to take care of year-to-year fluctuations in the average payouts PPPY. We express the risk loading as a function of (1) standard deviation of the distribution of payouts, (2) the number of participants (the larger the community, the lower the loading), and (3) the probability of defaulting that is defined as "acceptable" for the CBHI (usually this risk should not exceed 5%).

Estimation of per capita pure risk contribution depends on the two sets of data inputs: (1) the population characteristics, namely the risk profile of the community, measured by the frequency of occurrence (of events of various benefit types) and distributions of losses; (2) the condition parameters which are ultimately decided by the community, based on participants' need and willingness to pay.

In CBHI, the contribution is community rated. This rule implies that individual members are not differentiated based on individual risk factors (e.g., age, gender, or pre-existing conditions), and instead, each participant contributes the same amount to the scheme. The per-person contribution is calculated to ensure that the total contribution income from all insured members covers the expected health risk costs of the scheme (pure risk *plus* risk loading) and operating costs.

Modeling annual payout per individual for one particular benefit type: To estimate the expected or mean payout PPPY, that is, the pure risk (of a particular benefit type), information about the distribution of payouts (v) is necessary. However, when a CBHI is launched, the shape of the distribution is not known. Thus, the information about v is based mainly on the household survey conducted ahead of the implementation.

We assume (following a community-rating approach) that for all n participants in a scheme, the losses PPPY, $u_i = 1,2,\ldots,n$, are independent and identically distributed random variables. Then also the payouts PPPY, derived from u_i when condition parameters are applied $v_i = 1,2,\ldots,n$, are independent and identically distributed random variables with, say, expected or mean payout and standard deviation σ_v. In fact, the u_i are a special case of the v_i, if no condition parameters are applied. For the entire scheme, the average payouts follow the distribution $\overline{v}(n)=\frac{1}{n}\sum_{i=1}^{n} v_i$ with the same expected value μ_v and standard deviation ($\sigma_{\overline{v}} = \sigma_v/\sqrt{n}$). According to the law of large numbers, $\overline{v}$ converges (in stochastic terms, the convergence is in probability and almost surely) against μ_v as $n \to \infty$, this is why risk pooling makes sense. The Central Limit Theorem tells us something about the shape of the distribution of $\overline{v}(n)$ beyond the mean and standard deviation, namely that for large, the distribution $\overline{v}$ approximately follows a normal distribution (in stochastic terms: $\sqrt{n}\cdot\left(\overline{v}(n)-\mu_v\right)$ converges in distribution against the normal distribution with mean 0 and standard distribution σ_v). Hence, it is important to estimate the mean μ_v and standard deviation σ_v of the distributions $v_i = 1,2,\ldots,n$, as accurately as possible because μ_v is the pure risk cost and σ_v determines via $\sigma_{\overline{v}}$ the risk loading as shown in our subsequent calculation (See p. 13 (General formulas for the per capita contribution)).

Now, since we assume that the losses PPPY, $u_i = 1,2,\ldots,n$, of the community members are independent from each other and identically distributed random variables, we look at as many realizations of them (= the sample) as possible and then find a distribution that fits that sample. With that fitted distribution of the $v_i = 1,2,\ldots,n$, we calculate the mean/expected value and standard deviation of that distribution as a proxy for μ_v and σ_v. The sample we usually derive is from a baseline household survey where hundreds or thousands of community members have been asked to state the frequency and severity (costs) of all cost-generating health events by benefit type for a particular time period in the past (e.g., last 12 months for hospitalization).

We assume that the distribution of $u_i = 1,2,\ldots,n$, has a particular structure, that is, it is a compound Poisson distribution: The number of loss events N that a community scheme has to bear follows the Poisson distribution with expected value λ and the losses for each event X_1, X_2, $X_3,\ldots$, are independent and identically distributed random variables that are also independent of N, then the probability distribution of the total losses u of the community member conditioned on the number N of loss events is given as follows:

$$u \mid N = \begin{cases} \sum_{i=1}^{N} X_i, & \text{if } N > 0, \\ 0, & \text{if } N = 0. \end{cases}$$

The assumption that the number of occurrences follows a Poisson distribution is a common one. We assume a lognormal distribution can approximate $X_i(>0)$, but this is not a necessary condition for the procedure outlined here. If another distribution offers a better fit, that distribution should be used. However, in such a case, the coding (for simulation) needs to be done differently. Our final interest is in the payouts PPPY random variable v; and u is generated as an intermediary distribution. The random variable v can be derived from u by applying the condition parameters, which essentially modify the losses for each event $X_1, X_2, X_3,\ldots,$ to the payouts $Y_1, Y_2, Y_3,\ldots,$ and we have the following equation:

$$v \mid N = \begin{cases} \sum_{i=1}^{N} Y_i, & \text{if } N > 0, \\ 0, & \text{if } N = 0. \end{cases}$$

It is noted that now the payouts $Y_1,Y_2,Y_3,\ldots,$ are not necessarily independent or identically distributed anymore. For example, an annual cap could reduce the compensation for later loss events.

Table 5.3 provides a hypothetical example to differentiate between u and v.

Based on the distribution of severity of losses extracted from the baseline household survey data, the lognormal distribution of the $X_1, X_2, X_3,\ldots,$ is fitted (e.g., following a maximum-likelihood estimation). Note, all X_i follow the same distribution. The expected value λ of the Poisson-distributed number of occurrences N is estimated with the baseline

Table 5.3 Differentiating between Distributions of Actual Loss Incurred (u) and Payouts (v) under Limitations and Qualification

	The actual loss incurred (u) for consultation and medicine (individual events)			Distribution of annual individual loss (u)	Payouts (v) subject to event cap = 100, Family cap = 250			Distribution of annual payouts (v)
Individual	Event 1	Event 2	Event 3		Event 1	Event 2	Event 3	
1	—	—	—	0	—	—	—	0
2	65	—	—	65	65	—	—	65
3	—	—	—	0	—	—	—	0
4	275	—	—	275	100	—	—	100
5	370	—	—	370	100	—	—	100
6	222	—	—	222	100	—	—	100
7	22	—	—	22	22	—	—	22
8	116	—	—	116	100	—	—	100
9	352	—	—	352	100	—	—	100
10	292	—	—	292	100	—	—	100
11	22	—	—	22	22	—	—	22
12	103	159	357	619	100	100	50	250
13	62	271	356	689	62	100	88	250
14	26	43	393	462	26	43	100	169
15	59	—	—	59	59	—	—	59
16	184	—	—	184	100	—	—	100
17	—	—	—	0	—	—	—	0
18	269	—	—	269	100	—	—	100
19	86	63	—	149	86	63	—	149
20	252	31	—	283	100	31	—	131
Average PPPY				223				96

Note: Figures are hypothetical, in local currency.

household survey data as the average rate of occurrences. The mean and standard distribution of u can be easily calculated because it follows a compound Poisson distribution and we now know the distribution of N and that of the $X_1, X_2, X_3,\ldots$. However, to calculate the mean μ_v and standard distribution σ_v of v, we have to run a Monte Carlo simulation:

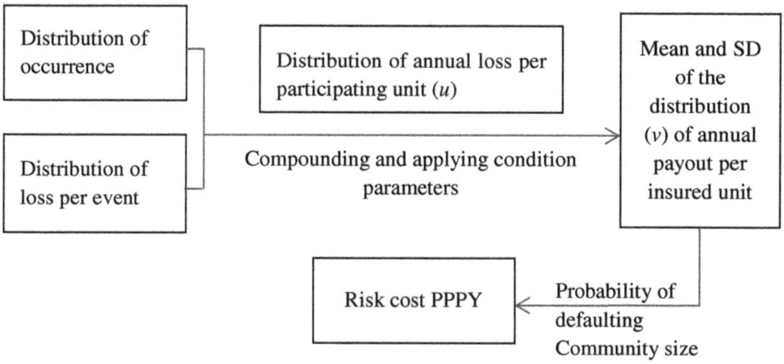

Figure 5.1 Key Steps for Estimating Risk Cost

Steps of simulation (Figure 5.1)

1. For every community member, $j = 1,2,\ldots,m$, generates a Poisson-distributed ($\lambda =$ average rate of occurrence) random number N_j modeling the frequency of loss events. Choose as large an m as possible.
2. For every community member, $j = 1,2,\ldots,m$, generates N_j lognormal-distributed loss values X_i^j, where $i = 1,2,\ldots,N_j$.
3. Apply for every community member $j = 1,2,\ldots,m$, the condition parameters (threshold, copayment, event cap, and annual cap) to derive from the loss values X_i^j the payouts Y_i^j for every $i = 1,2,\ldots,N_j$.
4. For every community member, $j = 1,2,\ldots,m$, determines the total payout $V^j := \sum_{i=1}^{N_j} Y_i^j$ (0 for $N_j = 0$).
5. Compute average and standard deviation of the m total payouts $v^j, j = 1,2,\ldots,m$, and set accordingly μ_v and σ_v.

Now, the pure risk component of the per capita contribution is given by μ_v and the risk loading can be calculated using σ_v and applying the Central Limit Theorem (as described above). Operating cost is location specific and depends on the size of the CBHI. It is higher in the initial years of operation (estimated at between 20% and 30%) and reduces gradually as the CBHI matures and increases in size.

General formulas for the per capita contribution

$$\text{Contribution PPPY} = \text{Pure Risk PPPY} + \text{Risk Loading PPPY} + \text{Operating Costs PPPY},$$

$$\text{Pure Risk PPPY} = \mu_v,$$

$$\text{Risk Loading PPPY} = Z_{\propto/2}\frac{\sigma_v}{\sqrt{n}},$$

$$\text{Operating Costs PPPY} = \text{Chosen as a certain percentage of Pure Risk PPPY},$$

where $Z_{\propto/2}$ *is such that* $Prob\left(W \geq Z_{\propto/2}\right) = \propto/2$ *for a random variable W from a standard normal distribution with mean* 0 *and standard deviation* 1 *and* $\propto/2$ *is the acceptable level of probability of defaulting (typically* 5%*) and n the expected number of community members in the pool.*

Note that the simulation process depends on the values of the condition parameters that apply to a particular benefit type. Some benefit types do not have condition parameters defined for them. In such situations, the mean and standard deviation of the distribution of payouts can be directly estimated from the distributions of the frequency of occurrence and severity of losses. The formulas for estimating the mean μ_v and

SELF-TEST QUESTIONS

1. Design a hypothetical benefits package, giving condition parameters for each benefit.
2. The two additive components of per capita contribution PPPY are (1) risk cost and (2) operating cost. How would you calculate the risk cost?
3. What are the risks and challenges faced while estimating the contribution per capita required to run a CBHI scheme? Does a commercial insurance scheme face similar or more/fewer challenges?
4. Describe the steps involved in calculating the mean μ_v and standard distribution σ_v of v, using a Monte Carlo simulation.
5. Using the law of large numbers, explain the usefulness of risk pooling in CBHI.
6. How does the Central Limit Theorem help in modeling annual payout per individual for any benefit type?

standard deviation σ_v of the distribution v in some special situations are given subsequently.

Modeling annual payout per household for one particular benefit type: We have so far considered one benefit type with condition parameters such as threshold, copayment, event cap, and annual individual cap. If the package is a family floater, that is, it has an annual family cap instead of an annual individual cap, the unit of participation changes from an individual to a family. The contribution per household per year (PHPY) is calculated in the following way: Fix a household size, say s, and do the same calculation as above, but consider the household (i.e., all participating members) as one unit, treating the annual family cap as the annual individual cap before. This increases the Poisson parameter λ of the average frequency of occurrence by the factor s. *Divide* the calculated premium by s to determine the contribution PPPY. Do this for all household sizes s. If the annual family cap is chosen household sizes s independent (what we generally do in CBHI), the contribution PPPY decreases as the household sizes s increases because the same cap applies to more household members and expected payouts per person are thus smaller. Based on the estimated distribution of numbers of participating household members (X% of household size 1, Y% of household size 2, and so forth), the average PPPY in a community can be calculated. One could now adjust through a bonus system the contribution per PPPY for different participating household sizes.

When there are no condition parameters: If there are no condition parameters applicable, that is, when u and v are identical, we actually do not need to simulate. Mean and standard deviation of u (and also of v) are given by the following formula, where $E(\lambda)$ denotes the expected value and $\mu_X = E(X_i)$ and $\sigma_X = \sigma(X_i)$ indicate the expected value and standard deviation, respectively, of the severity of loss for a loss event:

$$\mu_v = \mu_u = E(N) \cdot E(X_i) = \lambda \cdot \mu_X,$$

$$\sigma_v^2 = \sigma_u^2 = \lambda \cdot \left(\mu_X^2 + \sigma_X^2\right).$$

The first formula is an application of the law of total expectation and the second of the law of total variance. The values μ_X and σ_X can be estimated easily from the baseline household survey or from the severity of losses recorded in a sample of actual claims.

When there is no annual individual/family cap, but there is an event cap: In the absence of an annual cap, the payouts PPPY random variable is a compound Poisson distribution, where the number of loss events N is independent from the losses for each event Y_1, Y_2, Y_3,..., which is not the case when annual caps exist. Analogous to the case with no condition parameters, the mean and standard deviation of Y can be calculated, where $\mu_Y = E(Y_i)$ and $\sigma_Y = \sigma(Y_i)$ denote the expected value and standard deviation, respectively, of the payouts for a loss event:

$$\mu_v = \lambda \cdot \mu_Y,$$

$$\sigma_v^2 = \lambda \cdot \left(\mu_Y{}^2 + \sigma_Y{}^2\right).$$

The values μ_Y and σ_Y can be estimated easily from the baseline household survey (applying the condition parameters to the severity of loss data) or actual claim payout sample.

When the payout is defined as lump sum compensation: Benefits with lump sum compensation do not require any loss per event distribution. Say the lump sum compensation is F. Then $\mu_h = F$, $\sigma_h = 0$ and no simulation is required for (μ_v) and standard deviation (σ_v):

$$\mu_v = \mu_u = \lambda \cdot F,$$

$$\sigma_v^2 = \sigma_u^2 = \lambda \cdot F^2.$$

Modeling per capita contribution for wage loss compensation: Compensation for wage loss has a different set of parameters. Compensation is triggered by a threshold (a minimum number of days' stay in the hospital) and is capped by a maximum number of days' stay and by the lump sum amount per day. The required minimum number of days' stay multiplied by the amount per day is like a threshold, and the maximum number of days covered multiplied by the amount per day is like an event cap. Here the loss per event distribution is replaced by the distribution of the number of days' stay in the hospital multiplied by the rate per day, and it follows the same process as of any other benefit depending on whether there is an annual cap or not. The frequency of occurrence can be chosen the same as that of hospitalization (more precise would be to take the average frequency of occurrence of hospitalizations lasting at least the required minimum number of days). If there is no annual cap (which we have never had so far in any CBHI), mean μ_v and standard deviation σ_v are estimated as follows using the same principles explained above:

$$\mu_v = \lambda \cdot \mu_{\text{#days betw. min \& max}} \cdot r,$$

$$\sigma_v^2 = \lambda \cdot \left(\mu^2_{\text{#days betw. min \& max}} + \sigma^2_{\text{#days betw. min \& max}}\right) \cdot r,$$

where r is the wage loss compensation per day, $\mu_{\text{#days betw. min \& max}}$ and $\sigma^2_{\text{#days betw. min \& max}}$ are, respectively, the mean and standard deviation of the censored (after applying threshold and cap) distribution of the number of days' stay in the hospital.

Estimating aggregated contribution: So far, we have discussed the process of estimating per capita contribution for each benefit type (risk type). However, risk loading is applied at the end on the total pure risk contribution of all benefits together, in the same way, that it is applied on an individual benefit. By now, we know how to calculate all means μ_v and standard deviations σ_v of the payout distributions v for individual benefits. Assuming all risk types are independent (which is a conservative estimate rather slightly increasing the risk loading), the mean μ_T and standard deviation σ_T of the total payouts $T = \sum_{\text{Benefit type}} v_{\text{Benefit type}}$ are given by the following formula:

$$\mu_T = \Sigma \mu_v,$$

$$\sigma_T^2 = \Sigma \sigma_v^2.$$

Then

$$\text{Contribution PPPY} = \text{Pure Risk PPPY} + \text{Risk Loading PPPY} + \text{Operating Costs PPPY},$$

$$\text{Total Pure Risk PPPY} = \mu_T,$$

$$\text{Total Risk Loading PPPY} = Z_{\frac{\propto}{2}} \frac{\sigma_T}{\sqrt{n}},$$

$$\text{Operating Costs PPPY} = \text{Chosen as a certain percentage of Pure Risk PPPY},$$

where $Z_{\propto/2}$ *is such that* $\text{Prob}\left(W \geq Z_{\propto/2}\right) = \propto/2$ *for a random variable W from a standard normal distribution with mean* 0 *and standard deviation* 1 *and* $\propto/2$ *is the acceptable level of probability of defaulting (typically* 5%*) and n the expected number of community members in the pool.*

Presentation of benefits package in the form of calculator: Under the model presented here, the ultimate choice of the benefits package is left to the community. It is done it two stages. After calculating the means μ_v and standard deviations σ_v of the payout distributions for a particular benefit type v for a wide range of combinations of thresholds, copayments, event caps, and annual caps for each benefit, those μ_v and σ_v values are inputted in an Excel-based application (Figure 5.2) as background information. A user can select a benefits package of her/his choice by entering the values of condition parameters that define her/his package. The user can also set the acceptable risk of bankruptcy $\alpha/2$, approximate community size n, and level of operation costs loading; percent discount to be given to large families and proportion of the participants' population that might be benefitting from such discount.

The application instantly calculates the pure risk contribution for the benefits package, risk loading, and final chargeable contribution. The application also gives a visual presentation of a chance of defaulting and distribution of total contribution on different benefits for the selected package. The calculator is displayed and explained in a meeting with community leaders/members, where a few packages (usually 3–5 in number) are shortlisted for detailed consideration by the participants. The shortlisted packages are then pictorially depicted on a board, known as CHAT

Benefit	Threshold	Event Cap	Family Cap	Pure Risk Premium
Hospitalization		3000	10000	111
Injury	0	700	3000	99
Lab (only OPD)	0			0
Imaging (only OPD)	0	1000	5000	116
Transport (for hospitalization) Fixed		1000		42
Caesarean Delivery Fixed				0
Wageloss	Start Day	Last Day	Rate	25
	4	9	100	
OPD				
TOTAL				393
Community Size	5000			
Chance of Bankruptcy	5%			
Risk Loading	4%			17
Premium with Risk Loading				409
Admin Cost	20%			82
Total Premium Payable PPPY				491

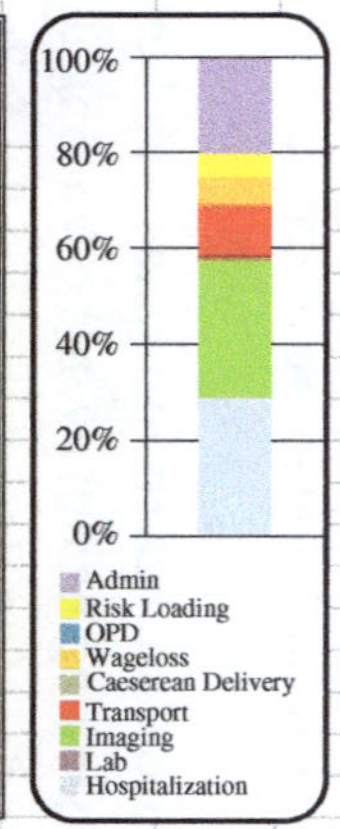

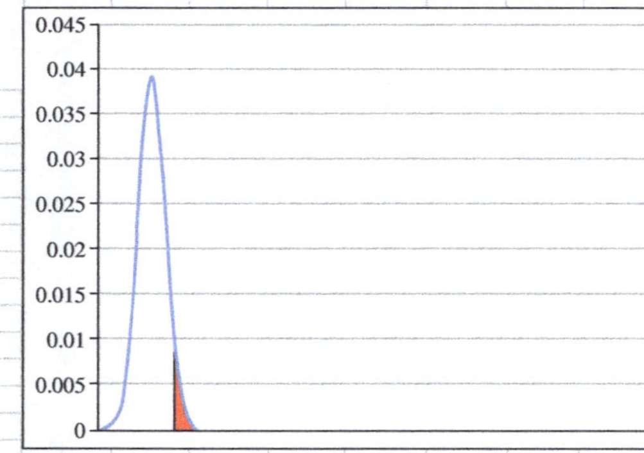

RISK TO THE SCHEME	5%
PREMIUM PPPY	491

Figure 5.2 Contribution Calculator

board. Copies of the CHAT boards are distributed in the villages where people discuss, debate, and conclude about the final package.

Source of data for identification of risks: Identification and assessment of risks are based on data collected before the implementation process begins, through a household survey of a sample of the scheme's target population. The household survey contains questions on the number of hospitalizations and other health events and losses incurred due to these occurrences. Once a CBHI is launched, the calculation of contributions in subsequent years can be adjusted based on the claims data recorded in the MIS system used (please also see Chapter 14).

Pricing Calculator

Designing a benefits package (i.e., the aggregate of the types of benefits for a specified premium) is an essential task for the administrators of the scheme. This requires the basic knowledge of data collection and statistics discussed so far.

Premium computation for health insurance requires us to know first the number of cost-generating health events occurring during a particular period. The standard cost-generating events are the following:

- hospitalization
- OPD consultations
- purchase of medicines
- imaging
- lab test
- maternity

The costs incurred differ for each event and every individual.

SELF-TEST QUESTIONS

1. Under the MIA model, the ultimate choice of the benefits package is left to the community. Describe the two stages in which this is carried out.
2. Explain the calculation for per capita contribution for wage loss compensation.

We do not know the exact amount beforehand, and we have to work with an expected value.

Another problem is how to get an idea about the total expenses. Many people do not incur any expenses; a few incur massive amounts.

So let us assume, in a community, the *expected* total expenditure on health for 1 year is E. Total number of people in the community is N. Assuming all other costs as zero, the premium PPPY can be calculated as follows:

$$\text{PPPY} = \frac{E}{N}.$$

If I is the total number of illnesses that would occur in the community, then $\frac{I}{N}$ is the incidence of illness in the community. *It can also be interpreted as the average number of illnesses that would occur to each.*

E is the total expenditure, therefore $\frac{E}{I}$ is the average cost per illness.

The above formula can be written thus:

$$\text{PPPY} = \frac{E}{N} = \left(\frac{I}{N}\right)\left(\frac{E}{I}\right).$$

The advantage of this formula is that the incidence rate and the average cost of illnesses may come from different sources. Second, the incidence rate remains fixed for quite some time, but the cost of treatment may change very quickly. The above formula reflects such a possibility.

Example — In a community with a population of 1,000, the yearly incidence rate of illness is 0.04. The average cost of treatment per illness episode is ₹5000. What should the premium be?

Note: Premium is PPPY unless stated otherwise.

$$\frac{I}{N} = 0.04, \frac{E}{I} = 5{,}000,$$

then $P = 0.04 \times 5{,}000 =$ ₹200.

If L is the total number of people who fall ill, then $\frac{L}{N}$ is the proportion of people who suffer from an illness and $\frac{E}{L}$ is the average cost of treatment per person. The formula reflecting this is given as follows:

$$\text{PPPY} = \frac{E}{N} = \left(\frac{L}{N}\right)\left(\frac{E}{L}\right).$$

If there are F families in a community, then the Premium Per Family Per Year (PPFPY) is calculated as follows:

$$\text{PPFPY} = \frac{E}{F} = \left(\frac{f}{F}\right)\left(\frac{E}{f}\right),$$

where f is the number of families affected by illnesses, f/F is the proportion of families affected by illnesses, and E/f is the average cost of treatment per family.

Thus, incidence and corresponding costs are the two variables required for premium calculation. If the incidence is expressed as the proportion of families likely to experience illness, the cost should also be the average cost per family and not the average cost per person:

$$\text{Premium} = f\,(\text{incidence, the average cost of treatment}).$$

Some events are not considered worth insuring as they are events that are certain to occur. These include immunization, preventive health check-ups, etc. To allow the community to choose what they wish to insure, we calculate the premium for each type of event separately. This means we must get incidence and cost data for each of these events. What are the sources of these data? Sometimes information is available from secondary sources. However, in CBHI, the incidence and cost depend on the local situation that a household survey has to be carried out for calculating premiums.

Simulation is drawing a large random sample from a distribution. For this, we have to know the shape and parameters of distribution — whether it is normal or Poisson, its mean and standard deviation, and λ. We need answers to two questions:

(1) Who may be hospitalized and how many times? (The number of health events follows Poisson distribution.)
(2) What would be the cost of each hospitalization event? (Individual hospitalization cost "usually" follows lognormal distribution.)

In fact, it is difficult to find the proper distribution of medical costs as it may follow the gamma distribution, log-logistic distribution, or yet another distribution. Sometimes, we prefer to take random samples from the original distribution we received from the survey instead of any "approximate" distribution.

In the premium calculation, the cap is equivalent to the sum assured, i.e., the maximum amount one can get during the year. A cap can be applied to an event or generally to the benefit type. The threshold is the amount payable by the insured before the right to reimbursement arises. Caps, thresholds, and copayments reduce uncertainty and moral hazard and help lower the premium.

SELF-TEST QUESTIONS

1. In a community with a population of 1000, the yearly incidence rate of illness is 0.03. The average cost of treatment per illness episode is ₹4,500. Estimate the premium per person per year.
2. Define simulation. What information do we need for simulation?

KEY TERMS

- **Annual individual/family cap:** This is the maximum amount payable for a specific benefit type for the entire policy period to an individual or a family.
- **Benefits package:** A benefits package is a combination of benefit types (e.g., hospitalization, lab test, imaging, transport) with limitations and qualifications applying to each type, together with its price.

(*Continued*)

(*Continued*)

- **Community rating:** It implies that individual members are not differentiated based on individual risk factors (e.g., age, gender, or pre-existing conditions), and instead, each participant contributes the same amount to the scheme.
- **Copayment:** This is the percentage of total claims borne by each participant.
- **Episode:** An episode is the span of treatments a person receives simultaneously or consecutively in the course of a single illness or associated illnesses.
- **Event cap:** This is the maximum amount payable per event claimed.
- **Experience rating (or Experience Modification Factor):** It is a method to adjust the premiums based on the health history of those covered.
- **Frequency of occurrence:** It is the average number of loss-generating health events per person per year (PPPY) in the community.
- **Gross premium:** The gross premium is the pure premium plus the loadings.
- **Loadings:** In addition to the insurance rate, there are other expenses (e.g., sales expenses (aka acquisition costs), claims processing costs, and profit) which are added. They are called Loadings.
- **Pure premium:** The pure premium is obtained by multiplying the price (or the rate) per unit of liability by the number of units insured.
- **Risk rating:** It is the practice of charging each person the premium reflecting that person's probability (aka frequency) of a risk multiplied by that person's amount of damage (aka severity), rather than the (lower) average cost of the risk pool in which the person participates, due to a lower frequency, or a lower severity, or both.
- **The severity of loss:** It measures the impact of an event as an average loss per event.
- **Threshold:** This is the minimum amount payable by the participant before entitlement to any payout from CBHI. A participant who incurred a loss below the threshold is not entitled to payouts from the CBHI, and payouts are due for losses beyond the threshold. Stated differently, the threshold is the self-insured part of the total loss.

Bibliography

Biener, C. (2013) Pricing in Microinsurance Markets. *World Development*, 41(1), 132–144.

Dror, DM and Jambhekar, S (eds.) (2016) *Microinsurance Business Processes Handbook*. New Delhi: Social Re Consultancy (Pvt) Ltd and Micro Insurance Academy.

Chapter 6

Estimating Willingness to Pay*

LEARNING OBJECTIVES

Upon completion of this chapter, the reader should be able to:

- Describe the three ways used in the study for expressing estimated premiums and actual payments
- Explain the two-pronged approach adopted in this chapter to assess the gap between WTP estimates and actual payment made by CBHI members
- Explain the reason for the gap between the estimated premiums and actual payments for CBHI
- Describe how the Heckman two-stage sample-selection model is applied to analyze the predictors of actual payment
- Discuss the relationship between household size and enrolment size
- Understand the role of financial and insurance literacy in aiming to achieve greater coverage of CBHI in the informal sector

*This chapter originally appeared as a part of Ms. Arpita Chakraborty's Ph.D. thesis, co-authored by Arpita Chakraborty, Atanu Majumdar, and David M. Dror, and supervised by Prof. Dr. Biswajit Dhar (Centre for Economic Studies and Planning, School of Social Sciences, Jawaharlal Nehru University, New Delhi).

Abstract

Actual community-based health insurance (CBHI) premium payments often fall short of Willingness-to-Pay (WTP) estimates. This study examines the gap between the estimated premiums and actual payments for CBHI by analyzing data from 3,685 households in rural India. Descriptive statistics are used to analyze the gap between the estimated premium and actual payments. Heckman two-stage sample-selection model is applied to analyze the predictors of actual payment, subject to household enrolment in CBHI. The estimated premiums were 0.50–1.26% of per-capita gross domestic product (PCGDP). The actual payments were ~50% of the estimates. The gap resulted as households enrolled fewer family members than expected. Further analysis indicates that a quadratic function (to estimate expected enrollees from the household) combining with a fixed premium (expressed as a percentage of PCGDP) can better predict actual income. Heckman analysis indicates that focusing on greater awareness and financial literacy can lead to an increase in actual payments.

Chapter Outline

Voluntary and contributory health insurance (HI) coverage, notably the coverage provided to grassroots groups in the informal sector and settings of poverty and rurality is paying much attention to estimating Willingness to Pay (WTP). Two principal reasons explain this interest: firstly, because this model embraces the policy that *the price determines the benefits*, rather than the other way around. This issue has been discussed in detail in Chapter 5. As the price determines what benefits the CBHI can cover, the discussion about the desirable benefits package starts with an estimate of the price. Secondly, the emphasis in WTP is on the word *willingness*; the CBHI model is not satisfied with being *inclusive,* because the binary nature of this adjective (excluded/included) does not suitably qualify the role of the community, let alone that of each individual in the decision at hand. Simply saying *inclusion* does not provide information about the quality, intensity, and degree of acceptance of the relationship between each individual and the whole set. After all, the feudal order was inclusive, as were the communist regimes. In our context, we relate to the groups and the individuals that participate as "active agents of change rather than as passive recipients of dispensed benefits."[1] The true expression of voluntary enrollment is *inclusion + acceptance*. Therefore, we make recurring use of terms that echo the proactive choice: willingness-to-pay, voluntary membership, community-based, consensus, and welfare gains.

Considerable attention is given to the discussion of WTP in the book: *Financing Micro Health Insurance: Theory, Methods, and Evidence.*[2] That discussion dwells in detail on several methods to estimate WTP. This chapter complements the previous discussion by making available various research tools for implementers wishing to perform WTP estimates. More importantly, we deal here with a difficulty that has plagued WTP estimates regardless of the method used to obtain them.

The gap between the actual income of CBHI schemes and the estimated premium

Notwithstanding the improvements in methods to estimate the WTP of prospective members of CBHI, it turned out that many schemes could not collect the income projected by the WTP estimates. This raised two questions: how big is the gap between estimated and actual income; and what might be the explanation for the gap, and how could such an explanation lead to a better estimate of the actual premium income of CBHI schemes. This is the subject matter of this chapter.

Introduction

Community-based health insurance (CBHI) has been proposed as an alternative model to provide health insurance coverage for poor people (Jain, 2017), notably because of the low outreach of government-sponsored plans (e.g., in India in 2015–2016, only about one-fourth of the population was covered by subsidized government-sponsored

[1] Sen, A. (1999) *Development as Freedom*, Oxford: Oxford University Press, Preface.

[2] Dror, DM (2018) *Financing Micro Health Insurance: Theory, Methods, and Evidence*. Singapore: World Scientific Publishing. *World Scientific Series in Health Investment and Financing* Vol. 2, number 10944, March. ISBN 978-981-3238-47-3, p. 552. DOI:https://doi.org/10.1142/10944.

health insurance schemes (IIPS and ICS, 2017)) and the partial coverage by those plans (Prinja *et al.*, 2017).

The financial sustainability of CBHI schemes rests mainly or entirely on premium income. Therefore, they must ensure that the premium would cover the administration and claims costs. When fixing the premium, the schemes must balance two considerations: too high might be perceived as expensive and too low could lead to unattractive packages. Both situations could reduce voluntary uptake. This is why CBHI have adopted the practice of estimating willingness-to-pay (WTP) upfront and there is abundant literature on this topic (Ahmed *et al.*, 2016; Basaza *et al.*, 2017; Binnendijk *et al.*, 2013; Dong *et al.*, 2003; Dror *et al.*, 2007; Nosratnejad *et al.*, 2016, 2017). However, the practice of investigating the declared WTP has overlooked the possibility that members, when enrolling, would pay less than their declared WTP. Such eventuality could expose CBHI schemes to insolvency risks that they cannot quickly remedy in the short run. We know from several studies that this gap between the estimated premium and actual payments is not merely hypothetical when people consider several specific healthcare services. In a study as early as 1972 for a pure and quasi-public good, it was found that there exists a difference between the hypothetical and actual values (Bohm, 1972). For hunting permits, it was found that the stated WTP values were 60–200% higher than the actual payment (Heberlein and Bishop, 1986). In an Asthma management program in the USA, only 12% of the participants paid the amount they said they would (Blumenschein *et al.*, 2001). In Timor-Leste, only 16% of the respondents in a WTP study for eyeglasses paid the price they said they would agree to pay (Ramke *et al.*, 2009). In Nigeria, only 76% of the respondents who expressed willingness to purchase insecticide-treated bed nets (ITBN), did so (Onwujekwe *et al.*, 2001). Similarly, in India, around 35% of the respondents who expressed their WTP for ITBN, did not do so in practice (Bhatia and Fox-Rushby, 2003). In Thailand, the declared "Yes" for payment for oral care for pre-school children far exceeded the actual "Yes" (Ryan *et al.*, 2017). A recent study on quality-adjusted life years in Germany raised doubts on the validity of the survey-based WTP estimates (Ahlert *et al.*, 2016). A review based on 111 articles on the usage of contingent valuation (CV) method to estimate WTP in healthcare concluded that the development and presentation of the hypothetical scenario, proposed payment methods, risk perception, time frame for *ex-ante* and *ex-post* analysis were the critical reasons for the gap in stated WTP and actual payment (Smith, 2003). Hausman (2012) suggested that the differences between stated preferences (measured through CV) and the actual behavior arise because the preferences are not unclearly defined.

As for WTP for CBHI, a recent study of the reasons behind the gap between estimated premium values and actual payments could not offer a solution to estimating the gap or an entirely satisfactory explanation why it occurs (Ryan *et al.*, 2017). An earlier publication examined which elicitation technique for health microinsurance among rural or resource-poor persons in the informal sector was most accurate (using data from 14 studies of WTP from several low- or middle-income countries), without conclusive results (Dror and Koren, 2012). Yet others pointed out that estimating the premium of the CBHI schemes by relying on WTP ignored people's ability to pay (Cookson, 2003; Schmidt *et al.*, 2006), or that the traditional way of estimating WTP ignores the gap between the actuarial price of the package and affordability of the target population (Dong *et al.*, 2003). Finally, it has been shown that the classical WTP studies collected individual estimated premiums when in the context of many CBHI schemes the decisions reflect group consensus rather than individual choice (Dror *et al.*, 2018).

Therefore, in this study we offer a novel two-pronged approach to assess the gap: first, we develop a new method to validate the expected revenue of CBHI plans by juxtaposing the actuarial first estimate of the premium with the consensus of the target audience (hereafter *estimated premium*) (Dror *et al.*, 2014). Then, we estimate the *actual payments* of the same target groups by using real data of their CBHI over three years. The purpose of this article is to provide replies to the following four research questions:

(1) What were the agreed values of the *estimated premium* for the CBHI coverage that the target groups determined by consensus? We express the values of the *estimated premium* in three ways: (i) nominally; (ii) as a percentage of monthly per capita food expenditure (MPCE/food) (following Binnendijk *et al.*, 2013); and (iii) as a share of per

capita gross domestic product (PCGDP) (following Nosratnejad *et al.*, 2016).

(2) What did the households pay to enroll their members in those same CBHI plans? Here also, we express *actual payments* in nominal units, and as a percentage of MPCE/food, and as a share of PCGDP.

(3) What was the gap between the estimated premium and actual payments (the difference between the findings in Questions (a) and (b)) and how can it be explained?

(4) What factors could give a better prediction of actual payments, so that CBHI schemes would be less exposed to the risk of a gap between estimated premium and actual payments?

Materials and Methods

Scheme description

Within the activities of a large EC funded project (2009–2014) on the impact of CBHI schemes on health-seeking behavior and financial protection, the Micro Insurance Academy (New Delhi) engaged with three Non-Government Organizations (NGOs) in the study locations ("the implementing field partners") to set up and operate three CBHI schemes in rural India. Two schemes were in Pratapgarh and Kanpur-Dehat (two districts in Uttar Pradesh), and one scheme in Vaishali district (in Bihar). The data of these CBHI schemes were used for the analysis.

We obtained Ethical clearance in 2010 before the baseline survey (for study design, sample selection, and survey instruments) from the Ethics Committee of the University of Cologne (knowledge partners in this project). In 2015, we obtained a follow-up approval from the Ethics Committee of the Micro Insurance Academy, New Delhi (research lead in the project), to ascertain that the study design and questionnaires conformed to the practices in India on ethical requirements.

The target population of this study consisted of all the households with at least one member enrolled in a Self-Help Groups (SHGs) in March 2010 (total 3,685 households, 1,283 in Pratapgarh, 1,039 in Kanpur-Dehat and 1,363 in Vaishali). Baseline information was collected from all these 3,685 households during March–May 2010 through a census of the target population. These 3,685 households were then divided into 48 clusters, of around 45–65 households each, based on geographic proximity (Doyle *et al.*, 2011). The 48 clusters were randomly assigned into three waves of implementation: Wave-1 (April-2011 to March-2012), Wave-2 (April-2012 to March-2013), and Wave-3 (April-2013 to March-2014).

During the Wave-1, ~1/3 of the households (1,335 households) were offered to join insurance. In Wave-2 and Wave-3, another 1,244 and 1,106 households were offered to enroll in CBHI. The households in the three groups (Waves 1, 2, and 3) were mutually exclusive (Table 6.1 contains the details).

Estimation of premium amounts

The baseline survey included questions on the frequency and severity of healthcare risks and local health seeking practices along with corresponding expenditures, which differed across the locations. Based on that information, 4–6 benefits packages options were prepared by actuarial scientists and presented to the participants during an awareness campaign. After the awareness campaign, the target households participated in a group activity called CHAT (Choosing Health-plans All Together) (Dror *et al.*, 2014) at the SHG level, to narrow the selection down to a single package that would be offered by the CBHI scheme to all its members in that location. The options included inpatient care, maternity care, and wage-loss compensation in Pratapgarh; inpatient and outpatient benefits in Kanpur-Dehat; and medical tests and outpatient care in Vaishali. The premium amounts of the benefits options varied from INR 157 to INR 297 per person per year (PPPY) (Table 6.2).

Participants in the CHAT exercise were then invited to join the CBHI by paying the premium. The annual premium was payable upfront and in full. 525 of the 1,335 eligible households joined in Wave-1 (1,806 individuals out of 7,722). 538 of the 1,244 eligible households joined in Wave-2 (1,542 individuals out of 6,481). And 373 of the 1,106 eligible households joined in Wave-3 (1,017 individuals out of 5,692). Expressed in percentages, 39%, 46% and 37% of the eligible households (23%, 24% and 18% of eligible individuals) joined CBHI in Wave-1, Wave-2, and Wave-3 respectively.

Table 6.1 Detailed Time Line of the CBHI Schemes

2010	March	• Received the list of all the SHG members affiliated to the implementing NGOs in study locations
2010	March–May	• Baseline survey of 3685 households (1283 in Pratapgarh, 1039 in Kanpur-Dehat and 1363 in Vaishali), a Spatial survey of the study locations
2010	June	• Clustering of the 3685 HHs using baseline survey data (quantitative and spatial) so that each cluster contains roughly equal number of HHs (total 48 clusters) and in the same geographic location (to control information spill over); each cluster was then randomly assigned in three waves of implementation (1/3rd in each wave). O Year-1 of implementation (April-2011 – March-2012) — Wave-1 clusters in treatment (1335 households); Wave-2 (1244 households), and Wave-3 (1106 households) clusters in control (total 2350 households in control) O Year-2 of implementation (April-2012 – March-2013) — Wave-2 clusters in treatment (1244 households) and Wave-3 (1106 households) clusters in control O Year-3 of implementation (April-2013 – March-2014) — Wave-3 clusters in treatment (1106 households)
		Preparatory Stage of Year-1 – 2010–2011
2010	July–October	• Initiation consultation workshop, design workshop, awareness tool development workshop, benefit option consultation workshop (finalization of 4–6 options using baseline data and inputs from SHG representatives), a training workshop for an awareness campaign
2010–2011	Nov–Feb	• Awareness campaign for the treatment population (1335 Wave-1 households), followed by benefit option finalization process
2011	March	• Enrolment process in CBHI for the treatment group (wave-1 HHs); 525 households enrolled
2011	April	• CBHI scheme launch. For one-year (2011–2012), enrolled people enjoyed the coverage of CBHI. No new enrolment during this period.

		Year-2 of Implementation — 2011–2012*
2011	Jul–Oct	• Benefit option consultation workshop, a training workshop for an awareness campaign
2011–2012	Nov–Feb	• Awareness campaign and benefit option finalization process for the treatment population (1244 households of Wave-2)
2012	March	• Enrolment and renewal process in CBHI; 538 households enrolled from the Wave-2 group
2012	Mar	• Midline survey of 3318 HHs (same baseline questionnaire)
2012	April	• CBHI scheme launch, for one year (2012–2013), the enrolled people enjoyed the coverage of CBHI. No new enrolment during this period.
		Year-3 of Implementation — 2012–2013*
2012	Jul–Oct	• Training workshop on Benefit option consultation before the awareness campaign
2012–2013	Nov–Feb	• Awareness campaign and benefit option finalization process for the treatment population (1106 households of Wave-3)
2013	March	• Enrolment and renewal process in CBHI for the treatment group; 373 households joined from Wave-3 group
2013	Mar	• Endline survey of 3307 HHs (same baseline questionnaire)
2013	April	• CBHI scheme launch, for one year (2013–2014), the enrolled people enjoyed the coverage of CBHI.

Note: *HHs that did not join CBHI in the first place when offered, could not join in the following years.

Table 6.2 Description of Benefit Options Offered under CBHI Schemes

	Pratapgarh				Kanpur-Dehat						Vaishali					
Package	1	2	3	4	1	2	3	4	5	6	1	2	3	4	5	6
Outpatient Care																
Lab test (pppy)											200	200	100	200	200	100
Imaging tests (pppy)											300	300	200	300	300	200
Wage loss (per day)	100	100		100	75	100	75	100	75	100	0	100	100	0	100	100
Days of coverage	3–8	3–8		3–8	4–13	4–13	4–13	4–13	4–13	4–13		4–9	4–9		4–9	4–9
Consultation with medicine					Yes	Yes	Yes	Yes	Yes	Yes	Yes	Yes	Yes	Yes	Yes	Yes
Inpatient Care																
Hospital fee (pppy)	5000	5000	6800	6000	3000	4000	5000	6000	7000	4500			2000			2000
Maternity-C-Section	1400	1400	1400	1400												
Transport		200		100	100	100	150	150	200	200						

Life Insurance																
Natural death														30000	30000	30000
Accidental death														75000	75000	75000
Disability due to an accident														37500	37500	37500
Premium per person per year (in INR)																
PPPY in Year-1	157	162	176	176	192	221	243	270	290	192	187	197	236	248	258	297
PPPY in Year-2				250						192		197				
PPPY in Year-3				250						199		197				
Package selected in Year-1				Final						Final		Final				
Package selected in Year-2				Final						Final		Final				
Package selected in Year-3				Final						Final		Final				

Note: The amounts under coverage for each item are in Indian rupee; pppy means per person per year.

Data

The study population for our analysis included all the households that were offered to join CBHI under three Waves of implementation: Wave-1 group for Year-1, Wave-2 group for Year-2 and Wave-3 group for Year-3. Data for this study originate from six sources:

(1) *Benefit Option Selection Process*: In this analysis, differently from conventional (individual) WTP elicitation methods, we consider the premium of the package that was selected by the target population in each year as a result of the consultations as each household's *estimated premium* PPPY. In Table 6.2, we mark as "Final" the package and premium that the members retained in each location and year. The estimated premium is identical for all members in each location and year, as only one package was offered after the consensus decision, at only one premium. We were able to validate complete data for 1,335 households in Year-1 (433, 378 and 524 from Pratapgarh, Kanpur-Dehat, and Vaishali, respectively), 1,181 households (out of 1,244 households) in Year-2 (433 in Pratapgarh, 341 in Kanpur-Dehat and 407 in Vaishali) and 996 households (out of 1,106 households) in Year-3 (363 in Pratapgarh, 275 in Kanpur-Dehat and 358 in Vaishali).

(2) *Household Survey*: The household surveys conducted during baseline, midline, and endline queried about socioeconomic and demographic details of the households, insurance, and CBHI understanding, outpatient and inpatient care episodes, corresponding expenditure and how households procured funds to pay for healthcare services. These three datasets served as our source of socioeconomic, demographic, and health details of the CHAT participants during the three years.

(3) *Management Information System (MIS)*: The MIS of the three CBHI schemes contained all the information on the price of the package that each scheme chose, the membership, and payments made. From the MIS, we obtained the actual enrolment status of all households, the number of members enrolled from each family, and the premium paid. We consider the amount that households spent as the *actual payments*.

(4) *National Sample Survey* (*NSS*): We estimated the monthly per capita food expenditure (MPCE/food) of the rural households in our three districts, following the methodology described by NSSO (National Sample Survey Organisation, 2013), using the unit level data of the Consumption Expenditure Survey conducted in 2011–2012. The rationale behind using MPCE estimates from NSSO is that we aimed to provide estimated premiums and actual payments that could be replicated using the information available from secondary sources, avoiding the resource-intensive method of primary data collection.

(5) *Directorate of Economic & Statistics* (*DES*): We obtained from DES websites the district-level PCGDP information for the study years of the relevant three districts (DSE-Bihar, 2014; UP-DES, 2016).

(6) *Census India 2011*: We collected village-level information from the Census 2011 village directories, available from the "village amenities" series of "District Census Handbook" (Census of India, 2011).

Around 20–44% of the study population was categorized as scheduled caste/scheduled tribe (Table 6.3). Average MPCE was about INR 1,150–2,200. While in Pratapgarh and Kanpur-Dehat most had a savings account in banks, in Vaishali, only a minority had such accounts (25–44%). Coverage by RSBY (a government-sponsored hospital insurance scheme) was much higher in Vaishali (around 48–66%) than in the other two locations (<1/3rd). The reported incidence of outpatient events was higher in Pratapgarh and Kanpur-Dehat than Vaishali. Overall, access to village primary and secondary schools was best in Kanpur-Dehat, followed by Vaishali and then Pratapgarh.

SELF-TEST QUESTIONS

1. Describe the methodology adopted in this study for estimation of premium amounts.
2. What were the health benefit options offered to the target population?

Table 6.3 Descriptive Statistics of the Household and Village Indicators — Mean ± Standard Deviation

	Pratapgarh			Kanpur-Dehat			Vaishali		
Indicators	Year-1	Year-2	Year-3	Year-1	Year-2	Year-3	Year-1	Year-2	Year-3
Household socio-economic status									
Schedule caste/Schedule tribe (Yes = 1)	0.36 ± 0.48	0.42 ± 0.49	0.36 ± 0.48	0.23 ± 0.42	0.21 ± 0.41	0.28 ± 0.45	0.39 ± 0.48	0.34 ± 0.47	0.32 ± 0.46
Monthly per capita expenditure (INR)	1148 ± 580	1264 ± 647	1627 ± 922	1806 ± 1351	1631 ± 816	2263 ± 1206	1368 ± 895	1583 ± 798	1824 ± 1065
Highest education in the family	9.18 ± 3.44	9.66 ± 3.66	9.77 ± 3.88	9.60 ± 3.33	9.72 ± 3.50	10.1 ± 3.68	7.25 ± 4.08	7.39 ± 4.13	7.67 ± 3.95
Financial literacy and insurance subscription									
Household have savings account (Yes = 1)	0.63 ± 0.48	0.69 ± 0.46	0.65 ± 0.47	0.46 ± 0.49	0.60 ± 0.48	0.68 ± 0.46	0.25 ± 0.43	0.41 ± 0.49	0.48 ± 0.50
Household enrolled in RSBY (Yes = 1)	0.18 ± 0.38	0.20 ± 0.40	0.28 ± 0.45	0.13 ± 0.34	0.29 ± 0.45	0.57 ± 0.49	0.47 ± 0.49	0.49 ± 0.50	0.69 ± 0.46
Household enrolled in any other insurance (Yes = 1)	0.27 ± 0.44	0.33 ± 0.47	0.31 ± 0.46	0.23 ± 0.42	0.29 ± 0.45	0.45 ± 0.49	0.19 ± 0.39	0.39 ± 0.48	0.33 ± 0.47

Household's health events									
Number of outpatient events	2.59 ± 1.47	2.41 ± 1.71	2.88 ± 1.83	2.21 ± 1.42	2.52 ± 1.60	3.22 ± 1.86	1.80 ± 1.33	2.40 ± 1.64	2.94 ± 1.80
Number of hospitalization cases	0.13 ± 0.37	0.18 ± 0.44	0.14 ± 0.39	0.20 ± 0.51	0.11 ± 0.32	0.14 ± 0.38	0.19 ± 0.44	0.12 ± 0.33	0.18 ± 0.42
Presence of children < 12 years (Yes = 1)	0.79 ± 0.40	0.80 ± 0.39	0.79 ± 0.40	0.76 ± 0.42	0.75 ± 0.43	0.76 ± 0.42	0.85 ± 0.35	0.85 ± 0.34	0.86 ± 0.34
Presence of adult > 65 years (Yes = 1)	0.28 ± 0.44	0.20 ± 0.40	0.24 ± 0.43	0.16 ± 0.37	0.16 ± 0.37	0.18 ± 0.39	0.20 ± 0.40	0.17 ± 0.37	0.16 ± 0.37
Insurance understanding									
Score of insurance and CBHI understanding	6.64 ± 3.42	7.72 ± 2.08	7.88 ± 2.47	7.89 ± 3.61	7.66 ± 3.46	7.92 ± 2.52	6.41 ± 3.52	7.49 ± 2.82	7.72 ± 2.51
Village characteristics									
Number of primary schools	1.44 ± 0.97	1.12 ± 0.75	0.79 ± 0.80	2.35 ± 1.02	2.53 ± 1.95	2.40 ± 1.68	2.18 ± 2.78	1.86 ± 1.96	2.10 ± 2.01
Number of secondary schools	0.78 ± 0.41	0.92 ± 0.53	0.61 ± 0.65	1.30 ± 1.13	1.25 ± 0.82	1.23 ± 0.73	1.05 ± 0.99	0.74 ± 0.87	0.86 ± 0.79
Bank in village (Yes = 1)	0.45 ± 0.49	0.12 ± 0.32	0.05 ± 0.22	0 ± 0	0.13 ± 0.33	0.03 ± 0.17	0.27 ± 0.44	0.11 ± 0.32	0.40 ± 0.49
Market place in village (Yes = 1)	0.52 ± 0.50	0.29 ± 0.45	0.20 ± 0.40	0.12 ± 0.32	0.34 ± 0.47	0.52 ± 0.49	0.10 ± 0.30	0.13 ± 0.34	0.32 ± 0.46
Observations	*433*	*433*	*363*	*378*	*341*	*275*	*524*	*407*	*358*

Methods

We expressed the *estimated premium* (both per person per year (PPPY) and per person per month (PPPM)) and *actual payments* in nominal values PPPM over the years, as well as in percentages of:

(1) *Food expenditure*, which was calculated from the NSS data for the lowest one-third MPCE tertile of the rural population in the three study districts (denoted MPCE/food). We took the MPCE amounts of the lowest economic tertile (bottom 33%) for rural areas in the study districts as that tertile corresponds to our study population. The NSSO data were available for the year 2011–2012. Using the price inflator/deflator (calculated from district level nominal and real GDP), we estimated the MPCE/food for the study years.
(2) *PCGDP* at the district level, collected from the DES.

We used descriptive statistics (mean, standard error of the mean (SEM)) to estimate the actual payments in the three locations.

The significance of the difference between the estimated premium expressed as a percentage of MPCE/food and PCGDP across years was tested by applying independent sample *t*-testing. The same method was followed to check the significance of the difference between the changes in actual payments over the years. For the difference between the estimated premium and actual payments in the same year, significance was tested using paired sample *t*-test.

As mentioned earlier, 37–46% of the eligible households (18–24% of eligible individuals) were enrolled in CBHI. Neither did all the eligible households join the insurance nor did all the members from the enrolled households join. Previous analysis with this study population found that household's social background, financial liabilities, and educational achievements were the main determining factors of households enrolment (Panda *et al.*, 2013). Households could not negotiate the premium as that was decided at the group level but could adjust their spending by enrolling fewer members from their family. Given the method of attributing estimated premiums based on group decisions, we must overcome possible bias in estimating the predictors of the actual payments by households (in PPPM). We resolve this by applying The Heckman two-stage sample selection model (Heckman, 1979), which allow correcting for selection bias problems. In the first step, we estimate the probability of a household to join the CBHI using a probit model specification, which can be expressed as:

$$\text{Prob}\ (\text{D}=1 \mid \text{Z}) = f(\text{Z}\ (\text{SES, FLI, HVP, IU, VILL})) \tag{1}$$

Where D is 1 if the household is enrolled in CBHI, 0 otherwise.

Z is a vector of explanatory variables.

In the second stage, the households' self-selection bias to enroll in CBHI is corrected by incorporating a transformation of the predicted probabilities at the household level as an explanatory variable to predict insured households' actual payments (AP, in PPPM). This can be represented as:

$$\text{AP}^* = \beta^* X + \varepsilon \tag{2}$$

Here AP is not observed if the household is not enrolled in CBHI. The conditional expectation — that households only pay for family members that have joined CBHI — can be expressed as:

$$E(\text{AP} \mid X, D = 1) = \beta^* X + E(\varepsilon \mid X, D = 1) \tag{3}$$

Where Z and X are vectors of characteristics representing the socio-economic status (SES), financial literacy (FLI), health and vulnerability profile (HVP), insurance understanding (IU) and village level characteristics (VILL) with $\text{X} \subset \text{Z}$. Those are all the variables that predict the actual payment by the household based on the predicted probability of household enrolment decisions.

In the second model, the village level indicators are not used as explanatory variables under the assumption that intra-household payment decisions are independent, i.e., households decide irrespective of what other peer households' decisions on this issue.

In the final model, SES represents a vector capturing the socio-economic characteristics of the household (caste, monthly per capita expenditure, the highest number of completed years of education in the family and household size). Here we use the MPCE information collected during baseline, midline, and endline surveys to capture the economic status of the household concerning its peers in that location.

Households' financial literacy (FLI) is represented by dummies capturing whether any member of the family has a savings account, is enrolled in another insurance, notably the Government hospitalization insurance scheme for the below-poverty-line population (called Rashtriya Swasthya Bima Yojana (RSBY)) or any other insurance scheme.

The number of outpatient episodes (during the last one month) and inpatient episodes (during the last one year), and presence in the family of children below 12 years and the elderly above 65 years serve as the proxy for households' health and vulnerability profile (HVP).

Households' insurance and CBHI understanding (IU) are captured by a set of 13 questions covering the respondents' knowledge and understanding of various insurance principles and operational aspects of insurance (in general) and CBHI (in particular) (Panda *et al.*, 2015).

VILL includes the village level indicators (number of primary and secondary schools, banks, marketplace) representing the access to education and financial services.

We used the Ordinary Least Square (OLS) regression to analyze the predictors of actual premium payments (in PPPM) by the households.

The analysis was done separately for each location and each of the three years to take account of the fact that each CBHI plan had a different benefits package (Table 6.2), and because of the different socioeconomic and demographic characteristics of the households in the three locations (Table 6.3).

SELF-TEST QUESTIONS

1. Discuss the three ways used in the study for expressing estimated premiums and actual payments.
2. In analyzing the predictors of actual payments by the enrolled households (in PPPM), describe how the study seeks to resolve the issue of selection bias regarding households' enrollment in CBHI.

Results

Estimated premium

Expressed in nominal terms in the light of selected benefits package

The estimated premium PPPY in Pratapgarh in Year-1, Year-2, and Year-3 were INR 176, INR 250, and INR 250. In Kanpur-Dehat, participants choose a benefits package costing INR 192 PPPY in years 1 & 2, and INR 199 PPPY in Year-3. In Vaishali, the chosen package by the participants was INR 197 PPPY in all three years (Table 6.2).

The average nominal *estimated premium* in PPPM in Pratapgarh was INR 14.67, INR 20.83 and INR 20.83 respectively in years 1, 2, and 3. In Kanpur-Dehat, the nominal estimated values were INR 16.00, INR 16.00, and INR 16.58 PPPM in years 1, 2, and 3, respectively. In Vaishali, the nominal estimated values were INR 16.42 PPPM for all the three years (Table 6.4).

Expressed as a percentage of food expenditure

Following the method proposed by Binnendijk *et al.* (2013), we measured the estimated premium as a percentage of MPCE/food (Table 6.4). The estimated premium as a percentage of MPCE/food was 4.03%, 4.61% and 3.39% in Pratapgarh in years 1, 2 and 3 respectively; 3.92%, 3.16%, 2.46% in Kanpur-Dehat in years 1, 2 and 3 respectively; and 4.05%, 3.69% and 3.13% in Vaishali, in years 1–3, respectively.

Expressed as a percentage of per capita GDP

Following Nosratnejad *et al.* (2016), we also measured the estimated premiums as percentages of PCGDP (Table 6.4). The GDP data is readily available from secondary sources in most countries, notably India, and this expression informs the value of WTP relative to a coherent measure of each country's economic output. PCGDP is often highly correlated with the welfare of a country (Jones and Klenow, 2016). Moreover, this measure can obviate the need to obtain primary data, and it establishes a proper basis for international comparisons.

Table 6.4 Estimated Premium Over the Years — in Nominal Per Person Per Month (PPPM, in INR), as % of Monthly Per Capita Food Expenditure (MPCE-Food) and as % of Per Capita Gross District Domestic Product (PCGDP)

	Year-1	Year-2	Year-3
Pratapgarh			
In nominal (PPPM, INR)	14.67	20.83	20.83
As a percentage of MPCE-Food	4.03	4.61	3.39
As percentage of PCGDP	1.13	1.26	1.09
Changes in Estimated-WTP as % of MPCE-Food over the years		0.58***	–1.22***
Changes in Estimated-WTP as % of PCGDP over the years		0.12***	–0.18***
Sample Size	433	433	363
Kanpur-Dehat			
In nominal (PPPM, INR)	16.00	16.00	16.58
As a percentage of MPCE-Food	3.92	3.16	2.46
As percentage of PCGDP	0.72	0.55	0.50
Changes in Estimated-WTP as % of MPCE-Food over the years		–0.77***	–0.70***
Changes in Estimated-WTP as % of PCGDP over the years		–0.17***	–0.05***
Sample Size	378	341	275
Vaishali			
In nominal (PPPM, INR)	16.42	16.42	16.42
As a percentage of MPCE-Food	4.05	3.69	3.13
As percentage of PCGDP	1.12	0.85	0.77
Changes in Estimated-WTP as % of MPCE-Food over the years		–0.36***	–0.56***
Changes in Estimated-WTP as % of PCGDP over the years		–0.26***	–0.08***
Sample Size	524	407	358

Note: ***P < 0.01 of independent sample *t*-test.

The values of estimated premiums as % of PCGDP have been 1.12%, 1.26% and 1.08% in Pratapgarh, 0.72%, 0.55% and 0.50% in Kanpur-Dehat, and 1.12%, 0.85% and 0.77% in Vaishali in years 1, 2 and 3 respectively.

Estimated premiums as % of GDP in Pratapgarh first increased from 1st to 2nd year and then dropped, but in Kanpur-Dehat and Vaishali, there was a decreasing trend.

Actual payments

Expressed in nominal terms

The average actual payments PPPM of the enrolled households in the three locations, and over the three years were somewhat unstable (Table 6.5). In Pratapgarh, the actual nominal payments PPPM were INR 8.78 (SEM ± 0.28), INR 10.63 (SEM ± 0.41) and INR 10.89 (SEM ± 0.44) in years 1, 2, and 3 respectively. In Kanpur-Dehat, the actual nominal payments PPPM were INR 9.20 (SEM ± 0.42), INR 10.31 (SEM ± 0.38) and INR 8.68 (SEM ± 0.42) in years 1, 2, and 3, respectively. Also, in Vaishali, the actual nominal values PPPM were INR 11.03 (SEM ± 0.26), INR 9.88 (SEM ± 0.27) and INR 8.01 (SEM ± 0.30) respectively in years 1, 2, and 3 (Table 6.5).

Expressed as a percentage of food expenditure

Expressed as a percentage of MPCE/food, the actual payments represented 2.41%, 2.35% and 1.77% in Pratapgarh in years 1, 2 and 3 respectively. The corresponding figures in Kanpur-Dehat were 2.26%, 2.03%, and 1.29% in Year-1, Year-2, and Year-3 respectively. Moreover, in Vaishali, the average actual payments values were 2.72%, 2.22%, and 1.53% of MPCE/food in years 1–3, respectively (please see Table 6.6 for SEM values).

The actual payments as a percentage of MPCE/food in the three locations decreased over time, and except for the change between Year-1 and Year-2 in Pratapgarh, the decrease was statistically significant.

Table 6.5 Actual Payments Over the Years PPPM (INR), and as % of Estimated Premium by the Enrolled Households — Mean and Standard Error of Mean (Mean ± SEM)

	Year-1	Year-2	Year-3
Pratapgarh			
Actual payments — PPPM (INR)	8.78 ± 0.28	10.63 ± 0.41	10.8 ± 0.43
Actual payments — % of MPCE-Food	2.41 ± 0.08	2.35 ± 0.09	1.77 ± 0.07
Actual payments — % of PCGDP	0.68 ± 0.02	0.64 ± 0.02	0.57 ± 0.02
Changes in Actual payments as % of MPCE-Food over the years		–0.06	–0.58***
Changes in Actual payments as % of PCGDP over the years		–0.04	–0.07**
Actual payments as % of Estimated premium	59.9%	51.0%	52.3%
Sample Size	174	180	142
Kanpur-Dehat			
Actual payments — PPPM (INR)	9.20 ± 0.41	10.31 ± 0.37	8.68 ± 0.37
Actual payments — % of MPCE-Food	2.26 ± 0.10	2.03 ± 0.07	1.29 ± 0.06
Actual payments — % of PCGDP	0.41 ± 0.02	0.35 ± 0.01	0.26 ± 0.01
Changes in Actual payments as % of MPCE-Food over the years		–0.22*	–0.74***
Changes in Actual payments as % of PCGDP over the years		–0.06**	–0.09***
Actual payments as % of Estimated premium	57.5%	64.4%	52.4%
Sample Size	109	134	116
Vaishali			
Actual payments — PPPM (INR)	11.03 ± 0.26	9.87 ± 0.26	8.00 ± 0.29
Actual payments — % of MPCE-Food	2.72 ± 0.07	2.22 ± 0.06	1.53 ± 0.06
Actual payments — % of PCGDP	0.75 ± 0.02	0.51 ± 0.01	0.38 ± 0.01
Changes in Actual payments as % of MPCE-Food over the years		–0.50***	–0.69***
Changes in Actual payments as % of PCGDP over the years		–0.23***	–0.14***
Actual payments as % of Estimated premium	67.2%	60.2%	48.8%
Sample Size	242	224	115

Note: ***$P < 0.01$, **$P < 0.05$, *$P < 0.1$ of independent sample *t*-test.

Expressed as a percentage of PCGDP

The values of actual payments as % of PCGDP in Pratapgarh have been 0.68%, 0.64% and 0.57% in Year-1, Year-2 and Year-3 respectively; in Kanpur-Dehat, the values were 0.41%, 0.35% and 0.26%; and in Vaishali, the values were 0.75%, 0.51% and 0.38%.

It is noteworthy that in all three locations, the actual payments (when expressed as % of PCGDP) have decreased significantly over time (except for Pratapgarh between Year-1 and Year-2).

The gap between the estimated premium and actual payments

Expressed in nominal terms

The actual payments PPPM were considerably lower than the estimated premium PPPM in all locations and all years (Table 6.6). In nominal terms, the actual payments were INR 5.89 less than estimated premium (59.9% of estimated premium), INR 10.20 (51.0%) and INR 9.94 (52.3%) in years 1, 2 and 3 in Pratapgarh; INR 6.80 less than the estimated premium (57.5% of estimated premium), INR 5.69 (64.4%) and INR 7.90 (52.4%) in years 1, 2 and 3 in Kanpur-Dehat; and in Vaishali INR 5.38 less than the estimated premium (67.2% of estimated premium), INR 6.54 (60.2%) and INR 8.41 (48.8%) in years 1, 2 and 3. The differences were statistically significant throughout (paired t-test).

Expressed as percentage of food expenditure

When expressed as percentages of MPCE/food expenditure, in Year-1, Year-2, and Year-3 respectively, in Pratapgarh, the gaps were 1.62, 2.26, and 1.62 percentage points; in Kanpur-Dehat the differences entailed 1.67, 1.12 and 1.17 percentage point; and in Vaishali, 1.33, 1.47, and 1.60. These differences were statistically significant (paired t-test).

Expressed as a percentage of PCGDP

Similarly, when the gap between estimated premium and actual payments is expressed as a percentage of PCGDP for Year-1, Year-2, and Year-3

Table 6.6 Gap between Estimated Premium and Actual payments Over the Years — in Nominal PPPM (in INR), as % MPCE-food and as % of PCGDP

	Year-1		Year-2		Year-3	
Indicators	Mean	SEM	Mean	SEM	Mean	SEM
			Pratapgarh			
In PPPM (INR)	5.89***	0.28	10.20***	0.41	9.94***	0.44
In % of MPCE/food	1.62***	0.08	2.26***	0.09	1.62***	0.07
In % of PCGDP	0.45***	0.02	0.61***	0.02	0.51***	0.02
Sample Size	174		180		142	
			Kanpur-Dehat			
In PPPM (INR)	6.80***	0.42	5.69***	0.38	7.90***	0.38
In % of MPCE/food	1.67***	0.1	1.12***	0.07	1.17***	0.06
In % of PCGDP	0.30***	0.02	0.20***	0.01	0.24***	0.01
Sample Size	109		134		116	
			Vaishali			
In PPPM (INR)	5.38***	0.26	6.54***	0.27	8.41***	0.3
In % of MPCE/food	1.33***	0.07	1.47***	0.06	1.60***	0.06
In % of PCGDP	0.37***	0.02	0.34***	0.01	0.39***	0.01
Sample Size	242		224		115	

Note: ***P < 0.01 of paired *t*-test.

respectively, the values were 0.45, 0.61 and 0.51 in Pratapgarh; 0.30, 0.20 and 0.24 in Kanpur-Dehat and 0.37, 0.34 and 0.39 in Vaishali.

Difference between the estimated premium and actual payments by households

Table 6.7 contains the data on the difference between the total estimated premium that households had to pay and the premium they paid. In this table, the figures are presented per household (rather than PPPM as in Tables 6.4 and 6.5) because this counting is more pertinent to the understanding of the phenomenon. As already noted in the PPPM data, the

Table 6.7 Difference between Estimated Premium and Actual Payments from the Enrolled Households under the CBHI Schemes Over the Years (Mean ± SEMean)

Indicators	Year-1	Year-2	Year-3
Pratapgarh			
Total premium to be paid if all members joined CBHI (INR)	1081 ± 36	1481 ± 25	1481 ± 27
Total premium paid by the household (INR)	607 ± 23	707 ± 22	675 ± 20
% of premium collected than declared	56%	48%	46%
Household size	6.14 ± 0.21	5.93 ± 0.1	5.92 ± 0.11
Total no. of members joined CBHI from a family	3.45 ± 0.13	2.83 ± 0.09	2.7 ± 0.08
Kanpur-Dehat			
Total premium to be paid if all members joined CBHI (INR)	1101 ± 35	1072 ± 21	1138 ± 22
Total premium paid by the household (INR)	583 ± 27	635 ± 22	560 ± 17
% of premium collected than declared	53%	59%	49%
Household size	5.76 ± 0.19	5.58 ± 0.11	5.72 ± 0.11
Total no. of members joined CBHI from a family	3.04 ± 0.14	3.31 ± 0.11	2.82 ± 0.08
Vaishali			
Total premium to be paid if all members joined CBHI (INR)	1048 ± 21	994 ± 15	1064 ± 15
Total premium paid by the household (INR)	702 ± 20	572 ± 12	572 ± 15
% of premium collected than declared	67%	58%	54%
Household size	5.56 ± 0.13	5.04 ± 0.08	5.4 ± 0.08
Total no. of members joined CBHI from a family	3.6 ± 0.11	2.9 ± 0.06	2.9 ± 0.08

actual payments were lower than the estimated premiums in all locations and years. In Pratapgarh, the gap was INR 443 (–42%) in Year-1, INR 815 (–54%) in Year-2, and INR 767 (–52%) in Year-3. In Kanpur-Dehat, the gap was INR 561 (–49%), INR 421 (–39%), and INR 602 (–53%) in Year-1, Year-2, and Year-3, respectively. Finally, in Vaishali, the picture is similar: a considerable gap of INR 331 (–32%), INR 437 (–45%), and INR 573 (–53%) in Year-1, Year-2, and Year-3 respectively.

In all three locations, the gap widened considerably from Year-1 to Year-3 in nominal values.

This gap begs an answer to the question of why households paid less than their estimated premium when they were involved in repeated group discussions and group decisions on the price of the package.

A closure look at the enrolled household size reveals that the households enrolled an average of 3.45, 2.83 and 2.70 members in Year-1, Year-2, and Year-3 respectively as against their total household size of 6.14, 5.93 and 5.92 in these three years. Similarly, households in Kanpur Dehat enrolled 3.04, 3.31, and 2.82 members, while the average household size was 5.76, 5.58, and 5.72 in Year-1, Year-2, and Year-3, respectively. Following the similar trend, in Vaishali, the average enrolment size from a household was 3.6, 2.9 and 2.9 as against the average household size of 5.56, 5.04 and 5.4 in Year-1, Year-2 and Year-3 respectively.

To identify the relationship, the household size and enrolment size from a family was plotted in a two-way scatter diagram (Figure 6.1). The observations lead us to examine the hypothesis that the enrolled number increases as the household size increases, but at a decreasing rate, with a tendency toward zero growth, indicating that at some stage, an increase in total household size does not lead to additional enrolment. The rationale underlying this assumption is that enrolling all members of a large household might be too expensive (especially if the number of breadwinners is small), whereas small households have a smaller margin to adjust. We build the model of such enrolment distribution, to predict the expected number of enrollees relative to the total household size.

If we assume that the rate of increase decreases linearly i.e.,

$$\frac{\partial E}{\partial S} = -aS + b \qquad (4)$$

where E is the number of enrolled, S is the household size and $a > 0$

$$\Rightarrow E = -a\frac{s^2}{2} + bS + c$$

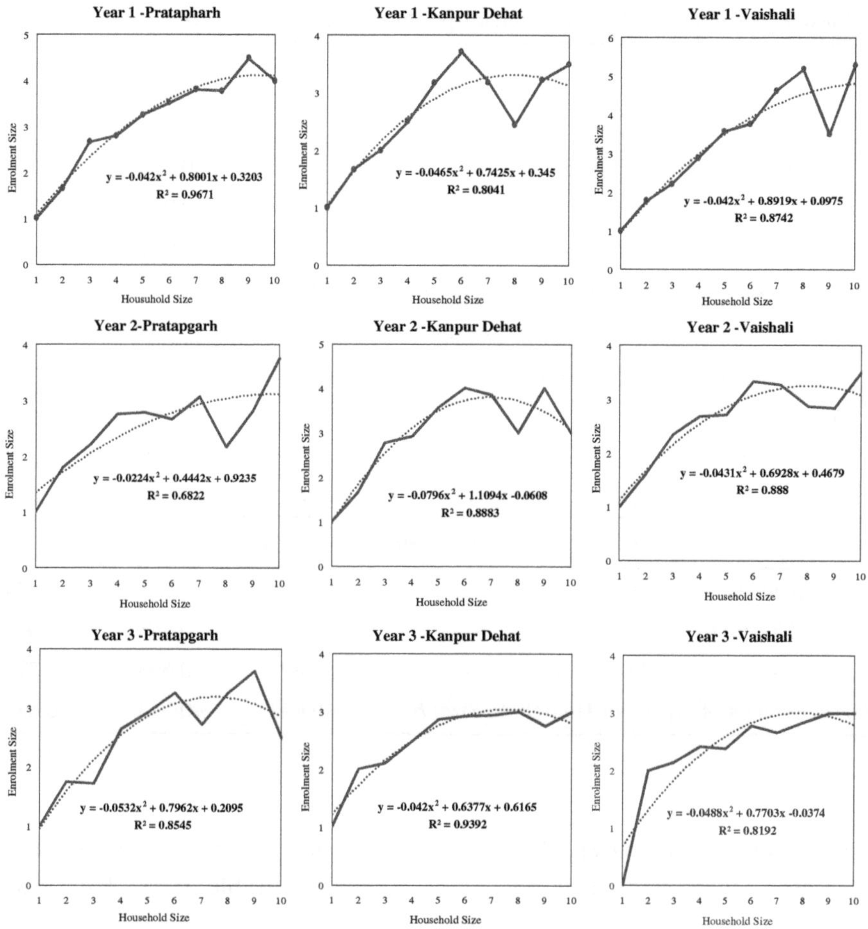

Figure 6.1 Relation between Enrolment Size and Household Size in the Study Locations over the Years

This implies that E is quadratic in S and c is the constant. Applying this quadratic relationship between enrolment (E) and household size (S) yielded very good predictions (with high R-square values) up to a limited household size of 10 (Figure 6.1).

Further analysis of the ratio of enrolment size to household size revealed that the relationship between these two is non-linear, i.e., as

Table 6.8 Estimates of Actual Payments per Family in Study Locations over the Years

Coefficients	Year-1	Year-2	Year-3
Pratapgarh			
Actual payments as % of PCGDP: α	0.688	0.663	0.553
Intercept Term: *C*	0.320	0.924	0.210
Coefficient of Household Size: *a*	0.800	0.444	0.786
The coefficient of Square of Household Size: *b*	–0.042	–0.022	–0.053
Kanpur-Dehat			
Actual payments as % of PCGDP: α	0.408	0.347	0.281
Intercept Term: *C*	0.345	–0.061	0.617
Coefficient of Household Size: *a*	0.743	1.109	0.638
The coefficient of Square of Household Size: *b*	–0.047	–0.080	–0.042
Vaishali			
Actual payments as % of PCGDP: α	0.749	0.528	0.424
Intercept Term: *C*	0.098	0.468	–0.037
Coefficient of Household Size: *a*	0.892	0.693	0.770
The coefficient of Square of Household Size: *b*	–0.042	–0.043	–0.049

household size increases, the number of enrolled from that family first increases, then stagnates, and then decreases (Table 6.8). This was confirmed in all the three locations and all the years.

Combining the findings, we can then represent the actual expected payment as:

$$\text{PACT} = \alpha * (\text{PCGDP}) \times \left\{ -a\frac{s^2}{2} + bS + c \right\} \quad (5)$$

Where PACT is the total actual premium paid by a household and α is actual payments, PPPM expressed as a percentage of PCGDP. The corresponding values of α, *a* and *b* for our study populations for the three years are shown in Table 6.8.

SELF-TEST QUESTIONS

1. Summarize the findings of the study concerning:
   (i) The significance of the difference between the estimated premium expressed as a percentage of MPCE/food and PCGDP across years
   (ii) The significance of the difference between the changes in actual payments over the years
   (iii) The significance of the difference between the estimated premium and actual payments in the same year
2. Summarize the relationship between household size and enrolment size, as observed in the study.

Predictors of actual payments made by the households

The results of the analysis on the predictors of actual premium payment using the Heckman two-stage selection model is provided in Tables 6.9A–6.9C for Pratapgarh, Kanpur-Dehat, and Vaishali respectively (refer to columns with heading "Actual Payment").

The *actual payments* in PPPM were positively and significantly associated with MPCE in Pratapgarh in Year-1 and Year-2 (Table 6.9A). Household size was a negative and significant predictor in Year-1 and Year-3. Households' ownership of a savings account and affiliation to RSBY was negatively and significantly correlated in Year-1. Among the households' health and vulnerability indicators, the number of hospitalizations and the presence of children were negatively linked to actual payments in Year-2. The score of insurance and CBHI understanding were positive predictors in Year-1 and Year-2.

In Kanpur-Dehat, actual payments were positively associated with MPCE in Year-3 and negatively associated with household size in Year-1 and Year-2 (Table 6.9B). Households' ownership of savings accounts was a positive predictor in Year-1 and Year-2. The vulnerability of family members to diseases (represented by children below 12 years of age and adults above 65 years of age) were positively linked in Year-1. Insurance and CBHI understanding were positive predictors in Year-2 and Year-3.

Surprisingly, in Vaishali, the highest education level in the family was negatively correlated with actual payment in Year-3 (Table 6.9C). Like the other two locations, here also, household size was a negative predictor in Year-2 and Year-3. Ownership of savings account was positively linked with actual payments in Year-3. While the number of outpatient events, and the presence of children were negative predictors in Year-1 and Year-3, respectively, the presence of elderly members was a positive predictor in Year-2. Furthermore, in Vaishali, insurance and CBHI understanding were positively associated with actual payments in Year-1 and Year-3.

Discussion

In this chapter, we analyze the expected income of CBHI schemes before their launch and the actual income in the first three years of operations. This analysis is essential to inform managerial decisions on the financial sustainability of operations. Many practitioners have applied well-known Contingent Valuation elicitation techniques to estimate WTP, which have, however, been questioned as these methods overlook the actuarial and affordability aspects (Dong *et al.*, 2003). Moreover, these methods can at best only estimate the projected income of the CBHI schemes before launch, whereas it is necessary first to validate the accuracy of these WTP estimates, and secondly to obtain more reliable estimates of actual income from premiums. In this study, we tried an alternative approach of combining actuarial methods and results of experiments by involving the end-users in group settings in package design and premium selection rather than relying on individual perspectives to estimate the WTP.

Moreover, we express estimated premiums and actual payments in three ways, which give more insights into the real value of the results in the specific context of each scheme and location. The expression of WTP in nominal terms is the most common, but least comparable across locations and over time because nominal units do not accurately reflect the purchasing power or the market exchange rates. Hence, two other methods have been used to express the estimated premium and actual payment estimates. Of these two, data on PCGDP is available on an annual basis in the public domain in most countries, whereas information on household food expenditure is survey-based and its sourcing from private informants involves cost.

Table 6.9A Predictors of Actual Payments (in PPPM) by Households Over the Years using Heckman Two-Stage Selection Method — Pratapgarh

	Year-1		Year-2		Year-3	
Indicators	Actual payments	Household enrolment	Actual payments	Household enrolment	Actual payments	Household enrolment
Household Enrolment Status in CBHI	—	12.19	—	12.15	—	12.15
	—	(0)	—	(0)	—	(0)
Household socio-economic status						
Schedule caste/Schedule tribe (Yes = 1)	0.193	0.00177	–0.811	–0.000217	0.764	–0.000183
	(0.551)	(1,059)	(0.668)	(924.3)	(0.823)	(1,087)
Monthly per capita expenditure (INR)	0.00124**	–3.47e-06	0.00201***	–1.72e-07	0.000737	–2.05e-07
	(0.000601)	(0.737)	(0.000631)	(0.734)	(0.000522)	(0.573)
Highest education in the family	–0.0502	–0.000181	–0.0798	–3.51e-05	0.0638	–1.01e-05
	(0.0844)	(149.4)	(0.102)	(146.8)	(0.120)	(137.1)
Household size	–0.615*	–0.000177	–0.788	–3.07e-05	–0.916**	–3.10e-05
	–0.342	(232.8)	–0.587	(250.9)	–0.277	(258.5)
Financial literacy & insurance subscription						
Household have savings account (Yes = 1)	–0.888*	–0.00111	–0.661	–0.000159	0.624	–0.000299
	(0.524)	(963.4)	(0.755)	(968.2)	(0.813)	(1,029)
Household enrolled in RSBY (Yes = 1)	–1.125*	0.00101	–1.146	–0.000820	–1.449	–0.00138
	(0.628)	(1,293)	(0.824)	(1,039)	(1.028)	(1,096)
Household enrolled in any other insurance (Yes = 1)	–0.497	0.00481	0.733	0.00205	–0.378	0.00180
	(0.538)	(1,107)	(0.692)	(1,231)	(0.752)	(1,330)

(Continued)

Table 6.9A *(Continued)*

	Household's health events					
Number of outpatient events	0.191	–0.000211	–0.0337	0.000110	0.0260	5.00e-05
	(0.168)	(369.3)	(0.211)	(300.2)	(0.201)	(312.1)
Number of hospitalization cases	0.305	–0.00128	–1.344*	0.000317	0.0253	–0.000727
	(0.705)	(1,148)	(0.787)	(1,195)	(1.024)	(1,172)
Presence of children <12 years (Yes = 1)	0.600	–0.000232	–1.849*	–0.000305	–0.278	–0.000207
	(0.774)	(1,160)	(0.974)	(1,307)	(1.056)	(1,370)
Presence of adult >65 years (Yes = 1)	–0.288	–0.00744	0.201	0.000244	–1.362	–0.00130
	(0.611)	(1,032)	(0.819)	(1,156)	(0.953)	(1,082)
	Insurance understanding					
Score of insurance and CBHI understanding	0.033**	–1.33e-05	0.158*	1.92e-07	0.203	4.28e-05
	(0.042)	(180.1)	(0.116)	(205.4)	(0.214)	(197.9)
	Village characteristics					
Number of primary schools	—	–0.000142	—	–0.000261	—	–5.07e-05
	—	(1,784)	—	(1,735)	—	(2.053)
Number of secondary schools	—	–0.000267	—	—	—	–0.000468
	—	(4,531)	—	—	—	(2,007)
Bank in the village (Yes = 1)	—	–0.00170	—	—	—	—
	—	(2,208)	—	—	—	—
The market place in the village (Yes = 1)	—	–0.000852	—	–0.00268	—	–0.00123
	—	(4,236)	—	(1,004)	—	(1,395)
Constant	11.37***	–6.098	14.03***	–6.092	13.09***	–6.098
	(1.707)	(2,574)	(1.916)	(2,905)	(2.687)	(2,396)
Observations	174	433	180	433	142	363

Note: Standard errors in parentheses; ***$P < 0.01$, **$P < 0.05$, *$P < 0.1$.

Table 6.9B Predictors of Actual Payments (in PPPM) by Households Over the Years using Heckman Two-Stage Selection Method — Kanpur-Dehat

Indicators	Year-1 Actual payments	Year-1 Household enrolment	Year-2 Actual payments	Year-2 Household enrolment	Year-3 Actual payments	Year-3 Household enrolment
Household Enrolment Status in CBHI	—	12.17	—	47.99	—	12.15
	—	(0)	—	(1.839e+09)	—	(0)
Household socio-economic status						
Schedule caste/Schedule tribe (Yes = 1)	–1.027	–0.000588	–1.381	7.924	0.368	–0.000698
	(0.819)	(1,133)	(0.848)	(3.161e+07)	(0.616)	(1,275)
Monthly per capita expenditure (INR)	0.000107	–1.49e-07	0.000507	0.00370	0.000545*	–1.17e-07
	(0.000266)	(0.338)	(0.000482)	(16,981)	(0.000296)	(0.575)
Highest education in the family	–0.0428	–4.21e-05	0.0677	0.395	–0.0896	–2.10e-05
	(0.113)	(156.6)	(0.106)	(1.447e+06)	(0.0758)	(158.3)
Household size	–1.560**	–7.99e-05	–1.016*	–1.268	–0.915	–1.67e-05
	(0.147)	(258.5)	(0.119)	(4.688e+06)	(0.259)	(331.2)
Financial literacy & insurance subscription						
Household have savings account (Yes = 1)	1.789**	–0.000182	1.766***	–0.250	–0.584	–0.000169
	(0.741)	(1,005)	(0.682)	(6.273e+06)	(0.627)	(1,185)
Household enrolled in RSBY (Yes = 1)	0.633	–8.13e-05	–0.742	–5.616	0.487	0.000372
	(0.987)	(1,432)	(0.725)	(3.277e+07)	(0.584)	(1,129)
Household enrolled in any other insurance (Yes = 1)	0.592	–0.000105	–0.584	–10.85	0.106	0.00112
	(0.807)	(1,258)	(0.738)	(3.880e+07)	(0.584)	(1,291)

(*Continued*)

Table 6.9B (*Continued*)

	Household's health events					
Number of outpatient events	−0.0343	−0.000141	−0.119	1.801	0.103	2.05e-05
	(0.274)	(355.8)	(0.219)	(7.804e+06)	(0.169)	(356.7)
Number of hospitalization cases	0.311	0.000102	0.777	−5.230	−0.168	0.00122
	(0.783)	(1,022)	(0.963)	(2.293e+07)	(0.682)	(1,633)
Presence of children <12 years (Yes = 1)	2.522***	−0.000637	0.0948	12.74	−0.845	−0.000153
	(0.969)	(1,299)	(0.895)	(4.797e+07)	(0.825)	(1,529)
Presence of adult >65 years (Yes = 1)	2.275**	−0.00104	0.648	−0.427	0.138	−0.000172
	(1.043)	(1,250)	(0.800)	(2.055e+08)	(0.721)	(1,590)
	Insurance understanding					
Score of insurance and CBHI understanding	0.0356	−7.26e-06	0.0865*	1.153	0.0705**	5.20e-05
	(0.129)	(136.5)	(0.102)	(4.452e+06)	(0.118)	(228.5)
	Village characteristics					
Number of primary schools	—	−0.000179	—	−4.605	—	−0.000102
	—	(645.5)	—	(1.377e+07)	—	(631.5)
Number of secondary schools	—	−9.17e-05	—	4.798	—	0.000206
	—	(679.6)	—	(1.544e+07)	—	(1,264)
Bank in the village (Yes = 1)	—	—	—	20.50	—	—
	—	—	—	(5.817e+07)	—	—
The market place in the village (Yes = 1)	—	−0.00290	—	−5.203	—	1.80e-05
	—	(1,476)	—	(1.620e+07)	—	(1,472)
Constant	16.91***	−6.130	13.27***	−39.27	13.51***	−6.090
	(1.944)	(2,555)	(1.629)	(1.337e+08)	(1.855)	(3,243)
Observations	109	378	134	343	116	275

Note: Standard errors in parentheses; ***P < 0.01, **P < 0.05, *P < 0.1.

Table 6.9C Predictors of Actual Payments (in PPPM) by Households Over the Years using Heckman Two-Stage Selection Method — Vaishali

	Year-1		Year-2		Year-3	
Indicators	Actual payments	Household enrolment	Actual payments	Household enrolment	Actual payments	Household enrolment
Household Enrolment Status in CBHI	—	12.15	—	12.15	—	40.71
	—	(0)	—	(0)	—	(2.166e+09)
	Household socio-economic status					
Schedule caste/Schedule tribe (Yes = 1)	0.431	0.000140	–0.190	0.00316	0.597	2.667
	(0.546)	(992.9)	(0.448)	(1,216)	(0.552)	(1.470e+07)
Monthly per capita expenditure (INR)	6.92e-05	–4.34e-08	0.000494	7.93e-08	0.000291	0.000758
	(0.000291)	(0.440)	(0.000341)	(0.634)	(0.000281)	(2,794)
Highest education in the family	–0.102	–1.92e-06	–0.0699	5.60e-05	–0.127**	0.0900
	(0.0692)	(115.3)	(0.0582)	(127.9)	(0.0593)	(164,942)
Household size	–0.561	–4.44e-06	–1.033*	7.29e-05	–0.792***	–2.324
	(0.456)	(234.3)	(0.187)	(349.0)	(0.159)	(4.004e+06)
	Financial literacy & insurance subscription					
Household have savings account (Yes = 1)	–0.186	0.000378	0.205	0.00173	0.924**	2.024
	(0.569)	(1,064)	(0.501)	(1,150)	(0.454)	(4.394e+06)
Household enrolled in RSBY (Yes = 1)	–0.186	–8.55e-05	–0.716	0.000700	–0.0863	–2.722
	(0.520)	(857.5)	(0.444)	(958.7)	(0.479)	(3.856e+06)
Household enrolled in any other insurance (Yes = 1)	–0.897	–0.000166	0.379	0.00504	0.447	–1.319
	(0.680)	(1,057)	(0.461)	(1,317)	(0.538)	(4.913e+08)

(Continued)

Table 6.9C *(Continued)*

	Household's health events					
Number of outpatient events	−0.455**	1.25e-05	−0.0937	0.000215	−0.0994	−0.217
	(0.178)	(356.1)	(0.153)	(354.5)	(0.138)	(1.677e+06)
Number of hospitalization cases	0.681	−0.000110	−0.439	−0.000588	0.483	−4.326
	(0.559)	(994.3)	(0.735)	(1,438)	(0.573)	(2.117e+06)
Presence of children <12 years (Yes = 1)	−0.297	6.93e-05	0.238	0.000541	−1.531*	9.972
	(0.892)	(1,196)	(0.708)	(1,430)	(0.787)	(1.853e+07)
Presence of adult >65 years (Yes = 1)	−0.857	−0.000141	1.911***	−0.000323	−0.490	−3.279
	(0.636)	(1,065)	(0.641)	(1,281)	(0.652)	(3.158e+06)
	Insurance understanding					
Score of insurance and CBHI understanding	0.218**	4.80e-05	0.0787	0.000249	0.320***	−1.265
	(0.106)	(146.1)	(0.0993)	(162.3)	(0.117)	(1.753e+06)
	Village characteristics					
Number of primary schools	—	−3.85e-07	—	−0.000325	—	—
	—	(269.8)	—	(850.4)	—	—
Number of secondary schools	—	0.000101	—	−0.000412	—	7.615
	—	(878.9)	—	(1,274)	—	(2.008e+07)
Bank in the village (Yes = 1)	—	−1.54e-05	—	0.00272	—	−8.507
	—	(2,201)	—	(4,345)	—	(2.808e+07)
The market place in the village (Yes = 1)	—	−0.000977	—	−0.00187	—	−7.684
	—	(1,423)	—	(1,387)	—	(2.345e+07)
Constant	14.32***	−6.081	14.03***	−6.062	11.33***	−6.770
	(1.516)	(1,917)	(1.244)	(2,394)	(1.670)	(4.480e+06)
Observations	242	524	224	407	115	359

Note: Standard errors in parentheses; ***P < 0.01, **P < 0.05, *P < 0.1.

Moreover, MPCE/food estimate may not be an accurate estimate of the spending capacity of poor households due to various conditional and unconditional cash transfer schemes targeting the weaker segment of the society primarily, but which are not easily recorded for each household everywhere. PCGDP data are based on the macro scale, reflecting changes in the country's overall economic activity. Therefore, we prefer the measure of estimated premiums to be expressed as a percentage of PCGDP.

The nominal *estimated premium* PPPM was around INR 14.67–INR 20.83 in Pratapgarh, INR 16.00–16.58 in Kanpur-Dehat and INR 16.42 in Vaishali over the three years (Table 6.4). When expressed as MPCE/food over the years, the values were approximately 2.46–4.61%, reasonably remindful of the benchmark 4.5% of food expenditure that was estimated in 2013 in comparable areas in rural India (Binnendijk *et al.*, 2013). Estimated premium values were around 0.50–1.26% of PCGDP in our study locations, lower than the benchmark findings (below 2% of PCGDP per household in rural areas) reported in 2016 in a systematic review on WTP in LMICs (Nosratnejad *et al.*, 2016).

Across the board, the household's actual payments toward their health insurance by CBHI plans were only around 49–67% of the estimated premiums in nominal values (around INR 8.01–11.01 PPPM; Tables 6.5 and 6.6). When expressed as % of PCGDP, the actual payments were around 0.26–0.75%. The gap between the estimated premiums and actual payments was statistically significant for all the locations and all the years (Table 6.6). These results reveal that in fact, households paid only around 45–63% of their *estimated premium*, which they could do by adjusting (downward) the number of family members enrolled (Table 6.7).

This could be because when household members selected a package in the group setting, they were keen to join a consensus on the "price" (and composition) of the package (Dror *et al.*, 2014). However, the data presented in Table 6.7 suggests that there was a difference between the household's contribution to group choice and the households' actual intention to pay. Once the group set the benchmark, households could not negotiate the price of the package by opting for a cheaper choice. So, each household adjusted its actual payments by enrolling only part of the family members in the insurance. It is noteworthy that households were able to adjust the total payment for health insurance while simultaneously accommodating the group consensus on the price and composition of the benefits package that their community agreed on. The consequence for the schemes was that actual payment was substantially and significantly less than estimated amounts.

The findings on the significant gap between estimated and actual payments validate the concern about the financial sustainability of the CBHI schemes and necessitate the search for better predictors of actual payments than merely relying on estimated premiums.

We analyzed the predictors of actual payments by the enrolled households (in PPPM) while using the Heckman sample selection model to correct for the selection bias regarding households' enrollment in CBHI. The regression results of actual payments by households showed that the economic status (a proxy for ability to pay), represented by MPCE of the household, was a positive determinant in Pratapgarh (Table 6.9A–C). There was a stronger negative linkage between actual payments and household size in all years in all three locations (Table 6.9A–C). The shape of the ratio of {enrolled to total household size} was quadratic in our study population, which means that the ratio initially increases with an increase in household size, but then at some point, the growth stagnates (Figure 6.1). A previous study (meta-analysis of factors affecting WTP for CBHI (Nosratnejad *et al.*, 2016)) concluded that family size was consistently correlated with higher WTP for CBHI. Our findings confirm that family size is a predictor, with the caveat that this relationship is not consistent. The quadratic shape seems to give a good fit between the ratio (enrolled/household size) and the household size, up to 10 persons. This suggests that actual premium payments can be expressed better as a function of PCGDP (Table 6.5) and the expected number of members joining from a family, which in turn is a non-linear function of household size (Equation (5)).

Indicators of households' financial literacy and health-related vulnerability could not offer a consistent and significant predictor of actual payments (contrasting the findings by Basaza *et al.* (2017)). The effects of formal education on premium payment were not a significant determinant either (Basaza *et al.*, 2017; Nosratnejad *et al.*, 2017).

However, insurance and CBHI understanding (represented by the scores of correct answers to some questions) provide some explanation. The score was positively related in six out of nine instances.

We conclude that the household size, ability to pay (proxy: MPCE of the household) and insurance and CBHI understanding are the best predictors of actual premium payment. This conclusion points to the need to include structured insurance education and financial literacy in the efforts to extend health insurance coverage of informal sector populations in LMIC. This conclusion also points to the need to explicitly teach about the relevance of insurance as a risk mitigation strategy from elementary schools everywhere where insurance uptake is voluntary.

Limitations

Given the study design, each CBHI offered its target population a single benefit package and corresponding premium. The decision was reached after iterative consultations with the group before each location, before the launch of the CBHI, and groups decided by consensus. This process restricted the variation in the estimated premium that could have been apparent if each household had decided independently of all others.

Conclusions

The first important insight is that there is a large gap between the estimated premium and the actual amounts that households paid for CBHI. The gap is about 50% of the estimated values. This shortfall in estimated income exposes the CBHI schemes to a high risk of deficits in the early years, which could lead to their financial default. Based on this finding, we conclude that the estimated premium is an unreliable predictor of expected income of CBHI schemes. The remedy is to look closely at other parameters of the target population that can be expected to provide a more accurate prediction of actual payments.

The second valuable insight from this analysis is that it would be possible to predict the actual earnings of CBHI schemes by using two essential pieces of information: firstly, the premium expressed as a percentage of PCGDP, and secondly the household size information of the target population. These pieces of information are easily available, one from secondary sources and the other from enrolment forms. Estimating actual payments by using PCGDP information and a quadratic relation with household size (which gives a prediction of the estimated number of people enrolled) produces a more realistic and reliable projection of income for CBHI schemes. The two advantages of applying this proposal for the projection of income are, first, a better prediction of expected income, and secondly, obviating the need for time- and resource-intensive sourcing of premium estimates (through the collection of primary data), which, as shown, deliver unreliable overestimates of expected income. This analysis, and the proposed new method of estimating the income of CBHI schemes is a significant value-addition to the existing literature because it shifts the focus to actual payments and away from grossly inaccurate premium estimates.

The Last key insight from this analysis is that the actual income of the schemes can be increased when the targeted households understand the advantages of CBHI coverage. This points out that a higher level of financial and insurance literacy can potentially be instrumental for greater coverage of CBHI in the informal sector of developing countries. Such training on an ongoing basis is an indispensable contributor to the promotion of universal health coverage and financial protection.

SELF-TEST QUESTIONS

1. The findings of the study reveal that households paid only around 45–63% of their estimated premium. Give the primary reason for this.
2. Discuss the two-pronged approach adopted in this chapter to assess the gap between WTP estimates and actual payment made by CBHI members.
3. Although the expression of WTP in nominal terms is the most common, it suffers from certain drawbacks. Explain these shortcomings and describe how these can be overcome using alternative WTP measures discussed here.
4. The study concludes that the estimated premium is an unreliable predictor of expected income of CBHI schemes. Suggest alternative parameters that can provide a more accurate prediction of actual payments.

KEY TERMS

- **CHAT (Choosing All Together):** An innovative method whereby the community can select the benefits package according to their need and willingness to pay through a consensus.
- **Enrollment:** The process by which a member of the community makes an informed decision to participate in the CBHI by paying the contribution and agreeing to abide by all its rules and business processes.
- **Benefits package:** The name of the full list of benefits that a participant can expect from CBHI Schemes, together with the conditions, limitations, and qualifications (e.g., threshold or cap) that apply to each benefit type. Each risk category has its own benefits package. Each benefits package commands a specific contribution amount payable.

Bibliography

Ahlert, M, Breyer, F, and Schwettmann, L (2016) How You Ask is What You Get: Framing Effects in Willingness-to-Pay for a QALY. *Social Science & Medicine*, 150, 40–48. https://doi.org/10.1016/j.socscimed.2015.11.055.

Ahmed, S, Hoque, ME, Sarker, AR, Sultana, M, Islam, Z, Gazi, R, and Khan, JAM (2016) Willingness-to-Pay for Community-Based Health Insurance among Informal Workers in Urban Bangladesh. *PLOS ONE*, 11(2), e0148211. https://doi.org/10.1371/journal.pone.0148211.

Basaza, R, Alier, PK, Kirabira, P, Ogubi, D, and Lako, RLL (2017). Willingness to Pay for National Health Insurance Fund among Public Servants in Juba City, South Sudan: A Contingent Evaluation. *International Journal for Equity in Health*, 16, 158. https://doi.org/10.1186/s12939-017-0650-7.

Bhatia, MR and Fox-Rushby, JA (2003). Validity of Willingness to Pay: Hypothetical Versus Actual Payment. *Applied Economics Letters*, 10(12), 737–740. https://doi.org/10.1080/1350485032000129575.

Binnendijk, E, Dror, DM, Gerelle, E, and Koren, R (2013) Estimating Willingness-to-Pay for Health Insurance among Rural Poor in India by Reference to Engel's Law. *Social Science & Medicine*, 76(1), 67–73. https://doi.org/10.1016/j.socscimed.2012.10.006.

Blumenschein, K, Johannesson, M, Yokoyama, KK, and Freeman, PR (2001) Hypothetical Versus Real Willingness to Pay in the Health Care Sector: Results from a Field Experiment. *Journal of Health Economics*, 20(3), 441–457. https://doi.org/10.1016/S0167-6296(01)00075-3.

Bohm, P (1972) Estimating Demand for Public Goods: An Experiment. *European Economic Review*, 3(2), 111–130. https://doi.org/10.1016/0014-2921(72)-90001-3.

Census of India (2011) Village Directory, District Census Handbook; Office of the Registrar General & Census Commissioner, India. Retrieved May 23, 2017, from http://www.censusindia.gov.in/2011census/dchb/DCHB.html.

Cookson, R (2003) Willingness to Pay Methods in Health Care: A Skeptical View. *Health Economics*, 12(11), 891–894. https://doi.org/10.1002/hec.847.

Dong, H, Kouyate, B, Snow, R, Mugisha, F, and Sauerborn, R (2003) Gender's Effect on Willingness-to-Pay for Community-Based Insurance in Burkina Faso. *Health Policy*, 64(2), 153–162. https://doi.org/10.1016/S0168-8510(02)00144-6.

Doyle, C, Panda, P, Poel, EV de, Radermacher, R, and Dror, DM (2011) Reconciling Research and Implementation in Micro Health Insurance Experiments in India: Study Protocol for a Randomized Controlled Trial. *Trials*, 12(1), 224. https://doi.org/10.1186/1745-6215-12-224.

Dror, DM and Koren, R (2012) The Elusive Quest for Estimates of Willingness to Pay for Health Microinsurance. In *Protecting the Poor: A Microinsurance Compendium: Vol. II* (pp. 156–173). Retrieved from https://papers.ssrn.com/abstract=2151384.

Dror, DM, Majumdar, A, and Chakraborty, A (2018) The Effect of Consensus on Demand for Voluntary Micro Health Insurance in Rural India. *Risk Management and Healthcare Policy*, 11, 139–158.

Dror, DM, Panda, P, May, C, Majumdar, A, and Koren, R. (2014). One For All and All For One: Consensus-Building within Communities in Rural India on their Health Microinsurance Package. *Risk Management and Healthcare Policy*, 139. https://doi.org/10.2147/RMHP.S66011.

Dror, DM, Radermacher, R, and Koren, R (2007) Willingness to Pay for Health Insurance among Rural and Poor Persons: Field Evidence from Seven Micro Health Insurance Units in India. *Health Policy*, 82(1), 12–27. https://doi.org/10.1016/j.healthpol.2006.07.011.

DSE-Bihar (2014) District Domestic Product 2004–05 to 2011–12. Retrieved February 28, 2018, from http://www.dse.bih.nic.in/.

Hausman, J (2012) Contingent Valuation: From Dubious to Hopeless. *Journal of Economic Perspectives*, 26(4), 43–56. https://doi.org/10.1257/jep.26.4.43.

Heberlein, TA and Bishop, RC (1986). Assessing the validity of contingent valuation: Three field experiments. *Science of the Total Environment*, 56, 99–107. https://doi.org/10.1016/0048-9697(86)90317-7.

Heckman, JJ (1979) Sample Selection Bias as a Specification Error. *Econometrica*, 47(1), 153–161. https://doi.org/10.2307/1912352.

IIPS and ICS (2017) *National Family Health Survey (NFHS-4), 2015–16: India.* Mumbai, India: International Institute for Population Sciences.

Jain, N (2017) *Role of Government-Funded and Community-Based Health Insurance Schemes in Moving Toward Universal Health Coverage in India.* Bethesda, MD: Abt Associates, Inc.

Jones, CI and Klenow, PJ (2016) Beyond GDP? Welfare across Countries and Time. *American Economic Review*, 106(9), 2426–2457. https://doi.org/10.1257/aer.20110236.

National Sample Survey Organisation (2013) *Key Indicators of Household Consumption Expenditure in India.* New Delhi, India: Ministry of Statistics and Programme Implementation.

Nosratnejad, S, Rashidian, A, Akbari Sari, A, and Moradi, N (2017) Willingness to Pay for Complementary Health Care Insurance in Iran. *Iranian Journal of Public Health*, 46(9), 1247–1255.

Nosratnejad, S, Rashidian, A, and Dror, DM (2016) Systematic Review of Willingness to Pay for Health Insurance in Low- and Middle-Income Countries. *PLoS ONE*, 11(6). https://doi.org/10.1371/journal.pone.0157470.

Onwujekwe, O, Chima, R, Shu, E, Nwagbo, D, and Okonkwo, P (2001) Hypothetical and actual willingness to pay for insecticide-treated nets in five Nigerian communities. *Tropical Medicine & International Health*, 6(7), 545–553. https://doi.org/10.1046/j.1365-3156.2001.00745.x.

Panda, P, Chakraborty, A, and Dror, DM (2015) Building Awareness to Health Insurance Among the Target Population of Community-Based Health Insurance Schemes in Rural India. *Tropical Medicine & International Health*, 20(8), 1093–1107. https://doi.org/10.1111/tmi.12524.

Panda, P, Chakraborty, A, Dror, DM, and Bedi, AS (2013). Enrolment in Community-Based Health Insurance Schemes in Rural Bihar and Uttar Pradesh, India. *Health Policy and Planning*. https://doi.org/10.1093/heapol/czt077.

Prinja, S, Chauhan, AS, Karan, A, Kaur, G, and Kumar, R (2017) Impact of Publicly Financed Health Insurance Schemes on Healthcare Utilization and Financial Risk Protection in India: A Systematic Review. *PLOS ONE*, 12(2), e0170996. https://doi.org/10.1371/journal.pone.0170996.

Ramke, J, Palagyi, A, du Toit, R, and Brian, G (2009) Stated and Actual Willingness to Pay for Spectacles in Timor-Leste. *Ophthalmic Epidemiology*, 16(4), 224–230. https://doi.org/10.3109/09286580902999447.

Ryan, M, Mentzakis, E, Suthi, J, and John, C (2017) External Validity of Contingent Valuation: Comparing Hypothetical and Actual Payments. *Health Economics*, 26(11), 1467–1473. https://doi.org/10.1002/hec.3436.

Schmidt, J-O, Mayindo, JK, and Kalk, A (2006) Thresholds for Health Insurance in Rwanda: Who Should Pay How Much? *Tropical Medicine & International Health*, 11(8), 1327–1333. https://doi.org/10.1111/j.1365-3156.2006.01661.x.

Smith, RD (2003) Construction of the Contingent Valuation Market in Health Care: A Critical Assessment. *Health Economics*, 12(8), 609–628. https://doi.org/10.1002/hec.755.

UP-DES (2016). District Domestic Product (New Base Year 2011–2012). Retrieved February 26, 2018, from http://updes.up.nic.in/STATE%20ACC%20STATISTICS/NDDP%20&%20GDDP/statedomestic(b)_ddp%2011-12.htm.

Chapter 7

Estimating Capital Requirements to Scale Health Microinsurance*

LEARNING OBJECTIVES

Upon completion of this chapter, the reader should be able to:

- Estimate community-based health insurance (CBHI) operating costs
- Estimate CBHI claims reserve
- Estimate CBHI loan requirements
- Estimate interest earned
- Estimate loan repayments installments
- Understand the sustainability parameters of insurance plans
- Interpret financial sustainability using a prototype plan
- Interpret the sensitivity of capital requirements to varying levels of claims ratio and confidence level
- Interpret return on investment
- Understand the policy repercussions of the study

---

*This chapter originally appeared in *The Geneva Papers on Risk and Insurance Issues and Practice*, (2019), 44(3), 410–444, authored by David M. Dror, Atanu Majumdar, and Nihar Jangle.

Abstract

Our objective is to estimate the capital required to launch, scale and sustain the operation of health microinsurance plans. We develop algorithms to estimate operating costs, capital or loan requirements, interest earned, repayments, and scaling projections. We check the plausibility of assumptions using the data of two CBHI plans. A prototype plan covering 40,000 persons in India requires USD 62,477 to offset deficits in the initial years if its long-term operating costs are not to exceed 20% of the premium and the claims ratio is to stabilize at around 70%. The probability of bankruptcy is fixed at 0.1% (i.e., 1 in 1,000). Fifteen years are required (after a five-year moratorium) to repay the loan in full plus interest at 5% p.a. in USD (10.96% in Indian rupees). It is possible to attain sustainability of health microinsurance schemes by providing the necessary initial capital as a loan and being very attentive to five parameters: enrollments, premiums, operating costs, renewal rates, and claims ratio.

Chapter Outline

CBHI plans are designed to enable deprived sections of society face their health costs more efficiently when not much thought has been given to the financial aspects of managing this risk without CBHI. In this chapter, we use empirical data from two plans, and a standard costing methodology, to design a prototype CBHI plan. With the prototype plan, we answer three fundamental business questions: Can CBHI plans be operationally sustainable? Can the plans also repay loans they took at inception and still achieve full sustainability? What is the social impact of the initial investment in a CBHI plan? We show that the amount of seed capital is low, that CBHI plans can repay the capital, at commercially relevant interest rates. The subsequent scaling up of CBHI plans can also generate considerable additional resources for health care. We stress that the assumptions and data used to develop the model must be verified and calibrated to every specific situation.

Introduction

One of the pain-points of the world's development goals is achieving affordable and equitable financing of health insurance. This global issue has particularly critical ramifications for informal sector populations and rural poor in low- and middle-income countries (LMIC). A recent systematic review (Asante *et al.*, 2016) concluded that "... healthcare financing in LMICs benefits the rich more than the poor ... there are impediments to making health care more accessible to the poor ..." According to the World Bank and the World Health Organization, "800 million people spend at least 10 percent of their household budgets on health expenses for themselves, a sick child or another family member. For almost 100 million people these expenses are high enough to push them into extreme poverty" (World Bank, 2017; Magdalena, 2013). This situation reflects the sad reality that most LMIC cannot effectively mandate universal health coverage. LMIC governments cannot allocate enough funds for premium subsidies that render such insurance affordable for resource-poor persons. Therefore, offering insurance coverage to most of the world's population is not a realistic option, and most risks remain uninsured (*The protection gap*).

In the absence of top-down solutions, mutuals, cooperatives and community-based organizations (MCCOs), notably CBHI plans[1] offer bottom-up health insurance known as "health microinsurance"[2] where funds are equitably pooled from resource-poor families, based on their willingness and ability to pay. CBHIs function at a small scale in rural and impoverished areas mainly in South Asia and Sub-Saharan Africa. CBHI plans make efforts to address the challenges of implementation at the grassroots level and do not pay much attention to the financial aspects until the plans are exposed to a shortage of fund due to the withdrawal of grants. Thus, they fail to attract (commercial) capital investment and remain dependent and small forever.

We, however, strongly feel that every CBHI plan can also be a compelling business proposition. We think differently, as we have implemented multiple schemes in India and Nepal without a single rupee of subsidy to premiums. If CBHIs can attract impact investors, to bring about

[1] In India, the term *scheme* is commonplace, while the term *plan* is unusual. We use *scheme* to refer to the field evidence and to the prototype.

[2] The term *microinsurance* used in this chapter means insurance schemes implemented through a community-based governance structure.

a paradigm shift that should support them to scale and adopt more inclusive, more efficient and more impact-oriented governance. The purpose of this chapter is to elaborate methodologies to estimate both the capital needs of CBHI plans and the viability of the terms under which investors would agree to make the capital available.

The assumptions (e.g., on the trends in premiums, the number of households enrolled, average insured from each household) are explained in context. Wherever possible, we use the operational data of two CBHI plans, one in Bihar, India (Dror *et al.*, 2009), and the other in Banke, Nepal (Dror *et al.*, 2014) to uphold the assumptions or replace them with "ground truthing" facts.

Data and Methods

Data

The data originated from the following CBHI plans: *Swasthya Kamal*, promoted by Sanchay Credit Co-op for members of Nidan NGO in Vaishali district, Bihar state (India); and *Sanjeevani* promoted by Nirdhan NGO for clients of Nirdhan Utthan Bank Limited (NUBL) in Banke district located in the Terai (flatlands), Nepal. The prototype scheme used in this article is an extrapolation of implementation experience of the Micro Insurance Academy (MIA) in India and Nepal.

We extracted data from the MIA-developed management information system application (MIA-MIS). This application is described in the *Microinsurance Business Processes Handbook* (Dror and Jambhekar, 2016). We used U.S. daily overnight rates (Treasury Direct, 2016), treasury yield curve rates (US Department of the Treasury, 2016), and Indian government bond yields (US Department of the Treasury, 2016), as well as U.S. Dollar/Indian Rupee FX spot rates (X-Rates, 2016; XE.com, 2016), to calculate forward exchange rates. Forward conversion rates for US$ are used to calculate loan and repayment installments, assuming that loans are taken and repaid in US$. Expenditures and claims cost were estimated in INR. We used the exchange rate 1 INR = 1.60 NPR to convert NPR to INR.

Estimating Operating Costs

A plan's operating costs are the sum of three major components: (i) start-up costs, (ii) acquisition costs, and (iii) routine administrative costs. Start-up costs reflect one-time expenditures incurred in the first year, including setting up infrastructure and organizing awareness campaigns. Start-up costs depend on the community's geographical spread. Acquisition costs are incurred when enrolling new households and renewing existing households. Acquisition costs reflect the cost of additional field staff, engaged for house-to-house visits during the enrollment period to assist with application forms and to collect premiums. Routine administrative costs are the costs of maintaining the plan's three-tiered governance structure that CBHIs typically have (Dror, 2016). The first tier consists of claims committees (CCs), each serving around 700 households participating in 60 to 80 women's groups, called "Self-Help Groups" (SHGs) in India and "Self-Reliant Groups" (SRGs) in Nepal. CCs are composed of representatives of SHGs/SRGs (one representative for 10–12 SHGs/SRGs). Each CC employs one salaried "scheme activist" to provide service to policyholders and support the CC members in processing claims. The second tier consists of coordination committees (CoCos), which oversee the operation of up to five CCs (3,500 households). CoCo membership is composed of representatives of the participating CCs. Each CoCo employs one salaried "scheme coordinator" and maintains an office where records of all transactions are kept. Claims processing happens at CC and CoCo levels. CC and CoCo members receive a "sitting fee" from the plan for meetings, but no salaries. The third tier, the Federation, is composed of representatives of the field partner (usually NGOs active in organizing the network of SHGs/SRGs) and CoCo members. The Federation employs one salaried project coordinator and one salaried accountant and oversees the activities of up to three CoCos (10,500 households). See Figure 7.1.

In analyzing the prototype plan, we assume that 2017 is the launch year, that the costs are calculated in INR, and we apply an annual inflation factor (10%) to estimate the standard costs for the successive years. We take the standard cost data of 2016 (because scheme data were available

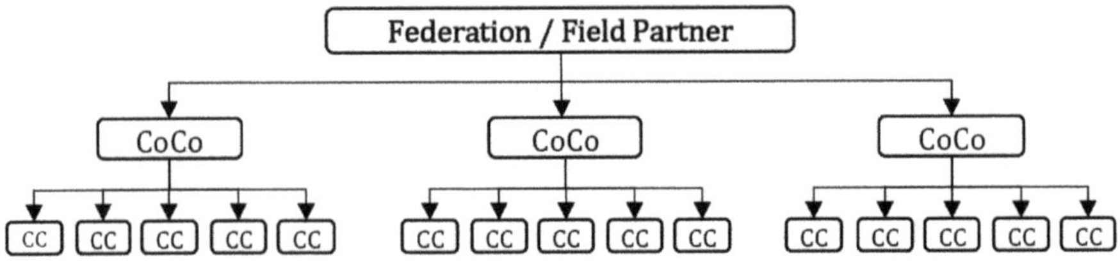

Figure 7.1 Governance Structure of the CBHI Scheme

up to this year). The start-up cost in the base year is the lump sum amount of INR 1,000,000 (US$ 14,948) that was given to each field partner as a grant at the beginning of a scheme to set up the infrastructure and initiate awareness programme in their captive area.

The estimated acquisition cost during the first year was based upon the experience of the scheme. A facilitator (community-based field staff) working part-time during the enrollment period can enroll on average two new households per day, costing INR 150 (US$ 2.24) per day (in the base year). Productivity doubles when renewing enrolled households compared to new households. Thus, the acquisition costs depend on the number of new households and the renewal rates in each scheme. Total acquisition costs at the launch year and the subsequent years are estimated based on this assumption and an annual inflation factor of 10%.

The base year's routine administrative costs (standardized) at the three levels of governance are shown in Tables 7.1, 7.2, and 7.3. It is recalled that one CC is set up for every 700 households, one CoCo for every five CCs, and three CoCos for one Federation. Thus, one saturated scheme should have 10,500 households. A new unit (CC or CoCo) is formed when the units formed previously reach saturation.

The routine administrative costs (standardized) at the CC level gradually decrease over time, and the average cost per household reduces approximately 38% from US$ 2.61 to US$ 1.63 over five years' period (at the present value of the base year). The average costs (standardized) per household at the CoCo and Federation levels are estimated at US$ 0.86 and US$ 0.56 respectively. Total routine administrative costs for the future years are estimated by applying the above assumptions and an annual inflation factor of 10%.

Table 7.1 Standard Administrative Cost at Claims Committee (CC) Level

	Plan activist @ INR 5000/ person/ month	Communication for activist @ INR 250/ person/month	Conveyance for activist @ INR 500/ person/month	Claims processing meeting expenses @ INR 2100/ month	Stationery during enrollment	Total annual cost at claims committee level (INR)	Total annual cost at claims committee level (NPR); conversion rate INR 1 = NPR 1.60	Total annual cost at claims committee level (USD); conversion rate USD 1 = INR 66.90
Year 1								
No. of months	12	12	12	12				
Annual cost	60,000	3000	6000	25,200	28,000	122,200	195,520	1826.61
Year 2								
No. of months	8	8	8	12				
Annual cost	40,000	2000	4000	25,200	28,000	99,200	158,720	1482.81
Year 3								
No. of months	6	6	6	12				
Annual cost	30,000	1500	3000	25,200	28,000	87,700	140,320	1310.91
Year 4								
No. of months	4	4	4	12				
Annual cost	20,000	1000	2000	25,200	28,000	76,200	121,920	1139.01
Year 5 onward								
No. of months	4	4	4	12				
Annual cost	20,000	1000	2000	25,200	28,000	76,200	121,920	1139.01

Number of households at the saturation level = 700

Table 7.2 Standard Administrative Cost at Coordination Committee (CoCo) Level

Cost items	Details	No. of persons	No. of months	Amount (INR)	Total annual cost at CoCo level (INR)	Total annual cost at CoCo level (NPR); conversion rate INR 1 = NPR 1.60	Total annual cost at CoCo level (USD); conversion rate 1USD = INR 66.90
Plan coordinator	@ INR 9000/ person/month	1	12	108,000	202,200	323,520	3022.42
Rent	@ INR 2000/month		12	24,000			
Electricity & water	@ INR 500/month		12	6000			
Communication & telephone	@ INR 250/month		12	3000			
Internet	@ INR 500/month		12	6000			
Stationery	@ INR 500/month		12	6000			
Computer maintenance	@ INR 1000/month		12	12,000			
Local conveyance	@ INR 500/person/ month	1	12	6000			
Claims processing meeting expenses	@ INR 2100/month		12	25,200			
Meeting with external stakeholders, govt	@ INR 500/month		12	6000			

Number of households at the saturation level = 3500

Table 7.3 Standard Administrative Cost at Federation Level

Cost items	Details	No. of persons	No. of months	Amount (INR)	Total annual cost at CoCo level (INR)	Total annual cost at CoCo level (NPR); conversion rate INR 1 = NPR 1.60	Total annual cost at CoCo level (USD); conversion Rate USD 1 = INR 66.90
Project coordinator	@ INR 24,000/person/month	1	12	288,000	396,000	633,600	5919.28
Accountant	@ INR 7000/person/month	1	12	84,000			
Communication and telephone	@ INR 500/person/month	2	12	12,000			
Local conveyance	@ INR 500/person/month	2	12	12,000			

Number of households at the saturation level = 10,500

SELF-TEST QUESTION

1. Explain the three major components of a plan's operating costs.

Estimating Claims Reserve

The capital of a CBHI serves two purposes: capital required for claims settlement and capital required for operations. The capital required for payment of claims, called *reserve*, consists of two parts: the expected claims for the year and the amount needed to pay claims that exceed the expected amount (IRMI, 2017). We calculate the reserve so that it protects the plan with 99.9% probability, i.e., the chance that claims exceed the total reserve should not be higher than 1 in 1,000. The optimum level of the reserve (expected value of claims plus the amounts required to cover shortfalls) at the beginning of each year is estimated as follows:

$$R_i = (\mu_i + \sigma_i \cdot Z_{0.999}) \cdot h_i \cdot a_i \tag{7.1}$$

where,
R_i = capital required for claims settlement in year i of the plan
μ_i = expected payout per person in year i
σ_i = standard error of the mean of payout per person in year i
$Z_{0.999}$ is such that $\text{Prob}\{X \leq Z_{0.999} \mid X \sim N(0,1)\} = 0.999$
h_i = number of households enrolled in year i of the plan
a_i = average number of insured from each enrolled household in year i.

Note that $\mu_i = p_i \cdot r_i$, where p_i is the premium per capita in year i, and r_i is the expected claims ratio for the year i.

Individual claims usually follow the lognormal distribution. Since individual claims can be assumed as identical and independently distributed (iid) random variables, their properly normalized sum "approximately" follows a normal distribution according to the Central Limit Theorem. The distributions of individual random variables do not matter as long as they are identical and independent. Thus, the average individual payout, which is an estimate of pure risk premium, follows the normal distribution with some mean and variance. On this point, we follow the lead of others who have posited the same assumption (Houston, 1960; Biener, 2013). We are aware that the assumption of independently and identically distributed individual payouts may be challenged in health insurance, and we discuss the justification of its application in this case, as well as its limitations, in the Limitations section. We assert that the pure risk premium per person per year (PPPY) is the mean of this distribution. To estimate the variance of the distribution, we assume a constant rate of the coefficient of variation. This assumption implies that if the mean increases over time, the standard deviation also increases proportionally. This assumption is reasonably fair. To be on the safe side, we have assumed a large value (10) for the coefficient of variation, higher by more than 1.5 times the value we have observed in our MIS dataset.

SELF-TEST QUESTION

1. Discuss the assumptions made while estimating the optimum level of the reserve at the beginning of each year.

Estimating Loan Requirements

The total capital requirement (T_i) for the ith year is then given by:

$$T_i = C_{operating,i} + R_i \tag{7.2}$$

where $C_{operating,i}$ is the Total Operating Cost and R_i is the required reserved for claims cost in the ith year of the scheme.

The primary source of income of CBHI plans is the premium collected from insured households. Total premium income P_i for the scheme in year i is

$$P_i = p_i \cdot h_i \cdot a_i \tag{7.3}$$

where, p_i, h_i, a_i are as explained above.

Premium income plus the operating balance carried forward may not suffice to meet the plan's capital requirement, especially in the first few years. CBHI plans can have other income as well, e.g., from interest on investments. When premiums plus other income plus the balance brought forward are insufficient, the plan needs to finance the gap with a loan. Hence, the operating results of a plan in a particular year i must satisfy the following equation:

$$B_i + P_i + M_i + I_i = C_{claims.i} + C_{operating,i} + L_i + B_{i+1} \tag{7.4}$$

where,
B_i = operating balance (opening) at the beginning of year i
M_i = loan taken at the beginning of year i
I_i = interest earned in year i
$C_{claims,i}$ = aggregated claims costs in year i
L_i = loan repayment in year i
P_i and $C_{operating,i}$ are as explained earlier.

Clearly, $B_i = 0$ when i is the first year of the plan. The need for a loan arises when $T_i > B_i + P_i$.

We assume that repayment is made in years with an operating surplus, when no loan is needed the following year, i.e., repayment in any given year is not made by taking a new loan in that year. Hence,

$$M_i \geq \max\left(T_i - B_i - P_i, 0\right) \tag{7.5}$$

To estimate the loan requirements M_i in future years, we assume that the aggregated claims costs $C_{claims,i}$ are best estimated by the expected value of the assumed claims ratio for the ith year, r_i, viz. $C_{claims,i} = P_i \cdot r_i$.

Estimating Interest Earned

The amount available at the beginning of the year in excess of the capital required for the year may be invested and can earn interest income. Thus, we estimate income from interest as follows:

$$I_i = \left(B_i + P_i + M_i - T_i\right) \cdot s \tag{7.6}$$

where s is the annual rate of interest. We assume that s remains constant over the years and $s = 8\%$ per annum (typical interest rate for fixed deposits in India).

Estimating Loan Repayment Installments

The repayment schedule of the loan and interest amounts must simultaneously fulfill the loan agreement while lowering the plan's risk of defaulting when required to pay amounts exceeding their ability. The cheapest strategy to do both would be for the plan to take the lowest loan amount M_i each year, so that (5) is fulfilled with an equal sign. Stated differently, the strategy would be to repay only at the end of a year when a new loan is not required for the following year. Mathematically,

$$L_i = \begin{cases} 0, \text{ if } \ M_{i+1} > 0 \\ \min\left(B_{i+1} + P_{i+1} - T_{i+1}, B_{i+1}, \ \textit{outstanding loan}\right), \text{ if } \ M_{i+1} = 0 \end{cases} \tag{7.7}$$

The actual value of L_i also depends on the interest rate payable. The most likely scenario is that the plan borrows enough money in launch year i_0 to cover its needs in the coming years and repay in several annual installments. The repayment installments could include the option of applying a moratorium (for the first few years, say m years) followed by installment amounts increasing annually by a factor (say $k \geq 1$). The most common repayment scenario would consist of equal annual installments starting in year i_0; $m = 0$ and $k = 1$. If all M_i are converted to a single loan of M' taken at the beginning of the first year at interest rate d, then the formula for the 1st (non-zero) installment, L_{i_0} is given by

$$L_{i_0} = \begin{cases} \dfrac{M'(1+d)^m (1+d-k)}{1-\left(\dfrac{k}{1+d}\right)^n} & \text{for } k \neq 1+d \\ \dfrac{M'(1+d)^m (1+d)}{n} & \text{for } k = 1+d \end{cases} \tag{7.8}$$

Sequential installments can be computed by multiplying L by k. We estimate M' through a process of iteration with the present value of all loan amounts as the first approximation of M'. While computing the present value, we apply a discount rate equivalent to the assumed interest rate (of 8%) to find the first approximation of the lump sum amount to be borrowed in the launch year. We can now find the lowest loan amount M' starting from the initial approximation, with $B_i \geq 0$ for all $i \geq i_0$. The single loan amount at the launch year M' is a function of expected operating costs, claims costs, premium income and interest earned.

So far, we have assumed the currency of loans and repayments to be constant, using the currency of the country of implementation (INR, NPR). However, if foreign lenders demand repayments in a foreign currency, we must consider exchange rate fluctuations. Loan M_i and repayment installments L_i can be expressed in US$ by applying current exchange rates for the base year and forward exchange rates for consecutive years. This could mean variable amounts in local currency for equal repayment installments in US$ and a different actual interest rate in local currency (for borrowing US$). We calculate the local repayment installments using forward exchange rates over the next 20 years. Equivalent interest rate in INR on borrowing (in US$) is estimated using the IRR function of MS Excel.

Findings

We build a prototype plan based on the evidence collected from the two CBHI plans and certain assumptions on operating costs for a well-implemented plan (introduced in the Data and Methods Section). Each of these two provides insights into good and bad practices that affect performance. In 2016, the plans were 3 and 6 years old and did not offer scope for analysis with longitudinal datasets. We study the impacts of various factors on the sustainability and scalability of the prototype plan. Table 7.4 provides the necessary information, referred to in multiple places in this article. There was no borrowing involved as these schemes were the beneficiaries of grants (in the initial years).

Recalling that a CBHI plan has two types of costs (claims and operating) and that claims costs fluctuate based on the statistical distribution describing them, it is impossible to forecast the plan's exact amount payable for claims in any given year. However, within a given confidence interval, the expected claims cost per person can be estimated for a given benefits package. Operating costs also change from year to year, based on the expansion and rates of inflation. The two keys to CBHI plan

Table 7.4 Primary Details of the Implemented Plans

Location	Year	Number of house holds	Number of individuals	Average number of insured per HH	Premium in local currency	Premium PPPY (USD)	Total premium (USD)	Claims cost (USD)	Claims ratio (%)	Cumulative claims ratio (%)	Current year's net surpluses in USD (premiums over claims)	Cumulative net surpluses (USD)	Cumulative net surpluses as a % of cumulative premium
Bihar	2014	1697	3662	2.16	220.00	3.68	13,492.55	8576.03	64	64	4916.51	4916.51	36
	2015	1271	2840	2.23	245.00	3.84	10,904.25	9023.04	83	72	1881.21	6797.72	28
	2016	1316	3147	2.39	250.00	3.74	11,760.09	8702.37	74	73	3057.72	9855.44	27
	Total						36,156.88	26,301.44			9855.44		
Banke	2011	1670	4173	2.50	252.00	3.51	14,660.48	6438.45	44	44	8222.03	8222.03	56
	2012	3270	7880	2.41	399.09	4.48	35,279.95	20,420.36	58	54	14,859.59	23,081.62	46
	2013	4180	11,870	2.84	392.34	4.21	49,990.29	32,386.81	65	59	17,603.48	40,685.10	41
	2014	3612	12,232	3.39	424.66	4.42	54,091.69	47,964.42	89	70	6127.27	46,812.37	30
	2015	3826	13,703	3.58	501.63	4.91	67,304.61	46,234.21	69	69	21,070.40	67,882.77	31
	2016	3560	12,582	3.53	503.69	4.71	59,206.28	41,227.11	70	69	17,979.17	85,861.94	31
	Total						280,533.30	194,671.35			85,861.94		
All	2011	1670	4173	2.50		3.51	14,660.48	6438.45	44	44	8222.03	8222.03	56
	2012	3270	7880	2.41		4.48	35,279.95	20,420.36	58	54	14,859.59	23,081.62	46
	2013	4180	11,870	2.84		4.21	49,990.29	32,386.81	65	59	17,603.48	40,685.10	41
	2014	5309	15,894	2.99		4.25	67,584.24	56,540.45	84	69	11,043.79	51,728.88	31
	2015	5097	16,543	3.25		4.73	78,208.86	55,257.25	71	70	22,951.61	74,680.49	30
	2016	4876	15,729	3.23		4.51	70,966.37	49,929.48	70	70	21,036.89	95,717.38	30

sustainability are: stabilizing the claims ratio and optimizing the operating costs.

In this section, we first analyze which sustainability parameters determine the financial sustainability of a prototype plan. For this, we study the Bihar and Banke plans' performances against these sustainability parameters.

Sustainability Parameters of Insurance Plans

Given the governance structure of a prototype CBHI plan (explained in the Data and Methods Section), total operating costs claims cost, and plan income all depend on the following *sustainability parameters* when standard costing (based on the assumptions described in the Data and Methods section) is applied:

1. Number of enrolled households.
2. The average number of insured members from each household.
3. Premium PPPY.
4. Excess of premiums over claims ratio (1 minus claims ratio).
5. Renewal rate.

The number of enrolled households determines the required number of CC and CoCo, which influences operating costs. When the number of enrollees increases, we can reasonably expect a decrease in per capita operating costs. However, this relationship is not strictly monotonic, because maintaining a CC or a CoCo has a fixed cost even if it serves a suboptimal number of households. The per capita operating cost decreases up to a certain number of households (assuming a certain average number of insured members per household), which is the saturation point for a CC or a CoCo. When a new CC or CoCo is formed, the marginal costs increase, and then gradually decrease as the number of enrolled households increases (distributing the fixed cost of the Federation over a more substantial number of households). The second important factor for the per capita operating cost is the average number of persons insured in each household. Because the cost of acquiring and serving a household remains

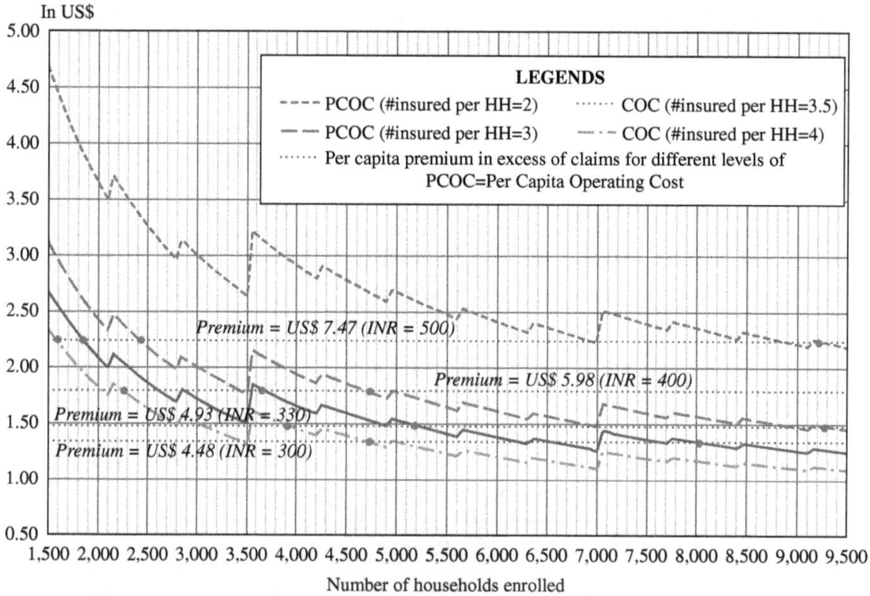

Figure 7.2 Per-capita Operating Cost and Sustainability Points for Different Levels of Enrollment and Premiums (Assumptions: Renewal Rate = 0%, Claim Ratio = 70%)

the same irrespective of the number of its insured members, per capita operating costs decrease when the average number of insured members in each household increases. Figure 7.2 illustrates these phenomena.

For simplicity, we assume in this illustration a conservative renewal rate of 0% and a claims ratio of 70%. We apply the plans' "long-term" per capita operating cost (achieved in the fourth year of operation as the operating cost decreases until the fourth year and then stabilizes, ignoring inflation). A plan is *sustainable* when the excess of per capita premium over claims is consistently higher than the per capita operating costs.

We then compare the per capita balance of premiums over claims for different premium levels with the per capita cost of operation for households with different averages of insured persons from each household; the results (summarized in Table 7.5) show that sustainability is achievable through different trajectories. The claims ratio is assumed to be

Table 7.5 Number of Households Needed to Achieve Plan Sustainability (Claims Ratio is Assumed to be 70%, Renewal Rate = 0%)

	Premium levels (PPPY)			
Average number of insured from each household	USD 4.48 (INR 300, NPR 480)	USD 4.93 (INR 330, NPR 528)	USD 5.98 (INR 400, NPR 640)	USD 7.47 (INR 500, NPR 800)
4.0	4700 HHs	3900 HHs	2250 HHs	1600 HHs
3.5	8000 HHs	5200 HHs	3650 HHs	1850 HHs
3.0	Never	9350 HHs	4700 HHs	2450 HHs
2.0	Never	Never	Never	9200 HHs

Table 7.6 Number of Households Needed to Achieve Plan Sustainability (The Assumptions are a Claims Ratio of 70%, a Renewal Rate of 50%)

	Premium levels (PPPY)			
Average number of insured from each household	USD 4.48 (INR 300, NPR 480)	USD 4.93 (INR 330, NPR 528)	USD 5.98 (INR 400, NPR 640)	USD 7.47 (INR 500, NPR 800)
4.0	4400 HHs	3700 HHs	2000 HHs	1500 HHs
3.5	7150 HHs	4600 HHs	2500 HHs	1800 HHs
3.0	Never	7950 HHs	4450 HHs	2350 HHs
2.0	Never	Never	Never	7950 HHs

70%, the renewal rate = 0%. A plan is sustainable with only 1,600 households that enroll four members from each household, paying a premium of US$7.47 (INR 500, NPR 800) PPPY. However, with a premium of US$4.48 (INR 300, NPR 480) PPPY, such a plan can never reach sustainability with an average of three or fewer insured members from each household. A balanced combination of the sustainability parameters may be when the premium = US$4.93 (INR 330, NPR 528) PPPY, the number of households = 5,200, the average number of insured per household = 3.5 and expected claims ratio = 70%. These estimates of the sets of the sustainability parameters apply a conservative assumption of 0% renewal rate (which increases the acquisition costs). A plan can achieve sustainability with fewer households when its renewal rate improves (Table 7.6). With a renewal rate of 50%, sustainability is confirmed even when the number of enrolled households is 3–32% lower, depending on the average number of insured members in each household and level of premium PPPY.

SELF-TEST QUESTION

1. Enumerate the CBHI sustainability parameters identified in the study, and discuss the impact of each parameter on the scheme's sustainability.

Analysis of Pilot Plans Sustainability Parameters

Table 7.4 contains the data to show the trajectories of the two plans with different sustainability parameters. Each plan began with a modest number of enrollments. Figures 7.3 and 7.4 illustrate how well the Bihar and Banke plans, respectively, have performed by reference to the five sustainability parameters, and how their performance should improve to achieve sustainability.

Banke has surpassed four of the five sustainability parameters multiple times in the last six years, (the exception being the number of households).

The Bihar plan is younger, and it is too early to comment on its progress. Thus far, this plan has already surpassed one of the sustainability parameters once in the last three years.

A Prototype Plan from Launch Onward

Table 7.7 shows the evolution of a prototype plan over time. Beyond the standard costing, this table contains assumptions on the evolution of the five sustainability parameters. The previous section showcases that these assumptions are optimistic but not unrealistic. As the claims ratio is a random variable that cannot be projected into the future, we assume it equals the expected claims ratio every year. However, since we calculated the reserve so that it protects the plan with 99.9% confidence, a random variable with an expected value of 70% as the claims ratio would show scenarios with very similar results.

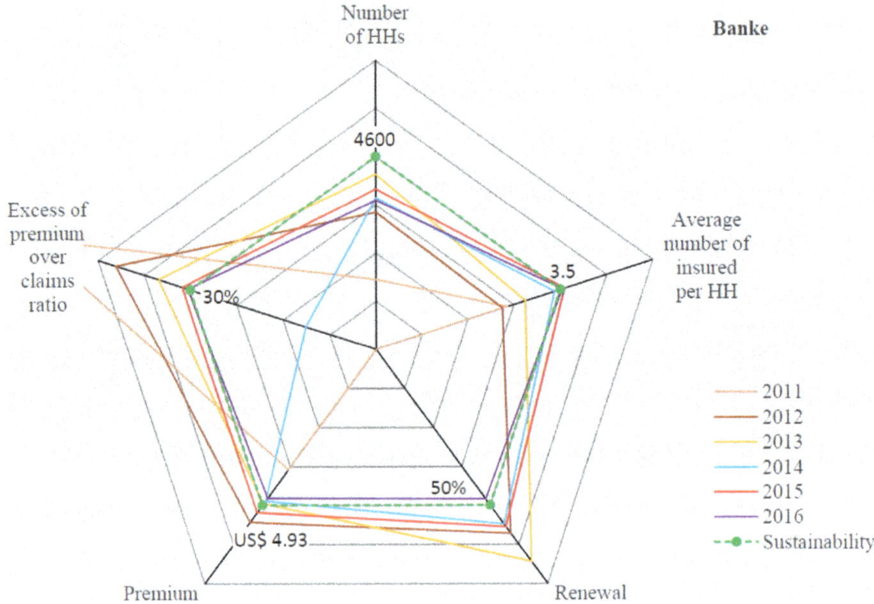

Figure 7.3 Performance of the CBHI Scheme (Banke, Nepal)

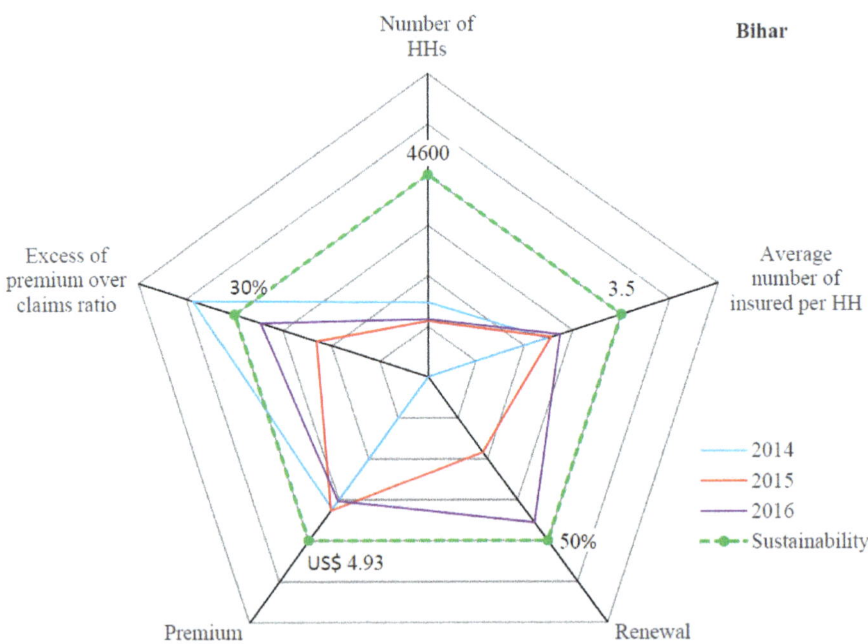

Figure 7.4 Performance of the CBHI Scheme (Bihar, India)

Table 7.7 The Evolution of a Prototype Plan and Its Capital Requirements

Year	Number of households	Average number of insured per HH	Number of individuals	Renewal rate (%)	Premium per capita (INR)	USD exchange rate (INR per USD 1)	Premium per capita (USD)	Rate of change in premium (INR) (%)	Premium income (USD)	Claims ratio expected (%)
2017	1400	2.00	2800	0	363.00	71.06	5.11		14,303	70
2018	2800	2.25	6300	25	399.30	75.34	5.30	10	33,392	70
2019	4200	2.50	10,500	40	439.23	79.78	5.51	10	57,806	70
2020	5,600	3.00	16,800	45	483.15	84.43	5.72	10	96,139	70
2021	7,000	3.50	24,500	50	531.47	89.29	5.95	10	145,834	70
2022	8,400	3.60	30,240	60	584.62	94.39	6.19	10	187,297	70
2023	9,800	3.75	36,750	70	643.08	99.64	6.45	10	237,185	70
2024	10,000	3.80	38,000	70	707.38	105.16	6.73	10	255,626	70
2025	10,000	3.90	39,000	70	778.12	110.99	7.01	10	273,424	70
2026	10,000	4.00	40,000	70	855.94	117.04	7.31	10	292,538	70
2027	10,000	4.00	40,000	70	941.53	123.52	7.62	10	304,892	70
2028	10,000	4.00	40,000	70	1,035.68	130.39	7.94	10	317,725	70
2029	10,000	4.00	40,000	70	1,139.25	137.42	8.29	10	331,614	70
2030	10,000	4.00	40,000	70	1,253.17	144.81	8.65	10	346,162	70
2031	10,000	4.00	40,000	70	1,378.49	152.71	9.03	10	361,064	70
2032	10,000	4.00	40,000	70	1,516.34	160.99	9.42	10	376,752	70
2033	10,000	4.00	40,000	70	1,667.98	169.65	9.83	10	393,273	70
2034	10,000	4.00	40,000	70	1,834.77	178.71	10.27	10	410,676	70
2035	10,000	4.00	40,000	70	2,018.25	188.18	10.73	10	429,014	70
2036	10,000	4.00	40,000	70	2,220.07	198.07	11.21	10	448,343	70

(Continued)

Table 7.7 *(Continued)*

Year	Upper boundary of the expected claims ratio with 99.9% CI (%)	Claims cost (USD)	Total operating cost (INR)	Total operating cost (USD)	Operating cost (as % of premium)	Deficit/ surplus (as % of premium)	Capital requirement for claims payment (USD)	Total operating cost (USD)	Total capital requirement (USD)	Capital requirement in addition to premium income (USD)
2017	111	10,012	2,142,360	30,147	211	– 181	15,859	30,147	46,006	31,703
2018	97	23,374	1,442,260	19,144	57	– 27	32,474	19,144	51,619	12,712
2019	91	40,464	2,129,068	26,686	46	– 16	52,667	26,686	79,352	12,954
2020	87	67,297	2,575,645	30,506	32	– 2	83,342	30,506	113,848	6178
2021	84	102,084	3,192,675	35,758	25	5	122,238	35,758	157,996	
2022	82	131,108	4,233,145	44,848	24	6	154,406	44,848	199,254	
2023	81	166,029	5,035,290	50,535	21	9	192,793	50,535	243,328	
2024	81	178,938	5,655,538	53,782	21	9	207,305	53,782	261,087	
2025	81	191,397	6,208,712	55,940	20	10	221,347	55,940	277,287	
2026	81	204,777	6,829,583	58,355	20	10	236,417	58,355	294,772	
2027	81	213,424	7,512,542	60,819	20	10	246,401	60,819	307,220	
2028	81	222,408	8,263,796	63,379	20	10	256,772	63,379	320,151	
2029	81	232,130	9,090,175	66,149	20	10	267,996	66,149	334,146	
2030	81	242,313	9,999,193	69,051	20	10	279,754	69,051	348,805	
2031	81	252,745	10,999,112	72,024	20	10	291,797	72,024	363,821	
2032	81	263,727	12,099,023	75,154	20	10	304,475	75,154	379,629	
2033	81	275,291	13,308,926	78,449	20	10	317,827	78,449	396,276	
2034	81	287,473	14,639,818	81,921	20	10	331,891	81,921	413,812	
2035	81	300,310	16,103,800	85,579	20	10	346,711	85,579	432,290	
2036	81	313,840	17,714,180	89,434	20	10	362,332	89,434	451,766	

The plan can enroll at least 1,400 households with at least two insured members from each household. At least two additional CCs are required every year up to the 7th year of operation. From the 8th year onward, the plan reaches 10,000 households and maintains that level. The average number of insured members in each household increases from 2 in the first year to 3.5 in the 5th year and 4 in the 10th year. This level is maintained from the 10th year onward. We assume that the plan starts in 2017 with a per-capita premium of INR 363 (US$5.11). Premiums increase by 10% in local currency (INR) every year merely to keep up with inflation, also assumed to be 10%. So, the present value of the net increase in premium equals zero. In reality, the compound annual growth rate (CAGR) in per capita premium was 14.86% in Banke (after five years) and 6.60% in Bihar (after two years). The plot (Figure 7.5) shows annual operating costs as a percentage of premium income over the years of the prototype plan.

The operating costs are 211% of the earned premium in the first year, 57% in the 2nd year, 46% in the 3rd year, 32% in the 4th year and 25% in the 5th year. The per capita operating costs stabilize at 20% of the premium PPPY. Hence, the high deficit that the prototype plan suffers in the early years drops in subsequent years, and from the 5th year onward the plan retains a surplus (ignoring financing costs for the moment).

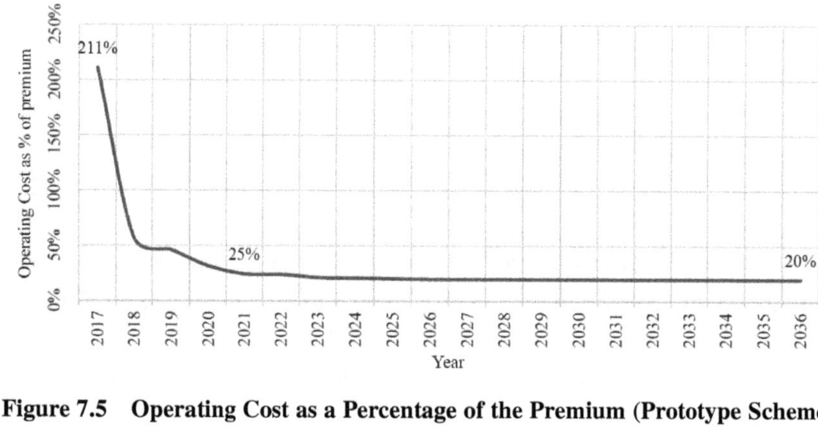

Figure 7.5 Operating Cost as a Percentage of the Premium (Prototype Scheme)

SELF-TEST QUESTION

1. In Figure 5, we see a remarkable fall in operating costs as a percentage of the premium. Investigate the reasons based on the given data.

Capital Requirements for the Prototype Plan

The prototype plan (assumed to launch in the year 2017) requires additional capital to cover its operating costs in the first four years. Some capital is also required to constitute a reserve for claims payment. Table 7.7 shown capital requirements.

CBHI plans have hitherto relied on grant support to fulfill capital shortfalls. Sourcing capital commercially requires adding financial returns to investors at competitive rates. We examine here the viability that CBHI plans can guarantee repayment with interest.

Applying the capital requirements formulas (explained in the Data and Methods Section), the following estimated amounts are required: US$31,703 (INR 2,252,944) in the 1st year of the plan; US$12,712 (INR 957,660) in the 2nd year; US$12,954 (INR 1,033,501) in the 3rd year; and US$6,178 (INR 521,619) in the 4th year, adding up to US$63,547 (INR 4,765,724) (Table 7.7). If the loan at launch is for the full cumulative amount, its estimated present value is US$62,477 (INR 4,439,804). The operating results of borrowing that amount from the outset for 20 years are presented in Table 7.8.

Loan repayment and closing balance are considered at the end of each year. The following year's annual exchange rates have been used for conversion of loan repayment from US$ to INR and of closing balance from INR to US$. The rate of interest on the loan is 5% in US$.

As can be seen, the plan generates a surplus of US$429,531 (INR 89,515,636) in 20 years, after full repayment of the loan amount plus interest at 5% in US$ (@10.96% in INR). We assume the loan is repaid in 10 equal yearly installments (US$10,326 each) starting from the 6th year. A moratorium of 5 years is required until the plan starts to generate operating surpluses. The expected loan account transactions are given in Table 7.9.

Table 7.8 The Operating Results of Borrowing from the Outset for 20 Years of Operation (For the Prototype Plan)

Year	USD exchange rate	Opening balance C/F (INR)	Premium income (INR)	New loan at beginning of year (INR)	New loan at beginning of year (USD)	Interest earned on long-term investable capital (INR)	Expected claims cost (INR)	Total operating cost (INR)	Loan repayment (INR)	Loan repayment (USD)	Operating balance (after repayment) (INR)	Operating balance (after repayment) (USD)
2017	71.06	0	1,016,400	4,439,804	62,477	174,949	711,480	2,142,360			2,777,313	36,866
2018	75.34	2,777,313	2,515,590			112,332	1,760,913	1,442,260			2,202,063	27,601
2019	79.78	2,202,063	4,611,915			38,638	3,228,341	2,129,068			1,495,208	17,709
2020	84.43	1,495,208	8,116,970			0	5,681,879	2,575,645			1,354,654	15,172
2021	89.29	1,354,654	13,020,973			21,502	9,114,681	3,192,675			2,089,774	22,140
2022	94.39	2,089,774	17,678,762			76,890	12,375,133	4,233,145	1,028,925	10,326	2,208,222	22,162
2023	99.64	2,208,222	23,633,067			127,689	16,543,147	5,035,290	1,085,887	10,326	3,304,654	31,426
2024	105.16	3,304,654	26,880,604			218,433	18,816,423	5,655,538	1,146,110	10,326	4,785,621	43,118
2025	110.99	4,785,621	30,346,787			348,550	21,242,751	6,208,712	1,208,562	10,326	6,820,934	58,281
2026	117.04	6,820,934	34,237,400			524,761	23,966,180	6,829,583	1,275,552	10,326	9,511,780	77,004
2027	123.52	9,511,780	37,661,141			737,938	26,362,798	7,512,542	1,346,435	10,326	12,689,083	97,319
2028	130.39	12,689,083	41,427,255			989,822	28,999,078	8,263,796	1,419,048	10,326	16,424,238	119,520
2029	137.42	16,424,238	45,569,980			1,286,103	31,898,986	9,090,175	1,495,350	10,326	20,795,810	143,610
2030	144.81	20,795,810	50,126,978			1,633,046	35,088,885	9,999,193	1,576,996	10,326	25,890,760	169,537
2031	152.71	25,890,760	55,139,676			2,037,580	38,597,773	10,999,112	1,662,462	10,326	31,808,668	197,581
2032	160.99	31,808,668	60,653,643			2,507,644	42,457,550	12,099,023			40,413,382	238,215
2033	169.65	40,413,382	66,719,008			3,192,316	46,703,305	13,308,926			50,312,475	281,535
2034	178.71	50,312,475	73,390,909			3,980,168	51,373,636	14,639,818			61,670,098	327,726
2035	188.18	61,670,098	80,729,999			4,884,295	56,511,000	16,103,800			74,669,593	376,987
2036	198.07	74,669,593	88,802,999			5,919,324	62,162,100	17,714,180			89,515,636	429,531

Table 7.9 Loan Account of the Prototype Plan

Year	Loan a/c at the beginning of the year (USD)	Interest accrued on loan (USD)	Loan a/c after accrual of 5% interest (USD)	Loan repayment at the year end (USD)	Loan a/c at year end (USD)
2017	62,477	3124	65,601	0	65,601
2018	65,601	3280	68,881	0	68,881
2019	68,881	3444	72,325	0	72,325
2020	72,325	3616	75,941	0	75,941
2021	75,941	3797	79,738	0	79,738
2022	79,738	3987	83,725	10,326	73,399
2023	73,399	3670	77,068	10,326	66,742
2024	66,742	3337	70,079	10,326	59,753
2025	59,753	2988	62,740	10,326	52,414
2026	52,414	2621	55,035	10,326	44,708
2027	44,708	2235	46,943	10,326	36,617
2028	36,617	1831	38,448	10,326	28,121
2029	28,121	1406	29,528	10,326	19,201
2030	19,201	960	20,161	10,326	9835
2031	9835	492	10,326	10,326	0

The Sensitivity of Capital Requirements to Varying Levels of Claims Ratio and Confidence Level

Table 7.10 contains the sensitivity analysis of the capital requirements at varying levels of the (expected) claims ratio and the protection level chosen for the CBHI plan. All other parameters remain as described earlier for the prototype plan.

The analysis shows that at an expected claims ratio of 70% the drop in the capital requirements is highest when the protection level is reduced from 99.9% to 99%. Further reductions in the protection level (from 99% to 98%, or 97%, etc.) result in smaller marginal reductions in capital requirements.

Moreover, when the expected claims ratio is increased (from 70%, 71%, etc. up to 74%), the capital requirements increase exponentially.

Table 7.10 Capital Requirement for Different Combinations of Claim Ratio and Protection Level (Other Parameters of the Prototype Remain Fixed)

Claim ratio (%)	Protection level (%)	Capital requirement (one-time loan) (USD)	Equal annual repayment instalment (USD)	Reduction in capital requirement (%)
70.0	99.90	62,477	10,326	
	99.00	58,250	9628	6.76
	98.00	56,742	9379	9.18
	97.00	55,785	9220	10.71
	96.00	55,066	9101	11.86
	95.00	54,480	9005	12.80
71.0	99.90	64,655	10,686	
	99.00	60,368	9978	6.63
	98.00	58,839	9725	9.00
	97.00	57,868	9565	10.50
	96.00	57,138	9444	11.63
	95.00	56,544	9346	12.55
72.0	99.90	66,878	11,054	
	99.00	62,486	10,328	6.57
	98.00	60,935	10,072	8.89
	97.00	59,951	9909	10.36
	96.00	59,210	9787	11.47
	95.00	58,608	9687	12.37
73.0	99.90	72,583	11,997	
	99.00	64,875	10,723	10.62
	98.00	63,031	10,418	13.16
	97.00	62,033	10,253	14.53
	96.00	61,282	10,129	15.57
	95.00	60,672	10,028	16.41
74.0	99.90	90,297	14,925	
	99.00	74,544	12,321	17.45
	98.00	69,684	11,518	22.83

(*Continued*)

Table 7.10 (*Continued*)

Claim ratio (%)	Protection level (%)	Capital requirement (one-time loan) (USD)	Equal annual repayment instalment (USD)	Reduction in capital requirement (%)
	97.00	67,035	11,080	25.76
	96.00	65,399	10,809	27.57
	95.00	63,964	10,572	29.16
74.5	99.90	Initial loan capital cannot be repaid		
	99.00	83,990	13,882	
	98.00	78,411	12,960	6.64
	97.00	75,503	12,479	10.10
	96.00	74,404	12,298	11.41
	95.00	74,161	12,258	11.70
74.7	99.90	Initial loan capital cannot be repaid		
	99.00	Initial loan capital cannot be repaid		
	98.00	83,764	13,845	
	97.00	82,596	13,652	1.39
	96.00	81,197	13,421	3.06
	95.00	80,206	13,257	4.25
74.9	99.90	Initial loan capital cannot be repaid		
	99.00	Initial loan capital cannot be repaid		
	98.00	Initial loan capital cannot be repaid		
	97.00	90,738	14,998	
	96.00	88,544	14,635	2.42
	95.00	86,653	14,322	4.50
75.0	99.90	Initial loan capital cannot be repaid		
	99.00	Initial loan capital cannot be repaid		
	98.00	Initial loan capital cannot be repaid		
	97.00	Initial loan capital cannot be repaid		
	96.00	Initial loan capital cannot be repaid		
	95.00	Initial loan capital cannot be repaid		

The impact of the protection level on the capital requirements also increases. When the claims ratio is assumed to range between 74% and 75%, a CBHI plan can only be operated with positive closing balances if the protection level is chosen not too high. However, this increases the risk of collapse of the CBHI plan in a year of above-average claims. Moreover, when the expected claims ratio is 75%, no CBHI plan can be operated sustainably, i.e., irrespective of the size of the initial loan, the plan would be unable to repay it and would not be able to maintain a positive closing balance in later years.

Higher expected claims ratios can be managed, if specific parameters of the prototype plan are changed, e.g., increasing the premium per capita (which might not be doable in the context of microinsurance), extending the loan moratorium or repayment period, lowering the rate of interest payable on the initial loan, or applying varying repayment installments (instead of equal annual installments).

SELF-TEST QUESTION

1. Suggest ways in which higher expected claims ratios can be managed?

Operating Results and Socioeconomic Impact of the Prototype Plan

Although the administrative structure of a prototype plan can cover 42,000 individuals in 10,500 households, we assume a more conservative saturation point at 40,000 individuals in 10,000 households. This saturation is achieved for the first time in the 10th year of operation. The plan remains under the loan cycle for 15 years (moratorium for the first five years followed by ten years of repayment).

Figure 7.6 provides some key insights into how a plan achieves financial sustainability while total capital requirements continue to expand as enrollment and inflation increase. Premium income covers the yearly claims cost in the early years, and from the 5th year on, it also covers

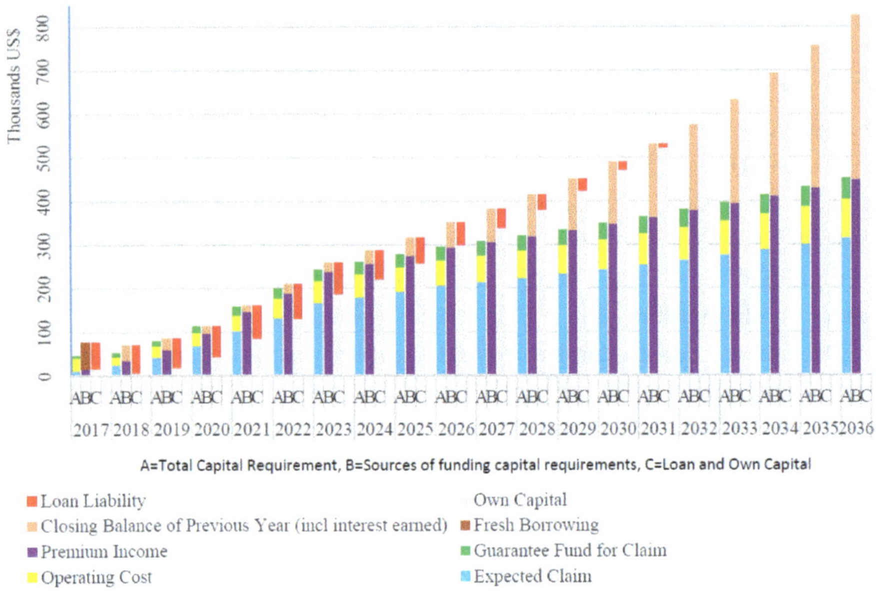

Figure 7.6 Sources and Utilization of Fund

operating costs. The plan achieves operational sustainability in year 5. The loan account credit balance keeps increasing up to the 5th year, then starts to decrease, reaching zero by the end of the 15th year (Table 7.9). At this point, the plan becomes debt-free, showing its full sustainability. Premium income alone in any particular year is never enough to protect the plan with 99.9% confidence. However, the premium income plus the closing balance of the previous year (including interest income) ensure this level.

Figure 7.6 depicts the balance at the beginning of each year during the prototype plan's first 20 years' operation, yearly capital requirements, and loan balance. The plan generates 444,890 policy-years within the first 15 years and 644,890 policy-years in 20 years. Every US$1 borrowed mobilizes premium income of US$52 in the first 15 years and $85 in 20 years.

The burden of repayment is not too high with a moratorium during the first five years. Total interest payable on the borrowed capital is 1.25% of the total premium income of the first 15 years and 0.77% of the total premium income of 20 years. The highest debt-to-income ratio (DTI)

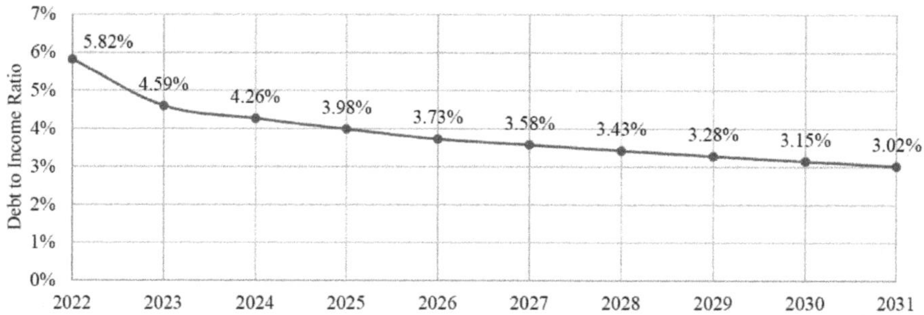

Figure 7.7 Debt to Income Ratio

(ignoring interest income) is 5.82% in the first repayment year and drops to 3.02% in the last repayment year (Figure 7.7).

The plan would need to borrow US$1.56 per insured individual, or only US$0.10 per policy-year when distributed over 20 years. During the same 20 years, the plan would pay benefits amounting to US$5.77 per policy-year, or a total of about US$3.72 million (assuming 70% of the collected premiums).

Return on Investment

The financial projections are based on an interest rate of 5% in $ (10.96% in INR), a reasonable rate for impact investors who expect their investments to produce a significant positive social and governance improvement for the underserved populations. As we see, the interest load increases considerably when the local currency is devalued against the US$. For example, given the forward exchange rates of US$ *vis-à-vis* INR for the period 2017–2032, we estimate that an annual US$ interest rate of 10% is equivalent to 16.25% in INR, 11% in US$ is equivalent to 17.31% in INR and so on (Figure 7.8).

The interest rate has no impact on the amount borrowed if the moratorium is granted. Investors might seek higher interest, which yields higher returns and higher NPV for them but adversely affects the plans' year-end results and their ability to retain assets. Specifically, the higher the interest rate applied, the longer it takes for the operating balance to

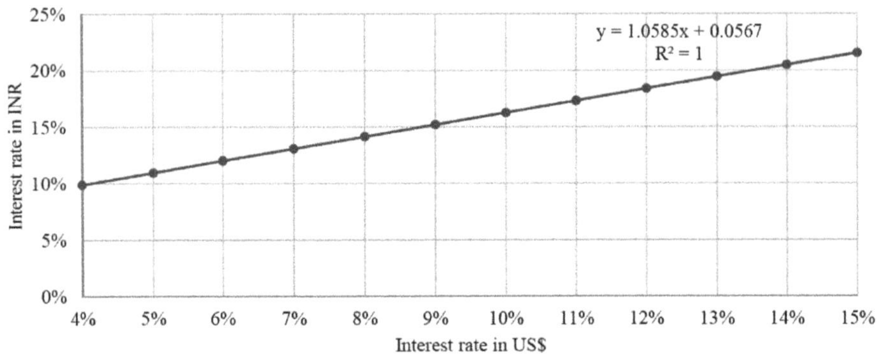

Figure 7.8 Conversion of Interest Rates from USD to INR

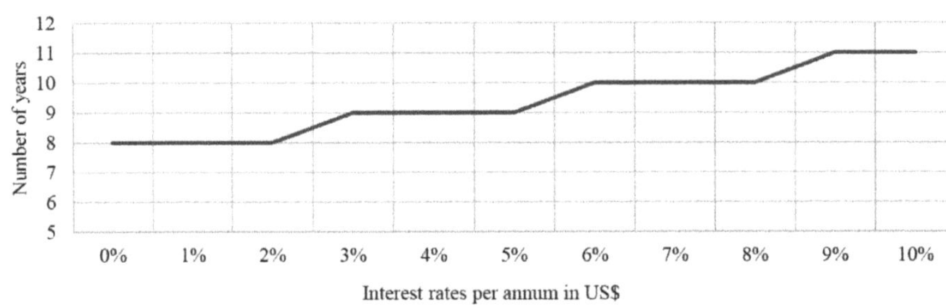

Figure 7.9 Number of Years Required for Operating Balance to Exceed Loan Liability (at Different Interest Rates)

exceed the loan liability. This length of time required until plans can generate enough operating surplus to pay interest without taking additional loans is shown in Figure 7.9 for different interest rates, up to the highest rate that still allows plans to maintain sustainability.

As a reference, the average U.S. Treasury interest rate is 2.37% over terms of 10 and 20 years. This benchmark leaves sufficient margin for commercial negotiations on a trade-off between the interest rate payable by plans and the repayment moratorium period they need before starting to repay the loan without risking deficits or cash-flow stress.

Another indicator of the tolerable interest rate is the share of total interest load as a percent of earned premiums. This percent should be low because a high rate could make it very unlikely that a plan could reach full sustainability even in 20 years. The share of interest payments as premium income for different interest rates is shown in Figure 7.10.

Investors also consider the net present value (NPV) of investments (Figure 7.11). The NPV of the initial investment of US$62,477 is

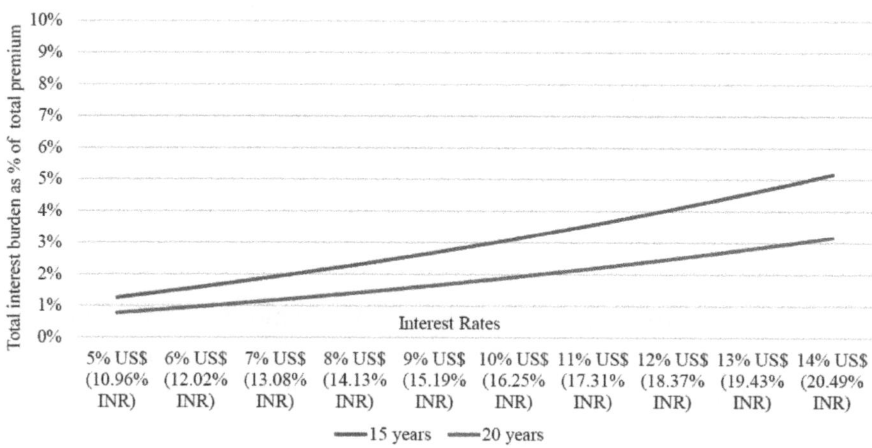

Figure 7.10 Total Interest Burden as % of the Total Premium Collected in 15 and 20 years (at Different Interest Rates)

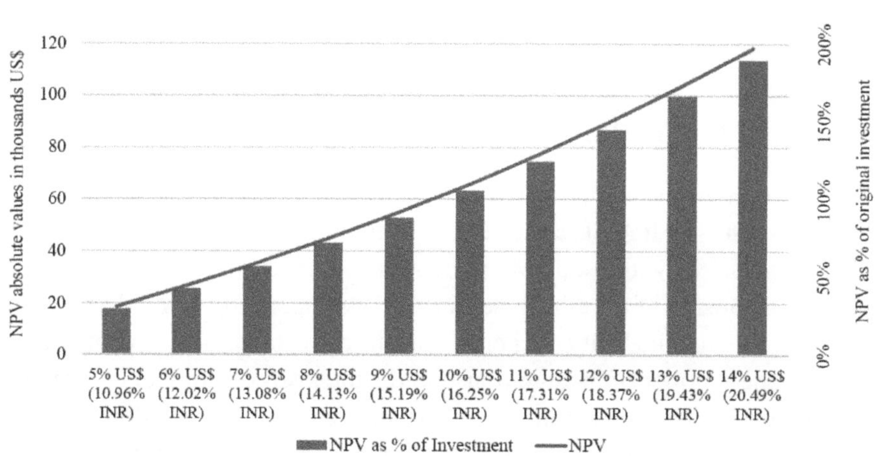

Figure 7.11 Net Present Value (NPV) for Varying Interest Rates

estimated at US$18,455 (30% of the original investment) when the annual US$ interest rate on borrowing is 5%, and at US$118,268 (189% of the original investment) when the annual US$ interest rate on borrowing is 14%. Calculation of NPV is based upon the annual discounting rate of 2.37%, which was the highest rate of interest for the US treasury bond.

SELF-TEST QUESTION

1. Give some indicators of tolerable interest rate, and discuss their impact on the plan's sustainability in the coming years.

Discussion

The prototype CBHI plan was designed using empirical data from two plans (with six and three years of operations in 2016, respectively) and a standard costing methodology, to answer three fundamental business questions:

(1) Can CBHI plans be operationally sustainable?
(2) Can the plans also achieve full sustainability when repaying loans, which they take at inception, to ensure solvency and operating costs?
(3) What is the social impact of the initial investment in a CBHI plan?

Attaining Operational Sustainability

A CBHI plan has two major cost components — claims costs and operating costs. Our findings are that the two plans' claims ratios varied from 44.0% to 88.7%, with a combined cumulative average of 69.8%, leaving on average 30.2% of premium income to cover operating costs. The plans' operational sustainability depends on five sustainability parameters, namely: the number of insured households, the average number of insured persons from each household, renewal rates, claims ratios and premiums PPPY. Operational sustainability can be reached with multiple combinations of these factors (Tables 7.5 and 7.6). The two pilot plans have not yet achieved operational sustainability. The Banke plan performed well, and with a small increase in the number of enrolled households and premium PPPY, it is on track to reach the desired performance. The Bihar plan is farther away from sustainability and needs to register significant increases in the number of enrolled households and the number of insured members from each household.

We also developed a general prototype plan (Tables 7.7 and 7.8) which gives projections of the sustainability parameters from the launch of a new plan up to 20 years. In year 5, the prototype plan could achieve operational sustainability covering 7,000 households or 24,500 individuals. At maturity, the plan could cover 10,000 households or 40,000 individuals. However, neither the CBHI plans that are in operation nor the prototype plan can ensure operational sustainability from the first year without additional capital.

Attaining Full Sustainability after Repaying Capital Costs

We can now deal with the second question: at what point can CBHI plans reach a year-end balance with a surplus over their operating costs plus loans payable (full sustainability)?

CBHI plans are often launched after a donor agrees to provide grant funds to cover the gap between their per capita operating costs and the excess of claims over premiums. Both CBHI plans analyzed here received start-up help from inception, one for five years, and the other for three years. However, since grants are not forever, we disregard this option here.

As CBHIs are mutual-aid plans (in which all members collectively own all assets, and only members can own the assets), they cannot raise money by selling equity to investors. Nor can CBHIs pay dividends. Hence, to cover deficits, CBHIs' sole fund-raising option is borrowing.

Borrowing by CBHIs raises two questions:

(1) Can plans repay the amount at a reasonable rate of interest?
(2) Are the assumed repayment-terms attractive for investors?

The average DTI ratio for the prototype plan (Figure 7.7) informs the first question. The DTI is between 5.82% and 3.02% when the annual $ interest is 5%; DTI is between 13.02% and 6.74% when the US$ interest rate is as high as 14%. However, the higher the interest rate, the longer it takes the CBHI plans to start repaying loans without having to take new loans. As already explained, CBHIs need a debt-repayment moratorium for the first few years, and the higher the interest rate, the longer the repayment moratorium period. When the total interest burden is expressed as a share of the plan's premium income, it is estimated at 1.25% when the annual interest rate is 5% US$ for 15 years, and 0.77 with a 5% US$ annual interest rate for 20 years. Regarding the absolute value, it is US$0.09 per policy-year over 15 years, and $0.06 when the total amount of interest is amortized over 20 years. This overhead is very much within the paying capacity of CBHI plans' target population.

Scaling Up

It has been demonstrated that each CBHI can reach sustainability when they borrow at reasonable interest rates at the outset and enroll up to 40,000 individuals. The scaling-up rate depends both on the size of the loan and on the interest rate negotiated (Table 7.11). From this analysis and the experience gathered in in-field projects showcased in this article, we conclude that there is a demand for voluntary and contributory (even unsubsidized) health insurance even among low-income people when such insurance is provided through a self-managed community-based scheme, at affordable premiums. Such CBHI plans require start-up capital, which they can repay with interest in full.

Social Impact

We have proved that a one-time investment of US$ 62,477 per CBHI plan can ensure its sustainable operations, gradually providing permanent health insurance cover to 40,000 individuals or 10,000 households. Stated differently, it is possible to provide contributory and voluntary health insurance even to indigent persons in rural settings in South Asia with an initial one-time loan of only US$ 1.56 per person.

Table 7.11 Scaling Up as a Function of Loan Capital and Interest Rate

									(if annual interest rate received from the plan is @ 3.5% (USD)			
Initial loan = investment (USD million)	No. of plans	# HHs (million)		# Individuals (million)		Claims (expected claims ratio = 70%)			Plans' capital minus outstanding loan at year end (USD million)			NPV 15 years with treasury interest rate @2.37% pa (USD million)
		Year 5	Year 10+	Year 5	Year 10+	Year 5	Year 10	Year 15	Year 5	Year 10	Year 15	
1	16	0.11	0.16	0.39	0.64	3.89	17.85	36.46	(0.83)	0.71	3.41	0.12
5	80	0.56	0.80	1.96	3.20	19.46	89.24	182.28	(4.17)	3.53	17.06	0.60
10	160	1.12	1.60	3.92	6.40	38.92	178.48	364.56	(8.33)	7.05	34.12	1.19
25	400	2.80	4.00	9.80	16.00	97.29	446.19	911.40	(20.83)	17.63	85.30	2.98
50	800	5.60	8.00	19.60	32.00	194.58	892.38	1822.80	(41.65)	35.26	170.60	5.96
100	1600	11.20	16.00	39.20	64.00	389.17	1784.77	3645.60	(83.30)	70.53	341.20	11.92

(*Continued*)

Table 7.11 *(Continued)*

	(if annual interest rate received from the plan is @ 5% (USD)				(if annual interest rate received from the plan is @ 10% (USD)				(if annual interest rate received from the plan is @14% pa (USD)			
	Plans' capital minus outstanding loan at year end (USD million)				Plans' capital minus outstanding loan at year end (USD million)				Plans' capital minus outstanding loan at year end (USD million)			
Initial loan = investment (USD million)	Year 5	Year 10	Year 15	N NPV 15 years with treasury interest rate @2.37% pa (USD million)	Year 5	Year 10	Year 15	NPV 15 years with treasury interest rate @ 2.37% pa (USD million)	Year 5	Year 10	Year 15	NPV 15 years with treasury interest rate @ 2.37% pa (USD million)
1	(0.92)	0.52	3.16	0.30	(1.26)	(0.27)	2.08	1.05	(1.57)	(1.10)	0.89	1.89
5	(4.61)	2.58	15.81	1.48	(6.28)	(1.34)	10.41	5.27	(7.85)	(5.51)	4.44	9.46
10	(9.22)	5.17	31.61	2.95	(12.56)	(2.68)	20.81	10.54	(15.70)	(11.03)	8.87	18.92
25	(23.04)	12.92	79.03	7.38	(31.39)	(6.71)	52.03	26.35	(39.26)	(27.57)	22.18	47.31
50	(46.08)	25.84	158.06	14.76	(62.78)	(13.42)	104.06	52.69	(78.52)	(55.13)	44.37	94.61
100	(92.16)	51.67	316.13	29.53	(125.57)	(26.84)	208.12	105.38	(157.05)	(110.27)	88.73	189.23

Moreover, at the end of 15 years, the CBHI plan would have repaid the loan in full plus interest and accumulate additional assets that would exceed three times the initial loan (Closing Operating Balance at the end of 15 years equals US$ 197,581; divided by US$ 62,477 = 3.16). Within that period, each CBHI would generate new resources for health amounting to 52 times the initial capital borrowed, 70% of which would be paid back to the insured in the form of claims, and the insured community would own all surpluses after the admin costs. These financial indicators of impact are significant for the ongoing social impact in the form of welfare gains of the insured member.

The social impact of this investment includes a much broader range of positive effects. The entire framing of the theory of demand for health microinsurance in the informal sector departs from the models/assumptions applied in rich countries (Dror *et al.*, 2014), favoring factors affecting enrollment in CBHI plans (Panda *et al.*, 2014; Dror *et al.*, 2016; Eling *et al.*, 2014), an important issue being building awareness to health insurance rather than applying partner-agent sales techniques among the target population of CBHI plans in rural India (Panda *et al.*, 2015). Another important aspect is that instead of basing the pro-poor discourse on subsidies and conditional cash transfers, we focus on the willingness to pay for voluntary health insurance by the beneficiaries themselves (Nosratnejad *et al.*, 2016; Binnendijk *et al.*, 2013), which is encouraged through consensus-building regarding benefits package design (Dror *et al.*, 2014). Finally, there are multiple positive health, financial and governance impacts of being insured by CBHI (Dror *et al.*, 2016).

Specifically, health insurance improves health-seeking behavior by increasing timely healthcare utilization, and by reducing the risk being caught in the trap of iatrogenic poverty (Meessen *et al.*, 2013), by reducing hardship financing (Binnendijk, 2012). Basing ourselves on the incidence rates observed in various baseline studies associated with CBHIs in India and Nepal, we can emit an estimate that each CBHI plan would provide partial support to over 17,500 cases of hospitalization events over 15 years (total policy years in 15 years 444,890 × 4% = 17,796, the approximate incidence rate for hospitalization = 4%). The number of outpatient events that would be partially or fully repaid by each CBHI plan would be very much larger. Furthermore, the most significant impact of the invested capital would be that it would lead to the creation of a market for health insurance at the base of the pyramid for people who today are uninsured and unable to obtain or afford health insurance. This can occur with a loan of only $1.56 per person. In summary, we submit that our analysis of the sustainability of CBHI plans identifies five sustainability parameters:

1. The number of enrolled households; the larger the number of enrolled households, the more significant the social impact.
2. The average number of insured members from each household; the larger the average number enrolled per HH, the more inclusive the plan (covering more female members, children, elderly).
3. Premium PPPY: The higher the per capita premium, the more comprehensive the health insurance coverage.
4. Excess of premium income over claims ratio (1 minus claims ratio): The claims ratio is a measure for value-for-money for the insured.
5. Renewal rate: The renewal rate is a measure of the satisfaction of the insured.

Each of the parameters makes it easy to monitor whether a CBHI plan is on track toward operational and full sustainability, as well as to measure social impact through easily verifiable objective indicators. Other positive impacts, e.g., changes in health-seeking behavior, reduction in out-of-pocket expenditure, reduction in hardship financing, improvement in the quality of life, etc., are much more difficult to measure especially in the short term.

SELF-TEST QUESTION

1. Describe the social impact of investment in CBHI plans. Do you think the positive benefits of investment in CBHI plans outdo the benefits of subsidies and conditional cash transfers?

Limitations

The analysis of the business case of CBHI is subject to some limitations. For one, we assumed that the operating costs of prototype plans follow a standard costing methodology. This requires strict monitoring of the activities of the key activists that implement each plan. All estimates are based on the assumptions of the model parameters such as the number of households in the scheme, the number of insured per household, renewal rates, premiums, the rate of interest on investment, claims ratio and variance of the payout distribution. The estimate for the capital requirement changes if the values of these parameters change. The model does not account for adverse selection and moral hazard, as these two factors are heavily controlled in the proposed model of community-based health microinsurance. Adverse selection is controlled by encouraging en-block affiliation. Community-level vigilance, free-flow of information within the community about its members' behavior and decision-making at the CBHI level (by the CC and CoCo) reduce the exposure of the CBHI to moral hazard to almost zero.

Furthermore, we did not include costs related to the provision of technical assistance, which are additional to those for which plans are responsible. Further research may reveal how technical assistance costs can be reduced and whether they can be included in the business case if more plans are launched simultaneously or phased in.

Another limitation is our assumption that individual payouts are independently and identically distributed. This assumption is crucial to justify the application of the Central Limit Theorem in estimating the reserve for any given protection level (see Data and Methods section). It is well known that under certain circumstances health incidents are not independently distributed, e.g., in cases of epidemic outbreaks in confined regions. Therefore, the reserve which protects the plan with 99.9% probability seems to be underestimated. However, the counterpoint to retain in our context is that health microinsurance schemes, which are not social health insurance programs, only provide limited coverage. Many cost items that would be particularly sensitive to the impact of epidemics, such as medicines, are typically not covered by such schemes. Hence, it is legitimate to assume that claims are closer to being independently distributed in health microinsurance schemes that are studied here than in health incidents in large commercial or social plans in rich countries. As covariate risks cannot be covered through such schemes, reinsurance of a scheme's pool would be ideal (Bonnevay *et al.*, 2002). As CBHI plans reach a larger scale and more plans are established in more countries, the attraction of reinsurance to these markets would improve. Finally, epidemic outbreaks of catastrophic dimensions are likely to be covered through interventions of the government or the international community.

Conclusions

The analysis set out to estimate the capital required for a CBHI plan to be able to scale up to 40,000 insureds, with full financial sustainability. We have applied stringent standards to measure the plans' ability to pay annual claims and administrative costs every year, (even under the high administrative load in the early years) and have shown that a health microinsurance/CBHI plan requires capital (as a loan) to launch, estimated at US$62,477 for a plan launched in 2017. We have also shown that the CBHI plans can repay such loans (while simultaneously paying the claims and operations costs) at commercially relevant interest rates. Capital requirements per person are estimated at a one-time loan of US$1.56.

The scaling up of CBHI plans can generate considerable additional resources for health care. For every $1 of capital borrowed at inception, each prototype plan can mobilize US$52 as premium income over 15 years, and US$85 over 20 years. This revenue would be generated from people who today are completely uninsured and pay for their health care out of pocket. This effect of being insured is of interest not merely for the insured, but also Governments and international development agencies, because we demonstrate higher uptake of health insurance among rural and informal sector groups without reliance on enforcing mandated enrollment and without reliance on subsidies to premiums.

Our analysis identified five easily measurable sustainability parameters, which inform impact investors on financial sustainability and the social impact of their investment. It was shown that to operate sustainably and reach its maximum scale of up to 40,000 insured persons; each CBHI plan should achieve not only a high absolute number of members but also multiple members per household and high renewal rates.

Our analysis highlights that a judicious combination of five sustainability parameters, together with seed capital at launch can bring long-term sustainability to a health microinsurance scheme under a regime of zero subsidies even in low-income communities. The five sustainability-controlling parameters are the number of enrolled households, an average number of insured members from each household, the PPPY, excess of premiums over claims ratio (1 minus claims ratio) and renewal rate. Scaling-up can be achieved by replicating similar CBHI plans with customized benefits packages across a country instead of relying on one national scheme with a vast number of enrollees with a uniform benefits package and premium for all. Stand-alone CBHI plans must have the autonomy to strive towards the most realistic combination of the five sustainability parameters based on the local context. The launch capital is estimated accordingly. The data exhibited of the already functioning CBHI plans that deploy a coherent mutual-aid, or co-op, business model confirm that they have achieved or are about to achieve viable results, as measured against the five sustainability parameters.

The first policy ramification of this analysis is that impact investors who want to generate compelling social and governance outcomes, in addition to reasonable financial returns, could provide the capital that CBHI plans must borrow. The financial returns have already been mentioned. The social effects include extending health insurance coverage to previously uninsured rural populations, and the governance gains flow from large-scale standardization of rule-based participatory management of these mutual-aid plans. As the amount per CBHI plan is modest, this investment opportunity can suit investments ranging from a modest ticket size (a few million US$) to large size (hundreds of millions of US$).

The second policy ramification is that governments and policymakers seeking these results in low-income settings may contribute by creating a supportive regulatory environment to launch, operate and capitalize CBHI plans or similar forms of microinsurance. Governments could also consider suitable risk collateral arrangements.

Finally, with investments and suitable regulations that facilitate risk transfer from CBHI plans to larger entities, the (re)insurance industry, which today is absent from the development of voluntary and contributory enrollment of CBHI plans, may develop a new market to securitize the financing of health insurance through reinsurance of outlier risks written by CBHI plans.

KEY TERMS

- **Acquisition costs:** These costs are incurred when enrolling new households and renewing existing households. These costs reflect the cost of additional field staff, engaged for house-to-house visits during the enrollment period to assist with application forms and to collect premiums.
- **Claims committee (CC):** The executive body (composed of community representatives) that decides on the claims the participants submitted.
- **Coordination Committee (CoCo):** The body entrusted by the scheme's owners-participants to oversee the operations of the CBHI scheme.
- **Central Limit Theorem (CLT):** In probability theory, the central limit theorem (CLT) establishes that, in some situations, when independent random variables are added, their properly normalized sum tends toward a normal distribution(informally a "bell curve") even if the original variables themselves are not normally distributed.[3]
- **Reserves:** The capital required for claims payments. It consists of two parts: the expected claims for the year and the amount needed to pay claims that exceed the expected amount (IRMI, 2017).
- **Routine administrative costs**: The costs of maintaining the plan's three-tiered governance structure that CBHIs typically have.
- **Start-up costs:** These reflect one-time expenditures incurred in the first year of the scheme, including setting up infrastructure and organizing awareness campaigns.
- **Sustainable plan:** A plan is sustainable when the excess of per capita premium over claims is consistently higher than the per capita operating costs.

Bibliography

Asante, A, Price, J, Hayen, A, Jan, S and Wiseman, V (2016) Equity in Health Care Financing in Low- and Middle-Income Countries: A Systematic Review of Evidence from Studies Using Benefit and Financing Incidence Analyses. *PloS One* 11 (4), e0152866.

---

[3]https://en.wikipedia.org/wiki/Central_limit_theorem (accessed on April 25, 2019).

Binnendijk, E, Dror, DM, Gerelle, E and Koren, R (2013) Estimating Willingness-to-Pay for Health Insurance among Rural Poor in India by Reference to Engel's Law. *Social Science & Medicine*, 76(1), 67–73.

Binnendijk, E, Koren, R and Dror, DM (2012) Hardship Financing of Healthcare among Rural Poor in Orissa, India. *BMC Health Services Research*, 12, 23.

Biener, C (2013) Pricing in Microinsurance Markets. *World Development*, 41(C), 132–144.

Bonnevay, S, Dror, DM, Duru, G, and Lamure, M (2002) *A Model of Microinsurance and Reinsurance*, Chapter 7 in Dror DM, Preker AS (Editors): *Social Reinsurance: A New Approach to Sustainable Community Health Financing* (Washington), World Bank & ILO, 2002, pp. 153–186

Dror, DM (2014) Health Microinsurance Programs in Developing Countries. In *Encyclopedia of Health Economics*, ed. AJ Culyer, pp. 412–421. San Diego: Elsevier.

Dror, DM, Chakraborty, A, Majumdar, A, Panda, P, and Koren, R (2016) Impact of Community-Based Health Insurance in Rural India on Self-Medication & Financial Protection of the Insured. *The Indian Journal of Medical Research*, 143(6), 809–820.

Dror, DM and Firth, LA (2014) The Demand for (Micro) Health Insurance in the Informal Sector. *The Geneva Papers on Risk and Insurance Issues and Practice*, 39(4), 693–711.

Dror, DM, Hossain, SAS, Majumdar, A, Pérez Koehlmoos, TL, John, D and Panda, PK (2016) What Factors Affect Voluntary Uptake of Community-Based Health Insurance Schemes in Low- and Middle-Income Countries? A Systematic Review and Meta-Analysis. *PLOS One*, 11(8), e0160479.

Dror, DM and Jambhekar, S (eds.) (2016) *Microinsurance Business Processes Handbook*. New Delhi, India: Social Re Consultancy (Pvt) Ltd and Micro Insurance Academy.

Dror, DM, Majumdar, A, Panda, P, John, D, and Koren, R (2014) Implementing a Participatory Model of Micro Health Insurance among Rural Poor with Evidence from Nepal. *The Geneva Papers on Risk and Insurance — Issues and Practice*, 39(2), 280–303.

Dror, DM, Panda, P, May, C, Majumdar, A, and Koren, R (2014) 'One for All and All for One": Consensus-building within Communities in Rural India on their Health Microinsurance Package. *Risk Management and Healthcare Policy*, 7, 139–153.

Dror, DM, Radermacher, R, Khadilkar, SB, Schout, P, Hay, F-X, Singh, A, and Koren, R (2009) Microinsurance: Innovations in Low-Cost Health Insurance. *Health Affairs*, 28(6), 1788–1798.

Eling, M, Pradhan, S, and Schmit, JT (2014) The Determinants of Microinsurance Demand. *Geneva Papers on Risk and Insurance: Issues and Practice*, 39(2), 224–263.

Fusion Media Limited (2016) India Government Bonds. India Bond Yield Rates. Available at https://in.investing.com/rates-bonds/india-government-bonds (accessed 9 September 2016).

Houston, DB (1960) Risk Theory. *The Journal of Insurance*, 27(1), 77–82.

IRMI (2017) Claims Reserve Insurance Glossary 2000. Available at https://www.irmi.com/term/insurance-definitions/claims-reserve (accessed 3 March 2017).

Kutzin, J, Yip, W, and Cashin, C (2016) Alternative Financing Strategies for Universal Health Coverage. In *Handbook of Global Health Economics and Public Policy*, ed RM Scheffler, Vol 1, pp. 267–309. Singapore: World Scientific Publishing Co.

Meessen, B, Zhenzhong, Z, Damme, WV, Devadasan, N, Criel, B, and Bloom, G (2003) Editorial: Iatrogenic Poverty. *Tropical Medicine & International Health* 8(7), 581–584.

Messner, W (2013) *Making the Compelling Business Case - Decision-Making Techniques for Successful Business Growth.* Houndsmills, UK: Palgrave Macmillan.

Nosratnejad, S, Rashidian, A and Dror, DM (2016) Systematic Review of Willingness to Pay for Health Insurance in Low and Middle-Income Countries. *PLoS One*, 11(6). https://doi.org/10.1371/journal.pone.0157470 (Accessed 16th Aug 2019).

ODI (2016) Private Investment, Public Money: Evaluating Development Impact. ODI — Evidence, Ideas, Change. Available at https://www.odi.org/events/4341-private-investment-public-money-evaluating-development-impact (accessed 4 January 2016).

Panda, P, Chakraborty, A, and Dror, DM (2015) Building Awareness to Health Insurance among the Target Population of Community-Based Health Insurance Schemes in Rural India. *Tropical Medicine & International Health* 20 (8): 1093–1107. https://doi.org/10.1111/tmi.12524.

Panda, P, Chakraborty, A, Dror, DM and Bedi, AS (2014) Enrolment in Community-Based Health Insurance Schemes in Rural Bihar and Uttar Pradesh, India. *Health Policy and Planning*, 29(8), 960–974.

Raban, M, Dandona, R, and Dandona, L (2013) Variations in Catastrophic Health Expenditure Estimates from Household Surveys in India. *Bulletin of the World Health Organization*, 91, 726–735.

The World Bank (2017) *Tracking Universal Health Coverage: 2017 Global Monitoring Report. 122029*. Washington, D.C.: The World Bank.

Treasury Direct (2016) *Overnight Rates*. Washington DC: U.S. Department of the Treasury, Bureau of the Fiscal Service.

US Department of the Treasury (2016) Daily Treasury Yield Curve Rates. Resource Center. Available at https://www.treasury.gov/resource-center/data-chart-center/interest-rates/Pages/TextView.aspx?data=yieldYear&year=2016 (accessed 9 August 2016).

XE.com (2016) USD / INR Currency Chart. US Dollar to Indian Rupee Rates. Closing Rate. Available at https://www.xe.com/currencycharts/?from=USD&to=INR&view=1D (accessed on 9 September 2016).

X-Rates (2016) Exchange Rate Average (US Dollar, Indian Rupee) — X-Rates. Indian Rupees per 1 US Dollar Monthly Average. Available at https://www.x-rates.com/average/?from=USD&to=INR&amount=1&year=2016 (accessed on 9 September 2016).

Selected Websites

The following website pertain to the content of this chapter:

- For more information on Central Limit Theorem go to https://en.wikipedia.org/wiki/Central_limit_theorem (Accessed on April 25, 2019).

Part 3

Implementation

Chapter 8

Insurance Awareness and Education

LEARNING OBJECTIVES

Upon completion of this chapter, the reader should be able to:

- Describe the core issues discussed during the initiation workshop
- Discuss the three insurance principles that are most relevant in the CBHI context
- Understand how mutual aid insurance is an extension of informal rules-in-use in rural settings
- Explain the role of the facilitator in CBHI awareness
- Describe the various awareness tools used for insurance awareness in rural settings
- Understand the relevance of gaining the trust of the target group and sharing risk exposure information with them directly and transparently
- Discuss the welfare gains associated with insurance

Abstract

The concept of insurance is novel to the target community of micro-insurance, and therefore, the success of a community-based health insurance (CBHI) scheme largely rests on the understanding and acceptance of insurance by the population. The objective of this chapter is to focus on the activities involved in creating insurance awareness and education among the mostly illiterate and innumerate members of the community. Three core issues are identified to discuss an understanding of the value proposition of insurance, the business process of CBHI, and the role of the community in this enterprise.

Chapter Outline

The first chapter in this book laid out three fundamental features of social maturity that explain, partly, why informal sector population groups are interested in social institutions that enhance cooperation, equality, and collective welfare gains. Experience has shown that most communities in the informal sector are keen to engage in dialog on insurance when the discourse is about awareness of the advantages of insurance and the fairness of the process. Implementers are also interested in promoting insurance education and financial literacy among grassroots groups because evidence from the informal sector has shown that when grassroots groups understand how insurance works (*aware about insurance*) they are more willing to enroll (Panda *et al.*, 2015; Adewole, 2017; Dror *et al.*, 2016).

The awareness activities entail mainly group discussions with frequent Q&A. The awareness activities unfold in stages (please see Annex 1 provided in the supplementary material of Chapter 3), starting with an *initiation workshop* which, as its name suggests, takes place as soon as the contact with grassroots groups has been established. The purpose of this workshop is to impart an understanding of the value proposition of insurance, the business process of community-based health insurance (CBHI), and the role of the community in this enterprise. This broad topic is composed of the following three core issues:

(1) the rules of the game (or insurance principles);
(2) building trust about rationing decisions;
(3) the welfare gains associated with insurance.

The rules of the game (insurance principles)

Certain rules govern every human relationship. Considering that every person learns the rules of behavior with his/her family from infancy onward, it is quite intuitive for everyone to learn the *rules of the game* before engaging in a new cooperative exercise. Insurance is a transactional activity, in which the notion of fairness relies on the *good behavior* of everybody, which is captured by certain insurance principles. The principles must be explained, understood, and respected for fairness to prevail. The following three principles are the most relevant in our context:

(1) **Utmost good faith:** Every person entering into a contract of insurance must disclose all the pertinent facts about the risk that the insurance company underwrites. Withholding information is a breach of utmost good faith that can result in cancellation of the contract or rejection of claims.
(2) **The principle of insurable interest:** When entering an insurance contract, the insured person needs to have a legitimate interest in the insured risk. For example, a person has a legitimate insurable interest in his/her own health (and in some cases the health of dependents), but not in the illness costs of other people. Thus, he/she can only claim his/her own costs. An insurable interest must exist when the insurance coverage begins. If there is no insurable interest, there should be no insurance policy, and if a policy is issued on false claims, it would be null and void.
(3) **The principle of indemnity:** This principle posits that insurance should only serve to indemnify a cost-generating insured event, never to enrich the insured person. This principle explains why the insurance should compensate up to the amount of the damage/loss, but never more than actual loss minus compensation received from all other sources. It also explains why an insured person can never claim the same loss from two sources.

The initiation workshop is the occasion to explain rules of the game of implementing the community-based mutual insurance and how the rules (including the insurance principles) create the basis for fair play cooperation. The explanations provide a conceptual bridge between the common informal rules in use in rural settings on the one hand and the more formal business rules of the insurance scheme on the other hand. The informal norms are that relatives and peers (friends, neighbors, or coworkers) extend financial and other help to each other in times of (financial) distress. The amount of help is left to the discretion of the donor and creates an informal but tangible expectation that *the recipient has a personal obligation toward the donor* to reciprocate. Such informal assistance can bring some relief, but is limited, mainly because most resource-poor persons interact with others who cannot afford to provide much help, or for a long time, and because the informal help is not entirely free. Therefore, grassroots groups seek structures of mutual aid that can complement — not replace — the informal reciprocal support. Mutual aid is *a voluntary reciprocal exchange of resources and services for mutual benefit.* In practice, the mutual aid insurance enlarges the circle of people linked by reciprocity to include more than close relatives and standardizes a contribution that is neither discretionary nor one that creates a personal obligation between payer and recipient. Instead, the formalized standard of reciprocity is that each person contributes the same amount of money into a pool, on the express agreement of everybody that the contribution is neither a savings account that each person can withdraw nor a personal donation to a designated individual or one that implies a *personal obligation* of recipients of payouts. Instead, the contribution creates an obligation *of the pool* to pay specific predefined amounts only to those persons who are members, and only when certain predefined risks occur. Also, all agree that the group owns the pooled money collectively, but no single individual can benefit from the funds even if the individual is the manager who can sign off the money. Also, there is an explicit agreement of all that the money can be used only for the predefined purpose. The informal rule was *an obligation to help relatives* and peers, but with vagueness about the quantum. The formal, reciprocal arrangement *removes the personal obligation of the recipient to reciprocate* and introduces an element of a *deliberate choice to enroll* in a rule-based cooperative effort coupled with clarity about the quantum of the contribution. The change entails not only a shift from obligation to help but also the freedom to decide how much to give and to make a voluntary choice about participation, but without a choice of the amount of the contribution or the terms of the reciprocal obligation incumbent on all members of the mutual aid scheme. Each member thus becomes both donor and potential recipient. This dual role establishes more equitable interpersonal relations and constitutes a strong incentive for everybody to keep the rules of the game captured by the insurance principles. The other element that is very attractive is the nexus between predictable contribution and predictable compensation.

Explaining these rules of the game must be done in a manner that is easy to comprehend. The aim is to impress the community that the insurance/CBHI provides security. The purpose is *not* to *sell* a specific benefits package. The awareness campaign is conducted largely by local *facilitators*, whom the community identifies. Community members with artistic talents and creative traits are invited to draft awareness materials and develop tools during a special workshop (*awareness tools development workshop*). These include songs, lyrics, slogans, stories, posters, themes for posters, and wall paintings (please see Annex 1 provided in the supplementary material for this chapter). These tools are in the local language and reflect the daily lives of local people. During the campaign, different types of awareness tools are used to teach about insurance, raise scheme visibility, convey key scheme messages, and motivate community members to join. Facilitators use these community-produced tools. Annex 2 (refer supplementary material for this chapter) provides a repertoire of the awareness tools that have been developed by the Micro Insurance Academy.

Facilitators are the mainstay of this campaign, and their effectiveness in communicating the message translates into high enrollment rates into the scheme. An effective campaign increases both the number of enrollees and the intensity of their commitment to abide by the rules and regulations of the scheme and actively participate.

Discussions of the rules of the game include elaborate consultations about the administration of the mutual aid scheme and its governance. Every person wants to feel that paying a contribution into the pool (unrelated to any calamity to self or a relative) is not tantamount to throwing away money. The comfort zone occurs when the participants understand how the money flows and trust the people handling the pooled money to do so with diligence, fairness, and transparency. The awareness activities about the governance structure are the topic of Chapter 10 in this book.

Experience has shown that the personal contribution is initially small, and therefore, the assistance is limited. This raises the second issue, namely who decides what should be reimbursed? Who determines the priorities? As the decision moves from the private to the common domain of the group, it requires much dialog. The next section deals with the group to dialog on priority setting.

SELF-TEST QUESTIONS

1. Describe the core issues discussed during the initiation workshop.
2. Discuss the three insurance principles that are most relevant in the CBHI context. How are they different from the common informal rules-in-use in rural settings?
3. A teacher in a village decides to pay for the insurance coverage of 5 students. Which insurance principle does this violate? How?

Building trust in the rationing process (facilitator training)

The principle that enrollment is voluntary and that the contribution is community rated in nominal terms, coupled with low amounts paid, make it necessary to decide upfront on the priorities of the group for utilization of the pooled money. Considerable effort is devoted to obtaining a context-relevant assessment of the risks that the local population is exposed to (please see Chapters 3 and 5). Like with our method of communicating insurance principles through games, we had to find a useful way to share the summary results of the risk analysis in a customer-friendly way. There are two aspects to this challenge. One aspect is that we must gain the trust of the target group that their interests are placed front and center. The other aspect is that the information on risk exposure is complex and its simplification must not cloud the ability of the group to understand the essential findings and make an informed choice of priorities.

In developing our implementation process, we integrate the notion that trust is a central component of social solidarity and the cement used to produce cohesion within the social networks (Lomnitz Adler and Sheinbaum, 2005). We recognize that the CBHI can offer only a partial solution to the needs. Thus, the advocacy needs to stress the positive connotations of participating in the proposed social network notwithstanding the rationed benefits or the negative consequences for individuals who remain outside such a network. People must be convinced that the mutual solution is more relevant and more accessible than other formal insurance institutions on the market and much more attractive than being uninsured.

The local facilitators who animate the discussion of rules of the game (described previously) act at this stage as representatives of the scheme.

Facilitators are people who *know the 3 Rs* (basic reading, writing, and arithmetic skills), express willingness to promote scheme implementation, have a sound knowledge of their local community, have good communication skills, and can conduct group discussions.

The primary role of facilitators in the awareness campaign phase of implementation is to dispel reservations about the scheme and myths about its operations. Facilitators must demonstrate their confidence in the scheme by enrolling all their family members. Facilitators, once trained, can reach out to members in the target community both during group meetings and during door-to-door visits to present the scheme, answer all questions accurately and patiently, or refer the issues they cannot resolve to their supervisor (the field coordinator or, if necessary, the field manager).

Facilitators are trained to successfully organize a unique simulation game that we developed (called CHAT: Choosing Healthplans All Together), which deals with the substantive aspect of prioritizing the benefit types that the scheme should reimburse. The CHAT game is discussed in detail in Chapter 9. One of the reasons why facilitators must be from the target community is to convey the message that everyone in the community can comprehend the trade-off between cost and priorities for healthcare utilization. Therefore, everyone should participate in those discussions and have a voice in forging the consensus of the target community on the perceived priorities that the benefits package should cover. This message addresses the concern, prevalent in the informal sector, that people should be able to take decisions over their lives and for which they pay themselves. People do not trust outsiders with such decisions.

SELF-TEST QUESTION

1. How can we overcome the challenge of sharing the summary results of the risk analysis in a customer-friendly way with the community?

The welfare gains associated with insurance (how CBHI works for the members)

In insurance industry circles, there is an often-cited phrase as follows: "Insurance is sold, not bought." This phrase reflects the reality of people who buy insurance in one of two cases: They must buy insurance by law (with scary non-adherence penalties) or they must buy insurance to access something else they really want (like a house, or a job). The reality of most people in the informal sector worldwide is however completely different. The informal sector is, by and large, outside the reach of mandating. People in the informal sector have developed ways to save for certain life-cycle high costs (e.g., weddings or schooling), but not for healthcare costs. So, the discussion of the value proposition of insurance starts neither with the price nor with the benefits package, but with some basic concepts that explain how insurance can resolve such a problem.

For one, insurance is the practice of managing risks by *pooling* many similar risks (or including many persons in one risk portfolio). The primary mathematical reason why risk pools add value is that as the pool size increases, the distribution of costs becomes more normal (takes a bell shape).[1] Participation in a risk pool means that costs that could be catastrophic for an uninsured person become less catastrophic or not at all catastrophic with insurance. However, how can this abstract idea be demonstrated to grassroots groups in rural settings, where statistics are not the common universe of discourse?

We devised games to do just that. Games provide a relaxed setting for delivering important key messages. All the games are intended for group settings. The games lead to discussions within the group and help people understand concepts better than through classroom lectures. These games do not require any prior mathematical skill, and illiterate and innumerate people can participate in these. The facilitator adds interesting commentaries and anecdotes during the game to inject humor to the game. The game we devised to communicate the message that *pooling is better than no pooling* is called *Treasure Pot.* We precede it by another tactile game: we give each participant a small wooden stick and ask them to break it. Easy. Now, we give each participant another stick, but this time we ask everybody to tie all the sticks together and break the bundle. Very difficult or impossible. This simple demonstration becomes symbolic of *Strength*

[1] https://www.statisticshowto.datasciencecentral.com/probability-and-statistics/normal-distributions/central-limit-theorem-definition-examples/.

in numbers, of the hidden strength of the entire group when it pools its strength (money) to negotiate better healthcare services.

Other games that have been used to communicate basic principles include the following:

Game name: *Snakes and Ladders* — Key message: *frequency and extent of the loss can vastly differ and can be random.*

Game name: *Wheel of Fortune* — Key message: *frequency and extent of the loss can vastly differ and can be random.*

Annex 3 provided in the supplementary material for this chapter contains a description of the games.

Another aspect of welfare gains from insurance that is not captured by the price is that many people bear financial and logistical responsibility for the welfare of other family members, e.g., elderly parents or young children. So, when insurance (notably the CBHI) pays the costs of dependent relatives, these payments constitute welfare gains for the responsible adult. These welfare gains from insurance are particularly valuable for women because for the first time they can follow a predictable claims process to obtain money to fulfill their traditional role as caregivers in the family, replacing the uncertain outcome of negotiations with menfolk over money. Women value this form of welfare gains as much as their own payouts.

Selection of Tool

There are among the many awareness tools, each imparting a specific message. Each tool is distinct in its scope, material, and time required for its demonstration and target audience. Facilitators are the best judge of the best tool to deploy, depending on conditions like the group mood, available time, and needed materials, like a CD player. As a rule, tools of the same nature and giving the same message should not be used in one meeting. Also, the same tool should be used just once in a group. Facilitators should plan how to engage the group and carry along with them the demonstration aids needed. This includes a contingency plan in case the group size is not as anticipated, or people are in a hurry or required materials are not available. If a game cannot be played or movie cannot be screened, facilitators should make the best of the situation and tap their oratorical skills to impart information about the scheme.

Microinsurance Studies to Develop a Future Talent Pool

Microinsurance is expected to flourish in the future as a critical program (in the commercial and government sectors) to provide insurance cover to the people living at the base of the pyramid. There would be a simultaneous surge in demand for professionals with a comprehensive knowledge of microinsurance. The Micro Insurance Academy seeks to fill the gap in insurance education through courses offered online as well as tailor-made workshops (please see Annex 4 provided in the supplementary material for this chapter).

SELF-TEST QUESTIONS

1. What are the advantages of pooling of risks?
2. Explain the role of the facilitator in CBHI awareness, and why do you think he/she should be from the target community?
3. What are the factors the facilitator must keep in mind while selecting an awareness tool?
4. The target community of CBHI comprises many illiterate and innumerate persons. Describe the awareness tools that are best suited for the community members and highlight the contribution of the members in developing such tools.

KEY TERMS

- **Awareness tools development workshop:** It is a workshop where community members with artistic talents and creative traits are invited to draft awareness materials and develop tools.
- **CHAT (Choosing Healthplans All Together):** It is an innovative method whereby the community can select the benefits package according to their need and willingness to pay through a consensus.

(Continued)

(*Continued*)

- **Contribution:** The amount payable to join the scheme and gain access to the benefits specified in the benefits package is called contribution.
- **Initiation workshop:** It is a workshop to impart an understanding of the value proposition of insurance and the business process of CBHI, and assist the community in clarifying its role of this enterprise.
- **Mutual aid:** It means a voluntary reciprocal exchange of resources and services for mutual benefit.
- **Treasure pot:** It is a game devised to communicate the message that *pooling is better than no pooling.*

Annexes

The annexes for this chapter are available online as supplementary material at https://www.worldscientific.com/worldscibooks/10.1142/11505#t=suppl.

Bibliography

Adewole, DA, Akanbi, SA, Osungbade, KO, and Bello, S (2017) Expanding Health Insurance Scheme in the Informal Sector in Nigeria: Awareness as a Potential Demand-Side Tool. *The Pan African Medical Journal*, 27, 52.

Dror, DM, Hossain, SAS, Majumdar, A, Pérez Koehlmoos, TL, John, D, and Panda, PK (2016) What Factors Affect Voluntary Uptake of Community-Based Health Insurance Schemes in Low- and Middle-Income Countries? A Systematic Review and Meta-Analysis. *PLoS One*, 11(8), e0160479.

Lomnitz Adler, L and Sheinbaum, D (2005) Trust, Social Networks and the Informal Economy: A Comparative Analysis. *Review of Sociology*, 10(1), 5–26. https://akademiai.com/doi/abs/10.1556/RevSoc.10.2004.1.1.

Panda, P, Chakraborty, A and Dror, DM (2015) Building Awareness to Health Insurance among the Target Population of Community-Based Health Insurance Schemes in Rural India. *Tropical Medicine & International Health*, 20(8), 1093–1107.

Chapter 9

Community Involvement in Benefits Package Design

LEARNING OBJECTIVES

Upon completion of this chapter, the reader should be able to:

- Understand the need for community participation in health insurance package design
- Explain how price determines the package and not otherwise
- Discuss why insurance must focus on low-cost, frequent events rather than on rare events
- Explain the purpose of CHAT
- Describe the activities involved at the preparation stage of the CHAT exercise
- Explain the activities involved in the *Benefits Option Consultation Workshop* and the three rounds of CHAT

Abstract

Community-Based Health Insurance (CBHI) schemes are all about community participation, and the best example of this is the process of benefits package selection. Here we discuss how community members select the benefits package according to their need and willingness to pay through a consensus. The Choosing Healthplans All Together (CHAT) exercise uses an innovative participatory approach for benefits package selection by a community comprising largely illiterate and innumerate persons.

Chapter Outline

One of the reasons for low voluntary uptake of health insurance among the population in settings of poverty and rurality is that the benefits packages do not cater to their actual health care needs. It is self-explanatory that higher enrolment in contributory health insurance ensues only when the benefits packages are tailored around the perceived priorities of the target group, the services they can access, and the amount they agree to pay for those services. A simulation exercise called Choosing Healthplans All Together (CHAT) has been tried and tested to elicit the community's desirable benefits package. This chapter includes a detailed discussion of CHAT. Each package of benefits comes with a price. We designed a pricing application, which is also discussed here. This application makes it possible to show the community the price of any combination of benefits they choose. By attaching a precise price to any combination, the community can adapt its priorities to its willingness to pay. Even illiterate and innumerate persons can participate in CHAT. CHAT begins with the exploration of various possible combinations and concludes with the group establishing consensus on one package for the CBHI scheme.

Why should customers be consulted on health insurance package design?

Beneficiaries of health insurance in high-income countries with universal health coverage do not have any say in designing their benefits package. They do not perceive this as a problem as within the financial arrangement for the delivery of healthcare services[1] they can access a prescribed

[1]One of three systems: (i) A *single-payer system*: The government taxes its citizens to pay for healthcare. Service providers may be either government employees or private service providers. The United Kingdom is an example of the single-payer system. (ii) *Insurance mandate*: The government requires everyone to buy insurance. Germany is an example of

minimum benefits (PMB) package that includes inpatient, outpatient, and primary care. Beneficiaries are not required to determine a trade-off between their contribution and the services that they prioritize when neither their enrollment nor their contribution level is voluntary, and when membership gives them access to a basic standard that includes *all the care that is usually delivered by primary care physicians.*

The situation is entirely different in most low- and middle-income countries in general and radically different in the rural or peri-urban areas of those countries. In the settings of poverty and informality, people must pay when and where they seek care, at least partly, for most services. In such settings, voluntary prepayment can exist only when people know what to expect in return for their payment. However, it would have been pointless to merely ask people which services they would like to access, without also asking them how much they would agree to pay for those services. As the amount of money may change when the package covers the beneficiaries' priorities, we had to devise a mechanism to elicit this information.

When enrollment is voluntary, and there is no access to government-provided PMB, it is not only desirable but outright necessary to give beneficiaries a say in the design of the benefits package. Evidence confirms that success in catalyzing demand for health microinsurance in the informal sector depends on encouraging group dialog on perceptions of risk exposure, welfare gains from the insurance, quality of local health-care provision (Dror, 2018, pp. 67–91), and reaching consensus on the benefits package (Dror, 2018, pp. 93–111).

Focus on benefit types rather than on illnesses

When they are sick, people often describe their condition in terms of the diagnosis that their physician or specialist told them (e.g., cardiovascular,

---

this system. Switzerland is an example of this system with the variant that people can choose a lower premium with a higher deductible. People can also purchase complementary comfort. (iii) *A two-tier approach*: The government uses taxes to pay for basic government health services. Citizens can also opt for better services with supplemental private insurance. France is an example.

gastrointestinal, arthritic, allergic, cancer, diabetes). However, health insurers categorize the cost of services according to the type of provider, e.g., hospital, laboratory, imaging, consultation. Following health insurers' practice, we present the health services by the *benefit type* rather than by illnesses or medical specialties.

Price determines package, not the other way around

The business of commercial health insurance is supply driven, allowing the insurer to design different packages that reflect what the insurer wants to underwrite (or what the regulator obliges the insurer to include, if the government defines a PMB), with the corresponding price that the insurer presents as TIOLI (Take it or leave it).

Microinsurance is a demand-driven market, and it is easier to comprehend the price than the benefits package, especially at the outset of the consultation process, when the prospective customers are confused about what they want or how much they agree to pay.[2] Therefore, we developed a pricing application which can show the price of any combinations of benefits. This pricing application supports the decision-making process of the target group.

There is another reason why the price determines the package and not otherwise: The discussions are conducted by a group whose decision applies to all members. The group is thus under pressure to consider the *amount that everybody in this community can pay*, including certain resource-poor members. Hence, once the amount affordable by all/most members is known, the group needs to establish consensus on the fitted package.

[2]"To be honest, we still haven't got the product design right — we just don't know what the clients want." Leila Moonda from the South African Insurance Association said what many providers are secretly thinking. Testimonial included in: "7 things I learned from the Microinsurance Network field trip and workshop on microinsurance distribution." Available at https://www.microinsurancenetwork.org/community/blog/insights-and-perspectives/7-things-i-learned-min-field-trip-and-workshop-0.

SELF-TEST QUESTIONS

1. In high-income countries with universal health coverage, beneficiaries of health insurance do not have any say in designing their benefits package. Do you think this has an adverse impact on their coverage? Would you suggest a similar scenario for rural areas of low- and middle-income countries?
2. In microinsurance, price determines package, not the other way around. Comment.

Focus on low-cost and frequent rather than on rare events

A benefits package is useful when it includes protection against the risks most likely to cause health-related severe financial hardship. The risk most likely to cause hardship is a medical problem that the local health-care service can treat. Let us consider the two components of this equation.

It is well known that serious illnesses and accidents require hospitalization and that an episode of hospital stay is usually expensive. With the view to reducing the financial barrier of access to hospitalizations for the most vulnerable population, the Government of India launched in 2008 a subsidized hospital insurance for the below-poverty line (BPL) population.[3] Notwithstanding the good intentions and the genuine effort to reach out, this hospital insurance cannot serve as a general model of success because benefits are subject to too many conditions. For instance, anyone living in a region where there is no accredited hospital cannot benefit from that scheme (which pays only for care in accredited hospitals). Anyone who is classified as above poverty line (i.e., not BPL) before the hospitalization is not eligible

[3]Called Rashtriya Swastiya Bima Yojna (RSBY). In 2018, the Ayushman Bharat-National Health Protection Scheme (AB-NHPS) replaced RSBY. The AB-NHPS beneficiaries are those enrolled in RSBY, plus 11 occupational groups, and people entitled based on deprivation criteria.

(even if after paying for a hospitalization that household falls to BPL level). Moreover, anyone who suffers from an illness that is not listed among the approved procedures would not benefit from such insurance.

The broader issue here is that, while it is true that the cost of a single hospitalization can be prohibitive, it is also true that the aggregated costs of outpatient healthcare over long periods, or larger populations, may far exceed hospitalization costs. Most people in the informal sector understand the juxtaposition of *rare care versus expensive care*. They seek health insurance for expensive care, rather than health insurance that is limited to rare cases that occur once or twice in a lifetime.

In the informal sector, the local information on the incidence and severity of risk exposure (obtained through baseline surveys — see Chapter 3) also sheds light on the types of care that locals could consider expensive or rare. Implementers of health microinsurance should retain the main message that the benefits package should solve the financial hardship that can be caused by any care, and the way to estimate it is to look at the aggregate cost rather than at the average cost of a single episode of care.

A simulation exercise to elicit the desirable benefits package

The complexities of actuarial calculations are not easily understood, but everyone can understand that as we add benefits, the package becomes more expensive. Empirical evidence (Dror, 2007; Dror *et al.*, 2007) has shown that women are more perceptive about the healthcare needs of their families and the amount that can be paid from the household budget. Therefore, women take a dominant role in the first step of the multistage selection process. All three stages of the simulation exercise unfold in group settings. The exercise, called *Choosing Healthplans All Together* (CHAT) (Dror, 2018) starts with the exploration of various possible combinations and concludes when the group selects one package that the entire group endorses.

SELF-TEST QUESTIONS

1. The hospital insurance launched in 2008 by the Government of India for the BPL population is not considered to be a general model of success. Why?
2. A benefits package should solve the financial hardship that can be caused by healthcare costs. Comment on the type(s) of care that beneficiaries of microinsurance usually seek coverage for — expensive care or rare care cases. Why?

Choosing Healthplans All Together

Preparations

Before the CHAT exercise can unfold, it is necessary to prepare the decision support tools. This process is accomplished in three stages. First, the information on all types of cost-generating health events (hospitalization, laboratory testing, imaging, consultation, imaging, and medicines) and their cost distributions are extracted from the baseline dataset. In the second stage, this information is fed in a pricing algorithm (described in Chapter 5) to estimate pure-risk premium for infinitely many combinations of health events with different caps. The pricing algorithm also estimates risk loading (as a percentage of pure-risk premium) to be added to the pure-risk premium to protect the scheme from failing with a chosen probability. The final output of this stage is a premium calculator with a user-friendly interface which is presented in the third stage of the process known as Benefits Option Consultation Workshop.

Benefits Option Consultation Workshop

The initial feasibility review of the benefits packages and their prices takes place during the *Benefits Option Consultation Workshop*. The objective of this workshop is to narrow down the choice of benefits package options from infinitely many to just a few (four to five options) that would be used in CHAT rounds. The community leaders, who are the key participants in this workshop, take the first decision on the packages following deliberations and based on their knowledge of the community's willingness to pay. This workshop allows validating the findings of the baseline study as well as to moderate the perceptions of community leaders on the frequency and severity of various health events. After the workshop, the short-listed options are designed in a colorful format with icons for each benefit type (the *CHAT board*) (see Figure 9.1). The CHAT board is printed in two sizes — small and large.

Three rounds of CHAT

The first round of CHAT (CHAT 1) is played at the local community group level. Each member of the group gets the small CHAT board. The benefits packages are explained, and *each member chooses the benefits package* he/she feels suits best for that person's needs and willingness to pay. The members get several colored stickers (*bindi*) that represent the budget and use the stickers to show the package of their choice. Once all the members have made their individual choice, they discuss the merits of their choices in the group. Some members modify their choice after this discussion.

When this group exchange ends, each participant takes the CHAT board home. This stage of the discussions makes it possible for each participant to get inputs, proposals, and support from their family members. At this stage, each person can make changes to their choice according to the discussions with family members.

A week later, the groups meet again to engage in the second round of CHAT (CHAT 2). In this round, the objective is to reach *a group choice.* The facilitated debate of the individual choices leads to a discussion of preference that might be relevant for the entire group until there is an agreement of only one benefits package.

The third round (CHAT 3) takes place during the *Benefits Package Finalization Workshop* when representatives of all the groups meet to discuss each group's preferred package. The objective this time is to reach consensus on one benefits package that would apply for the entire scheme. The CHAT exercise ends when one benefits package is chosen for the entire community.

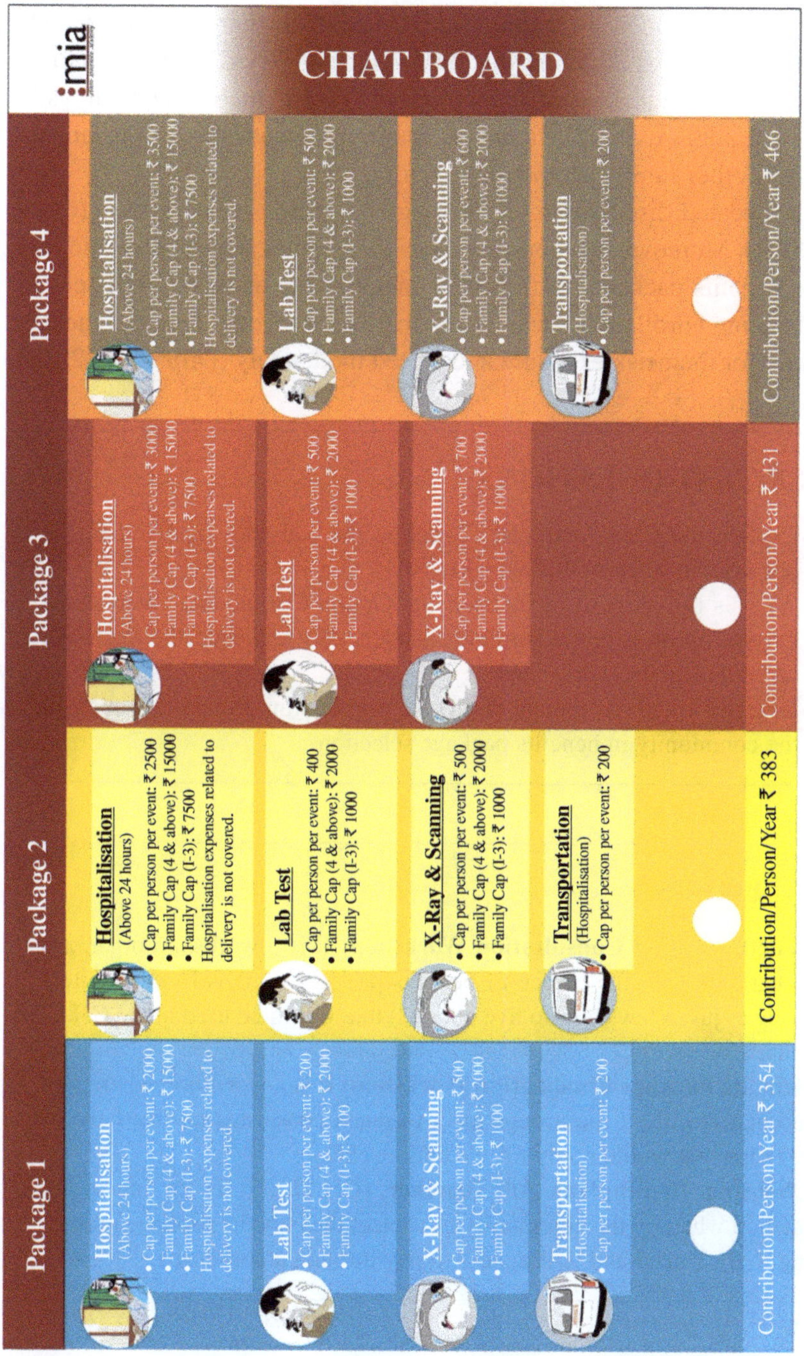

Figure 9.1 Representative CHAT board

Facilitators who were trained on the use of awareness tools accompany the discussions all along the three stages of CHAT and also participate in some discussions at the household level (their role there is to support the person who participated in group discussions to present the exercise to other family members).

The repeated discussions set the stage for increased consensus (Danis *et al.*, 2007). Moreover, the consensus has the double effect of consolidating a single benefits package for the entire membership of each CBHI scheme and enhancing enrollment because members trust that the benefits package is relevant for their risk exposure and priced moderately (Dror *et al.*, 2014).

SELF-TEST QUESTIONS

1. Explain the CHAT exercise. Describe the activities involved in the preparation stage of this exercise.
2. What is the purpose of the Benefits Option Consultation Workshop? Do you think a few community leaders can influence the decisions taken during the workshop?
3. Describe the three rounds of CHAT, highlighting the participation of the community in benefits package selection.

KEY TERMS

- **Benefits Option Consultation Workshop:** It is a workshop organized to narrow down the choice of benefits package options from infinitely many to just a few (four to five options) that would be used in the CHAT rounds.
- **Benefits Package Finalization Workshop:** It is a workshop where representatives of all the groups meet to reach consensus on one benefits package that would apply for the entire scheme.
- **Choosing Healthplans All Together (CHAT):** It is an innovative method whereby the community can select the benefits package according to their need and willingness to pay through a consensus.

Bibliography

Danis, M, Binnendijk, E, Vellakkal, S, Ost, A, Koren, R, and Dror, DM (2007) Eliciting Health Insurance Benefit Choices of Low-Income Groups. *Economic and Political Weekly*, 42(32), 3331–3335.

Dror, DM (2007) Why "One-Size-Fits-All" Health Insurance Products Are Unsuitable for Low-Income Persons in the Informal Economy in India. *Asian Economic Review*, 49(1), 47–56.

Dror, DM (2018) *Financing Micro Health Insurance: Theory, Methods, and Evidence*. In *World Scientific Series in Health Investment and Financing*, ed. AS Preker, Vol. 2. Singapore: World Scientific Publishing.

Dror, DM, Koren, R, Ost, A, Binnendijk, E, Vellakkal, S, and Danis, M (2007) Health Insurance Benefit Packages Prioritized by Low-Income Clients in India: Three Criteria to Estimate Effectiveness of Choice. *Social Science & Medicine*, 64(4), 884–96.

Dror, DM, Panda, P, May, C, Majumdar, A, and Koren, R (2014) One For All and All For One: Consensus-Building within Communities in Rural India on Their Health Microinsurance Package. *Risk Management and Healthcare Policy*, 7, 139–153, doi:10.2147/RMHP.S66011.

Chapter 10

The Governance Structure and Training the Key Actors

LEARNING OBJECTIVES

Upon completion of this chapter, the reader should be able to:

- Describe the three tiers of governance in CBHI, and explain the function of each key actor
- Understand the roles and responsibilities of each key actor, including the General Assembly of Participants
- Give the qualifications required for each key actor's position
- Describe the role of the ombudsman in grievance redressal according to the claim appeal process

Abstract

The governance structure of community-based health insurance (CBHI) comprises members of the community who are also the owners of the scheme. The model is driven by the *principle of subsidiarity* which posits that every social or economic issue should be dealt with at the most immediate (or lowest) level that can resolve it while respecting camaraderie and human dignity. We learn about the roles and responsibilities of each key actor and their contribution in the various business processes of the scheme.

Chapter Outline

The success of a CBHI lies largely in its organization structure which is comprised of persons selected by participants from their own community. While an effective governance structure can bolster the community's trust and willingness to participate in health insurance, the failure of a CBHI's governance can lead to both low enrollment and renewal rates of a scheme. In this chapter, we learn that the CBHI organization structure is designed to ensure three functions of governance — executive, oversight and mediatory. The qualifications of each key actor is outlined, and her/his role and responsibilities discussed *vis-à-vis* the business process, to give the reader a good understanding of the functioning of a CBHI.

The synergy between community-based health insurance and existing grassroots organizations

The desire of individuals to enhance welfare by cooperating with peers is as old as humanity. The efforts to structure collective action formally date back some 200 years, but much collective action has been informal. Today still, there are many individuals who work together to achieve common goals, e.g., by pooling resources and sharing knowledge. When the pooling of money and its redistribution extends to many individuals, it becomes necessary to define the rules governing those functions and the managerial (hierarchical) structure of the organization, even if it remains *informal* (i.e., not registered with a government) and *local* (i.e., limited to members in one location).

This book focuses on community-based mutual aid organizations that launch and operate Community-based Health Insurance (CBHI) schemes. For pragmatic reasons, an outside initiator [in our case it has been the Micro Insurance Academy (MIA)] may wish to cooperate with non-governmental organizations (NGOs) that are already engaged with grassroots groups locally in promoting a common goal like the self-help groups (SHGs) or a health-related activity. Cooperation with *implementing field partner organizations* or *partner organizations* accelerates outreach. It also introduces the notion of federating many clusters of contiguous small groups. Thus, from the outset, the organization of a CBHI scheme includes the local, cluster, and federation levels.

"Top-down" or "bottom-up"? The principle of subsidiarity applies

An organizational structure of three levels raises the following question: *Who is in command?* The answer that pertains to our model is as follows: apply the *principle of subsidiarity* which posits that every social or economic issue should be dealt with at the most immediate (or lowest) level that can resolve it while respecting camaraderie and human dignity. A *subsidiary* (higher) level should be involved with the resolution only when the local level cannot resolve the issue. *Subsidiarity* (social organization) combines well with *mutuality* (a form of ownership) and *solidarity* (behavior).

The CBHI organizational structure serves to ensure the following three functions of governance (Figure 10.1):

- *Executive* Carrying out the activities following rules and regulations
- *Oversight* Having the responsibility to ensure that the rules of the scheme are applied equitably to all the participants
- *Mediatory* Investigating complaints and refereeing disputes

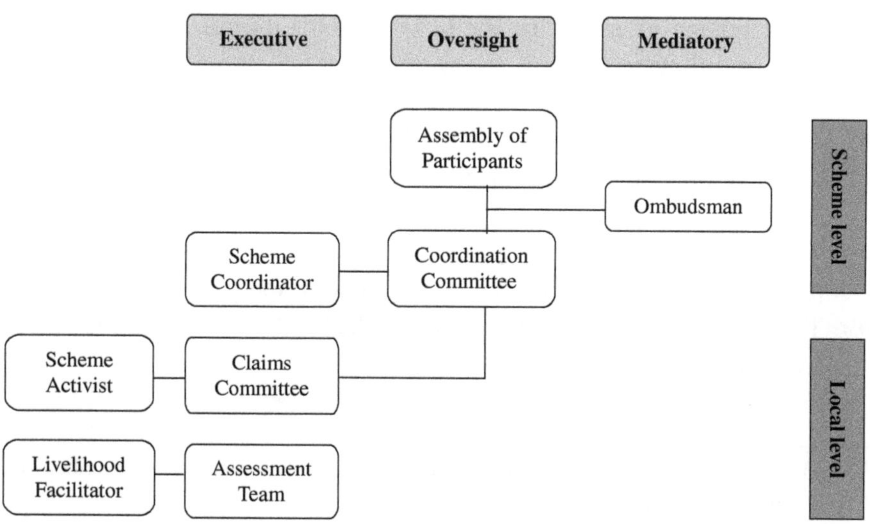

Figure 10.1 The Governance Structure of CBHI

In a CBHI, the Claims Committee (CC, at the local level) decides on the claims submitted by the participants. The Coordination Committee (CoCo, at the cluster level) supervises the decisions of several CCs for consistency with the reimbursement rules and fair adjudication. When a CBHI scheme has several CoCos, there is a federated level. The Assembly of Participants (the federated level) is the highest body that decides on issues extending beyond claims. The Ombudsman (independent, federal level) deals with complaints from beneficiaries about unfair or erroneous decisions by any person or body acting for the CBHI.

Governance

General Assembly of Participants

The *General Assembly* consists of all the scheme's enrolled participants. The General Assembly of Participants (GAP) exercise the role of the owner of the scheme. It takes decisions on policy and direction of the scheme; on continued functions or dissolution; on carrying forward reserves from previous years and utilization of funds; on the nomination or termination of community representatives and key actors; on changing the benefits package (and engaging in the CHAT[1] process from time to time).

In exercising its authority, the GAP upholds the rules of mutual aid societies as follows[2]:

- The General Assembly decides all the rules for the scheme. Every enrolled member has the right to participate in the GAP and its decisions.
- The balance of previous years is inherited collectively by all the participants. The money is never refunded to the participants.
- The GAP decides on the utilization of the funds in line with the objectives of the scheme.

[1] CHAT — acronym for Choosing Healthplans All Together. Chapter 9 described the CHAT process in detail.

[2] http://wiki.p2pfoundation.net/Mutual_Aid_Societies.

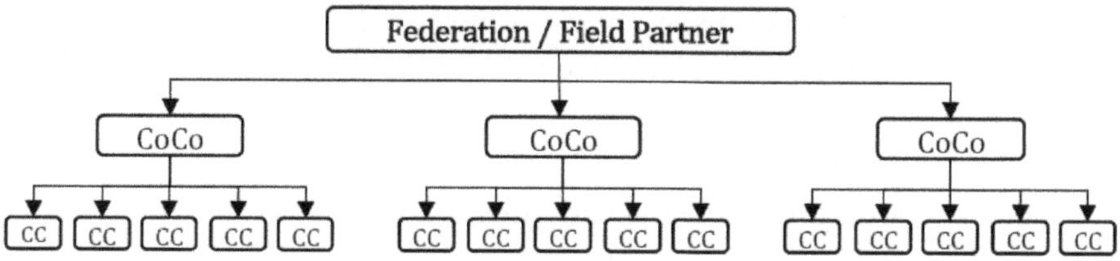

Figure 10.2 Three-Tiered Governance Structure

- No individual member can claim an identifiable share of the assets. If the mutual is dissolved, all assets must be handed over to another mutual, a charitable fund, or a relief fund.

Three-tiered governance structure

The governance structure of CBHI plans is three-tiered (Figure 10.2).

> **SELF-TEST QUESTIONS**
>
> 1. Describe the roles and functions of the GAP.
> 2. The principle of subsidiarity applies to the CBHI model. Comment.

The First Tier of Governance

The first tier of governance consists of CCs. Each CBHI scheme has several CCs, each serving around 700 households participating in 60–80 women's groups that are called SHGs in India and *self-reliant groups* (SRGs) in Nepal. CCs are composed of 7–9 representatives of SHGs/SRGs (one representative for every 10–12 SHGs/SRGs). They receive a *sitting fee* for meetings but no salaries. They may be replaced, but the CoCo maintains the same composition.

Functions of the CCs include the following:

- They employ the *scheme activists* (SAs) and decide his/her salary.
- They review and decide on the claims promptly.

- They ensure that claims are paid promptly after the decision.
- They maintain claims-related records for the duration of the cover. At the end of the cover period, all the documents are handed over from CCs to the CoCo.
- They support all the scheme activities in the field.

Meetings

- CCs meet at least once a month, and more frequently when required.
- A quorum of two-thirds of the CC members must be met in every meeting.
- Minutes are taken at all the meetings.

Reporting

- CCs report to the CoCo; each sends the CoCo a monthly claims status report.

Each CC employs one salaried SA to provide services to policyholders and support the CC members in processing claims. Each SA attends to 600 households or 3,000 participants covered under the scheme. The SA's duties include the following:

- mobilizes community members to become participants;
- Is involved in awareness creation before and after enrollment;
- helps the participants to complete enrollment forms, collects contributions, and distributes participant kits before coverage begins;
- helps participants file claims and disburses the payout as decided by the CC;
- records all CC-level monetary transactions;
- verifies details of household changes for participatory note modification.

SAs report to the CCs and coordinate all scheme-related issues with the SC.

The Second Tier of Governance

It consists of CoCos that oversee the operation of up to five CCs (3,500 households). Each CBHI has at least one CoCo. It consists of five to seven members, one nominated by the field partner, one or two representatives of the participants, and one from each CC that reports to the CoCo. CoCo members receive a *sitting fee* for meetings but no salaries from the plan. They may be replaced, but the CoCo maintains the same composition.

Functions of CoCo include the following:

- employing the *scheme coordinator* (SC) and deciding his/her remuneration/salary;
- maintaining the records and the management information system (MIS);
- overseeing the functioning of the CCs and ensuring that claims are processed promptly;
- initiating the financial audits of the CBHI;
- receiving grievances from participants and providing remedies for the issues raised;
- ensuring that scheme funds are used only in compliance with the decisions of the GAP.

Meetings

- The CoCo meets at least once a month, or more frequently when required.
- CoCo meetings are subject to a quorum; when two-thirds of the CoCo members attend the quorum is satisfied.
- The CoCo must keep minutes of all meetings.

Reporting duties

- The CoCo reports to the GAP.
- The CoCo can propose to the GAP guidelines for the better operation of the CBHI.

Each CoCo employs one salaried SC and maintains an office where records of all transactions are kept. The SC operates at the scheme level and is an employee of the CBHI. His/her duties consist of the following:

- enters the data related to enrollment, claims, participatory note modification, and renewal in the MIA-MIS;
- maintains the MIS and generates reports/documents on demand;
- maintains the scheme's books of accounts;
- is responsible for keeping the bankbook and ensures that the account passbook is updated;
- follows up with the External Insurer for matters related to risks underwritten;
- maintains the minutes of all the CoCo meetings;
- liaises between the CCs, CoCo, and other key actors on scheme-related operational issues.

The SC reports to the CoCo on all matters.

The Third Tier of Governance

It is the *Federation*. At this level, representatives of the field partner (usually NGOs active in organizing the network of SHGs/SRGs) and CoCo members meet. The Federation employs one salaried *project coordinator* and one salaried accountant to oversee the activities of up to three CoCos (10,500 households). Each scheme also has an *Ombudsman* who operates at the level of the Federation.

The *Ombudsman* is nominated by the GAP to act as the scheme's internal authority to investigate grievances submitted by the participants about decisions that concern them, as well as to mediate disputes between the CCs and the CoCo. The Ombudsman is autonomous in elaborating a solution to each case submitted. The Ombudsman informs the GAP on all the cases submitted and their solutions. There are no formal qualifications to become an Ombudsman, the only guideline being that he/she should be a person held in high regard by the majority of the community. The reason for the nomination of an Ombudsman is to provide a grievance resolution instrument, as participants cannot have recourse to a court of law or to formal arbitration. In practice, the mere fact that an Ombudsman was nominated avoided the need to have recourse to such an intervention.

SELF-TEST QUESTIONS

1. Discuss the three tiers of governance in CBHI and explain the function of each key actor.
2. Do you think having an ombudsman from among the community members is a prudent decision? Justify your answer.

Selection and training of key actors

The collective name for all the administrators of the scheme is *key actors*. Key actors are themselves members of the community where they then work. The participants select the candidates, who must express interest in working for the scheme. This selection process reflects the ownership of the scheme and ensures the involvement of the community.

The key actors undergo comprehensive training to enable them to carry out their responsibilities effectively. The training is conducted by a technical assistance (TA) provider who specializes in health microinsurance and who conducts the baseline survey (in our case, this was the MIA, New Delhi). The specific skill mix needed to catalyze demand for CBHI among grassroots groups is fundamentally different from that required to train insurance agents or underwriters, and the training is carried out *in situ* where the CBHI would then operate. Training modules have been designed for each key actor position, to impart the information and skills they require to perform their roles.

Scheme Activist

The module is meant to train SAs, both designated and currently serving in Community-Based Mutual Aid Schemes (CBHIs). It is designed primarily to help SAs learn skills they need to know to perform roles related to the following:

- mobilizing community members;
- helping community members to enroll and receive scheme benefits;
- networking with local stakeholders;
- promoting education and awareness of insurance;
- handling claims and contributing to participatory note modification.

The SA is the primary community mobilizer — taking the lead in an essential function in the community-based initiative. The term *community based* is used to describe an activity that is organized and takes place locally. This definition applies to all the activities within a CBHI — the enrollment, claims decision, and grievance redressal all unfold at the local level.

The SA represents the scheme and is the first point of contact for scheme participants. The SA is an executive actor at a local level.

Like all the other key actors, the SA belongs to the local community. The advantage is that the SA and community are familiar with each other. The SA is aware of community cultural practices and norms. These community-specific social norms influence CBHI communication and awareness strategy. Local information, especially about local resources and key influential persons is helpful when planning baseline studies, awareness, and obtaining support from key local stakeholders. Most important, the community knows the SA even before the launch of the scheme and therefore finds it more comfortable to trust the scheme. This also helps foster a local sense of scheme ownership.

The positioning of SAs at the local level makes them readily accessible to scheme participants. SAs work within the rules of CBHI decided by the GAP, the scheme owners. SAs also follow the guidelines as described by CBHI business processes.

SAs are executives of the CC and report to the CC.

The following are the required qualifications for SAs:

- certification of at least high school completion — sound knowledge of the 3 Rs — reading, writing, and arithmetic;

- fluency in communicating in the local language. SAs should speak community members' main language; knowledge of local dialects is desirable;
- familiarity with basic arithmetic is essential because keeping accurate financial records is part of the SA's job.

The applicants' essential basic communication and organizational skills are assessed during personal interviews. Some of these skills can be developed and refined through training and mentoring, given a desire for self-improvement.

Communication skills include verbal and non-verbal communication. The parameters to look out for are as follows:

- **Listening ability.** Does the individual talk regularly without stopping to listen to what others have to say?
- **Openness to others' ideas.** Being open to hearing out what the others have to say without being judgmental is an important quality of a good communicator.
- **Posture and personality.** Is the applicant's style open, interested, and appropriately friendly?
- **Clarity of message.** Is the applicant's language clear and concise?
- **Confidence.** Is the applicant confident? People are more likely to trust and follow a confident person rather than one who projects over-confidence or lack of it.
- **Respect.** People listen to a person who respects them — small gestures like being on time for a group meeting and arriving well prepared for the interaction.

These are the basic organizing skills that help the SA work efficiently. The SA should be able to plan his/her work within the guidelines of the scheme with a focus on the goals to be achieved.

SAs need to know about the following:

- the local community;
- basic concepts of insurance and how it works;

- the principles, governance structure, and business processes of CBHI, and how it works;
- the rules of the scheme decided by the General Assembly;
- benefits package — for each type of covered risk and any changes that occur for each coverage period.

Responsibilities

(i) **Community mobilization:** This is the central role of SAs. Community mobilization is a process of reaching out to all segments of a community and forging partnerships to help implement CBHI.
Through discussions, SAs encourages community members to implement and manage their scheme.

Through insurance education and awareness, the community becomes aware of the risks they have been coping with using resources available to them. This gives them a chance to talk about the vulnerabilities or threats to their lives and livelihoods. The SA explains how the paucity of resources aggravates their vulnerability to the financial burden of loss.

These discussions are best held in group settings so that people learn, understand, and identify the risk exposure through others' experiences. The take-home message is as follows: "If this can happen to someone in my community, it can also happen to me."

Discussions draw on personal experiences and sometimes local anecdotes. SAs should collect relevant local information before dialog with the community. Local examples give local context to discussions on risk and insurance. Local resources are discussed for their availability, accessibility, and community members' trust and satisfaction with them.

SAs demonstrate that the community needs a risk management mechanism like CBHI for protection from financial consequences of defined risks. It is essential to discuss in this context how CBHI builds on existing informal arrangements and creates a rules-based system equitable for all. The communal nature of scheme ownership and a local governance structure are highlighted. SAs have to be prepared to answer members' queries until they are satisfied.

(ii) **Help community members to enroll:** Enrollments are prospective members' first encounter with scheme participation — filling out enrollment forms, paying contributions, and signing the form as a promise to abide by scheme rules.

Through door-to-door visits or meetings in group settings, the SA explains the benefits package, answers further questions, and helps people with the paperwork.

The principle of *en bloc* affiliation is encouraged — all group members join the scheme with all their family members. This boosts solidarity within the scheme.

Understanding the concept of solidarity is important. It is related to scheme enrollment and underlines the whole CBHI effort — people come together to help each other in times of financial stress from defined risks. Solidarity is demonstrated through en bloc affiliation — no one is left out in the cold.

- For the health enrollment process, the SA should know the benefits package in detail. The benefits package describes the benefits for the contribution payable and the attendant limitations and qualifications. The prospective members must understand the benefits package to make an informed choice to enroll. Claims decisions are also based on the benefits package.
- A single enrollment form is filled in for each household and covers every enrolled member of that household.
- The contribution is collected in full before the start date of the policy, and a receipt is always given, stating the amount collected, not the total amount payable.
- The records of contributions received are updated in the Daily Collection Sheet.
- The second copies of money receipts and updated Daily Collection Sheets are submitted with the collected cash to the SC for data entry.
- After the enrollment period, the SA distributes the Participant Kits to the enrolled households.

(iii) **Help community members to file claims:** The claims are the most tangible benefit of coverage — proof of the value of insurance. The SA interacts with the community the most and is, therefore, best placed on teaching scheme participants how to file a claim. This instruction can be done at monthly group meetings or in claim disbursal meetings. Initially, the SA may proactively keep track of any insured cost-generating adverse health events in the enrolled households and help them submit a claim. The responsibility for submitting claims lies with the participant; the SA facilitates this process.

The role of the SA in claims is to facilitate claim submission, convey claim decisions to the claimants, and ensure disbursal of the claim amount within a specified time.

Note: The SA does not make claims decisions, it is the role of the CC.

The SA must know the benefits package in detail — claims are decided according to the benefits package in force.

- The SA stocks forms and makes them available to claimants on request. The SA may help the claimant fill in the claim form and gives a claim received acknowledgment. A separate claim form is filled for each health event.

Note: A participant may have experienced two cost-generating adverse events within a short period and is submitting both the claims simultaneously. In such cases, the participant has to fill in one claim form for each event with the relevant supporting documents.

- Within a household where several members experience the same illness, one claim form is filled for each member even though the illnesses may have coincided.
- The Principal Participant fills in the claim forms for each sick household dependent.
- The SA advises on the supporting documents required for claim submission and may assist the claimant in collecting bills, reports, and discharge notes from healthcare providers. All the documents are serially numbered and self-attested by the claimant.
- The SA hands over all the claim documents to the SC for data entry.
- In the case of claim-related queries, the SA helps the CC verify the claim details through visits to households and healthcare providers.
- The SA may attend the CC meeting but not participate in claims discussions. The SA disburses the claim payment with the help of CC members.

Note: When the claim is paid by check, the check may be drawn in favor of the Principal Participant in place of the dependent claimant.

(iv) **Support community members in participatory note modification:** The participatory note is a system-generated document that gives details on the enrolled household and applicable benefits package. The note is issued for each participating household. Changes may be required in case of change of participants or their profiles. In such cases, the SA assists the participant in requesting a modification in the note. The SA verifies the modification and reports to CC for endorsement. The modified note is generated by the SC and given to the participant by the SA.

(v) **Renewals:** Renewals or re-enrollments help participants to continue participating after the end of the cover period. The SA follows the renewal planning done by the CC. The SA's role in renewals is the same as in enrollments.

(vi) **Networking with local stakeholders:** Local information available to SAs helps them identify the key local stakeholders and resource persons for scheme participants. SAs meet with them and tell them about the scheme, stressing community ownership and management of an equitable, rules-based scheme. The CoCo decides on further action on points of mutual benefit recognized by the SA.

(vii) **Insurance education:** Community members need to understand the value proposition of insurance to make a voluntary, informed choice to enroll in the scheme. Insurance education is an ongoing process continuing well beyond the awareness and enrollment phases. SAs take every opportunity to tell people about the benefits of insurance. The MIA has developed an extensive repertoire of entertaining and informative awareness and insurance education materials like games, films, documentaries, and animations. SAs should be acquainted with the scope of each aid to select the best one for each occasion.

SELF-TEST QUESTION

1. Elaborate the SA's role in the various business processes of CBHI.

Claims Committee

The module is meant to train both the current and designated members of the CC on their roles and responsibilities within the CBHI governance structure.

The CC is an executive actor at a local level and deals with all the claims.

This is an expression of the principle of subsidiarity — functions that can be carried out efficiently in smaller units and at the local level should be carried out at that level and no higher. This is a fundamental CBHI principle.

A local-level committee is best placed to verify the authenticity of the claims because these events happen in their vicinity. Committee members are aware of any cost-generating adverse health events in their neighborhood, which leverages local information and reduces moral hazard. Claims are not decided by a faceless entity in a remote location (as in commercial insurance), but by community members whom the participants know. This increases the trust in the scheme, and people are less likely to submit fraudulent claims with intent to cheat.

The CC is an executive actor and does not decide the rules on which the claims are assessed. The CC decides all the claims submitted by the participants in accordance with the benefits package applicable for a particular cover period.

The CC is composed of designated community members. They are also scheme participants.

Seven to nine community representatives represent approximately 600 households or 3,000 participants covered under the scheme within a defined locality. The GAP can replace CC members keeping the same representative composition.

Qualifications required of CC members

- Fluency in communicating in local language — conversational, reading, and writing; knowledge of local dialects is desirable.
- Familiarity with basic arithmetic at least sufficient to understand the bills submitted, add bill amounts to arrive at claim amount, and understand the Claim Overview Document (COD).

- The same qualifications apply to those members designated to replace existing CC members.

Responsibilities

(i) **To decide on claims submitted by the scheme participants:**

This is the primary responsibility of the CC. No other key actor of the scheme can decide on claims except when CC refers claims to the CoCo, or a participant files a claim appeal.

The claim decision is always made in accordance with the benefits package selected by the participants for the cover period. There are no *ex gratia* payments — payments made on compassionate or similar grounds that are not a part of the benefits package are discouraged.

Only claims that conform to CBHI rules are accepted, and the amount payable is decided according to the benefits package and the COD. Claims that are not submitted within the stipulated time limit, not covered by the benefits package, or exceed the annual cap may be rejected. Some claims may require further verification or supporting documents before a decision can be taken — these are categorized as pending for further information.

A claim form is filled for each claim separately. The supporting documents required for claim submission are standard records maintained and shared with the patients by healthcare providers. The onus of providing supporting documents lies with the claimant. If a document is not submitted with the claim form, the claimant may seek reasonable time to arrange for the same from the healthcare provider.

In cases where hospitalization (or any benefit related to hospitalization like transport costs, costs of medicines pre- and post-hospitalization) is covered, the discharge card or discharge summary must be submitted with the claim. All the bills must be submitted in original.

Each CC member present in the meeting must scrutinize every claim submitted for a decision. They do not have to understand the details of the illness — diagnosis, investigation reports, or treatment particulars. The claim decision is independent of the diagnosis or illness category. This unique feature makes claim decisions at the community level possible. Reimbursement of expenditure is in accordance with the limits set in the benefits package irrespective of the disease condition.

(ii) **Support scheme activities:** CC members guide SAs' efforts in community mobilization. They may interact independently with community groups and encourage people to join the scheme. Through formal and informal interactions, they also advise participants on how to submit claims.

CC members also participate in awareness campaigns and help identify local resources and key stakeholders.

The members participate in training conducted for the scheme and help organize the training.

The schedule for CC meetings is decided at the beginning of the cover period and shared with all the key actors within the governance structure. The CC meets at least once a month but may meet more than once if required (a large number of claims, emergency claims).

A CC meeting always precedes the CoCo meeting — helps to prompt the release of claim amount by CoCo.

The quorum of at least two-thirds of the members is required for the meeting. Any meeting with less than a prescribed quorum is dismissed. The next date is announced, and the meeting takes place only when two-thirds of the members are present. An agenda is recommended for the meetings so that no topic is overlooked.

A register devoted to CC business is recommended for keeping meeting minutes during the cover period. The minutes are signed by all members present at the meeting.

Meeting register is maintained separately for each cover period. After the cover period, the register is maintained as a scheming record.

SELF-TEST QUESTION

1. Explain the roles and responsibilities of the CC.

Coordination Committee (CoCo)

The module is meant to train current and designated members of the CoCo on their roles and responsibilities within the CBHI governance structure.

By the end of the course, every CoCo member knows how to do the following:

- formulate guidelines for the scheme and confirm that rules are applied equally to all;
- supervise that scheme operations are in accordance with the CBHI business processes;
- ascertain that scheme funds are utilized only to pay valid claims and cover operational scheme costs;
- resolve any health claim appeals submitted by scheme participants and represent participants' grievances to External Insurer in case of crop and livestock claims;
- liaison with external stakeholders including the External Insurer (for livestock and crop enrollment and claims) on behalf of the scheme.

The CoCo is an oversight actor at the scheme level. The CoCo oversees the operations of the scheme on behalf of the owners of the scheme, i.e., GAP through formal and informal interactions.

The CoCo is the first level of appeal in health claims and represents the participant's grievances to the External Insurer in case of crop and livestock claims.

There is only one CoCo for every scheme.

The GAP decides on the rules of the scheme including the benefits package. It appoints the CoCo to ensure that the scheme operates by scheme rules and that they apply equally to all. As scheme managers, the CoCo cannot override rules made by the GAP but can only design guidelines for the key actors to follow.

The CoCo is composed of the following people:

- an equal number of members from each CC — a scheme can have more than one CC depending on the number of members enrolled (see Chapter 4, the formation of CC);

- a nominated representative from the field partner organization — to support and mentor the scheme functionaries and enhance trust within the scheme;
- one or two respected members from enrolled participants — helps give more credibility, acceptability, and representativeness to the CoCo.

Qualifications for CoCo members are as follows:

- Fluency in communicating in local language — conversational, reading, and writing. Knowledge of local dialects is desirable.
- Familiarity with basic arithmetic as they scrutinize the bills and decide on the claim amount payable in case of claim appeals.

The same qualifications apply to those members designated to replace existing CoCo members and to nominated field partner representative.

Every CoCo member must be familiar with the following:

- **The scheme benefits package:** This is the foremost rule of the scheme decided by the enrolled participants through consensus. Claims are always decided by the benefits package. Therefore, every CoCo member should be well versed in the benefits package provisions.
- **Scheme rules:** CBHI is a rules-based system, and CoCo has to ensure that the rules of the scheme are applied equally to all. Rules are decided by the scheme participants and may change. Every CoCo member must be up to date with the scheme rules.
- **Prescribed CBHI business processes:** These describe how the scheme is operated by its key functionaries and the roles and responsibilities of each within the governance structure.
- **Scheme outreach:** The number of SHGs or Common Resource Groups (CRGs) covered by the scheme, the total number of enrolled participants, and the options for scaling up.
- **Scheme assets and fund status:** Physical inventory of scheme assets (computer, printer, business stationery) and fund status (contribution

collected, reserves carried forward, claims paid, operational costs paid).

- **Scheme internal activities:** These include enrollment schedule for each risk category and the schedule of value-added services.

CoCo members work together as a team with each member contributing personal knowledge and experience to make the scheme work.

Responsibilities

(i) **To plan activities for the scheme and ensure adherence to prescribed processes:** On behalf of the GAP, the CoCo is responsible for carrying out scheme activities like awareness campaigns and enrollments for each risk category.

Planning is a process of deliberating and deciding on a course of action to achieve the desired result.

Preparatory work for enrollment starts around three months before the cover end date.

The scheme performance for the current cover period has to be reviewed for the following:

- number of members enrolled;
- members enrolled per household;
- households enrolled per SHG or CRG;
- number of claims received;
- total number of claim payments;
- operational expenses incurred.

The review is conducted with the help of TA. Such a review will help decide whether a change of benefits package is required, strategy for increasing enrollment, and strategy for scaling up.

Discussions can be initiated if a benefits package change is required. The benefits package of the scheme is always decided through consensus among the scheme participants, reached through the process of Choosing Healthplans All Together (CHAT). Planning an awareness campaign entails recruiting facilitators, scheduling awareness campaigns, and designing awareness tools with TA support.

(ii) **To ensure rules are applied equally to all:** Equity is a key feature of CBHI. The same rules apply to all participants. All participants have equal rights and responsibilities, pay the same contribution, and are entitled to the same benefits.

The rules of the scheme are decided by the GAP collectively within the framework of CBHI.

The CoCo members have to be up to date on scheme rules to ensure that the rules are applied equitably to all participants. This also applies to the benefits package.

- **Random checking of claims decided by the CC** — Claims are always decided according to the benefits package chosen by scheme participants. A claims sample review will demonstrate if the rules were followed during claims decisions or if any claims were settled without proper documentation, any *ex gratia* payment was made to a participant, or a receivable claim was rejected for unjustified reasons.
- **Addressing participants' grievances** — These are related to claims, key actors, External Insurer, and value-added services. The CoCo is the first level of appeal within the scheme in the grievance redressal mechanism. By attending to grievances, the CoCo ensures that participants are not deprived of their rights or entitlements within the scheme.

(iii) **To manage scheme funds:** At CoCo level, there is one bank account for each scheme. Three signatories are appointed from the CoCo for account operations. Of the three, one has to be the nominated representative of the field partner. This provision is designed to safeguard the scheme account and increase accountability within the participants.

The CoCo ensures that premium is paid to the External Insurer of livestock and crop covers within the stipulated time limits. The CoCo also monitors disbursal of payouts on receipt of the claim amount from the External Insurer.

The CoCo initiates any internal financial audit, to verify that the prescribed accounting processes are followed for all transactions at all levels within the scheme. The internal audit is not to be confused with a statutory audit, which is a legal requirement for any business entity.

The CoCo reports periodically to the GAP on the fund status.

(iv) **To decide on the remuneration of key actors:** The key actors are paid remuneration from scheme funds in amounts decided in consultation with the GAP. The CoCo ensures that the key actors' remuneration is paid within the stipulated time and against proper vouchers. The MIA-MIS accounts are updated, and a report is presented in the CoCo meeting.

(v) **To oversee the functioning of key actors:** As a part of its oversight functions, the CoCo also supervises the activities of the scheme key actors. The CoCo sets guidelines and plans activities for the scheme. The CoCo ensures that the rules of the scheme are followed at all times and that activity plans are followed.

The CoCo can ensure that the schedule for CC meetings is followed and that the required meeting quorum is present. A scrutiny of the CC meeting register helps the CoCo identify members who routinely skip meetings. The CoCo may recommend replacing such members. The CoCo can also monitor the claim turnaround time (TAT) measured from claim submission to claim settlement. The TAT report is available from MIA-MIS. A low TAT implies diligent claim settlement. Prompt reimbursement of their healthcare expenditure is in the interest of the claimants.

Insurance education and awareness creation are essential responsibilities of the SA. These help the community members make a voluntary, informed choice to join the scheme and benefit from it. It is particularly incumbent on the CoCo to confirm that these activities are part of regular interactions between scheme functionaries and the community.

(vi) **To act as a custodian of scheme assets:** On behalf of the GAP, the CoCo maintains and protects the scheme assets.

Completed enrollment and claim forms (with supporting documents) and MIA-MIS data are also scheme assets. The data in them have a value — decisions like a change of benefits package or types of value-added services can be based on them. The data can be used for research and impact evaluations (to see how beneficial the scheme has been for its participants).

The logbook is a record of scheme activities or events. The logbook can be maintained for recording activities like enrollment, meeting schedules, and value-added services.

In cases where livestock and crop covers are offered by the scheme, assets would include ear tags, tag applicators, and weather station logs. The CoCo is responsible for their provision and maintenance.

The CoCo meetings are held after the CC meeting(s). There could be a gap of 2–3 days between the CC and CoCo meetings. This gives the SC time to prepare Return Receipts (RRs) for the claims decided in the CC meeting(s).

CoCo meetings always follow CC meeting(s), to help CoCo's prompt release of claim amounts.

The schedule of the CoCo meetings is decided at the beginning of the cover period and shared with all the key actors within the governance structure.

The CoCo meets at least once a month and may meet more often if required — in any emergency (related to funds, bank account operations, etc.), during CHAT, or enrollment to review the activity status.

The quorum required for the meeting is at least two-thirds of the members. Any meeting with less than a prescribed quorum is dismissed. The next date is announced, and the meeting takes place only when two-thirds of the members are present.

An agenda is recommended for the meetings so that no topic is overlooked.

Keeping a CoCo meeting register during the cover period is advisable for recording meeting minutes. The minutes are signed by all meeting participants.

After the cover period, the register is maintained as a scheme record.

SELF-TEST QUESTION

1. Discuss the responsibilities of the CoCo. In case the committee is not satisfied with the performance of any key actor, what action can it take?

Scheme Coordinator

The module is intended to train current and designated SCs in the skills they need to do their job well in a CBHI. These include the following:

- data entry and report generation from MIA-MIS;
- accounting;
- record management;
- MIA-MIS maintenance;
- reporting scheme details to the CoCo.

The SC is the scheme anchor, an individual who can be relied on for support and stability.

The SC is an executive actor at the scheme level who handles all the scheme information.

Using MIA-MIS, the SC organizes and makes available on demand, relevant information for effective management of scheme activities.

The SC is recruited from the community. Unlike other key actors, the SC job requires technical skills in addition to people skills. The qualifications required are as follows:

- certificate of first degree (Bachelors or similar) in any discipline from a recognized university;
- basic computer knowledge and, at the minimum, English typing, MS Word, and Excel; certification in MS Office is a plus;
- ability to read, write, and type in English; conversational fluency is desirable but not mandatory;
- knowledge of accounting desirable, specifically bookkeeping.

There is one SC at the scheme level and he/she reports to the CoCo.

Once scheme membership reaches 40,000 members or 10,000 households, the scheme may employ more than one SC.

The SC is responsible for back-office scheme activities — data entry, bookkeeping, records management, and MIA-MIS maintenance.

Responsibilities

(i) **Data entry and generating reports from MIA-MIS:** CBHI uses standardized forms for each process. Each transaction generates data that need to be recorded systematically. MIA-MIS is a desktop application designed in-house by the MIA to streamline data management at the community level. Data related to all financial and non-financial transactions are recorded in the MIA-MIS — enrollment, claims, contribution collected, operating expenditure, and bank accounts operations.

System-generated documents like the participatory note, COD, RRs, and such others support the processes in the field. The SC makes these documents available to the key actors within stipulated time limits for smooth operations.

In addition to the system-generated documents, the SC generates reports on demand — e.g., reports on claims settled and members enrolled. These reports may be used to assess scheme performance and, by the CoCo, for decision-making.

(ii) **Accounting:** Bookkeeping is a major part of the SC's job. Bookkeeping is a recording of financial transactions of a business. Every organization/business entity has its bookkeeping system as a part of its accounting system. In CBHI, all financial transactions are entered in the Accounting module of MIA-MIS. Once entered in MIA-MIS, the receipts and vouchers are filed by category.

The SC receives the contributions collected with completed Enrollment Forms, Daily Collection Sheets, and a copy of the Money Receipt from the SA. The SC checks the cash against the amount payable specified on the Enrollment Form, the amount paid according to the Money Receipt, and the Daily Collection Sheet. The amounts mentioned should match the cash in hand. This is especially important in cases of partial payments or staggered payments made over the enrollment period.

The scheme bank account is at the CoCo level and can be accessed only by the CoCo signatories. The SC deposits the collected contributions and withdraws money for payment of claims and operating expenditures only under CoCo supervision. The SC is also responsible for updating the passbook regularly.

Accounting Basics

The SC does not have to have an accounting certification or work experience. Data entry in the Accounting module of MIA-MIS does not require any specialized accounting or accounting software knowledge. Familiarity with basic accounting terms suffices — these terms are discussed next.

In accounting, the two most important points to remember are as follows:

- All financial transactions are recorded — irrespective of the amount involved or value of the transaction. All monies received and spent have to be recorded.
- The discipline of recording has to be followed — these transactions should be recorded as soon as they occur to lay a paper trail. This trail starts with expenditure authorization and includes bills, receipts, vouchers, bank deposit slips, a record of checks issued, and account passbook.

These are definitions and explanations of elementary accounting terms. The SC is not expected to know the definitions verbatim but to understand the concepts and be familiar with the terminology.

Accounting is a systematic way of recording and reporting financial transactions to facilitate review and decision-making.

Receipts are records of money received — e.g., written assertion of money paid by participants.

Vouchers are records of expenses or money paid out — e.g., RRs for claims paid, stationery bills, and written acknowledgment of remuneration paid.

Bankbook is a record/register of deposits, withdrawals, and checks drawn on the scheme bank account.

Passbook is a record issued by the bank.

Physical cash balance is cash in hand, the amount not deposited in the bank.

Statement of accounts is a periodic summary of account activity with a start date and an end date.

Account activity includes receipts and payments to and from the scheme. These include contributions received, claims paid, and the premium amount transferred to the External Insurer.

Accounting Rules

The following are a few important accounting rules:

- Every financial transaction (receipt and payment) must be documented with a voucher and appended with supporting documents.
- Vouchers must contain the details of transaction: date, payee, amount, and purpose. There must be no overwriting, scribbling, or stains on the vouchers. The handwriting must be legible. In the case of any error in the entries, strikethrough the entry and sign it. Never tear out a voucher (vouchers are numbered); cancel it and save the hard copy.
- The bankbook must be reconciled with the passbook at least once a month to find and resolve any discrepancies between bank balance and accrued claim expenditure.
- The physical cash balance should be checked and reconciled with the cash book balance at the end of every day. This refers to any petty cash, cash withdrawn for claim payments, and operating expenses.
- Any discrepancies between the statement of accounts, cash in hand, bank passbook, receipts, and vouchers should be investigated and the investigation results communicated immediately to the CoCo.
- A statement of accounts should be prepared every month, summarizing receipts and payments, and a hard copy should be filed and submitted for the CoCo's perusal during its monthly meeting.

(iii) **Managing records:** The SC enters all the forms, receipts, and vouchers in the MIA-MIS. The hard copies are filed by category. Documents for the current cover period are turned over to the CC for its reference. Documents from previous cover periods are stored at the CoCo level. The hard copies are for reference. The same data can be obtained much more easily from MIA-MIS.

(iv) **MIA-MIS maintenance:** This is discussed in the MIA-MIS User Manual

The SC creates and stores a daily backup of MIA-MIS. This helps to retrieve information in case of system damage. The updated MIS is sent to the TA team fortnightly for scrutiny. This also adds a layer of backup security.

It is recommended that the SC be a part of MIA-MIS User Support Group to discuss problems and for peer-to-peer learning. TA support is available for troubleshooting any problems encountered in MIA-MIS operations.

(v) **Reporting scheme details to the CoCo:** The SC is the executive actor of the CoCo and functionally reports to the CoCo.

The SC assists in CoCo meetings by preparing monthly claims reports for discussion. The SC also prepares a statement of accounts and makes available the monthly receipts/vouchers and bank passbook for CoCo scrutiny.

SELF-TEST QUESTION

1. Why does the SC's job require technical skills in addition to people skills? If such skills are not available in any community member, what would you suggest?

Ombudsman

The module is intended to train designated Ombudsman of Community-Based Mutual Aid Scheme (CBHI) to assume the mediatory role within the scheme. The role is central to the scheme grievance redressal system.

The following topics are covered:

- role of Ombudsman within the governance structure;
- mediation process;
- grievance redressal according to the claim appeal process.

The Ombudsman is the mediator at the scheme level.

The Ombudsman acts as the final level of appeal in grievances related to health cover claims only.

Note: Mediation is always at the request of the claimant. The Ombudsman neither *suo moto* interferes in the claims process nor scrutinizes claims settled by the CC. The office of the Ombudsman provides a venue for grievance redressal if the claimant is dissatisfied with claim decisions by the CC and CoCo.

The Ombudsman is a respected member of the community who is also a scheme participant. The recommended qualifications are the following:

- Fluency in communicating in the local language — conversational, reading, and writing. Knowledge of local dialects is desirable.
- Familiarity with at least basic arithmetic — bills must be scrutinized to decide the claim amount payable.

The same qualifications apply to designated Ombudsman to replace the existing officeholders.

Each scheme has a sole Ombudsman who is responsible for health cover claims' grievance redressal on request.

The Ombudsman reports to the CoCo and the GAP.

Mediation

Mediation is a process for reaching an amicable solution facilitated by a third party. The solution must be agreeable to all the parties involved. The attempt is to end a disagreement or resolve a grievance without assigning blame to either party.

The Ombudsman's role is not to act as a presiding judge who hands down rulings. Rather it can be compared with the role of an elderly, well-respected, non-partisan family member who is approached to find solutions in case of differences between family members.

Responsibilities

(i) **Grievance redressal according to the claim appeal process:** The process described relates only to health cover claims.

A claimant follows the due process of claim submission — earliest intimation of the adverse event, completing the claim form, and appending supporting documents. The CC is responsible for claim decisions. The CC may accept, reject, or withhold the claim if proper documentation is lacking. Once the CC decides the claim, the SC enters the decision in the MIA-MIS and prepares the RR. The CC releases the claim amount for disbursement, and the claimant is reimbursed. If the claim is rejected or claim reimbursement amount is unsatisfactory, the claimant has the right to appeal the CC decision.

The CoCo is the first appellate level. The appeal is always made in writing. The SA may help the claimant draft the appeal.

All the claim-related documents are made available to the CoCo — claim form with supporting documents, COD, RR, and claim appeal.

The CoCo reviews the claim documents and may

- confirm the CC decision,
- may reject the claim even if it has been approved by the CC, and
- may increase the claim amount payable to the claimant.

The CoCo decision is entered in the MIA-MIS and is conveyed to the CC and claimant in writing.

In case of an increase in claim amount, the CC follows the claim payment process.

The CoCo decision is binding on the CC.

A claimant who is dissatisfied with the CoCo decision may appeal to the Ombudsman in writing. The appeal is submitted to the SA/CC and reaches the CoCo. The CoCo forwards the appeal and makes available all the claim documents to the Ombudsman.

The first appeal is always to the CoCo. The claimant cannot bypass the CoCo.

The Ombudsman carefully reads the claim documents and the decisions made by the CC and CoCo.

The Ombudsman convenes a meeting of the claimant, CC, and CoCo representatives. Each party is given an opportunity to explain the claim and the grievance or rationale of the decision. The Ombudsman hears the explanations and may make suggestions for reaching an amicable solution.

If discussions turn hostile or either party is adamant, the Ombudsman may then render a decision. This decision is binding on all.

The decision is always made in accordance with the benefits package and the scheme rules.

The decision is entered in MIA-MIS, and the CC is responsible for any further action required.

SELF-TEST QUESTION

1. Discuss the role of the ombudsman in grievance redressal according to the claim appeal process.

KEY TERMS

- **Contributory principle:** Everyone paying a contribution to participate in the scheme is called contributory principle.
- **Executive function:** It means carrying out the activities following rules and regulations.
- **Key actors:** It is the collective name for all the administrators of the scheme. Key actors are themselves members of the community where they then work.
- **Mediatory function:** It means investigating complaints and refereeing disputes.
- **Mutuality principle:** It means the scheme is owned by all participants. The enrolled participants decide on the rules by which the scheme should work.
- **Oversight function:** Having the responsibility to ensure that the rules of the scheme are applied equitably to all the participants is known as oversight function.
- **Subsidiarity principle:** It means that all decisions should be taken at the lowest level at which they can be taken, and only those decisions that cannot be taken at the lower level are passed on to a higher, subsidiary level of the community. This is the opposite of the top-down approach.

Bibliography

Dror, DM and Jambhekar, S (eds.) (2016) *Microinsurance Business Processes Handbook*. New Delhi: Social Re Consultancy (Pvt) Ltd and Micro Insurance Academy.

Dror, DM and Jambhekar, S (eds.) (2017) *Microinsurance Implementation — A Training Manual*. New Delhi: Social Re Consultancy (Pvt) Ltd and Micro Insurance Academy.

Selected Websites

The following website pertains to the content of this chapter:

- For more information on the structure and functioning of Mutual Aid Societies, go to http://wiki.p2pfoundation.net/Mutual_Aid_Societies.

Chapter 11

Enrollment into the Scheme

LEARNING OBJECTIVES

Upon completion of this chapter, the reader should be able to:

- Describe the actions that the CBHI scheme undertakes to enroll participants
- Understand and define the various technical terms used during various enrollment activities
- Explain the conditions that increase the propensity of the target population to sign up as participants
- Elaborate the emphasis on community rating and *en bloc* affiliation in the CBHI model

Abstract

Our objective is to describe the enrollment activities in community based health insurance (CBHI). The first part of the chapter describes the actions that the CBHI scheme undertakes to enroll participants. The second part deals with conditions that increase the will of the target population to enroll in the scheme. The emphasis on community rating and *en bloc* affiliation in the CBHI model are discussed. Trust in the scheme and an understanding of the functioning of the scheme are core factors which impact enrollment/renewal in the scheme.

Chapter Outline

Enrollment can have two distinct meanings as follows[1]:

- **Transitive meaning:** It describes the action of party A that influences party B (e.g., *In my role as the scheme activist, I enrolled Sarah Gandhi as a member in the Health & Happiness CBHI scheme*).
- **Intransitive meaning:** It describes a person's action (e.g., *I enrolled myself in the Health & Happiness CBHI scheme*).

This chapter deals with both meanings of enrollments. The first part describes the actions that the CBHI scheme undertakes to enroll participants. The second part deals with conditions that increase the will of the target population to enroll in the scheme.

Actions by the scheme to add new participants

When the awareness campaign and the Choosing Healthplans All Together (CHAT) process are concluded, the Scheme Activists (SAs) meet each household separately to effect the enrollment. The description of the specific actions of the SAs includes the following:

- *We visit 20 households and enroll at least 10 households every day.*
- *During the home visits, we try to convince the household head to enroll not just him/herself but all household members en bloc.*[2]
- *We help illiterate people fill the enrollment form.*
- *We verify the prospective participants sign (or thumb sign) to confirm that they accept the CBHI rules and the coverage terms.*
- *We collect the contribution and issue a receipt.*
- *We give each new member the Participant Kit (that contains policy documents).*

---

[1]An action verb that affects something or someone else (a direct object) is called a ***transitive verb***. An action verb with no direct object is called ***intransitive***. Some verbs, such as *arrive*, *go*, *lie*, *sneeze*, *sit*, and *die*, are always intransitive, as it is impossible to use them to describe affecting the action on someone else. Some verbs may be used both ways.

[2]*En bloc affiliation* means that all household members become insured at the same time.

- *We enter the data of all new enrollees into the MIA-MIS*[3] *on the day of enrollment.*
- *We attach the receipts to the enrollment forms, file them, and send the money to the Scheme Coordinator.*

The main technical terms that come up during these enrollment activities include the following:

Enrollment, renewal of coverage, expiration of coverage: These terms convey the business rule that enrollment is time bound. *Enrollment* of a participant for the first time requires registering the specific start and end dates. After the end date, the term *expiration of coverage* applies. An existing participant can extend coverage if this is done before the expiration of cover; this enrollment is called *renewal of coverage*.

Policy documents/participatory note: Every participant receives a printed document (the *participatory note*) that describes the terms of the benefits package, the start and end dates, the cost, and the contact details of key activists. We call this *participatory note* to distinguish it from the commercial term *policy document*. The participatory note is issued in the name of the household member who is affiliated with the grassroots group (e.g., self-help group (SHG) or common resource group (CRG)) and is listed as the *principal participant*. Other family members are registered as *dependents*. The participatory note is system generated.

Payment receipt: At the time of paying the contribution, each participant gets a receipt. There is only one receipt for the entire year because the CBHI collects the annual premium in full upfront. Usually, the amounts in question are very low, and staggered payments add administrative costs. The participant is supposed to keep the receipt for the entire coverage period. However, some people find it challenging to keep any paper for a long time and express concern that if they mislay the sole proof of payment, they could suffer an adverse consequence.

[3]MIA-MIS (Micro Insurance Academy-Management Information System) is a dedicated computerized information management application. See Chapter 13 for more details.

Community rating: The premium payable is the same for all the members of the household and the group, irrespective of age, gender, or pre-existing conditions. This pricing method is more equitable and is simpler to administer, considering that in the informal sector it is difficult to verify pre-existing conditions or even the exact age of many persons.

Enrollment period: For reasons of administrative convenience, coverage of all persons starts on one and the same date and is valid for one year. The enrollment period opens six weeks before the start date. During the enrollment period, SAs assist households in enrolling. Enrollments for coverage that starts later than the applicable date during the enrollment period require special permission from the scheme and attract different conditions.

Late joiner fee: Anyone who requests to join after the end of the enrollment period must agree to pay the full annual premium, even though claims are not receivable for costs incurred before the effective joining date. The premium for the period without coverage is called the *late joiner fee*. The late joiner fee is also applied when a principal participant wishes to include another dependent participant. The late joiner fee means merely that the contribution payable, i.e., the end date of the coverage and benefits applicable are the same as for the principal participant who enrolled during the enrollment period and whose coverage started from the start date.

SELF-TEST QUESTIONS

1. Describe the role of the SA in enrolling members to the CBHI scheme. What are the pros and cons of having a community member as the SA?
2. Insurance coverage for all members of a CBHI scheme starts on the same date with validity for one year. What solutions would you suggest for fine-tuning the premium to take into account the inclusion of newborns at mid-year (or reimbursement for those who die in mid-year)?

***En bloc* affiliation:** Households tend to enroll only part of the members of a household.[4] However, they cannot predict which household member

[4] See Chapter 6 of this book.

might incur a risk and how severe it might be. Therefore, the entire family runs the risk of catastrophic health expenditure when even a single household member is uninsured. This risk defeats the purpose of health microinsurance. Hence, during the enrollment period, the SA is trained to flag this risk with the view to encouraging households to enroll all members at once (called e*n bloc* enrollment).

SELF-TEST QUESTIONS

1. Define the term *community rating* and give its advantages.
2. What information does the *participatory note* provide? What is its equivalent in commercial insurance?
3. What is meant by *en bloc* affiliation and how does it benefit the members of the scheme?

Conditions that increase the propensity of the target population to sign up as participants

We recall that in our context, the voluntary enrollment occurs because people are unable to avail publicly financed coverage (this voluntary enrollment is called *substitutive coverage*). Health microinsurance schemes aim to achieve high penetration rates among their target groups. They can improve their pitch and success rate if they know the reasons that people invoke for enrolling (or for not enrolling). Testimonials about those reasons are often heard but rarely recorded during enrollment. However, it is possible to find some references to such testimonials in publications on this topic. We bring a few examples here:

- *I enroll because in our rural area we prefer management by the (name) non-governmental organization (NGO) with village-level responsibility of running the new health insurance scheme* (Gumber, 2002).
- *For me, a woman, the health insurance scheme makes it easier to get the healthcare I need. The government health insurance plan covers only hospitalizations* (Sarkar, 2007).
- *I joined because I am poor and need financial help when sick.*

- *As a woman heading a household, I enrolled to protect my family, like other women household heads in our village* (Sarker *et al.*, 2017).
- *I enrolled because when the SA assisted me in filling the form, it was so simple.*
- *I did not enroll in (in family-based health insurance scheme) because I heard that it is complicated to enroll and that I can get primary health care only in (name of facility) that is not good* (Thi Thuy Nga *et al.*, 2018).
- *I join because I could participate in selecting the benefits package and the price is affordable. After the discussion of the package [...], we all agreed* (Sarker *et al.*, 2017).
- *I joined so that my dependent son would be covered.*
- *I want to enroll, but I have no money now. Come back after the harvest season when I can pay.*
- *I did not enroll because I do not understand the benefits.*
- *It was a collective decision to enroll; there was a consensus on the package, and our opinions were considered* (Dror *et al.*, 2014).

SELF-TEST QUESTION

1. Describe the term *substitutive coverage* in the context of CBHI enrollment.

Understanding the motivations of people is essential for the community to succeed in enrolling many members in health microinsurance. Therefore, we bring a summary of recent publications on this topic.

One approach has been to attract a homogeneous target group. For instance, in India, four CBHI schemes enrolled only women who participated in an SHG: one scheme was exclusive for slum dwellers, one was only for farmers, two were for students, and some were only for socially backward groups (Bhageerathy *et al.*, 2017). A different approach has been to apply household-level membership, in which all household members are enrolled. The logic underlying this approach is that in the context of informality and poverty, households pool their resources in one kitty that must pay for all the care the household consumes. Such *en bloc* affiliation rule also reduces the risk of adverse selection by the CBHI (Likka *et al.*, 2018). There is empirical evidence (published in 2014; (Dror *et al.*, 2014)) that the most substantial effect on enrollments comes when the target population has an engaging social experience to reach a consensus on perceived priorities (more influential than price or package composition). Eight other studies (mentioned in a systematic review of the literature published 2018; Fadlallah *et al.*, 2018) confirm a higher likelihood to enroll in CBHI when community members felt a sense of solidarity (which was also mentioned in the 2014 study as "the intention that many members should benefit"). Six additional studies (cited in the 2018 paper) conclude that enrollments increase when benefits packages are tailored to the needs of the community (and enrollments decrease when packages are perceived as unsuitable).

SELF-TEST QUESTIONS

1. List the various methods discussed in the chapter to increase CBHI enrollment. Which of these do you find most effective? Why?
2. Past studies have shown that it is easier for the CBHI to target population to pay for insurance after the harvest period as then they have money to spare. However, the harvest season varies by location and crop. If you were to design a payment plan for a CBHI, how would you ensure that enrollment/renewal time takes into account the income fluctuations of the poor?

There is also empiric evidence that household size is positively associated with renewal decisions (Dror *et al.*, 2016). This finding supports our emphasis on *en bloc* affiliation. It also suggests that the initial restrictive pattern of prioritizing enrollment to insurance coverage within households (Panda, 2013) (i.e., the household head and the spouse come first, then the children of the household head, then other household members) at renewal households tend to increase membership if they had good experience with the insurance.

Trusting the process is influential as well. Trust includes the evaluation of scheme management (reinforced by positive claims experience) and the support of government to the CBHI (not necessarily financial support but regulatory recognition) (Bhageerathy, 2017; Likka *et al.*, 2018).

Finally, all the studies agree that when the target groups are familiar with how the scheme functions (through awareness and information campaigns on insurance concepts in general and CBHI schemes in particular), the enrollments increase.

KEY TERMS

- **Community rating:** It implies that individual members are not differentiated on the basis of individual risk factors (e.g., age, gender, or pre-existing conditions), and instead, each participant contributes the same amount to the scheme.
- ***En bloc* affiliation**: It means that all household members become insured at the same time.
- **Enrollment:** The process by which a member of the community makes an informed decision to participate in the CBHI by paying the contribution and agreeing to abide by all its rules and business processes is called enrollment.
- **Expiration of coverage:** After the end date of the policy, the term expiration of coverage applies. No benefits can be claimed after the expiration of coverage for events occurring after the end date.
- **Late joiner fee:** Anyone who requests to join after the end of the enrollment period must agree to pay the full annual premium, even though claims are not receivable for costs incurred before the effective joining date. The premium for the period without coverage is called the *late joiner fee*. The late joiner fee is also applied when a principal participant wishes to include another dependent participant.
- **MIA-MIS:** This is a database application that is designed and developed by the MIA for management of CBHI.
- **Participatory note:** A system-generated document issued in the name of the principal participant. There is one participatory note per risk category. This note is documentary evidence of enrollment. It gives the details of the household members covered by the CBHI.
- **Principal participant:** The member in whose name the participatory note is issued is known as principal participant.
- **Renewal of coverage:** An existing participant can extend coverage if this is done before the expiration of cover. This enrollment is called renewal of coverage.
- **Substitutive coverage:** Voluntary enrollment that occurs because people are unable to avail publicly financed coverage is called *substitutive coverage*.

Bibliography

Bhageerathy, R, Nair, S, and Bhaskaran, U (2017) A Systematic Review of Community-Based Health Insurance Programs in South Asia. *The International Journal of Health Planning and Management*, 32, e218–e231.

Dror, DM, Panda, P, May, C, Majumdar, A, and Koren, R (2014) One For All and All For One: Consensus-Building within Communities in Rural India on Their Health Microinsurance Package. *Risk Management and Healthcare Policy*, 147(7), 139–153, doi: 10.2147/RMHP.S66011.

Dror, DM, Hossain, SAS, Majumdar, A, Pérez Koehlmoos, TL, John, D, Panda, PK (2016) What Factors Affect Voluntary Uptake of Community-Based Health Insurance Schemes in Low- and Middle-Income Countries? A Systematic Review and meta-analysis. *PLoS ONE* 11(8): e0160479. doi:10.1371/ journal.pone.0160479.

Fadlallah, R, El-Jardali, F, Hemadi, N, Morsi, RZ, Abou Samra, CA, Ahmad, A, Arif, K, Hishi, L, Honein-Abou Haidar, G, and Akl, EA (2018) Barriers and Facilitators to Implementation, Uptake and Sustainability of Community-Based Health Insurance Schemes in Low- and Middle-income Countries: A Systematic Review. *International Journal for Equity in Health*, 17(1), 13.

Gumber, A (2002) *Health Insurance for the Informal Sector: Problems and Prospects* (p. 34). Available at https://www.researchgate.net/publication/237639773_Health_insurance_for_the_infor mal_sector_Problems_and_prospects (accessed 3 April 2019).

Likka, MH, Handalo, DM, Weldsilase, YA, and Sinkie, SO (2018) The Effect of Community-Based Health Insurance Schemes on Utilization of Healthcare Services in Low- and Middle-Income Countries. A Systematic Review Protocol of Quantitative Evidence. *JBI Database of Systematic Reviews and Implementation Reports*, 16(3), 635–651.

Sarkar, S (2007) Health Insurance for the Poor in Informal Sector. *Indus Journal of Management & Social Sciences*, 1(2), 129–146 (Fall 2007), pp. 138–139.

Sarker, AR, Sultana, M, Mahumud, RA, Ahmed, S, Islam, Z *et al.* (2017) Determinants of Enrollment of Informal Sector Workers in Cooperative-based Health Scheme in Bangladesh. *PLoS One*, 12(7), e0181706.

Thi Thuy Nga, N, FitzGerald, G, and Dunne, M (2018) Family-Based Health Insurance for Informal Sector Workers in Vietnam: Why Does Enrolment Remain Low? *Asia Pacific Journal of Public Health*, 30(8), 699–707.

Selected Websites

The following website pertain to the content of this chapter:

- For more information on factors influencing CBHI enrollment, go to https://www.microinsurancenetwork.org/groups/what-factors-affect-voluntary-uptake-community-based-health-insurance-schemes-low-and-middle.

Part 4

The Business Processes of Microinsurance

Chapter 12

The Business Processes of CBHI

> **LEARNING OBJECTIVES**
>
> Upon completion of this chapter, the reader should be able to:
>
> - Describe all the essential processes of CBHI, specifying the role of the key actors involved
> - Identify the threats to credibility faced by a CBHI
> - Explain the business rules for enrollment in CBHI
> - Explain the business rules for claims handling in CBHI
> - Understand the accounting business rules and fund management rules of CBHI

Abstract

Standardizing the business processes of a community-based health insurance (CBHI) enhances the efficiency of the scheme and thus encourages enrollment and future renewals. We discuss the standard CBHI processes for enrollment, claims decisions, claims payment, renewals, participatory note modifications, accounting, and fund management. The business rules define the periphery within which the scheme functions and clearly define the roles of the key actors of the scheme.

Chapter Outline

As there is no exchange of physical goods in a community-based health insurance (CBHI), the key differentiator for customers to evaluate the insurers are benefits package offerings and the quality of customer services. The business process is the backbone of reliable and excellent customer services.

This chapter deals with managing a CBHI scheme. Multiple key actors participate in performing a series of predictable repeated tasks to achieve a concrete goal (the *business process*). The business process is setting a standard pattern for all persons involved to follow, to ensure an optimal flow of information. Clarity about the business process is a necessary precondition for an identical application of the business rules to all persons in a similar situation. Clarity by all involved persons about the business process is a necessary precondition for an optimal flow of information and actions. The standard business process includes *business rules*, definition of *technical terms*, *flowcharts* describing the action, and *supporting forms* (for manual input of information) or screenshots (for automated input).

Different industries follow their dedicated business process. The CBHI business process is part of the category of *financial services*. The process includes assessing risks, pricing (rate making), issuing participatory notes (policies), renewing coverage, maintaining a roster of participants, claims handling, processing payments (collecting premiums and reimbursing claims), and keeping books of accounts. Even though we focus on health insurance, we do not deal with typical health business processes (which include medical assessments, drug approvals, electronic medical files, and managing the delivery of care).

Threats to credibility

The main reason for standardizing the business process is to pre-empt and reduce predictable and frequent problems of operating a management system that depends on inputs and actions by many stakeholders. The main threats are as follows:

- **Integration issues** — When it is necessary to integrate information from different sources of information, there is a risk of communication gaps and malfunctions. In the case of CBHI, the integration occurs between the participants' roster, information on the benefits package, and information on each claim submitted.
- **Bottlenecks** — A process can be slow, or even grind to a stop altogether, due to a human error or missing information.
- **Duplication of work and redundancy** — We want to reduce or avoid repeated or redundant data entry or decisions, to decrease errors and costs.
- **Lack of visibility** — The larger the number of steps required to complete a process, the more difficult it becomes to supervise the process for overall good performance. It also becomes challenging to oversee that each step delivers the expected outcomes promptly and accurately.

SELF-TEST QUESTIONS

1. Define the term *business process*. List the activities involved in the CBHI business process.
2. Discuss the main threats to credibility faced by a CBHI.

Business processes

The essential processes of CBHI are as follows:

I. ***Enrollment*** — Community members voluntarily join the scheme and undertake to abide by its rules.
II. ***Claims handling*** — Claim benefit availed by those eligible members of the scheme.
III. ***Policy modification*** — Modifications to existing policy document at the scheme and household level whenever applicable.
IV. ***Renewals*** — Re-enrollment into the scheme by the members for yet another policy period.

The key actors who maintain the records of participants, records of claims, and other scheme activities get support in completing their role by using the computerized management information system (Chapter 14) and by keeping robust bookkeeping.

The processes follow the business rules laid down and accepted by the governing assembly of the scheme, and the forms are standardized to fit in with its management information system.

Enrollment

Information on benefits package given in group settings

Before enrollment, each CBHI scheme conducts awareness and insurance education activities. Chapter 8 contains a detailed description of awareness campaigns and tools. The awareness campaign includes door-to-door visits and interactions in small groups to explain the benefits package and the processes and rules of the scheme. The main reason why we insist that enrollment should be an informed decision is that the processes and rules of the scheme cannot be modified on a case-by-case basis. Although the enrollment campaign takes place only during a few weeks each year, insurance education is a continuous effort and should continue throughout the policy period.

CBHI bears health risk in full without ceding any part to any external insurer. Technically, the scheme could explore the opportunity of top-up insurance of its outlier risks which would serve a similar purpose as reinsurance.

Business rules for enrollment in CBHI

(1) There is no age or gender restriction on enrollment.
(2) Every enrollee must submit a filled enrollment form.
(3) Every enrollee must sign (or thumb sign) the form, confirming acceptance of the governance rules of the CBHI and the terms and conditions of coverage.
(4) Every participant must pay the annual contribution in full before coverage starts.

(5) The scheme activist (SA) gives a receipt for every contribution collected.
(6) The benefits package (with its limitations and qualifications) remains valid for one year.
(7) The coverage ends on the same date for all participants.
(8) Every participating household should enroll all its household members together.
(9) Once a year, the community can decide to extend the validity of the benefits package or make changes to it.
(10) The SA is responsible for entering data of members and payments into the MIA-MIS.
(11) The SA is responsible for entering all data on the day when transactions occur.
(12) Every renewal must be completed before the end date of coverage to avoid a gap in the participant's protection.
(13) Every member who fulfills the enrollment rules receives the (system generated) participant kit, containing the participatory note, terms and conditions of the coverage, and a list of relevant contact persons.
(14) The *principal participant* is the household member who is affiliated with the self-help group (SHG) or common resource group (CRG).
(15) Other family participants are listed as *dependents.*
(16) Anyone who joins after the end of the enrollment period must pay the full annual contribution.
(17) Start date of coverage of late joiners is the effective day of payment, and the end date is the same as for the principal participant. The share of the contribution paid for the period when claims are not receivable is called *late joiner fee.*
(18) Additional member(s) of the household who join later than the principal participant must pay the late joiner fee.
(19) Once coverage takes effect, the contribution cannot be refunded.

Flowchart of the enrollment process

Information of health benefits package is given in group settings and during door-to-door visits, so that community members make an informed decision to join the scheme (Figure 12.1).

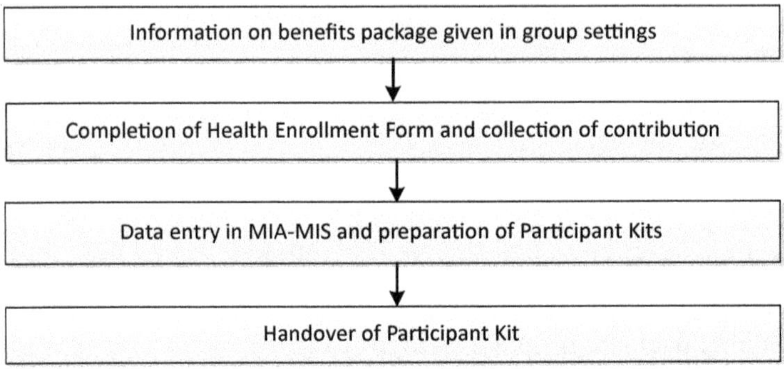

Figure 12.1 Enrollment Process

Enrollment Form (see Annex 1 provided in the supplementary material for this chapter): The *principal participant* (usually the woman who is a member of the SHG, even if she is not the head of the household) must fill and sign an enrollment form. All other household members who join the scheme are listed on the form as the *dependents*.

The SA may help to fill the enrollment form (Figures 12.2, 12.3, 12.4 and 12.5).

The information contained in the enrollment form is used to calculate the contribution due from that household.

The contribution must be paid in full for all the members enrolled in the scheme.

At the time of payment, the SA must issue a receipt to the person for the amount paid (see Annex 2 provided in the supplementary material for this chapter).

On the same day (or as soon as possible after that), cash must be deposited in the scheme bank account.

On the same day, the SC must enter the information recorded in the *enrollment form* and *money receipt* into the computerized MIA-MIS (Figures 12.6 and 12.7).

The SC generates the participatory note (see Annex 3 provided in the supplementary material for this chapter) for all enrollees who have paid the contribution in full.

The SC prepares the participant's kit containing the participatory note (that specifies the names of the enrolled members), an information sheet describing the benefits package applicable for the policy period, and contact information of the relevant SA.

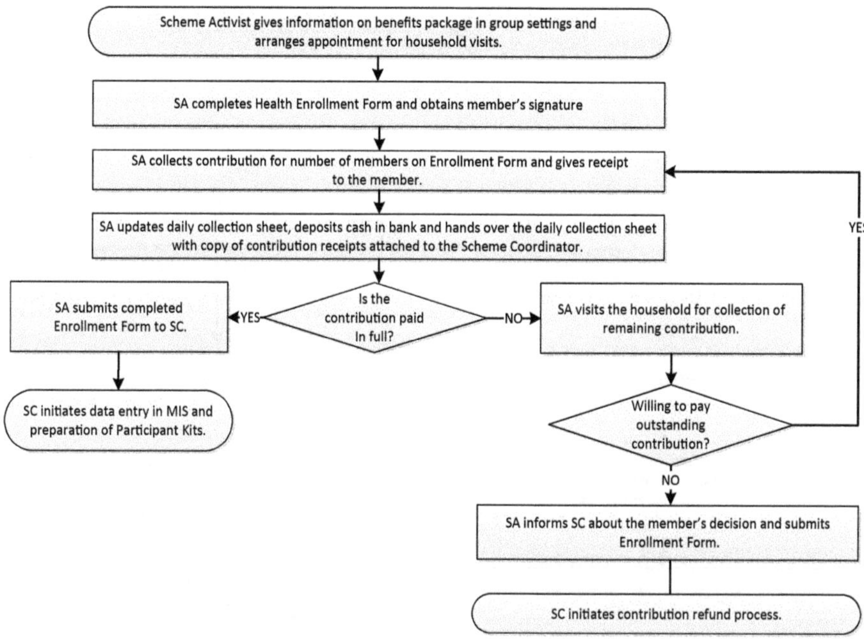

Figure 12.2 Completion of Health Enrollment Form and Collection of Contribution

The SA verifies the information on the participatory note and delivers the kits to the enrollee households within seven days of the cover start date. Any discrepancies are reported, and a new participatory note is generated after the changes are reflected in the system.

In rare cases of partially paid contributions, Participatory Notes are not generated and amount collected is refunded to the members. The member signs an acknowledgment for the money received and the transaction is closed in MIS.

Supporting forms and screenshots

See Annexes 1, 2, and 3 provided in the supplementary material for this chapter.

SELF-TEST QUESTIONS

1. What are the business rules for enrollment in CBHI? Identify the key elements that distinguish them from the business rules of traditional insurance.
2. Explain the enrollment process of CBHI with the help of a flowchart.
3. Discuss the roles of the SA and SC in the enrollment process.

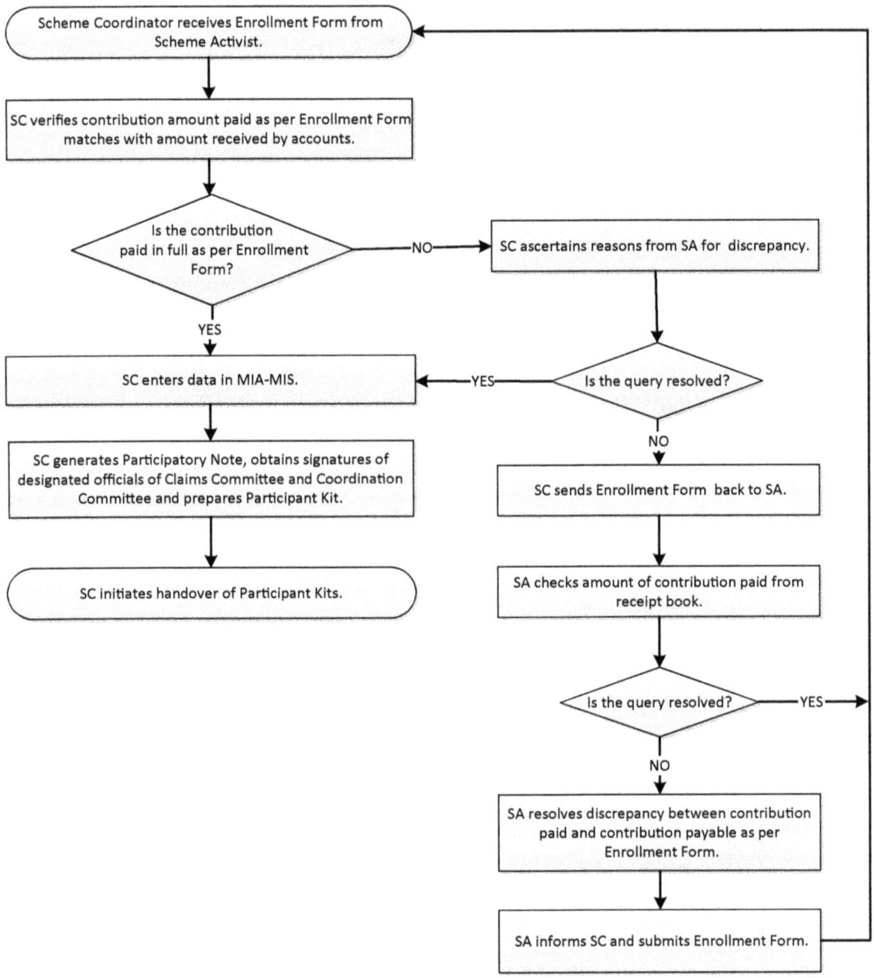

Figure 12.3 Data Entry and Preparation of Participant Kits

Claims Handling

Business rules for claims handling in CBHI

1. The claims handling process includes claim submission, claim decision, and claim payment (Figure 12.8).
2. Every principal participant can submit claims for reimbursement of costs that are included in the benefits package.

3. All claims must be submitted as soon as possible after the loss-generating event, and in any case no later than the end date of coverage.
4. All claims must be submitted with all the supporting documents.
5. Claims submitted without the supporting documents shall normally not be receivable.
6. The SA or the Claims Committee (CC) members may assist the participants in preparing the submission of claims (Figure 12.9).
7. The CC is the participant's point of contact for claims.
8. The CBHI, through the CC, decides on whether a claim is receivable in part or in full and on the maximum payable amount (Figure 12.10).
9. The CC obtains the maximum payable amount from the MIA-MIS, which calculates this amount taking into account the individual, event, and household cap that applies to each claim, by applying the rules stipulated in the benefits package.
10. The CC notes the authorized payment amount on the Claim Overview Document (COD) and Return Receipt (RR).
11. The full amount that the CC authorized is payable to the participant. No deduction is allowed (e.g., as commission or gratuity to intermediaries) (Figure 12.11).
12. The Coordination Committee (CoCo) is the adjudicator in matters related to claims.
13. A participant who has received less than the full amount mentioned in the RR may file a complaint with the CoCo whose responsibility is to ensure that the participant receives the full amount approved in respect of the claim(s) in question.
14. A claimant may file an appeal in case of disagreement over the reimbursement decision (Figure 12.12).
15. Claims are receivable for medical treatment outside the area of operations of the scheme.
16. Claims can be submitted on behalf of a deceased participant for medical care costs that arose until the person's death. Such claims shall be paid out to the principal participant or another name listed in the participatory note.
17. The CC cannot approve any *ex gratia* payments in case of adverse events.

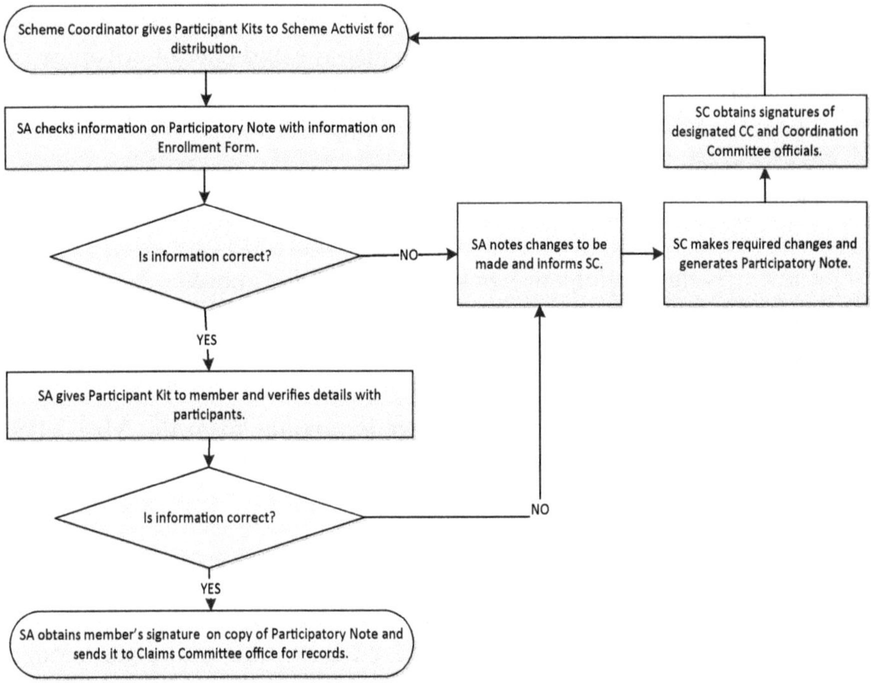

Figure 12.4 Handover of Participation Kits

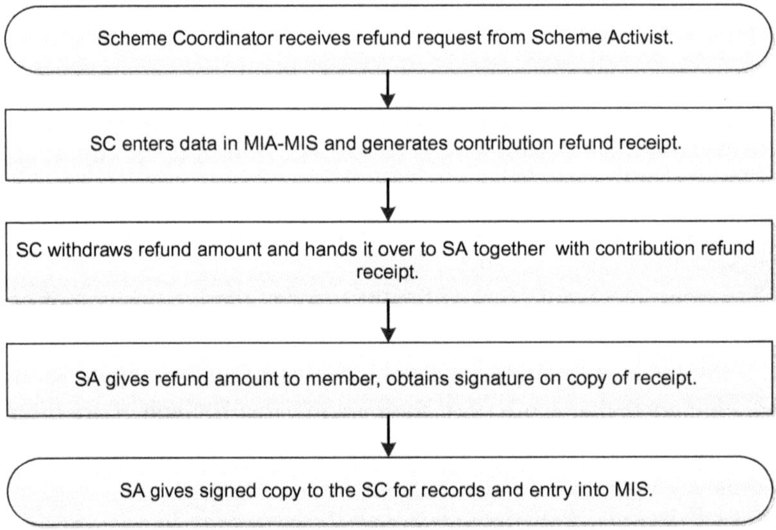

Figure 12.5 Refund of Contribution

Has the HH been enrolled before? If yes mention PHHID______________________________

Principal Participant					
Sl.no	First Name#	Middle name	Last Name	Sex	(1)Male (2) Female
1				Age	

Household Address and Other Details			
Address			
Village#		Name of SHG/group#	
PO		Block#	
District		State	
PIN Code			
Contact no.			

Dependents to be Insured					
Sl.no	First Name	Middle name	Last Name	Sex	Age
2					
3					
4					
5					
6					

Date Signature of PP

This field is mandatory. (For office use only. To be filled by the SA only)

Total Contribution Amount Payable				
Date	Money Receipt No.	Money Collected By	Total Money Received	Balance Amount if Any (H/L/A)

Figure 12.6 Screenshot of MIS Enrollment Window

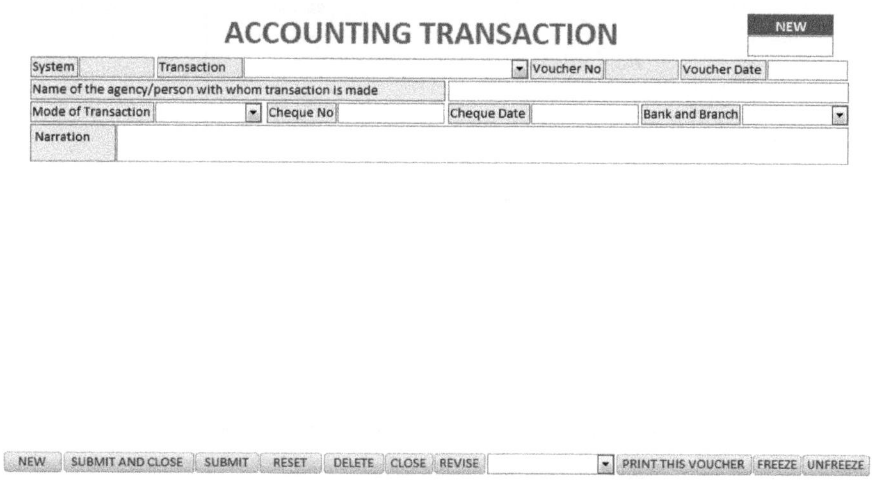

Figure 12.7 Screenshot of MIS Accounts Window

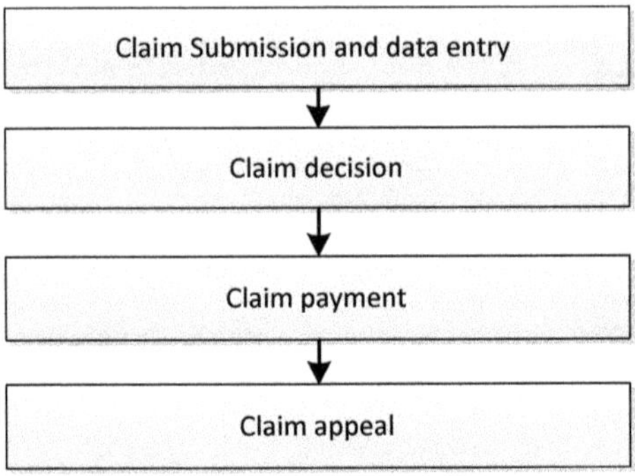

Figure 12.8 The Claims Process

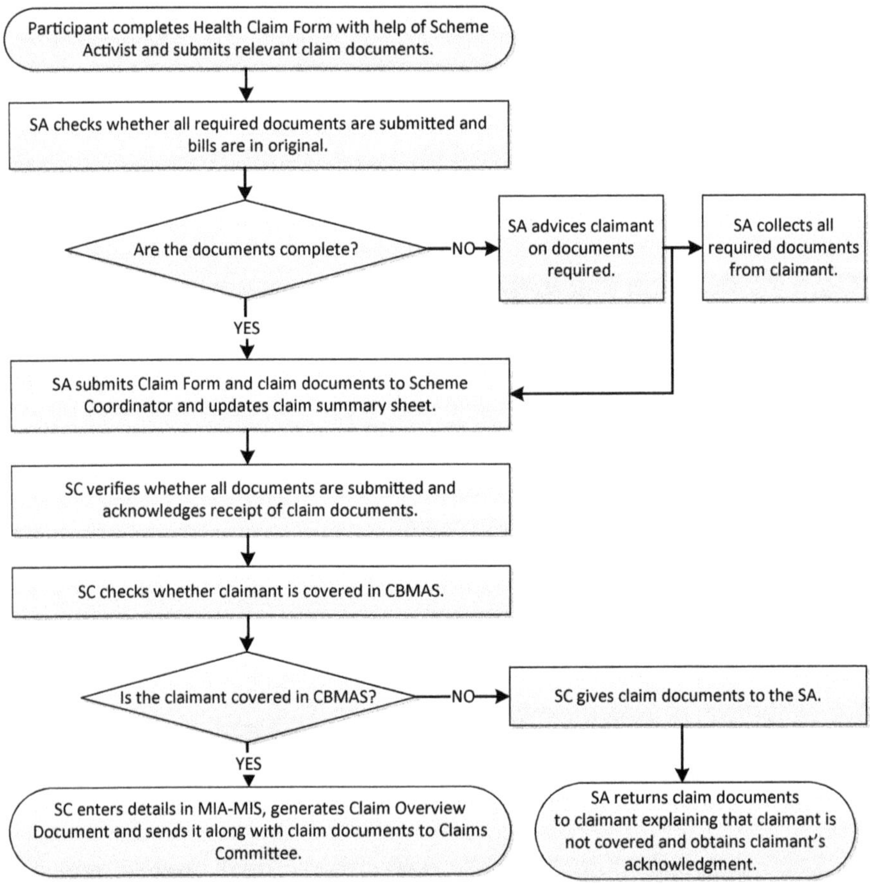

Figure 12.9 Health Claim Submission and Data Entry

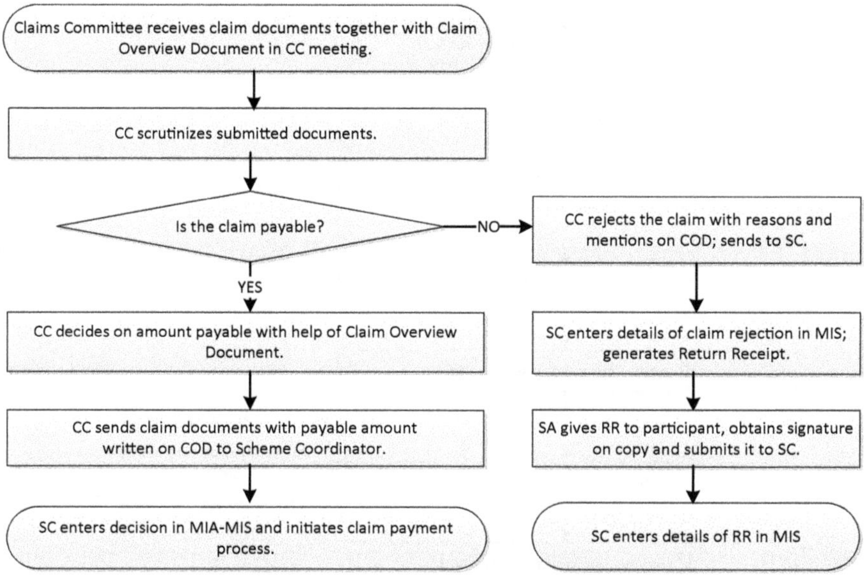

Figure 12.10 Health Claim Decision

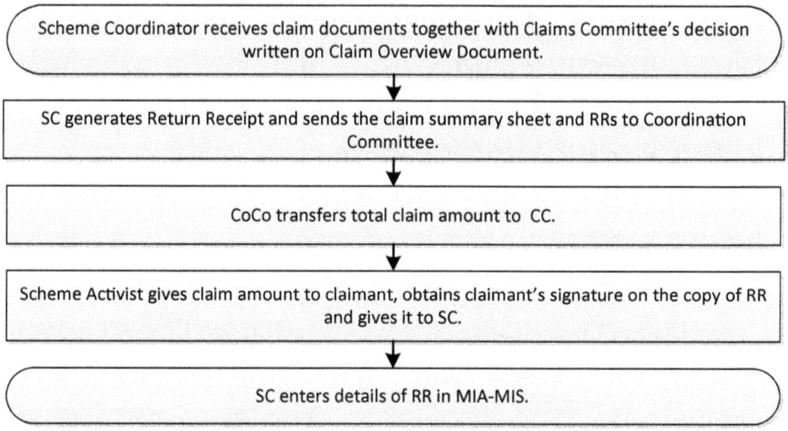

Figure 12.11 Health Claim Payment

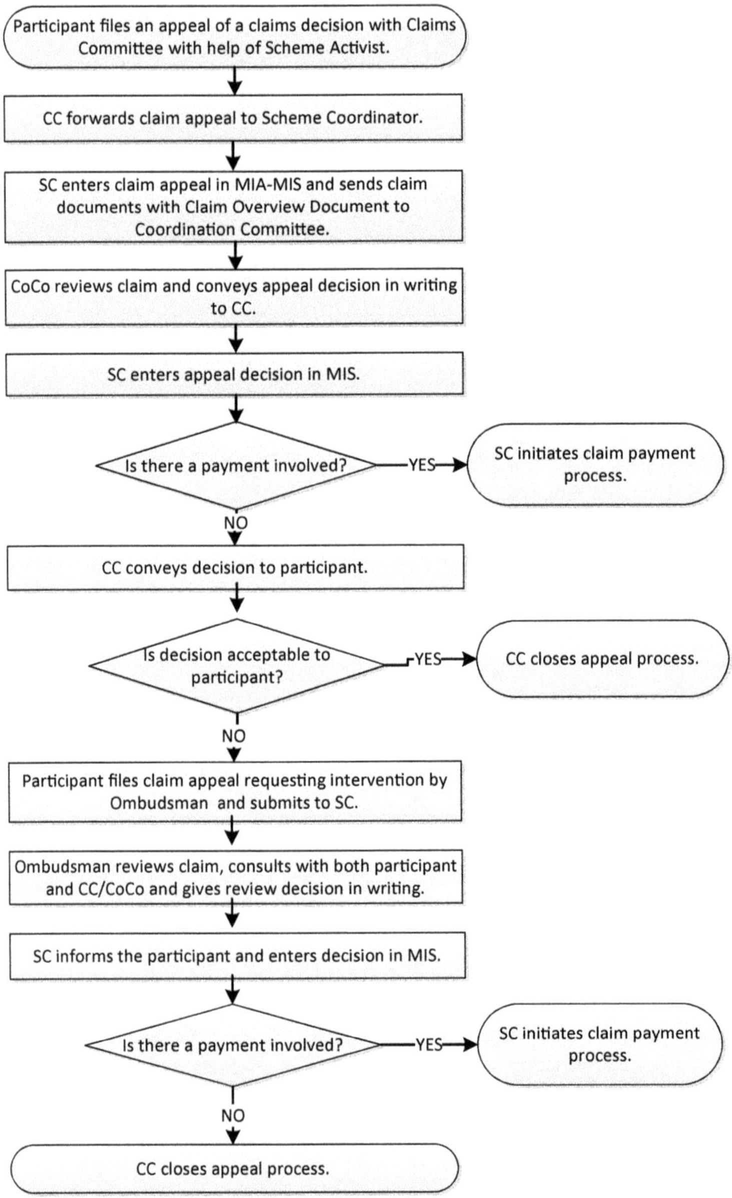

Figure 12.12 Claim Appeal

Flowcharts describing claims handling

The claim submission is the responsibility of the participant.

It is expected that the participant gives the earliest intimation of the occurrence of the adverse health event.

In any case, on discharge from the hospital, the participant has to fill in the Claim Form (see Annex 4 provided in the supplementary material for this chapter). She may take the help of the scheme functionary to fill in the details and get all the supporting documents in order. In case of hospitalization covered by the benefits package, the supporting documents are the discharge card issued by the treating hospital, photocopies of investigation reports, and all the bills in original. For other events, the supporting documents include notes by the treating physician, photocopies of investigation reports, and bill in original according to the type of claim raised.

The filled claim form with the supporting documents is submitted to the back office.

The details of the form and the documents are entered in the MIS, and a COD is generated (see Annex 5 provided in the supplementary material for this chapter).

The claim file is submitted to the CC for decision.

The COD gives information about claim history, caps, and thresholds applicable according to the benefits package (Figure 12.13). The CC decides on the claim amount payable.

On receiving the decision on claim and amount payable, the SC enters it in the MIS (Figure 12.14). An RR (see Annex 6 provided in the supplementary material for this chapter) is generated, and a check is issued for the same (Figure 12.15).

All claim payments are made by check.

The SA gives the claim amount to the claimant and obtains acknowledgment on the RR.

The RRs, along with other claim documents, are filed away in the office.

RR is generated even in case of rejected claims, and the decision is conveyed to the claimant.

The scheme provides for a grievance redressal mechanism for its participants.

System | Participatory Ref | Coverage Start Date | Coverage End Date

Benefit Package | Claim SI | Claim Ref | PHHID | Principal Participant

Patient's PUID | Patient's Name | Sex | Age

BILLS AND DOCUMENT

Sl no	Document Type	Date	Name of Issuing Agency	Nature of Issuing Agency	Type of Issuing Agency	Amount	Benefit

REMARKS

DETAILS OF HOSPITALISATION

Date From	Date To	Name of Hospital	Nature of Hospital

CLAIM CALCULATION

Benefit	Amount validated	Condition Parameters					Claim Already Decided (excluding this claim)		Amount Payable After Applying				
		Threshold	Co-pay	Event Cop	Annual Individual Cap	Annual Family Cap	Individual	Family	Threshold	Copay	Event Cap	Annual individual cap	Annual Family Cap
											Total		

Note: This document is generated from MIAMIS for use by Claims Committee only.

Figure 12.13 Claim Overview Document (COD)

(4) Claim Sharing Before Decision | (5) Claim Decision | (6) Claim Sharing After Decision | (7) Return Receipt

(1) Bills and Documents | (2) Hospitalisation Details | (3) Claim Overview Document

System L0A0011 | Claim Ref L0A0011002041 | Benefit Package SAN-H-1406005

Slno	Document Type	Date	Name of Issuing Agency	Nature of Issuing Agency	Type of Issuing Agency	Amount	Benefit
1	Bill	24-Aug-14	Bheri Hospital	Hospital	GOVT	3130	Hospitalisation
2	Transport Bill	24-Aug-14	Bheri Hospital	Hospital	GOVT	200	Transportation
3	Discharge Certi	24-Aug-14	Bheri Hospital	Hospital	GOVT		
4	Lab Test Report	24-Aug-14	Bheri Hospital	Hospital	GOVT		
					TOTAL	3330	

Record: 5 of 5 | No Filter | Search

Date of submission to IA	07-Oct-14	Claim Overview Document prepared by	LALSARI KHATR	Date submitted to CC	
Date of submission to IC	10-Oct-14	Date Claim Overview Document Prepared	12-Oct-14		12-Oct-14

Figure 12.14 Claim Data Entry

System Participatory Ref Benefit Package Claim SI Claim Ref

PHHID Principal Participant PUID Name Sex Age

DETAILS

Benefit	Amount approved	Amount available		Claim already approved		Amount payable after applying		Source of payment	
		Annual Individual cap	Annual family cap	Individual	Family	Annual Individual cap	Annual family cap	Payment from external underwriter	Payment from scheme
						Total			

Mode Of Payment	
Cheque No.	
Cheque Date	
Bank	

Signature of recipient	
Date	

For office only: If the claim is paid from any advance account then write below the details of person who took advance

Name Signature
Place Date

Figure 12.15 Return Receipt

An appellate system allows the claimant to submit a written complaint to the CoCo. The complaints usually refer to either a claim being dismissed or the claimant feels that the claim amount sanctioned is inadequate.

The CoCo peruses the claim documents and gives its decision, which is implemented by the Scheme Coordinator.

In case the claimant is not satisfied with the CoCo's decision, mediation is provided by the Ombudsman of the scheme on a written appeal by the claimant.

The decision of the Ombudsman is final and binding on the claimant and scheme functionaries.

Supporting forms and screenshots

See Annexes 4 and 5 provided in the supplementary material for this chapter.

SELF-TEST QUESTIONS

1. List the business rules to be followed for claims handling in CBHI.
2. Explain the health claim submission and data entry process of CBHI with the help of a flowchart. Discuss the role of the SA and SC in this process.
3. Explain the process by which health claims decisions are made. Would you suggest any changes to this process?
4. How can a participant file an appeal of a claims decision with the CC?
5. Once the CC approves the claim amount, how is the claim payment made to the claimant?

Participatory Note Modification

Business rules for claims handling in CBHI

1. The participatory note modification processes (Figures 12.16 and 12.17) comprise the following:
   - **Change in terms of the cover or benefits package:** The new benefits package and terms of the cover must be defined before the start of the coverage period. For this modification, the consent of the General Assembly is required, but changes are not recommended for an ongoing risk cover.

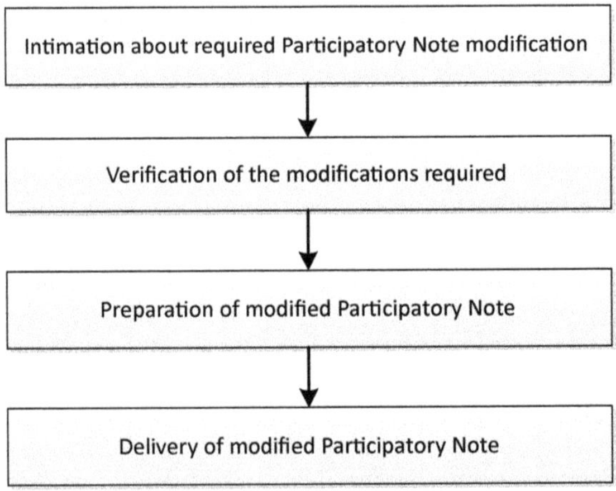

Figure 12.16 Health Participatory Note Modification Overview

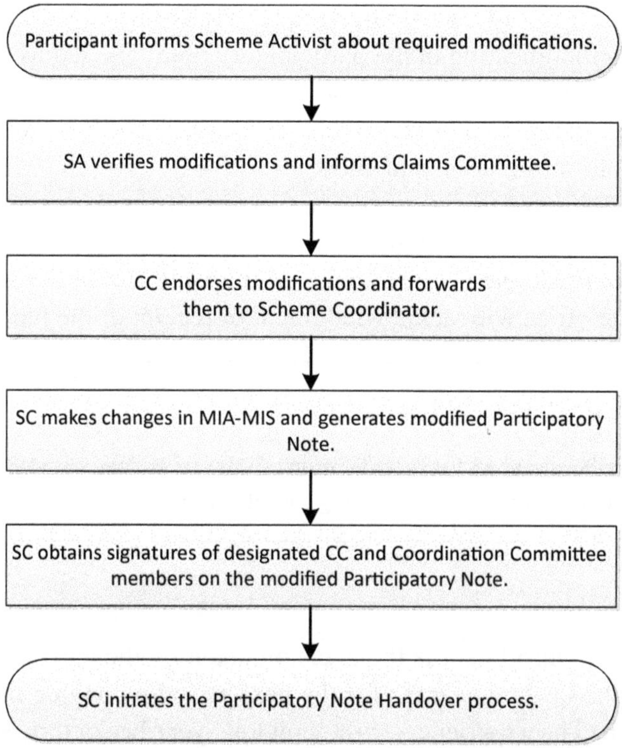

Figure 12.17 Health Participatory Note Modification Process

- **Change in any details of the individual household:** Any change in the details of the household must be reflected in the participatory note. This might also occur before cover starts. The participant must communicate changes, and those must be reflected in the MIS and all other records.

2. Reportable changes include a household change of address, addition or deletion from the family through birth, death, migration, and marriage.

Flowcharts describing participatory note modification

It is the participant's responsibility to inform about any changes in the household since enrollment. These could be a change of address and addition or deletion of a household member due to marriage, adoption, migration, or death.

The participant gives a written requisition describing the change and requesting a modification in the participatory note. The requisition is submitted to the SA or submitted in the scheme office.

The SA, being the closest to the participants, verifies the changes in the household information and endorses it.

The SC receives the confirmation from the SA and generates a modified participatory note from the MIS.

The modified note is given to the participant. The earlier note is submitted to the office with acknowledgment of receipt of the modified note.

SELF-TEST QUESTION

1. Describe the need for modifications to the participatory note. Explain the process followed for making modifications.

Renewals

Renewal or re-enrollment is the decision taken by the participant to continue with the health coverage for the next period by paying the requisite contribution. The experience of the previous year backs this decision.

High renewal rates are an indicator of a CBHI's success. The renewal process is, in principle, not different from the enrollment process.

The renewal process for existing participants unfolds in parallel to new participants' enrollment after an awareness campaign.

The benefits package may be modified and new benefits package is chosen by consensus (through CHAT) before the renewal period.

The process is like the enrollment process: filling the enrollment form, collecting the contribution, and handing over the participant kit.

A fresh participatory note is issued on renewal.

A list of existing participants from the MIS facilitates renewals.

Accounting and Fund Management

Business rules

1. Every scheme has an independent bank account with signatories to the account nominated from among the scheme functionaries.

2. All withdrawals are by check.
3. Every financial transaction (receipt and payment) must be documented with a voucher and supporting documents appended like the daily collection sheet (see Annex 7 provided in the supplementary material for this chapter).
4. All transactions are also entered in the accounts module of MIA-MIS.
5. Vouchers must contain the details of the transaction: date, payee, amount, and purpose.
6. The bank book should be reconciled with the passbook at least once a month.
7. The physical cash balance should be checked and reconciled with the cash book balance at the end of every day. Any discrepancies should be investigated, and the investigation results should be communicated immediately to the CoCo.
8. A statement of accounts should be prepared every month, summarizing receipts and payments, and a hard copy should be filed.

Fund management rules

9. If at the end of the year, the scheme has a surplus, the CoCo should evaluate the cash flow needs, and projected amount of money required every month to pay claims, and what amount could be considered for secure investments in callable debt. The CoCo should seek the advice of an external independent, responsible body on cash flow estimates and investment options.

SELF-TEST QUESTIONS

1. Describe the factors that influence the participants' decision to renew their enrollment.
2. Explain the accounting business rules and fund management rules of CBHI.
3. Briefly describe all the essential processes of CBHI. Do you feel these processes are transparent and can be followed by a community of mostly illiterate and innumerate persons?

KEY TERMS

- **Adjudicators:** The authority/authorized functionaries who decide on the claims submitted by the scheme participants are known as the adjudicators.
- **Annual family cap:** It is the maximum amount payable for the entire cover period to a group of participants that constitute one family.
- **Claim:** It is a requisition made by a participant for reimbursement of a loss incurred due to an adverse event covered by the benefits package.
- **Claimant:** The participant who submits the claim is the claimant.
- **CC (Claims Committee):** It is the executive body of community representatives that decides on the claims submitted by the participants.
- **CoCo (Coordination Committee):** The oversight body which manages the scheme on behalf of the scheme's owners–participants is called the CoCo.
- **Complaint:** It is a grievance by the claimant about claim settlement.
- **Contribution:** It is the amount payable to join the scheme and gain access to the benefits specified in the benefits package.
- **Cover end date:** It is the date on which the risk cover ceases to exist. No benefits can be claimed for events occurring after that date. All benefits claimed after the end date must be in respect of events that occurred before the end date.
- **Cover start date:** It is the date on which the risk cover begins.
- **Deduction:** Amount deducted from the total claim submitted under the benefits package is known as deduction.
- **Dependent:** It is the other household members enrolled in the scheme and are listed on the participatory note.
- **Enrollment:** The process by which a member of the community makes an informed decision to participate in the scheme by paying the contribution and agreeing to abide by all its rules and business processes is called enrollment.
- **Event:** It is an occurrence that, in context, generates losses to a participant.
- **Event cap:** The maximum amount payable per event is called event cap.
- ***Ex gratia* payment:** Any payment made to the claimant, not in keeping with the limitations and qualifications of the benefits package is *ex gratia* payment.
- **External Insurer:** Any commercial underwriter chosen by the community to cover certain risks is external insurer.
- **Family floater:** It is the package where at least one benefits type has an annual family cap.

(*Continued*)

- **Late joiner fee:** The share of the contribution paid for the period when claims are not receivable is called late joiner fee. A participant who decides to join the scheme after the policy start date has to pay the full contribution for the year, rather than the only partial contribution for the remaining policy period.
- **Limitations and qualifications:** These are descriptions of all the business rules that apply to a given benefit type.
- **Maximum payable amount:** It is the total amount payable as claims benefit to the claimant and is calculated according to the caps and thresholds defined by the benefits package.
- **MIA/MIS:** It is a database application, designed and developed by MIA, for management of CBHI.
- **Ombudsman:** An ombudsman is a respected member of the community, nominated by the General Assembly to act as the ultimate arbitration authority for settlement of disputes between a participant and the scheme.
- **Participant:** An enrolled member of the scheme is a participant.
- **Participatory note:** It is a system-generated document issued in the name of the principal participant and is a documentary evidence of enrollment. In health, it gives the details of the household members covered by the scheme.
- **Participatory note modification:** It is the process by which any changes are made in the details of the participatory note.
- **Participant kit:** It is a set of documents that are given to the participating household on enrollment. The kit includes the participatory note, list of important contacts within the scheme's governance structure, nearest healthcare providers, and claim forms.
- **Payment:** It is the disbursement of claim amount as decided upon by the CC.
- **Period of cover:** It is the duration from the start date to end date during which the risk cover is in force.
- **Principal participant:** The member in whose name the participatory note is issued is the principal participant.
- **Receivable claim:** Claims that are eligible for consideration based on the benefits package and time stipulation according to the scheme rules are called receivable claims.

(*Continued*)

(*Continued*)

- **Reinsurance:** The practice of an entity which underwrites risk to transfer portions of its risk portfolio to another entity to increase its capacity to meet huge risks is known as reinsurance.
- **Renewal:** A decision taken by the participant to remain a member of the scheme by paying the contribution for the next year is called renewal.
- **Submission of claim:** It is the process by which the claimant submits a filled claim form and supporting documents to an authorized scheme functionary.
- **Supporting documents:** It is the documents required to be submitted along with the claim form as documentary evidence of the occurrence and costs incurred for an adverse event covered by the benefits package.
- **Return Receipt:** It is an acknowledgment of receipt of claim amount signed by the claimant closing the claim transaction.

Annexes

The annexes for this chapter are available online as supplementary material at https://www.worldscientific.com/worldscibooks/10.1142/11505#t=suppl.

Bibliography

Dror, DM and Jambhekar, S (eds.) (2016) *Microinsurance Business Processes Handbook*. New Delhi: Social Re Consultancy (Pvt) Ltd and Micro Insurance Academy.

Dror, DM and Jambhekar, S (eds.) (2017) *Microinsurance Implementation — A Training Manual*. New Delhi: Social Re Consultancy (Pvt) Ltd and Micro Insurance Academy.

Chapter 13

Data in Microinsurance

LEARNING OBJECTIVES

Upon completion of this chapter, the reader should be able to:

- Understand the relevance of collecting, analyzing, and presenting data
- Describe the classification of data based on the source and nature of data
- Explain the available methods for data collection and their adaptability to various conditions
- Understand the ways of presenting findings through available data presentation methods — reports, tables, and graphs

Abstract

This chapter aims to introduce the relevance of data in establishing a microinsurance scheme. The success of a scheme rests in large part on the affordability of the benefits package (premium) and the relevance of the benefits it provides to the members. There are several combinations for such a solution, and identifying them requires using local, context-specific, and reliable data. Here we study the significance of data in microinsurance, the various types of data available, their sources, and methods to present the findings of the data analysis.

Chapter Outline

What are Data?

Today, one of the most recurring words in business and management parlance is *data*, describing both the facts and the applications using those facts. *Data* is the term used nowadays to describe numbers, characters, symbols, statistics, information, records, reports, photos, pictures, or material stored on cellular phones. Use of the term *data* refers to several distinct things, both mundane and exotic. Research data, administrative data, databases, databanks, and data packs are examples of a general descriptor (ordinary use); and terms like big data, data analytics, metadata are more mysterious descriptors. The term gained popularity with the advent of computer systems, and today the word conjures images of computers, advanced digital devices, large storages of archival material, and algorithms. The volume, variety, complexity, and the rapidity with which data can now be made available for analysis and decision-making are mind-boggling.

The word *data* originates from the Latin *datum*, which means, literally, "something given." Used in philosophy, *data* means things known or facts used as the basis of reasoning or calculation.[1] The early usage was restricted to research and allied fields. The dawn of the *digital era* (the period in human history characterized by the shift from an economy based on traditional manufacturing to information technology) popularized the term and has since been a predictable part of computer vocabulary. The term gained further acceptance since business entities treat information as an invaluable resource.

Data can be in the form of unprocessed, random facts that serve as the raw material for processing. We all gather such facts, knowingly or unknowingly, through our daily interactions. They could be a song we hear, a photo we watch, a report we read or publish, and conversations. Whatever we accumulate with our senses are raw facts. These facts are not always sorted and stored systematically; in fact, we forget many of them. They may or may not be relevant in their original form. Once we process data into something meaningful, we treat them as *information*.

---

[1] Available at https://www.merriam-webster.com/dictionary/data (accessed 12 February 2018).

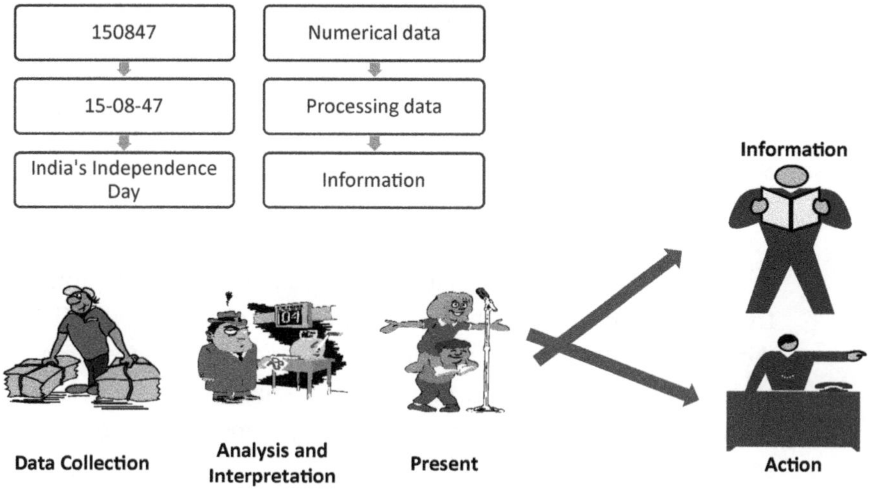

Figure 13.1 Data Tasks

Data and information are distinct, which however are frequently used interchangeably. So, what is the distinction between data and information? In culinary parlance, *data* are like raw vegetables and *information* is the dish prepared from those raw vegetables. The transformation from raw to edible comes about by cooking and adding condiments. Similarly, when data are collected, sorted, analyzed, and presented coherently, either as a narrative or as pictures, that information is used for triggering action (Figure 13.1).

Consider the following as an example of the difference between raw data and information.

Types of Data

Data[2] can be classified in the following ways:

1. Classification based on the sources of the data:
   (a) *Primary data* are collected from the source firsthand, for a purpose defined by the party that collects them. Primary data collection can be on a small or large scale. Blood testing is an example of a small-scale collection of primary data, performed specifically

[2]Data is plural of datum. But often data is used both as the singular and the plural.

to analyze one person's exposure to a specific illness at a specific period. An example of a large-scale firsthand primary data collection is the Population Census, conducted by the Government of India every 10 years.

(b) *Secondary data* are harvested (or sourced) from the party that has collected and processed them for a different purpose, i.e., secondhand use of a data set for purposes other than the original intent of the original collector of the data. Secondary data are sourced from published or unpublished sources. Examples of published data include data series of central, state, and local governments, technical and trade journals, books, magazines, newspaper reports, and publications by researchers. Unpublished sources of secondary data may include data sets that the original owner may wish to exploit for commercial purposes. Historical records of an organization are also secondary data.

2. Classification based on the nature of the data:

(a) *Quantitative data* can be expressed in numbers. Examples are age (25 years, 2 years 6 months), income (₹5,000 per day, ₹10,000 per month), education (completed 12 years of school), weight (75 kg), length (in centimeters, meters, kilometers), temperature (70 degrees Fahrenheit, 21.1 degrees Celsius), area (1 hectare, 10,000 square meters), and time (1 year, 52 weeks). There are many more quantitative categories (for volume, pressure, power, speed, and even for expressing the size of clothes or shoes).

(b) *Qualitative data* are descriptions which approximate or characterize but do not measure the attributes, characteristics, or properties of a thing or phenomenon. The descriptions can relate to physical attributes and properties, which cannot be expressed or defined in numbers. Examples are the perception of crop loss ("severe," "negligible"), attitude toward buying insurance ("smart move," "good value for money"), trust in certain processes, or loyalty between relatives. In statistics, qualitative data are often described as "categorical" data, meaning that they entail measurement of a specific category (hence, "categorical") expressed using natural spoken or written descriptive language rather than in numbers.

Often it can be difficult to distinguish between qualitative and quantitative data. Certain data may look quantitative but are qualitative. For example, age category mentioned in quantitative terms like "age between 5 years and 60 years" and income category (high-income, middle-income, low-income) when income is a range (between ₹500 per day to ₹15,000 per month) are other examples of category.

3. Classification of quantitative data as discrete or continuous
   (a) *Discrete data* describe the variables only with integer values, namely only in whole numbers. For example, a person can be hospitalized twice (2 times) or thrice (3 times) in a specific year, but never 2.7 times.
   (b) *Continuous data* can take any value, both whole numbers, and fractions. Examples include the time taken to reach the nearest hospital (1 hour 15 minutes or 1.25 hours). *It is a common practice to round off the continuous data to their nearest whole numbers.* For example, the very accurate description of a person's age could be 27 years 2 months 3 days 4 hours 5 seconds 6 milliseconds 8 nanoseconds 99 picoseconds and so on. However, for most purposes, 27 years would be sufficiently accurate.
   A different way to explain the distinction between discrete and continuous data is to say that we obtain discrete values by counting and continuous variables by measuring or calculating.
4. Classification based on the way data is ready to be searched/analyzed
   (a) *Structured data* are collected through "close-ended" questions, i.e., questions that allow the respondent to select a pre-defined response from multiple — but restricted — choices of answers. Example of a structured question:
   What type of facility did you visit when you were sick last time? (1) Public, (2) Private, (3) Charitable, (4) Others, (5) Can't say.
   (b) *Unstructured data* are collected through "open-ended" questions which allow the respondent to describe events, incidents, and perceptions. An example of an unstructured question:
   What was your experience during your most recent treatment at the hospital? (The interviewer should note verbatim the interviewee's evaluation.)
   The distinction between structured and unstructured data refers to the degree of organization of the information for ease of search operations. The search of structured data would be simple, by

using straightforward search algorithms. Searching unstructured data is time consuming and energy consuming because the lack of structure makes it necessary to compile the data first.

Example of an unstructured question: What types of facilities did you visit when you were sick last time? (*This is an open-ended question.*)

The answer could be: 3 months ago, I had severe diarrhea. My wife called the neighbors. They took me to the nearest hospital which is 5 kilometers from home. They refused to admit me, and told us, "No Doctor is available now, and so you should better go to town." They even arranged for transport by the ambulance. The ambulance took me to a nursing home in the town. Treatment was proper, but they charged us ₹10,000. (*The answer is noted verbatim.*)

The structured information was disguised in the above-mentioned response and includes the following details:

(1) The ailment for which hospitalization occurred: diarrhea;
(2) The distance of the nearest hospital: 5 kilometers;
(3) Reasons for refusal: non-availability of doctor;
(4) Mode of transportation: ambulance;
(5) Types of referral facility that treated: nursing home (private);
(6) Cost of treatment: ₹10,000;
(7) Perception about the quality of service: good;

5. Classification based on whether numbers can represent structured qualitative data.
   (a) *Ordinal* data describes data sets that can be put into a defined order within qualitative data. Example: income categories (rich, middle, and poor) can also be represented as rich = 3, middle income = 2, and poor = 1. It is also possible to establish an order such as rich > middle-income > poor.
   (b) *Nominal* data is the kind of data with which it is pointless to establish an order. Example: sex (male, female) can be codified as male = 0, female = 1. However, the female > male is incorrect (though the number of females > the number of males and can be expressed as quantitative data).

The data types can thus be summarized as

1. Primary or secondary
2. Quantitative or qualitative
3. Discrete or continuous
4. Structured or unstructured
5. Ordinal or nominal

SELF-TEST QUESTION

1. Differentiate between
   i. ordinal and nominal data;
   ii. structured and unstructured data;
   iii. discrete and continuous data;
   iv. data and information.

Methods of Data Collection

Data collection describes the sourcing of data by applying different methods. Data are collected to test hypotheses, evaluate outputs, and conduct research on operational, marketing, and other aspects of many fields. The Internet is nowadays the most important repository of (secondary) data in almost any domain, which makes it increasingly easy for anybody to collect vast amounts of information at any time, from (almost) any location in the world, within seconds. Mobile devices have revolutionized data collection by shifting record-keeping from paper documents to electronic files. The more convenient access to data raises the concern about "data integrity" (i.e., the assurance that the data are accurate and consistent over the entire life-cycle) to ensure accurate analysis with more and better data.

Some studies require the collection of primary data directly from the source. Other studies rely on secondary or historical data to perform the research objective. The purpose for which data are collected determines the most suitable method for data collection. The following are the most commonly used methods of data collection:

(1) collection of primary data;
(2) collection of administrative data;
(3) collection of baseline information;
(4) collection of secondary data.

Primary data collection methods

Users consider primary data as the most authentic and reliable, as they are collected firsthand for the defined purpose. The main advantage of collecting primary data is the ability to ensure focus and control of the process. The main downside is the cost and time required, which usually exceed other methods. The quality of the data depends on obtaining unbiased information, which is achievable when the questions are formulated with neutrality and clarity. Primary data collection is used extensively by researchers, academic institutes, governments, or private organizations.

The following types of data collected may determine the methods most suitable:

(a) quantitative;
(b) qualitative;
(c) mixed.

(i) Methods to collect quantitative data

Data that take a digital form can be measured or counted and are called quantitative data. Such data are processed in mathematical or statistical analysis and can also be presented graphically. The standard methods to obtain quantitative data include interviews, survey questionnaires, schedules, experiments/clinical trials, and observations.

I. **Interviews:** Interviews are direct exchanges between the interviewer and the respondent with the explicit permission of the respondent that the interviewer can record the information shared for use later. The loss of information is minimal in this two-way exchange. Interviews can be conducted face-to-face, as computer-mediated communication, or over the telephone. The response rate in personal interviewing is usually higher than when telecommunications are used. However, as computer-mediated techniques make it possible to reach respondents located remotely, and to cross-check responses, such interviews are used increasingly frequently. There are several structured techniques for such interviewing, e.g., Computer-Assisted Telephonic Interviews (CATI), Computer-Assisted Personal Interviewing (CAPI), Computer-Assisted Self Interviewing (CASI), and Computer-Assisted Web Interviewing (CAWI).

Quantitative interviewing consists of specific, "to the point" questions that leave less margin to nuance the replies compared to qualitative in-depth interviews.

II. **Survey questionnaires:** Commonly used for data collection, questionnaires consist of lists of questions that are structured to facilitate the replies of respondents. Questions can be close-ended (answers must be from listed responses), open-ended (answers can be in the form of free text), multiple choice (selecting one answer out of several confounding alternatives), dichotomous (yes/no), ranking, or ration scales. When designing a questionnaire, it is necessary to pay attention both to the subject matter of each question included and to its wording. The subject matter needs to inform the topic for which the questionnaire is conducted, and the wording should ensure that the respondent understands the meaning of the terms used (*cognition*). The quality of response depends on respondents' good comprehension of the questions asked. Therefore, in surveys, it is common to perform a *cognitive pre-test* to ensure that the respondents understand what the interviewer means when using the language of the questions, then reformulate ambiguous or confusing terms before fielding the survey to a large sample.

Questionnaires are either *administered* (by a surveyor, investigator, or interviewer) or *self-administered* (i.e., the respondents fill the answers themselves) or partially administered and partially self-driven. The questionnaires can also be mailed to the respondents or disseminated through the web. Using electronic media to get responses makes the data collection cheaper and enhances the outreach to scattered groups of people. Electronic administration of questionnaires is especially useful with literate respondents, but the response rate is lower than when an investigator administers data collection.

III. **Schedules:** Schedules are structured variants of questionnaires, in which the data collected is the response to a particular treatment, also known as a predefined "schedule." Scheduled studies usually require a controlled environment, e.g., clinical trials in the medical field. Sometimes researchers segregate the respondents in two groups to compare the results of an intervention in one group (labeled *treatment group*) to the results of no treatment or a placebo in an otherwise comparable group (labeled *control group*). In such an experiment, it is critical to maintain the same conditions for both groups throughout the experiment, with the view to avoid fact that unrecorded changes in the environment could affect the outcome. This technique is both labor intensive and time consuming and is therefore limited to experimental studies.

Schedules cannot be self-administered or mailed to respondents; they are always administered. Therefore, the quality of responses depends on the understanding and diligence of the numerator administering it.

The following are some examples:

(1) community schedule (general information on populations, occupations, ethnics, etc.) or household schedule (details of households, individuals, education, age, gender, income, etc.);
(2) opinion schedule (views or attitude of a different group of people regarding a specific issue);
(3) experiments/clinical trials.

IV. **Observation:** In this method, data collection is carried out like a clinical trial, but without segregating the population into groups. For example, 15 infected rats are kept in the observatory for a year to observe the changes in their conditions and activities before and after the introduction of certain medicines.

(ii) Methods to collect qualitative data

Qualitative data are data which quantitative data fail to answer as they are more subjective and explanatory. Collection of qualitative data revolves around the "why" and "how" questions. The answers are gathered mainly through interviews of respondents, individually or in groups. The interviews could be carried out as a one-time activity (to get clarity about a specific issue) or repeated (to measure changes over time).

Qualitative data provide depth to the study by assessing perceptions, emotions, feelings, motivation, and psychological and behavioral factors of the respondents. The flip side is that the subjective interpretation of insights cannot be generalized.

Unlike quantitative data collection methods, qualitative data collection methods are less stringent and more flexible, though often considered cost-intensive. As the information collected cannot easily be verified objectively, it is quite common to conduct group observations, focus group discussions (FGDs), in-depth interviews, and key informant interviews (KIIs).

These in-depth formal/informal conversations between interviewer and respondent(s) over a specific issue like an assessment of needs or planning any intervention, etc., are useful in collecting qualitative data. Responses are open ended. These are most suitable to gather individual opinions, feelings, and experiences about the topic of interest. Interviews help in studying divergence or outliers often not understood by quantitative studies.

The interviewer is physically present during interviews. However, such interviews can also be conducted telephonically or through another electronic medium, especially when the interviewer cannot visit the interviewee due to cost constraints or other limiting factors. Interviewers must be well trained to probe and extract the required information from the respondents and handle sensitive issues deftly during interviews.

In-depth interviews are usually conducted on a relatively smaller sample than quantitative studies. Overall, qualitative interviews have a higher response rate than self-administered options. However, such interviews are often costly and time consuming and could be prone to bias and misinterpretation.

The data are collected in the form of interview notes or as tape recordings or typed verbatim during the interview.

I. **Observation:** A commonly used method, it is a participatory technique wherein the researcher becomes a part of the research group or context and observes and collects data about the topic of interest (behavioral study, collating psychological differences, cause identification of disease patterns, etc.). It is a long-term intensive technique because it takes time for a researcher to become part of any study group. It is an unstructured data collection usually done in a free and flexible manner without any pre-defined schedule unlike in quantitative observations. The collected data may be in the form of field notes, sketches, audiotapes, photographs, or video recordings, etc.

This method is time consuming and uneconomical but provides an in-depth understanding of the subjects. Since the observer is involved with the group, it is prone to observer bias. The observer may also cause changes in group dynamics thus affecting the observations.

II. **Focus group discussions (FGDs):** This is a group activity to explore insights about the topic of group interest, i.e., group attitude, behavior, beliefs, or perceptions rather than individual as in individual interviews. Discussions are held in groups about pre-defined and specific topics of interest. Group settings help in validating responses and identifying outliers. Groups range from 6–12 people or depend on the capacity of the facilitator in handling large groups. Literacy is not a constraint to get a response.

FGDs are useful in exploring the research hypothesis.

These are time consuming, and views may be driven by most intellectual or outspoken individual/s. Discussions may lead to conflicting results or divergence from the topic of discussion.

(iii) Mixed methods to collect data

As the name suggests, this approach of data collection includes both quantitative and qualitative methods of data collection. Data gathered using this approach are usually most reliable, and results are considered more robust than either of the individual approaches. The quality of quantitative data can be improved using a qualitative approach to study outliers. Qualitative study before questionnaire design helps to avoid problems like question misinterpretation, non-response, developing sensitive questions, etc. Collecting data using this approach helps triangulation which increases the credibility of findings. This data collection approach is best suited for studying impact evaluation, improving research design, or developing and expanding intervention.

Administrative data collection methods

Administrative data is a specific form of collecting data primarily for administrative purposes (not research). Government departments and other organizations usually collect data to keep stock of the demographics, regulated transactions (e.g., land ownership), and record-keeping of licensed activities (e.g., the practice of medical or legal professions), as well as to keep track of the delivery of a service. In modern societies, administrative data collection is widespread and covers most domains of ordinary life (e.g., the government registers every birth and death in a country; companies keep records of all employees, shops keeping records of each accounting transactions, the authorities keep records of all vehicles in use, community health insurance schemes register every health claim).

Administrative data are called *administrative* to denote both the primary use and the origin of the right to collect such data.[3] The official source is the organizational unit responsible for implementing an administrative regulation (or group of regulations), for which the source of statistical data is the corresponding register of units or transactions.

Administrative data are captured through the Management Information System (MIS) of government departments and other organizations.

Baseline data collection methods

A variant of primary data collection is the exercise called baseline study (or simply baseline) which consists of recording and measuring conditions in a given location before launching an intervention project. Baseline studies also define the basis against which it would be possible to compare the effects or impact of the intervention by making comparisons at different points of time.[4] The most common method to collect baseline data is to conduct a household survey. Baseline studies often collect data on many aspects of the target population, including socioeconomic determinants, behavioral and educational aspects, occupational details, health-related issues, and social dynamics. Chapter 3 in this book describes the purpose of baseline studies (and provides examples of how to create the questionnaire).

Like with other forms of primary data collection, household surveys are costly and time consuming. Therefore, there is an ongoing effort to develop alternative methods that could yield equally good data faster and cheaper. Chapter 4 in this book provides a detailed explanation of a method to estimate context-specific morbidity and healthcare utilization.

---

[3]The Statistical Data and Metadata exchange (SDMX 2009).

[4]IFRC, Baseline Basics, 2013.

Similar efforts to develop alternatives to household surveys were motivated by the concern that the self-declared information might deliver less reliable information than analytical information. For example, declared willingness to pay for health insurance (collected as part of household surveys) have been less accurate than alternative methods of estimation. This is elaborated in Chapter 6 of this book.

Methods to collect secondary data

Data that the direct user did not collect, but harvested from other sources (be those individuals, private organizations or official governmental) are secondary data.

Secondary data are often collected from raw data sets (e.g., official statistics) or analytical material (such as published reports and studies). The primary sources of secondary data include government publications, publications of intergovernmental bodies, universities, other research bodies, private companies, foundations or non-profits organization, trade associations, and similar organizations. The data published by the World Bank, The Organization for Economic Co-operation and Development (OECD), the International Monetary Fund (IMF), and the United Nations Development Program are particularly reputed to publish many secondary data sets. In India, the most comprehensive source of secondary data is the Population Census conducted by the Government of India every 10 years.

A final reminder that the largest source of documents that are in the public domain is the Internet.

SELF-TEST QUESTIONS

1. You have been given the task to organize the collection of local healthcare data to make changes to the existing CBHI health package. Time and money are significant constraints for this task. Which method would you adopt and why?
2. What are the advantages of using mixed methods of collecting data?
3. Differentiate between schedules and questionnaires.
4. Describe some methods to collect qualitative data. How is such data verified?

Sources of Data

Depending on the objective, data can be obtained from a variety of sources, both primary and secondary.

Primary sources of data

Data obtained firsthand from the source is *primary data source*, e.g., recording the personal information, perceptions, opinions, and attitudes that respondents communicate directly to someone conducting a survey or an interview. Primary data can include firsthand testimony or direct evidence, photographs, transcripts, personal narratives, memoirs of people, and any other data collected firsthand in its original form. Primary data collection allows defining a specific purpose or focus.

Administrative data

The Statistical Data and Metadata Exchange (SDMX 2009) defines administrative sources as "data holding containing information collected and maintained to implement one or more administrative regulations." The primary purpose of collecting such data is not research or statistical analysis.

Government departments and other organizations usually collect administrative data for registration, transaction, and record-keeping, usually during the delivery of a service. For instance, the government registers every birth and death in the country. Companies keep records of all employees from the time they join the organization. Shops keep records of all accounting transactions. Also, community health insurance schemes register every member, contribution collected, and health claim submitted.

Administrative data originate from an official source.[5] The organizational unit responsible for implementing an administrative regulation (or group of regulations) is the authoritative source of statistical

[5]The Statistical Data and Metadata exchange (SDMX 2009).

data, found in its corresponding register of units or transactions.[6] The administrative records cover many domains of normal life, including income, expenditure, property, professional accreditation, or civil status. The following are examples of sources of administrative data which record details of individuals and organizations:

- tax data (personal income tax, value-added tax (VAT), corporate tax, goods and services tax (GST));
- social security data;
- health/education records;
- registration of businesses/property/vehicles;
- identity cards/passports/driving license/professional accreditation;
- electoral register;
- register of farms;
- building permits or ownership of the real estate;
- published business accounts;
- internal accounting data;
- data held by private businesses (credit agencies, telephone directories, retailers with store cards, etc.).

Secondary data

Data that the direct user did not collect but harvested from other sources (be those official governmental records or records owned by individuals or private organizations) are secondary data. Secondary data are often extracted from raw statistics or from published reports and studies that include analytical material.

The primary sources of secondary data include government publications and documents that are in the public domain, including publications of international bodies, universities and other research bodies, private companies, foundations or non-profit organizations, and trade associations. Data that are nowadays found in the public domain cover almost all

[6]OECD, IMF, ILO, Interstate Statistical Committee of the Commonwealth of Independent States, "Measuring the Non-Observed Economy: A Handbook," Second Draft, Annex B, Glossary, Paris, 2002.

disciplines including socioeconomic indicators; climate-related data and analysis; development indexes; information relating to agriculture, industry, medical, technology, innovation; as well as predictions of various phenomena.

The data published by the World Bank, the OECD, the IMF, and the United Nations Development Program are particularly reputed and cited secondary data sets.

In India, the broadest source of secondary data is the Population Census conducted by the Government of India every 10 years. It includes demographic and socioeconomic characteristics of every individual, e.g., gender, age, educational level, employment status, occupation, access to household amenities, involvement in economic and non-economic activities, and many other details. Census data are used by many organizations, with the view to defining marketing strategies or to conduct research requiring socioeconomic information, as well as analyses that require data by region or other relevant segmentations.

Presentation of Data: Reports, Tables, and Graphs

Once the data are collected and analyzed, the next step is to present the findings through data presentation methods.

What is data presentation?

Simply defined, data presentation is the "ways of illustrating statistical results."[7]

"Data presentation includes the description of the table contents, with their data breakdowns. It should also include summary information on units of measurement, the period covered, adjustments to data (e.g., seasonal adjustments for time series) and availability of textual analysis of current-period development with the dissemination of the data."[8]

---

[7] Glossary of Terms (2014) by The Association of Corporate Treasurers.

[8] Glossary of Statistical Terms (2007) by The Organisation for Economic Co-operation and Development.

Data presentation process

The process of data presentation involves a sequence of actions beginning with collating information, organizing this information, followed by summarizing the crucial points, and finally communicating the information.

- **Collating:** The first step is to gather, collect, and combine information at one place from all possible sources like survey results, reports, publications, literature reviews, and other primary and secondary sources.
- **Organizing:** The collated information is then arranged in a systematic and more structured way in various content formats (like newsletter, reports, article, academic papers, etc.), tabulation, graphs, charts, etc.
- **Summarizing:** This involves briefing and highlighting the most important delivery points.
- **Communicating:** The information is communicated to the end-user using graphs, charts, maps, and other methods so that it becomes easier to understand.

Data Presentation Types

There are various forms of presenting data depending on the type of data collected and users of such data. The popular forms of data presentation can be categorized as follows:

1. Textual
2. Tabular
    i. One variable
        - Frequency distribution
        - Relative frequency distribution
        - Cumulative frequency distribution
        - Stem and leaf plot

    ii. Multiple variables
        - Cross-tabulation
3. Graphs and charts
    i. Bar chart
    ii. Pie chart
    iii. Word cloud

iv. Dot plot
v. Box plot
vi. Histogram
vii. Ogive graph
viii. Scatterplot
ix. Line chart
x. Maps

4. Other data presentation forms
   i. Infographics
   ii. Pictograph
   iii. Report

Textual

Data is presented in the form of text that explains the key facts and figures. This way of presentation restricts us to some extent because while working with big sets of information, this method may lead to ambiguity. For instance, textualizing the average age of the head of the household of microinsurance schemes in Bihar (India) could be possible, but stating the average age of the head of the household of each village where microinsurance schemes are running may not be a good idea.

Tabular

Tabular data presentation expresses the data in several rows and columns where the first row/column usually represents the names of fields explaining the underlying data. This is the most frequently used method of conveying information. Tabular data presentation makes large sets of data easy to interpret. Using this method of presentation one can compare two or more group sets effectively. Textual descriptions accompanied with data tables provide information clarity and increase the understandability. Most data analysis software tools provide a table as an output of big sets of data.

Frequency distribution (for one-variable data)

Data can be presented in a tabular form showing the frequency (or several occurrences) of items in each of several non-overlapping group classes.

This allows for quick summarization of data and is an easy way to interpret the occurrence of each group.

In Table 13.1, we have data on the education status of members enrolled in a health insurance scheme supported by MIA, operational in Pratapgarh district in Uttar Pradesh (India) from 2011 to 2013.

In Table 13.2, we can see the frequency distribution of the education status of the members of the scheme.

In this table, the frequency distribution shows that most of the members have never been to school or are illiterate.

Relative frequency distribution (for one-variable data)

In large data sets, the frequency distribution alone may not suffice for understanding the data, and therefore, it is useful to calculate the relative frequency distribution as well. The relative frequency distribution is a

Table 13.1 Education Status of Members Enrolled in a Health Insurance Scheme

PUID	First Name	Middle Name	Last Name	Sex	Age In Years	Age In Months	Education
L0A00080000101	Yasoda		Devi	FEMALE	50		16=Never been to school, illiterate
L0A00080000103	Niraj		Pal	MALE	14		09=CLASS IX
L0A00080000104	Satyam		Pal	MALE	18		03=CLASS III
L0A00080000105	Niraj		Pal	MALE	15		11=Class-XI
L0A00080000201	Ramkali		Pal	FEMALE	60		17=Never been to school, literate
L0A00080000203	Sachin		Pal	MALE	15		09=CLASS-IX
L0A00080000204	Sachin		Pal	MALE	16		11=Class-XI
L0A00080000301	Pyari		Devi	FEMALE	45		16: Never been to school, illiterate
L0A00080000302	Arti		Devi	FEMALE	15		10=CLASS X
L0A00080000501	Lalita		Devi	FEMALE	55		16=Never been to school, illiterate
L0A00080000503	Raja		Pal	MALE	58		05=CLASS V
...	...	...	...	...	...	...	...
...	...	...	...	...	...	...	...

Table 13.2 Tabular Data Showing the Frequency Distribution of the Education Status of Members of the Scheme

	Variable	Frequency Distribution	Relative Frequency Distribution
Codes	Education	Frequency	Percentage
01	CLASS I	98	5.3%
02	CLASS II	45	2.4%
03	CLASS III	43	2.3%
04	CLASS IV	46	2.5%
05	CLASS V	195	10.6%
06	CLASS VI	56	3.0%
07	CLASS VII	56	3.0%
08	CLASS VIII	177	9.6%
09	CLASS IX	68	3.7%
10	CLASS X	147	8.0%
11	Class-XI	38	2.1%
12	Class-XII	72	3.9%
13	DIPLOMA CERT	22	1.2%
14	GRADUATE	56	3.0%
15	POST GRADUAT	16	0.9%
16	Never been to school, illiterate	391	21.3%
17	Never been to school, literate	214	11.6%
18	PRE SCHOOLCHILD	100	5.4%

tabular summary of data showing the specific frequency as a percentage of total frequency for all group classes.

In Table 13.2, we can see that 11.6% of enrolled members are literate but have never been to a school, 5.4% fall in the category of pre-school child, and only 3% are graduates.

Cumulative frequency distribution (for one-variable data)

Sometimes we are interested in knowing the frequency of data corresponding to a particular class and classes falling above (or below) it.

Table 13.3 Cumulative Frequency of Claims Amount Reimbursed for a Health Scheme in Uttar Pradesh

	Frequency Distribution	Cumulative Frequency Distribution
Claim Reimbursed	Frequency	Cumulative Frequency
0-1000	6	6
1000-2000	5	11
2000-3000	55	66
3000-4000	18	84
4000-5000	14	98
5000-6000	44	142
6000-7000	5	147
>=7000	7	154

The cumulative frequency is calculated to give us this information, and it is calculated using a frequency distribution table.

Table 13.3 gives the cumulative frequency distribution of claims reimbursed for a health scheme. For each class, the cumulative frequency gives the number of claims which were reimbursed for an amount less than or equal to that class.

The frequency of claims in the range ₹2,000–3,000 is 55. The corresponding cumulative frequency for this class is 66. In other words, there exist 66 records of reimbursed claims, each over an amount less than or equal to the specified range.

Stem and leaf plot (for one-variable data)

This is a tabular data presentation method which helps in visualizing the shape of the distribution. In a stem and leaf plot, each data value is split into a "stem" (the first digit or digits) and a "leaf" (usually the last digit).

In Table 13.4, we present the turnaround time (TAT) of 39 claims made by members of a CBMAS health scheme in Uttar Pradesh, India for the year 2013.

The raw data (in days) is 5, 6, 7, 7, 7, 7, 7, 7, 8, 9, 9, 9, 10, 11, 12, 12, 14, 14, 14, 15, 16, 16, 16, 17, 18, 18, 18, 20, 22, 22, 26, 27, 29, 29, 32, 35, 38, 39, 39.

Table 13.4 Stem and Leaf Plot

TAT of 39 claims of CBMAS Health for the year 2013															
0	5	6	7	7	7	7	7	7	8	9	9	9			
1	0	1	2	2	4	4	4	5	6	6	6	7	8	8	8
2	0	2	2	6	7	9	9								
3	2	5	8	9	9										
Stem	Leaf														

The stem and leaf plot for this data (Table 13.4) shows that most of the claims were settled between 10 and 19 days. The minimum time to settle a claim was 5 days, whereas some claims took a maximum of 39 days to get settled.

Cross-tabulation (for multiple-variable data)

Cross-tabulation is a method for presenting data which have two or more mutually exclusive variables. This helps in depicting the relation between variables which may not be otherwise readily apparent.

Data can be presented using cross-tabulation include genderwise average scores of students of a class in each subject, age and genderwise population of a village, and countrywise data of average income, literacy, and longevity.

In Table 13.5, we show the genderwise claim count and the average claim amount reimbursed for 3 years for a CBMAS health scheme in Uttar Pradesh (India).

Graphs and Charts

Various graphical presentation techniques, such as graphs and charts, offer an excellent alternative to the tabular presentation of qualitative or quantitative information. Graphs and charts are effective ways of representing numerical data using points, lines, areas, and other geometric figures and symbols. Graphic presentation of data provides clear, more accessible, and quicker visual insight about the data than dipping down into numbers. Using this technique, one can visualize trends in data and easily compare different groups.

Table 13.5 Genderwise Claim Count and Average Claim Amount Reimbursed for a CBMAS Health Scheme

	Claim Count	Average of Amount Reimbursed	Claim Count	Average of Amount Reimbursed	Total Claim Count	Total Average of Amount Reimbursed
Year	FEMALE		MALE		TOTAL	
2011	27	3767.04	20	2459.30	47	3210.55
2012	25	3011.08	45	2218.44	70	2501.53
2013	7	2973.29	30	2794.07	37	2827.97
Total	59	3352.54	95	2450.93	154	2796.35

The most used graphs and chart forms are bar chart, pie chart, world cloud, dot plot, box plot, histogram, ogive, scatter diagram, and line chart.

Bar Chart: In a bar chart, categorical data are presented in the form of rectangular bars, where each bar represents a group category, and the length of each bar represents the corresponding quantity. The bars can be plotted vertically or horizontally.

The data given in Table 13.2 can be represented as a bar chart as in Figure 13.2.

Figure 13.2 shows that out of the total enrolled members, a majority has attained only primary education. It also shows a downward trend in education status after the primary level.

Pie Chart: A pie chart is a circular graphic presentation of data. The chart is divided into slices, each slice denotes a group category, and the size of the slice is proportional to the quantity it represents.

The pie chart in Figure 13.3 shows the data listed in Table 13.2 for the education status of enrolled members.

Word Cloud: Word cloud is a potent technique used to highlight popular words based on their frequency of use in a source of textual data. It is an informative image comprising words used in a text, and the size of each word indicates its frequency or importance in the text. This technique can be applied to the information collected through various qualitative interviews.

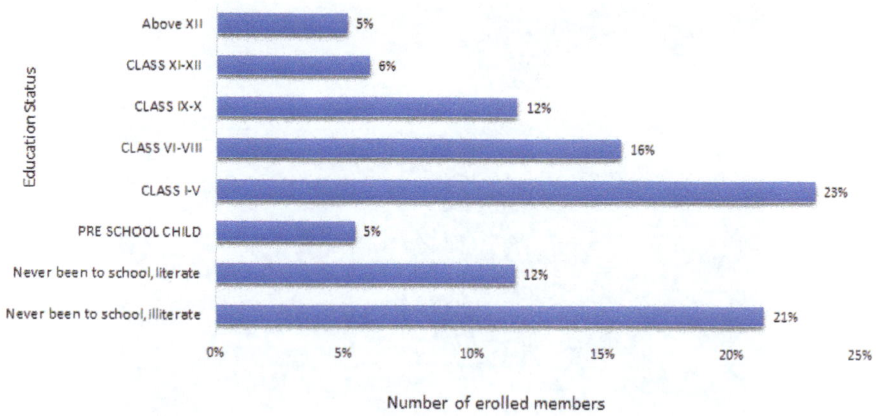

Figure 13.2 Bar Chart of Education Status of Enrolled Members

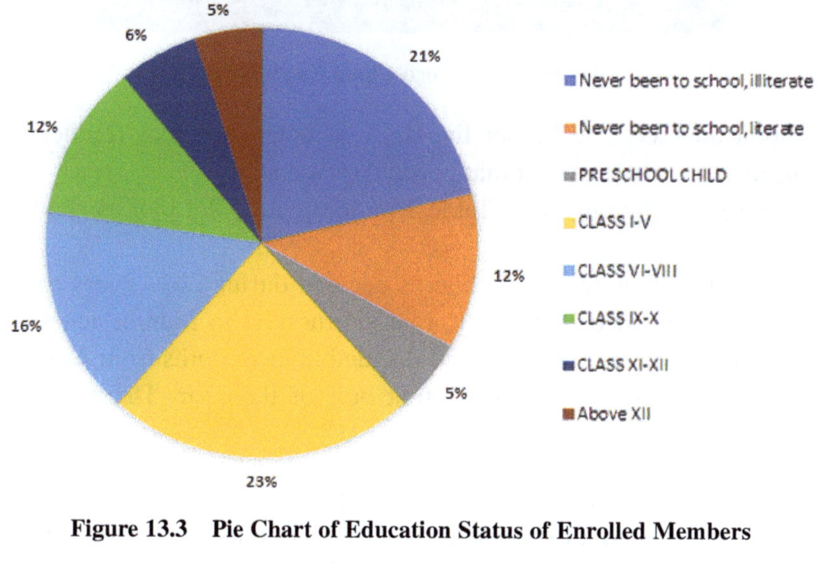

Figure 13.3 Pie Chart of Education Status of Enrolled Members

In Figure 13.4, we have a word cloud which has been created using a given text on the topic "data." We can see that the most frequently used words in the text were "information," "organization," and "collected."

Dot Plot: The dot plot is a graphical way of data presentation where each dot represents a data point, and the count is shown in each category as dots

Figure 13.4 Word Cloud Example[9]

one upon another. The higher the stack of dots, the more frequent the occurrence of data points in that particular category.

We use the data given in Table 13.6 to create a dot plot as shown in Figure 13.5.

The dot plot shows the 34 claims decided during 2013 every month, i.e., 4 claims decided in January, 1 in February, 3 in March, and so on. Most of the claims are received and decided in the months from August to December, in comparison to the first half of the year. There were no claims decided during April and September.

Box Plot: A box plot is a method for graphically representing statistical data on a plot through their quartiles. A rectangle is drawn from the first quartile to the third quartile, and a vertical line drawn inside indicates the median value. The lower and upper quartiles are shown as horizontal lines on either side of the rectangle.

In Table 13.7, we have the TAT of claims settlement for a CBMAS health scheme in Uttar Pradesh (India) from 2011 to 2013.

[9]Word cloud created through https://www.wordclouds.com/.

Table 13.6 Claims Amount Reimbursed for a Health Scheme in Uttar Pradesh for Claim Decisions for the Year 2013

Scheme Year	Claim Amount Reimbursed	Date Decision
2012-13	2054	17-Jan-13
2012-13	4100	17-Jan-13
2012-13	4500	17-Jan-13
2012-13	4500	19-Jan-13
2012-13	4300	19-Feb-13
2012-13	4500	29-Mar-13
2012-13	4400	29-Mar-13
2012-13	1100	29-Mar-13
2012-13	1100	20-May-13
2012-13	1100	20-May-13
2013-14	3032	20-Jun-13
2013-14	4100	20-Jun-13
...	...	...
...	...	...
...	...	...
...	...	...
...	...	...

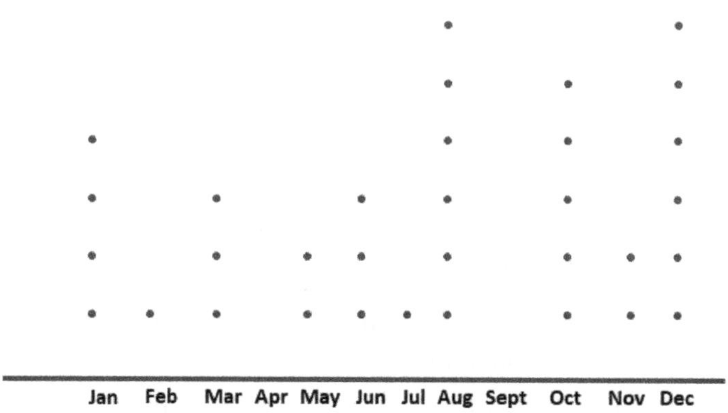

Figure 13.5 Dot Plot of Monthly Claim Decisions (2013)

Table 13.7 TAT of Claims Settlement for the Years 2011–2013

Turn Around Time		
2011	2012	2013
14	17	18
17	17	9
3	17	26
10	22	14
9	17	29
7	22	16
25	19	14
6	19	7
5	19	20
31	19	7
31	22	17
4	14	14
4	35	22
20	11	38
107	5	10
...	...	...
...	...	...
...	...	...

In Figure 13.6, the three plots suggest that the TAT has improved over the three years. In the third year, TAT has reduced considerably.

Histogram: The histogram is a graphical representation of frequency distribution using vertical rectangular bars. The width of each bar represents a class interval, and the length represents frequency.

In Table 13.8, we have the claims reimbursement amount of a health CBMAS in Uttar Pradesh (India).

In Figure 13.7, we plot a histogram showing the frequency of the claims reimbursement amount.

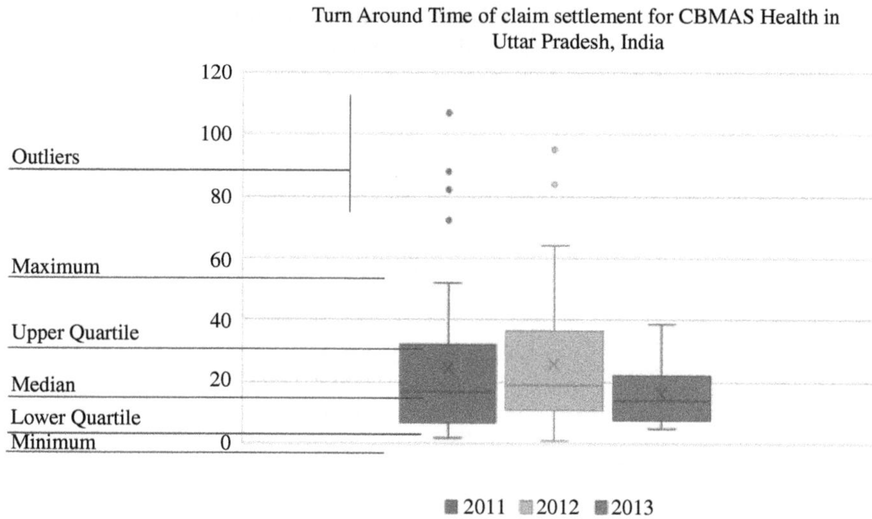

Figure 13.6 Box Plot of Claims TAT (2011–2013)

Ogive Graph: This graph represents the cumulative frequencies for the classes in a frequency distribution, and it is a continuous-frequency curve. This curve can be presented as "more than" and "less than" the cumulative frequency curve, where less than ogive shows accumulative frequencies, and more than ogive shows reducing frequencies.

We can represent the data of Table 13.8 in an Ogive graph (Figure 13.8).

Scatterplot: Scatterplot is a graphical technique used to plot two or more variables along the horizontal and vertical axis to understand the relationship between the variables. This plot provides an efficient way to study data trends, and the correlation between variables, or randomness. It is also called the XY plot.

In Table 13.9, we have a daily maximum temperature for January 2015 for two blocks — Vaishali and Bidupur.

Figure 13.9 gives the scatterplot for the data. We can see the relationship between the maximum temperature for the two blocks — Vaishali and Bidupur. Both the blocks show an increasing trend for the maximum temperature (through trend lines represented through small dots). Bidupur block is seen to be relatively hotter than Vaishali block (most of the circled dots are above the squared ones representing a higher maximum temperature in Bidupur).

Table 13.8 Claims Reimbursement Amount of a CBMAS health scheme in Uttar Pradesh (India)

Year	Claim Reimbursement
2011	0
2011	0
2011	0
2011	0
2011	700
2011	1250
2011	1300
2011	1600
2011	1600
2011	1600
2011	1600
2011	1602
2011	1699
2011	1871
2011	1980
2011	2000
2011	2137
...	...
...	...
...	...
...	...
...	...
...	...
...	...

Line Chart: A line chart or line graph is a type of chart which displays information as a series of data points (called "markers") connected by straight line segments. Such graphs are used to display quantitative values over a continuous interval or period. It helps in studying data trends and analyzing how the data have changed over time.

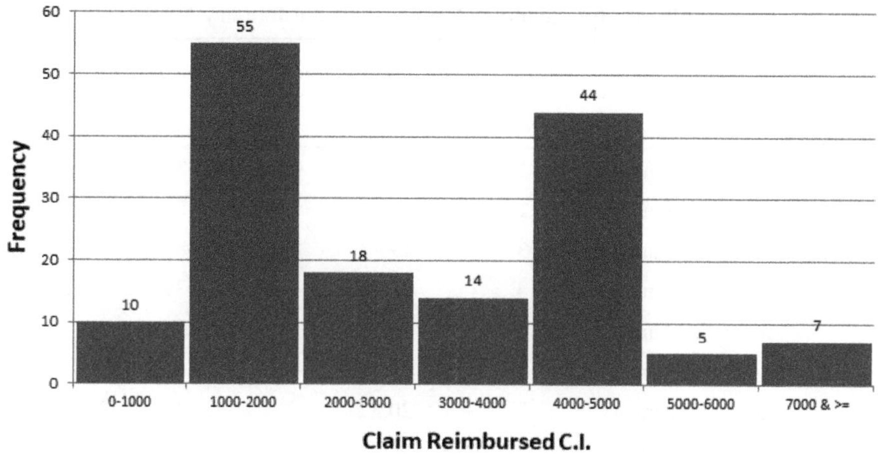

Figure 13.7 Histogram of Claims Reimbursement Amount

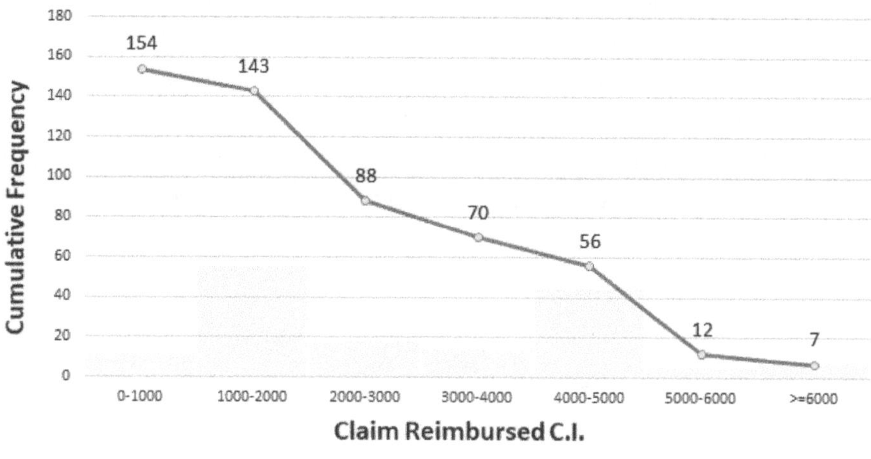

Figure 13.8 Ogive Graph of Claims Reimbursement Amount

In the Table 13.10, we have the claims reimbursement amount of a CBMAS health scheme in Uttar Pradesh (India). The line chart following this (Figure 13.10) depicts these data.

Maps: Maps are a diagrammatic representation of a geographical area separated through boundaries. Maps can serve as excellent infographics for making visually interactive informative comparisons within different geographies. Road maps, wind maps, river maps,meteorological maps,

Table 13.9 Daily Maximum Temperature for January 2015

			Daily Maximum Temperature in °C	
Year	Month	Day	Vaishali Block	Bidupur Block I
2015	January	1	24.76	25.34
2015	January	2	19.52	21.21
2015	January	3	19.43	20.85
2015	January	4	22.59	22.39
2015	January	5	19.05	21.34
2015	January	6	19.59	19.62
2015	January	7	20.32	21.4
2015	January	8	22.07	21.98
2015	January	9	16.94	19.22
2015	January	10	13.06	14.97
2015	January	11	14.52	15.37
2015	January	12	19.08	19.66
2015	January	13	16.26	17.81
2015	January	14	20.36	20.19
2015	January	15	24.24	24.41
…	…	…	…	…
…	…	…	…	…
…	…	…	…	…
…	…	…	…	…

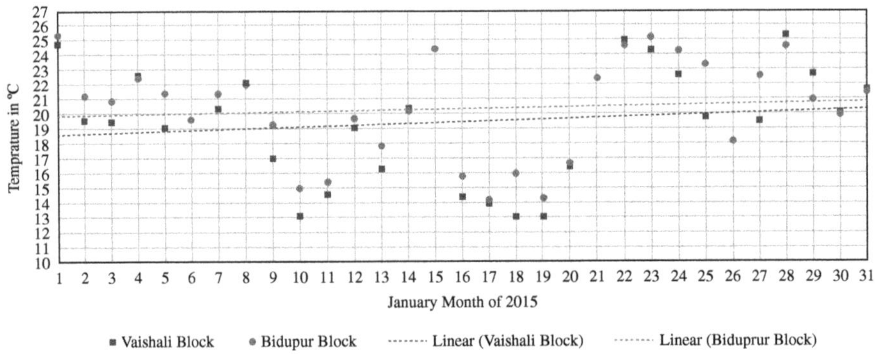

Figure 13.9 Scatterplot of Daily Maximum Temperature for January 2015 for Two Blocks — Vaishali and Bidupur

Table 13.10 Claims Reimbursement Amount of a CBMAS Health Scheme in Uttar Pradesh (India)

Claims Reimbursed Amount	Frequency
0-1000	10
1000-2000	55
2000-3000	18
3000-4000	14
4000-5000	44
5000-6000	5
7000 & >=	7

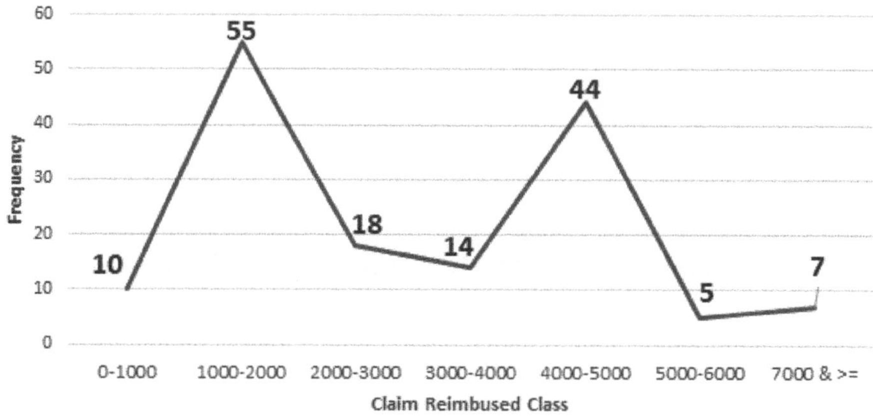

Figure 13.10 Line Chart of Claims Reimbursement Amount of a CBMAS Health Scheme in Uttar Pradesh (India)

maps with population comparisons, and maps showing comparison of agricultural produce are some good examples of map usage. Figure 13.11 shows the distribution of minerals in India.

Other data presentation forms

Infographics: Infographics is a widely used technique of data presentation which includes a combination of text, numerical data, and graphics. Graphics here include images, tables, charts, graphs, shapes, symbols, artistic drawing, and other graphic designs, etc. Infographics are designed to use little space but to give information a larger insight. This interactive

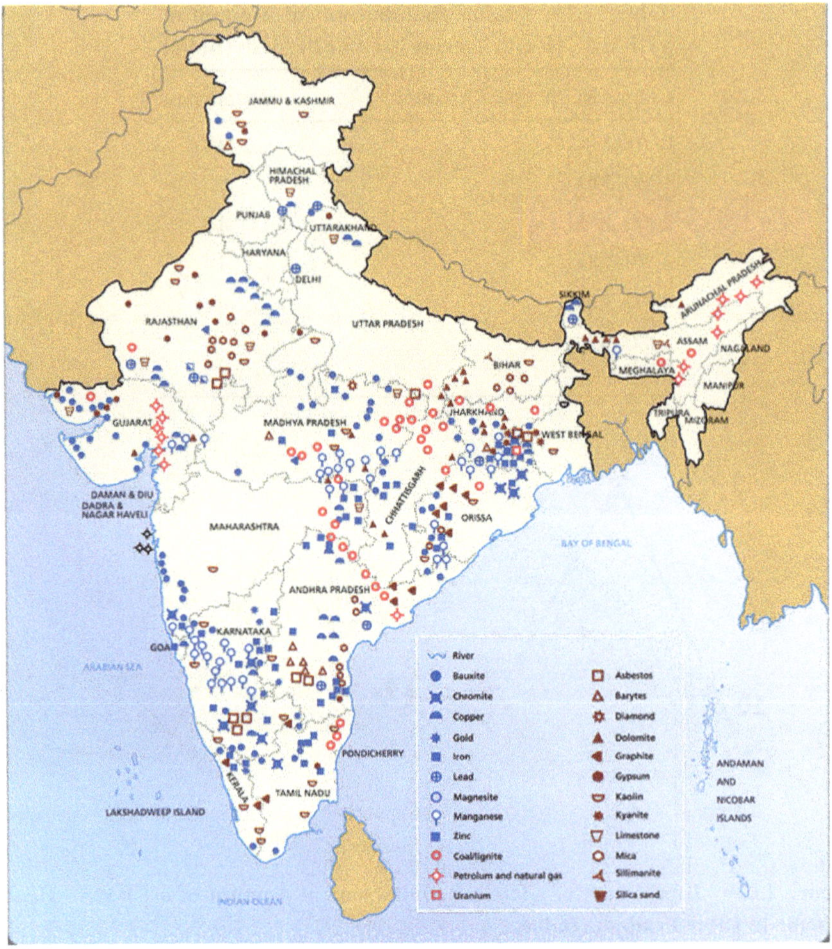

Figure 13.11 Mineral Distribution in India

Source: ENVIS Centre on Environmental Problems of Mining, http://ismenvis.nic.in/KidsCentre/Mineral_Distribution_in_India_13948.aspx.

and visually engaging presentation technique is trendy in cyberspace. Some of the common examples are road direction charts, country maps, train network maps, a webpage, etc.

In Figure 13.12, infographics have been used to depict various health packages.

Pictograph: The pictograph is a picture which conveys its meaning, i.e., these are pictorial illustrations, drawn in a manner to resemble physical

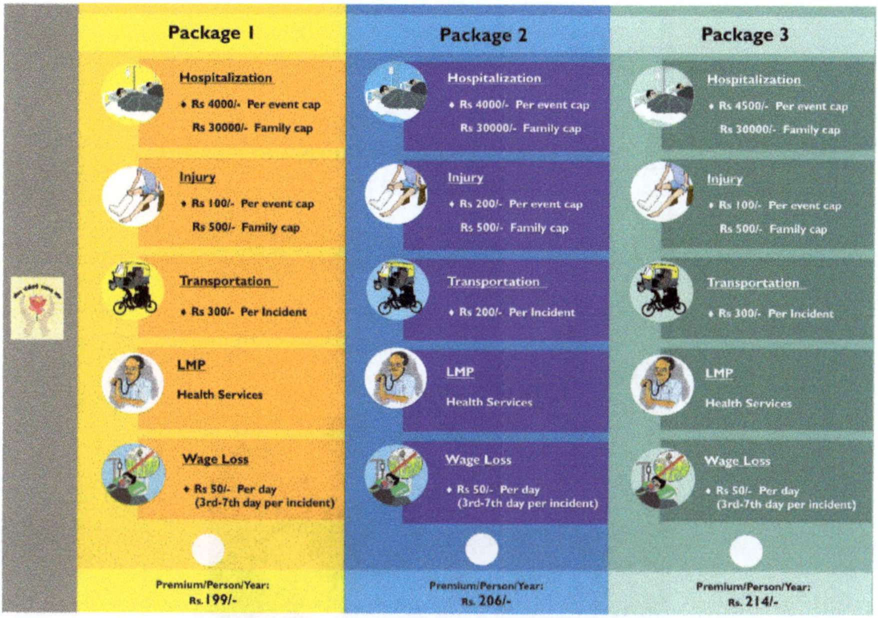

Figure 13.12 Micro Insurance Academy's Consensus Building Tool Called "CHAT Board," Uses Infographics to Show Different Health Packages

Figure 13.13 Sales of Cupcakes in a Week

objects, humans, activities, or messages to be conveyed. Road signs, directional signs, instructional signs, pictorial bar charts, etc., are some commonly seen examples of pictographs.

In Figure 13.13, the units of cupcakes sold in a week are represented using a pictograph.

Reports: Reports are technical and comprehensive presentation of data. Report writing usually follows a set basic format which includes an

Figure 13.14 Report Produced by Micro Insurance Academy

introduction, the body of the report, conclusion, and references. It is possible to present reports through written content or audio or audiovisual mediums. A written report may employ one or more data presentation techniques we discussed earlier in this chapter. It can also be a text-only report or a report with informatics, text, chart, graphs, maps, etc. Figure 13.14 shows a report produced by Micro Insurance Academy.

SELF-TEST QUESTIONS

1. If you are studying data trends and need to analyze how the data has changed over time, which type of graph/chart would you prefer to use?
2. When you have to understand the relationship between two or more variables, which graphical technique would you adopt?
3. The target population of a CBHI comprises mostly illiterate and innumerate persons. If you had to explain the various health benefits package options available to them, what graphical method would you use?
4. Suggest an appropriate method to present multiple-variable data.

KEY TERMS

- **Continuous data:** These are data that can take any value, both whole numbers and fractions.
- **Discrete data:** These data describe the variables only with integer values, namely only in whole numbers.
- **Focus group discussions (FGDs):** This is a group activity to explore insights about the topic of group interest, i.e., group attitude, behavior, beliefs, or perceptions rather than individual as in individual interviews.
- **Nominal data:** This is the kind of data with which it is pointless to establish an order.
- **Ordinal data:** It describes data sets that can be put into a defined order within qualitative data.
- **Qualitative data:** Data which are more subjective and explanatory, or which quantitative data fails to answer, are called qualitative data. Such data are descriptions which approximate or characterize but do not measure the attributes, characteristics, or properties of a thing or phenomenon.
- **Quantitative data:** These are data which can be expressed in digital form or can be measured or counted. Such data are required for mathematical or statistical analysis which can then be presented graphically.
- **Secondary data**: Data that the direct user did not collect but harvested from other sources (be those official governmental records or records owned by individuals or private organizations) are secondary data.

Issue Briefs

The following Issue Briefs contain advanced topics related to this chapter:

1. Using data for estimation, inference, and modeling.
2. Understanding population patterns.
3. Software applications used for data analysis and presentation.

Issue Brief I: Estimation, Inference, and Modeling

Estimation

We calculate central tendencies (mean, median, and mode) and the dispersion (range, variance, and standard deviation) of the dataset of annual health expenditure of three towns with a population of 300,000 inhabitants each. The graphical representations of these datasets are shown in Figure 1:

The dotted red lines are functions of x, i.e., values plotted against the horizontal or X-axis. The corresponding value of y can be represented as a function of x, i.e., $y = f(x)$.

This is always greater than or equal to zero, i.e., it never goes below X-axis.

The area under the curve is the sum of its (hypothetical) slices. If the area of the thinnest possible slice is dx, the total area would be an "integration $f(x)dx$ from minus infinity to plus infinity" and represented thus

$$\int_{+\infty}^{-\infty} f(x)\,dx.$$

For each curve, the area under the curve is 1.

The lines are a special function of x, where x is a population characteristic. This function of variable x is written as $f(x)$ and is called the *probability distribution function* or pdf.

The functional form of the dotted line is $f(x) = \frac{1}{\sigma\sqrt{(2\pi)}} e^{\frac{1}{2}\left(\frac{x-\mu}{\sigma}\right)^2}$, where μ (mean) and (standard deviation) are constants and called population parameters.

A pdf has two important properties:

- Values of $f(x)$ are always greater than zero, i.e., $f(x) \geq 0$.
- Total area under the curve is 1, i.e., $\int_{+\infty}^{-\infty} f(x)\,dx = 1$.

For each point on the X-axis, there is $f(x)$.

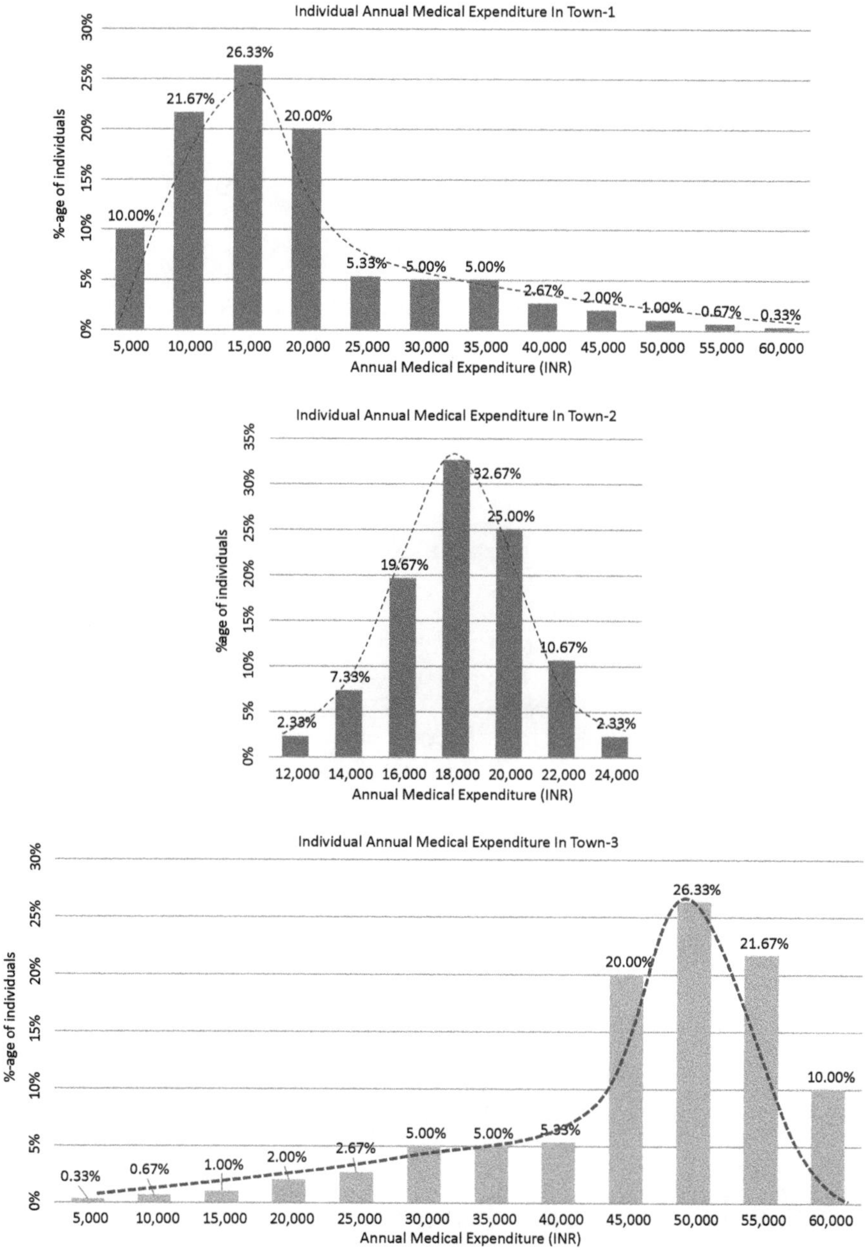

Figure 1 Healthcare Expenditure of Three Towns

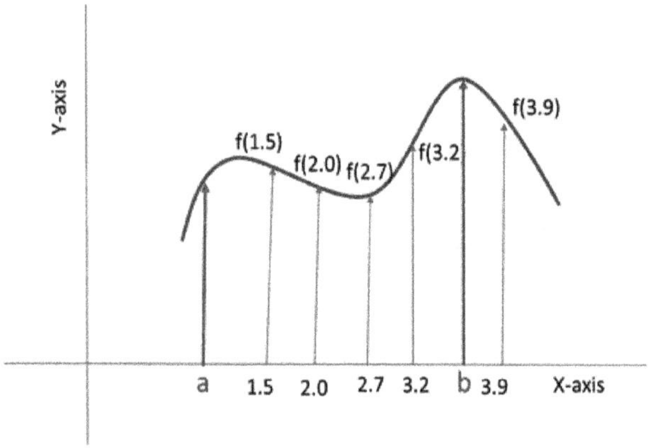

Figure 2 Area under the Curve from $x = a$ to $x = b$

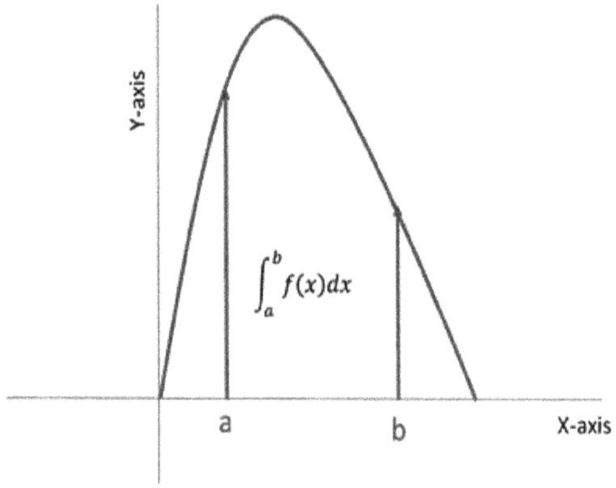

Figure 3 Calculating area under a curve by integration

The area under the curve from $x = a$ to $x = b$ is given as follows:

$$\int_a^b f(x)dx.$$

If x is the variable denoting annual health expenditure, a probability density function of x can be plotted as shown in Figure 3. If the total area under the curve is 1, then any part of it represents a percentage of the total population. It is possible to calculate the percentage of people whose annual health expenditure is between a and b. This probability is given by the following equation:

$$\int_a^b f(x)dx.$$

It is also possible to calculate the probability that a person spends less than a and is given as follows:

$$\int_0^a f(x)dx.$$

This is $F(a)$ where F is a cumulative distribution function (cdf).

The probability of a person spending less than b is $F(b)$, and it is calculated as follows:

$$\int_0^b f(x)dx.$$

Thus, $\int_a^b f(x)dx = F(b) - F(a)$.

A population represented by $f(x) = \frac{1}{\sigma\sqrt{(2\pi)}} e^{\frac{1}{2}\left(\frac{x-\mu}{\sigma}\right)^2}$ is called a normal population. If the values of the mean (μ) and the standard deviation (σ) are known, then the normal distribution is specified.

> In MS Excel, the normal distribution can be calculated using the formula NORM.DIST(a, μ, σ, TRUE).

There are other distributions like t-distribution, F-distribution, chi-square distribution, exponential distribution, logistic distribution, Pareto distribution, and others.

Pdf is calculated for continuous random variables. When the variable is discrete (i.e., the variable can take only whole numbers), probability mass function or pmf is calculated. In pmf, the integration symbol is replaced by a summation (Σ) symbol.

A binomial distribution is not used to compute probability when n (i.e., sample size) is very high. When n is very high, the binomial distribution is approximated as Poisson distribution. Binomial distribution can calculate the probability of x number of people out of n people that encounter a defined event, say hospitalized. Here x can never be more than n. Under the Poisson distribution, the probability of x (number of hospitalization cases) in the area can be calculated. Theoretically, x can be any value greater than 0.

> Population means a set of numbers — the set of all values of the population characteristics of interest corresponding to every individual/item of the population.

Estimation is estimating the population parameters like mean, variance, etc., to guess the best values for the parameters of the pdf and pmf functions. This helps to calculate the probability of some events and based on the estimated probabilities to forecast certain numbers related to the events.

The best estimator of the population mean is the sample mean. The sample mean is calculated thus

$$\overline{x} = \frac{1}{n}\sum_{x=1}^{x=i} x_i .$$

Sample variance is calculated as

$$s^2 = \frac{1}{n-1}\sum_{x=1}^{x=n} \left(x_i - \overline{x}\right)^2 .$$

The variance of the sample mean is called standard error of the mean (SEM).

Sample standard deviation is the square root of the above expression.

According to the Central Limit Theorem, the sample mean follows the normal distribution with mean μ and variance σ^2. That means that when the mean and standard deviation of a normal distribution are known, the probability can be easily calculated for any range of values.

Alternatively, if *F*(*a*) is given, the value of *a* can be found using the Excel function NORM.INV. When *F* is the CDF of the normal distribution with mean = 0 and standard deviation = 1, the distribution is called *standard normal distribution.*

The confidence interval of the mean is the range of the interval and the probability that the exact value of the population mean lies within that interval. The calculation of the confidence interval requires the value of population standard deviation.

Inference

Statistical inference is the process through which inferences about a population are made based on certain statistics calculated from a sample data drawn from that population.[10]

Let us understand this with an example from a community-based health insurance scheme. Though the example is hypothetical, this is an important decision required for an operational scheme.

A scheme fixed their premium on the assumption of an average 80 claims per year, but it received and settled 69, 71, 90, 99, and 95 claims in the past 5 years. Since the number of claims in the past 3 years exceeded 90, the management of the scheme thinks the premium should be recalculated based on an assumption of 90 claims per year. How can the management make an informed decision?

Basic knowledge of statistics is required here.

Let us assume the number of people in the scheme remains constant from the beginning (for simplicity).

Prima facie, the last 3 years' claim figures are closer to 90 than 80 and they more likely to come from a Poisson population with mean 90 than one with mean 80.

---

[10]Available at https://www.sciencedirect.com/topics/neuroscience/statistical-inference (accessed 26 May 2018).

The question is as follows: How unlikely is it for the claim figures to come from a Poisson population with mean 80 and how likely is it that they have come from one with mean 90?

The following are the two alternatives to decide upon:

(i) actual average for the number of claims per year is 80 — Null Hypothesis, written as H_0;
(ii) actual average for the number claims is 90 — Alternative Hypothesis, H_1.

If the actual average is 80 and one concludes otherwise, then it is a wrong decision. Similarly, if the actual average is 90 and one concludes otherwise, it is also a wrong decision. Here the actual is not known.

		Actual Situation	
		H_0 is True	H_1 is true
Your conclusion	Accept H_0 as True	✓	x
	Accept H_1 as true	x	✓

If H_1 is accepted as true though, in reality, H_0 is true, it is type I error. If H_0 is accepted when H_1 is true, it is type II error.

The scheme received 69, 71, 90, 99, and 95 claims in the last 5 years, i.e., 84.8 claims per year. What is then the probability of getting a sample mean of 80 if H_0 is true?

If we assume x is the number of claims received by the scheme and has a Poisson distribution with mean λ, which is unknown. Let be the average number of claims from a sample of size n. Applying Central Limit Theorem, we know approximately follows the normal distribution with mean λ and variance. So H_0 and H_1 can be written as follows:

Null hypothesis H_0: $\lambda = 80$;

Alternative hypothesis H_1: $\lambda = 90$.

For the example, $\lambda = 84.8$, sample size $n = 5$.

For null hypothesis H_0: $\lambda = 80$, the distribution of approximately follows normal with mean 80. This implies that $\frac{\bar{\lambda}-80}{\sqrt{80/5}}$ approximately follows standard normal (mean = 0, standard deviation = 1).

For alternative hypothesis H_1: $\lambda = 90$, the distribution of approximately follows normal with mean 90. This implies that $\frac{\bar{\lambda}-90}{\sqrt{90/5}}$ approximately follows standard normal (mean = 0, standard deviation = 1).

Under the null hypothesis, the expression $\frac{84.8-80}{\sqrt{80/5}} = 1.2$ is a sample (of size 1) from $N(0,1)$.

If a random sample is drawn from $N(0,1)$ what is the probability of arriving at a mean ≥1.2 as proposed under the null hypothesis?

In Excel, NORM.S.DIST(1.2, TRUE) = 0.115. If we reject the null hypothesis, the probability that we have made a mistake (type I error) is 11.5%. This is called the *p*-value. Ideally, type I error should not be more than 5%. Moreover, in some conservative situations, it can be even lower (1% or 0.1%). So, we can conclude H_0 is probably true, i.e., we disagree with the perception of the management.

For *p*-value of 0.05 (=5%) or smaller, we reject H_0.

NORM.S.INV(1 – 0.05) or $F(95\%) = 1.64$.

So, we reject H_0 if $\frac{\bar{\lambda}-80}{\sqrt{80/5}} \geq 1.64$ or $\bar{\lambda} \geq 86.56$.

Prob ($\bar{\lambda} \geq 86.56$, | H_0 is true) = 0.05. The range $\bar{\lambda} \geq 86.56$ is called critical region.

As long as $\bar{\lambda} < 86.56$, we would have accepted H_0 even when H_1 is true (and commit a type II error). What is the probability of this?

Prob ($\bar{\lambda} < 86.56$, | H_1 is true) = Prob $\left\{\bar{\lambda} < 86.56 \middle| \bar{\lambda} \sim N\left(\text{mean} = 90, \text{variance} = \frac{90}{5}\right)\right\}$

$$= \text{Prob}\left\{\frac{\bar{\lambda}-90}{\sqrt{\frac{90}{5}}} < \frac{86.56-90}{\sqrt{\frac{90}{5}}} \middle| \bar{\lambda} \sim N\left(\text{mean} = 90,\ \text{variance} = \frac{90}{5}\right)\right\}$$

$= \text{Prob}\left\{U < -0.811 \mid U \sim N(0,1)\right\}$

= NORM.S.DIST(–0.811, TRUE) = 0.209. This is the probability of type II error.

Type I error is usually denoted by α and type II error by β. In our previous example, $\alpha = 0.05$ and $\beta = 0.209$. Though we want to minimize both types of errors, we cannot reduce them both simultaneously. If type

I error decreases, the other increases. The convention is to fix type I error first and then type II.

$1 - \beta$ or 1 – type II error is also called the power of the test.

In summary, define the null hypothesis (H_0) and the alternative hypothesis (H_1). Find a test statistic (a function of the sample) and its distributions under H_0 and H_1. Fix type I error (type II error is fixed automatically). The sample size should be based on the acceptable level of type I error and type II error. The type II error does not matter when actually doing the test. Compute the value of the test statistic. Calculate the p-value. If p-value ≤ 0.05, reject the null hypothesis.

These days, various statistical software applications are available for testing, e.g., SPSS, Stata, R. All that is required is the dataset and entering suitable commands for testing.

Modeling

Modeling is nothing but exploring the relationship between two or more variables. We start with an initial assumption. Then we try to make it "precise" with the help of the sampled dataset and examine the "goodness of fit" for the model.

Correlation Coefficient: We introduce here an essential statistical measure which indicates the relationship between two variables (=population characteristics). If X and Y denote the two characteristics of the same object of the population, then we can measure the correlation coefficient between the two. Statistical definition of correlation coefficient is represented as follows:

$$\rho = \sqrt{\frac{\sum_{i=1}^{i=N}\left(x_i - \bar{x}\right)\left(y_i - \bar{y}\right)}{\sum_{i=1}^{i=N}\left(x_i - \bar{x}^2\right)\left(y_i - \bar{y}^2\right)}}.$$

Correlation coefficient of the population is denoted by ρ. When we compute the correlation coefficient between two variables from a sample, it is denoted by r. There is one very interesting property of ρ. It always lies between −1 and +1, that is, $-1 \leq \rho \leq +1$. The higher the absolute value of ρ, the stronger is the linear relationship between X and Y. $\rho > 0$ implies that Y increases when x increases and $\rho < 0$ implies that Y decreases when x increases. All statistical software and MS Excel readily compute the correlation coefficient from a given dataset. The Excel function for the computation of correlation coefficient is CORREL (Range 1, Range 2).

Example: The following table gives the income and expenditure on food of 52 families sampled from a locality. We want to check the following: Is there any relationship between the income of a household and its food expenditure?

Income	Expense on Food	Income	Expense on Food	Income	Expense on Food	Income	Expense on Food
14,800	6,200	12,000	6,700	18,500	8,100	13,200	5,600
13,900	5,600	13,800	6,000	13,300	5,800	15,800	7,300
17,900	8,300	15,800	7,600	19,000	9,200	6,600	2,800
12,700	5,400	16,300	6,600	16,100	8,400	6,100	3,900
7,800	4,900	6,300	3,400	13,400	6,700	13,500	5,900
12,200	5,800	11,400	5,600	11,600	6,400	12,000	4,900
18,500	8,200	17,800	7,300	16,500	7,700	10,500	5,900
5,900	2,900	6,900	3,100	17,400	7,300		
17,600	9,000	8,900	5,300	9,000	4,900		
10,000	5,200	13,500	6,000	15,200	6,600		
13,500	5,900	7,800	3,500	11,800	4,700		
10,600	5,500	17,500	8,700	19,900	8,600		
18,500	8,700	13,000	6,600	7,100	3,900		
11,900	6,200	10,700	6,200	16,100	7,200		
6,100	3,000	6,000	3,000	14,500	7,600		

The correlation between the two variables is estimated as 0.93889. This implies that there is a very strong linear relationship between income of the household and its expenditure on food. Let us look at the scatterplot chart of these two variables.

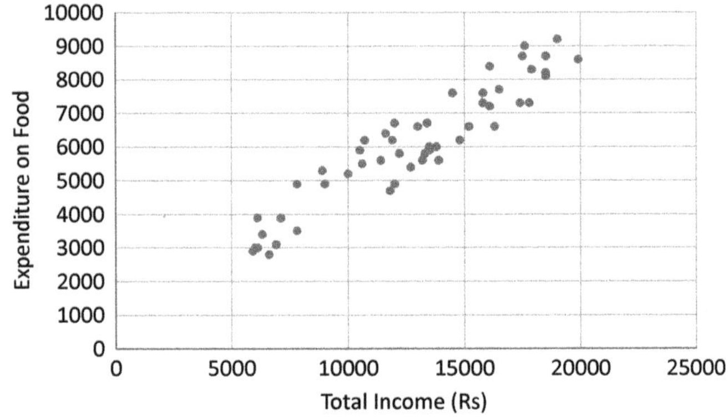

The scatterplot also suggests that there is a linear relationship between the total income of the household and its expenditure on food. Let X denote the annual income of the household and Y its expenditure on food. Then the relationship between Y and X can be written as $Y = a + bx$.

However, what are the values of a and b? One can draw many straight lines through the cluster of points. But which is the best one?

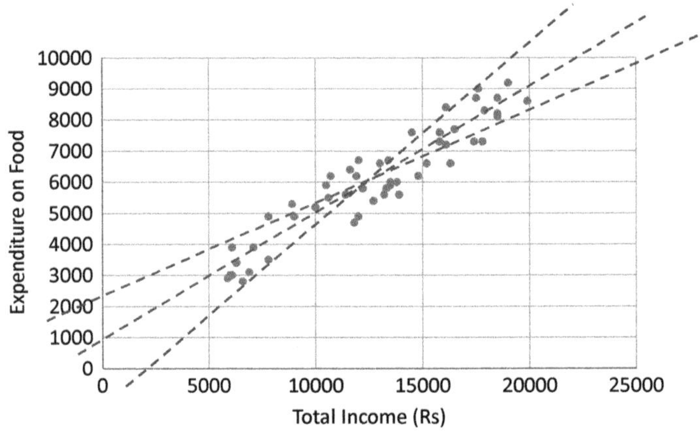

It can be proved that the equation of the best fitting straight line will be as follows:

$$y = \bar{y} + r\frac{\sigma_y}{\sigma_x}(x - \bar{x}), \tag{1}$$

where $\bar{y}$ = observed mean of y from the sample (expenditure on food),

$\overline{x}$ = observed mean of x from the sample (total income),
σ_y = standard deviation of y,
σ_x = standard deviation of x,
r = correlation coefficient between x and y.

Equation (1) can be rewritten as follows:

$$y = \left(\overline{y} - r\frac{\sigma_y}{\sigma_x}\overline{x} \right) + r\frac{\sigma_y}{\sigma_x}x.$$

***R*-square**: Once we have got the equation of the best fitted straight line, we can always predict a value of y for any given value of x. For any given value of x, you also have an observed value of y. Now for every x, you have two y's — one observed, and the other predicted. R the correlation between the observed and predicted values of y. R-square is simply the square of R. The higher the value of R-square, the better is the fit of the model.

Step-by-Step Guide to Modeling Using MS Excel

Select the points on the scatter plot and right click.

- Select Add Trendline from the dialog box

From the following dialog box, (Format Trendline) choose

- Linear
- Check-in Display Equation on Chart
- Check-in Display R-squared value on chart

You will find a best fitted straight line passing through the cluster of points. The equation of the straight line is also displayed on the chart.

Look at the Dialog Box Format Trendline. There are many options to choose from other than the linear one you have selected. A linear relation is just an assumption, and actually some other models like exponential or logarithmic polynomial may better fit the data. You can try various options. The R-square value will indicate how good fit your model is.

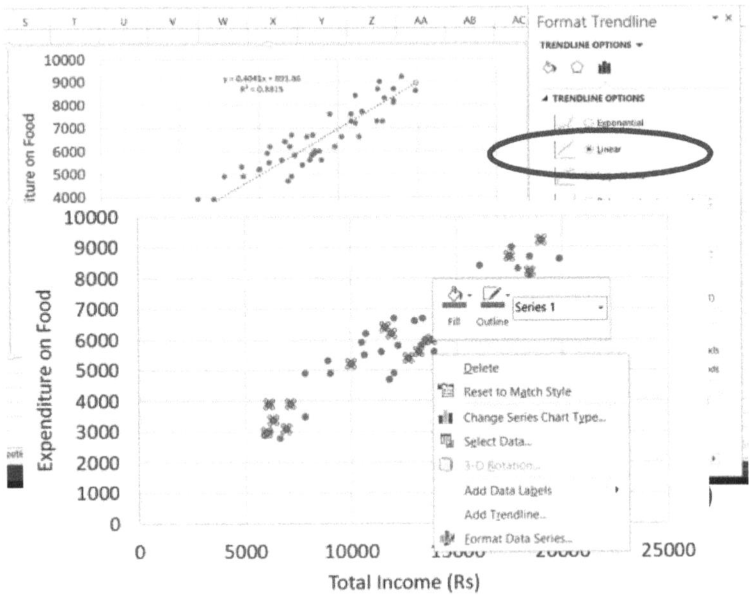

Modeling with More than One Variable

So far, we have modeled to predict Y with a single variable x. In reality, Y may be dependent on many variables X_1, X_2, X_3, ... In most cases, the relationship is linear. The assumption is $Y = a + b_1X_1 + b_2X_2 + b_3X_3 + \ldots + b_nX_n$. Moreover, the key challenge is to find the estimates of $b_1, b_2, b_3, \ldots, b_n$ from the observed values of Y and $X_1, X_2, X_3, \ldots, X_n$. Fortunately, the task is done by statistical software, and one just has to input the dataset and assumption through specific commands or functions.

Y is called dependent variables and X_i's are independent variables. Sometimes Y is called the outcome variables and X's are explanatory variables. When Y depends on two or more independent variables, the modeling is called multivariate modeling.

Logistic Modeling

The most common model is linear model as we have explained: $Y = a + b_1X_1 + b_2X_2 + b_3X_3 + \ldots + b_nX_n$, where we predict the value of Y from the values of X. Instead of linear, we can also use another model with the given dataset. You have to check which model gives the best fit for the dataset.

There is another type of model which does not predict the values of Y *per se*. For example, consider a situation where many people have joined the scheme, and at the same time many people have not joined the scheme. All people have their socioeconomic and sociodemographic characteristics such as their gender, age, income, education, etc. Can we conclude that people with a specific characteristic are more likely to join the scheme or more likely not to join the scheme. Note that Y's can be either 1 (joined) or 0 (not joined). So, predicting the values of Y does not make sense. Then what do we do? We try to predict the probability or odds that Y will be =1 or 0.

We assume that $\text{Prob}(Y=1)=\frac{e^{\sum_{i=1}^{i=n} b_i x_i}}{1+e^{\sum_{i=1}^{i=n} b_i x_i}}$. This is type of modeling is called logistic modeling.

This implies that $\text{Prob}(Y=0)=\frac{1}{1+e^{\sum_{i=1}^{i=n} b_i x_i}}$

OR $\frac{Prob(Y=1)}{Prob(Y=0)}=e^{\sum_{i=1}^{i=n} b_i x_i}$. This is called odds.

Now suppose one of the x_i's, say x_k, changes by one unit and other X_i's remain constant. Then

$$\frac{\frac{Prob(Y=1\mid x_k=k+1)}{Prob(Y=0\mid x_k=k+1)}}{\frac{Prob(Y=1\mid x_k=k)}{Prob(Y=0\mid x_k=k)}} = e^{b_k}.$$

This is called odds ratio of X_k.

If we take the log of both sides, we get the log odds ratio of X_k.

Hence, in the logistic model, the coefficients b_i's are the log odds ratios of the independent variables.

Again, there is software that calculates the values of b_i's from a given dataset.

KEY TERMS

- **Confidence interval of the mean:** This is the range of the interval and the probability that the exact value of the population mean lies within that interval.
- **Estimation**: Estimating the population parameters like mean, variance, etc. to guess the best value for the parameters of the pdf and pmf functions is known as estimation.
- **Modeling**: It means exploring the relationship between two or more variables.
- **Statistical inference**: It is the process through which inferences about a population are made based on certain statistics calculated from a sample data drawn from that population.

Issue Brief II: Understanding Population Patterns

Once we have a dataset of interest, the next step is to understand the data to be able to make necessary policy decisions. Region-specific data is used in the case of microinsurance, as this helps in understanding the socioeconomic indicators and health indicators about a community where a microinsurance scheme is to be launched. Since these indicators often display significant variations across regions in the same country or even state, we recommend the use of region-specific data for more efficient designing and pricing of benefits packages.

In this chapter, we use the term "population" figuratively to refer to the dataset which contains data about every element (i.e., an individual) of the population.

In statistics, population parameters are calculated using the given data, and this is thereafter used to understand patterns in the dataset. This helps in defining the characteristics of the given dataset.

Population characteristics help in answering questions related to estimation, forecast/prediction, and comparison of data.

We try to **estimate** something.

- How many hospitalization cases happen in a population of size 1,000 in a period of one year?
  We try to **forecast/predict** something.

- How many people are expected to join the insurance scheme in the next 10 years?
- How probable it is that a low-income household joins the insurance scheme?
  We try to **compare** two situations.

- Has the out-of-pocket expenditure reduced after the introduction of the insurance scheme?

In this chapter, we discuss the relevance of various population characteristics and the methods used to calculate them.

We use the health expenditure dataset shown in Table 1 to understand population patterns.

In the graph shown in Figure 1, we see that the values center around ₹15,000. A dataset tends to cluster around a central point. This property

Table 1 Health expenditure dataset

Amount (INR)	Number of Individuals	%-age
0	5	1.67%
5,000	25	8.33%
10,000	65	21.67%
15,000	79	26.33%
20,000	60	20.00%
25,000	16	5.33%
30,000	15	5.00%
35,000	15	5.00%
40,000	8	2.67%
45,000	6	2.00%
50,000	3	1.00%
55,000	2	0.67%
60,000	1	0.33%
Total	300	100.00%

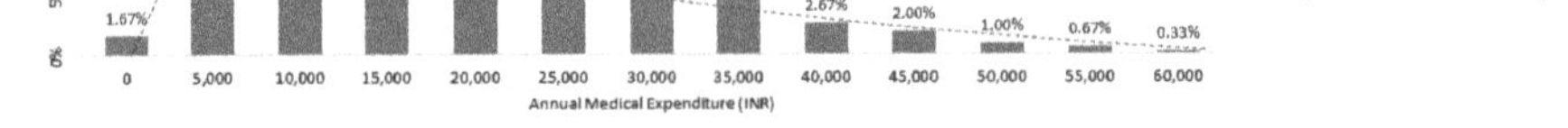

Figure 1

of the dataset is known as a central tendency. Similarly, all values of the dataset are usually not equal, and it has a spread. This property of the dataset is known as **dispersion**.

It is also essential to study whether the data points (individual values of a dataset) are uniformly distributed around the central point (**symmetric**) or skewed (**asymmetric**).

Population Characteristics

- **Central tendency:** The methods used to measure the central tendency of the dataset are mean, median, and mode. While the mean gives a good measure of the central tendency, it may not serve the purpose when the dataset contains few very large or very small values which are far away from the central values. These values, which are called "outliers," seem unlikely but are not impossible. Outliers are known to influence the mean profoundly, and therefore, they are either excluded from the calculation of mean or alternative measures of central tendency such as median or mode are calculated. In the health microinsurance context, the expenditure incurred in a high-expense surgery for one individual can be considered an outlier.
- **Dispersion:** The spread of the dataset is referred to as its dispersion. Dispersion is "some kind of an average" of distances of all values from its mean. If many values are located far away from the mean, dispersion would be high. Measures of dispersion are variance, standard deviation, and range.
- **Skewness:** The spread of the dataset may be symmetric or asymmetric around the central point. The Data Science jargon for this is *skewness.*
- **Distribution:** The dataset has a distribution, where $x\%$ of the values are equal to a, $y\%$ of the values are equal to b and so on. Sum of all percentages is 100% or 1. This is called probability distribution.

Understanding the Notations Used to Define the Population Parameters

Before we learn how to calculate the various population patterns, let us understand the notations used in the calculations.

X = a variable representing the population,

For example, X = annual individual health expenditure

X_i = value of the ith element of the population dataset.

For example, X_3 = annual health expenditure of the third individual. In reality, i may run from 1 to any number.

$$\sum_{i=1}^{i=N} X_i = X_1 + X_2 + X_3 + X_4 + \cdots + X_N.$$

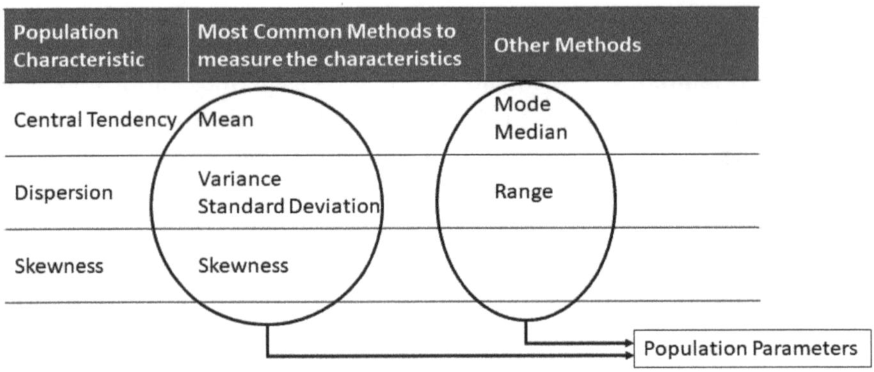

Figure 2

Σ (pronounced as "sigma") is the summation symbol. N is the total number of individuals in the population dataset.

A Measure of Central Tendency: Mean

Symbol: μ

Formula 1: $\mu = \frac{1}{N}\sum_{i=1}^{i=N} X_i.$

Explanation: Mean is nothing but the simple average we learned in our school days. When we sum over all the values of the population and then divide the sum by the total number of elements, we get the mean of the population. Every population has a mean.

Alternative Formulas of Mean

In our example, the population has 300 elements (i runs from 1 to 300) but 12 different values. If we define X_i as the ith **different value** of X and f_i as the number of times it repeats itself in the population, then

$$N = \sum_{i=1}^{i=12} f_i,$$

where f_i is the "frequency" of the ith different value of X. N is the total frequency.

Thus, the alternative formula for the mean is given as follows:

Formula 2: $\mu = \frac{1}{N}\sum_{i=1}^{i=12} X_i f_i$.

This formula is more convenient for calculation.

Note that the above formula can be written as $\mu = \sum_{i=1}^{i=12} X_i \left(\frac{f_i}{N}\right)$.

$\left(\frac{f_i}{N}\right)$ is the proportion of X_i in the population. $\left(\frac{f_i}{N}\right)$ is the **relative frequency**.

$\left(\frac{f_i}{N}\right)$ is also written as p_i. p stands for probability.

Many times, instead of f_i's and N, we are given the p_i's to define a population.

The third alternative formula for the mean is given as follows:

Formula 3: $\mu = \sum_{j=1}^{j=k} Y_j p_j$, where p_j is the probability of drawing Y_j.

All three formulas for mean discussed here are equivalent and produce the same result.

Exercise for Calculating Population Mean

j	Amount (INR) Y_j	Number of Individuals f_j	$Y_j \times f_j$	$f_j/N = p_j$	$Y_j \times p_j$
1	0	5	0	0.017	0
2	5,000	25	125,000	0.083	417
3	10,000	65	650,000	0.217	2,167
4	15,000	79	1,185,000	0.263	3,950
5	20,000	60	1,200,000	0.200	4,000
6	25,000	16	400,000	0.053	1,333
7	30,000	15	450,000	0.050	1,500
8	35,000	15	525,000	0.050	1,750
9	40,000	8	320,000	0.027	1,067
10	45,000	6	270,000	0.020	900
11	50,000	3	150,000	0.010	500
12	55,000	2	110,000	0.007	367
13	60,000	1	60,000	0.003	200
	Total	300	5,445,000	1	18,150

$$\mu = \frac{1}{N}\sum_{j=1}^{j=k} Y_j f_j = \frac{5{,}445{,}000}{300} = 18{,}150$$

$$\mu = \sum_{j=1}^{j=k} Y_j \left(\frac{f_j}{N}\right) = \sum_{j=1}^{j=k} Y_j p_j = 18{,}150$$

A Measure of Central Tendency: Median

Like the mean, the median is also a measure of central tendency.

If the values of the population dataset are arranged in ascending or descending order, then the middle-most value is called the median of the population.

- If the population has an **odd number** of elements, then you get a value precisely in the middle.

If X_i is the ith element of the population after arranging the values in ascending or descending order and the population size is N, then the median is the $(N + 1)/2$th value, i.e., median $= X_{N+1/2}$.

Let us look at the following example:

Population: {200, 100, 50, 70, 300, 40, 80, 150, 130, 135, 100}.

Count that the population has 11 elements. First, arrange the values in ascending (or descending order).

Arranged population: {40, 50, 70, 80, 100, 100, 130, 135, 150, 200, 300}.

The middle-most value is the sixth value, i.e., 100. So, median = 100.

- If the population has an **even number** of elements, then there is no value in the middle, or, there are two values in the middle. In such cases, the median is the average of the two middle-most values of the population dataset.

If X_i is the ith element of the population after arranging the values in ascending or descending order and the population size is N, then the median is the average of (N/2)-th and (N/2 + 1)-th values,

i.e., $\text{Median} = \dfrac{X_{N/2} + X_{N/2+1}}{2}$.

Let us look at the following example:

Arranged population: {40, 50, 70, 80, 100, 100, 130, 135, 150, 200, 300, 325}.

The middle-most values are the sixth and seventh ones, i.e., 100 and 130. So, median = (100 + 130)/2 = 115.

Probabilistic Definition of Median

Notice that since the median lies in the middle of the population dataset, there is an exactly equal number of elements which are **less than** the median and those which are more **than** the median.

In the population: {40, 50, 70, 80, 100, 100, 130, 135, 150, 200, 300}, N is odd, median = 100.

Prob (X_i's ≤ median) = Prob (X_i's ≥ median) = 6/11 = 0.545 ≈ 0.5 (when n is very large).

This understanding leads to the **probabilistic definition** of the median. Median is the value such that

Prob (X ≤ median) = Prob (X ≥ median) = 0.5.

If we cannot get a single value satisfying the condition, then the median is such that

Prob (X < median) < 0.5 AND Prob (X ≤ median) ≥ 0.5,

OR Prob (X > median) < 0.5 AND Prob (X ≥ median) ≥ 0.5 (both are equivalent).

We would need to calculate the cumulative frequency and cumulative probability before we calculate the median.

Cumulative frequency of $X_i = \sum_{j \le i} f_j$,

i.e., the number of elements which are less than or equal to X_i.

Example: Cumulative frequency of $X_3 = f_1 + f_2 + f_3$.

Cumulative probability of $X_i = \sum_{j \le i} p_j$. It is the probability that a sample of one unit drawn randomly from the population will be less than or equal to X_i.

In our example, using the cumulative frequency and cumulative probability, we arrive at a median value of 15,000.

i	Amount (INR) Yj	Number of Individuals fj	Cumulative Frequency (Less than type)	fj/N = pj	Cumulative Probability (Less than type) Prob(x<=Xi)	
1	0	5	5	0.02	0.017	*Does the middle value fall in this group ? NO. Cumulative Frequency<150, Cumulative Probability<0.5*
2	5,000	25	30	0.08	0.100	*Does the middle value fall in this group ? NO. Cumulative Frequency<150, Cumulative Probability<0.5*
3	10,000	65	95	0.22	0.317	*Does the middle value fall in this group ? NO. Cumulative Frequency<150, Cumulative Probability<0.5*
4	15,000	79	174	0.26	0.580	*Does the middle value fall in this group ? YES. Cumulative Frequency>150, Cumulative Probability>0.5*
5	20,000	60	234	0.20	0.780	
6	25,000	16	250	0.05	0.833	
7	30,000	15	265	0.05	0.883	
8	35,000	15	280	0.05	0.933	
9	40,000	8	288	0.03	0.960	
10	45,000	6	294	0.02	0.980	
11	50,000	3	297	0.01	0.990	
12	55,000	2	299	0.01	0.997	
13	60,000	1	300	0.00	1.000	
	Total	300		1		

Median Group
Median Value = 15,000

A Measure of Central Tendency: Mode

The mode is that value (out of all different values) of the population which has the highest frequency.

Probabilistic definition: Mode is that value of the population which has the highest probability to appear when a random sample of one unit is drawn from the population.

To calculate the mode, search for the highest frequency or highest probability. Both appear in the same row.

Let us look at the following example:

Amount (INR)	Number of Individuals	$f_i/N = p_i$
0	5	0.017
5,000	25	0.083
10,000	65	0.217
15,000	79	0.263
20,000	60	0.200
25,000	16	0.053
30,000	15	0.050
35,000	15	0.050
40,000	8	0.027
45,000	6	0.020
50,000	3	0.010
55,000	2	0.007
60,000	1	0.003
Total	300	100.00%

The highest frequency or highest probability is in the fourth row (= 4). Thus, mode = Y_4 = 15,000.

Which Measure of Central Tendency to Use — Mean, Median, or Mode?

We have discussed three measures of central tendency: mean, median, and mode.

For the annual individual health expenditure dataset of Town-1 we have the following values for three population parameters:

Mean = 18,150

Median = 15,000

Mode = 15,000

Note that while these values are not the same, they are close to each other.

Wherever possible we should use the mean as the measure of central tendency. However, at times mean is highly influenced by a few very large or very small values which are far away from the central values. They seem unlikely but are not impossible. These are called "outliers." In such situations, we should use median or mode as the measure of central tendency.

A Measure of Dispersion: Variance

Variance is used to measure the dispersion of a dataset. It is the average squared distances of all values of the population from its mean. The symbol for the variance of a population dataset is σ^2, which is given as follows:

$$\sigma^2 = \frac{1}{N}\sum_{i=1}^{i=N}(X_i - \mu)^2.$$

Like mean, there are three equivalent formulas for a variance.

When Y_j is the jth different value of the population with frequency f_j,there are k different values and p_j is the probability of drawing Y_j.

$$\sigma^2 = \frac{1}{N}\sum_{j=1}^{j=k}(Y_j - \mu)^2 f_j \quad \text{where } N = \sum_{j=1}^{k} f_j,$$

$$\sigma^2 = \frac{1}{N}\sum_{j=1}^{j=N}(Y_j - \mu)^2 \left(\frac{f_j}{N}\right),$$

$$\sigma^2 = \frac{1}{N}\sum_{j=1}^{j=N}(Y_j - \mu)^2 p_j.$$

In the following example, we calculate variance using the third formula.

j	Amount (INR) Y_j	Number of Individuals f_j	$Y_j \times f_j$	$f_j/N = p_j$	$Y_j \times p_j$	$Y_j - \mu$	$(Y_j - \mu)^2$	$(Y_j - \mu)^2 f_j$	$(Y_j - \mu)^2 p_j$
1	0	5	0	0.017	0	-18,150	329,422,500	1,647,112,500	5,490,375
2	5,000	25	125,000	0.083	417	-13,150	172,922,500	4,323,062,500	14,410,208
3	10,000	65	650,000	0.217	2,167	-8,150	66,422,500	4,317,462,500	14,391,542
4	15,000	79	1,185,000	0.263	3,950	-3,150	9,922,500	783,877,500	2,612,925
5	20,000	60	1,200,000	0.200	4,000	1,850	3,422,500	205,350,000	684,500
6	25,000	16	400,000	0.053	1,333	6,850	46,922,500	750,760,000	2,502,533
7	30,000	15	450,000	0.050	1,500	11,850	140,422,500	2,106,337,500	7,021,125
8	35,000	15	525,000	0.050	1,750	16,850	283,922,500	4,258,837,500	14,196,125
9	40,000	8	320,000	0.027	1,067	21,850	477,422,500	3,819,380,000	12,731,267
10	45,000	6	270,000	0.020	900	26,850	720,922,500	4,325,535,000	14,418,450
11	50,000	3	150,000	0.010	500	31,850	1,014,422,500	3,043,267,500	10,144,225
12	55,000	2	110,000	0.007	367	36,850	1,357,922,500	2,715,845,000	9,052,817
13	60,000	1	60,000	0.003	200	41,850	1,751,422,500	1,751,422,500	5,838,075
Total	Total	300	5,445,000	1.000	18,150	154050	6,375,492,500	34,048,250,000	113,494,167

$\mu = 18{,}150$

$$\sigma^2 = \frac{1}{N}\sum_{j=1}^{j=k}(Y_j - \mu)^2 f_j = \frac{1}{300}34{,}048{,}250{,}000 = 113{,}494{,}167 \qquad \sigma = \sqrt{113{,}494{,}167} = 10{,}653$$

Measure of Dispersion: Standard Deviation

Since variance inflates the actual distance, we can also consider the positive square root of the variance as a measure of dispersion. This is known as **standard deviation** and is denoted by small sigma (σ).

$$\text{Standard Deviation} = \sqrt{\text{Variance}}.$$

A Measure of Dispersion: Range

Range = maximum value – minimum value
The range is a quick measure of dispersion and easiest to calculate.
In the annual individual health expenditure dataset,
Range = 60,000 – 500 = 59,500.

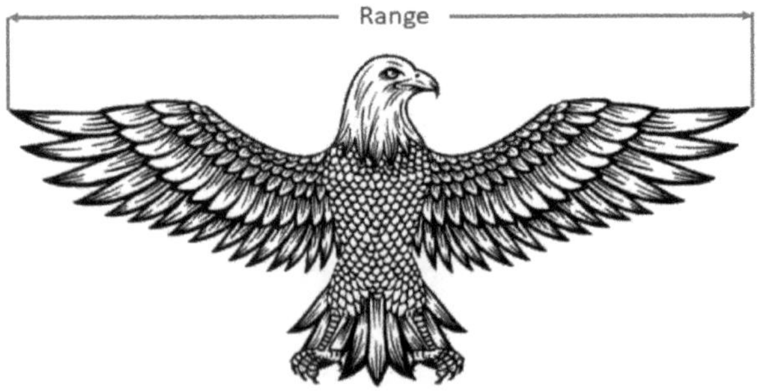

Measure of Skewness

The spread of the dataset may be symmetric or asymmetric around the central point. Skewness is the measure of the level of asymmetry. This is a shape parameter.

Measure of skewness:

$$\frac{\frac{1}{N}\sum_{i=1}^{i=N}\left(X_i-\mu\right)^3}{\sigma^3}=\frac{1}{N}\sum_{i=1}^{i=N}\left(\frac{X_i-\mu}{\sigma}\right)^3.$$

There is no standard symbol for skewness.

Like mean and variance, there are three equivalent formulas for skewness.

$$\text{Skewness}=\frac{\frac{1}{N}\sum_{i=1}^{i=N}\left(X_i-\mu\right)^3}{\sigma^3}=\frac{1}{N}\sum_{i=1}^{i=N}\left(\frac{X_i-\mu}{\sigma}\right)^3.$$

When Y_j is the jth different value of the population with frequency f_j, there are k different values and p_j is the probability of drawing Y_j.

$$\text{Skewness}=\frac{1}{N}\sum_{j=1}^{j=k}\left(\frac{Y_j-\mu}{\sigma}\right)^3 f_j.$$

$$\text{Skewness}=\sum_{j=1}^{j=k}\left(\frac{Y_j-\mu}{\sigma}\right)^3 p_j.$$

The following are a few graphical representations of different types of skewness.

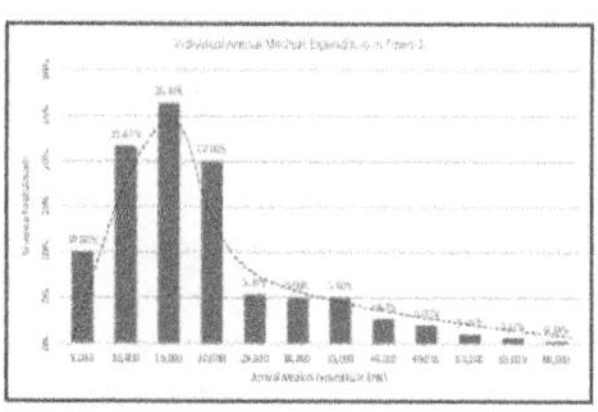

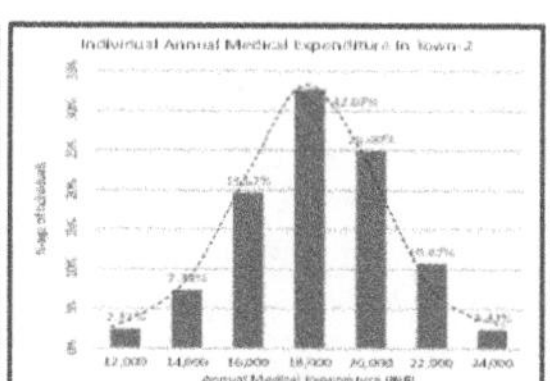

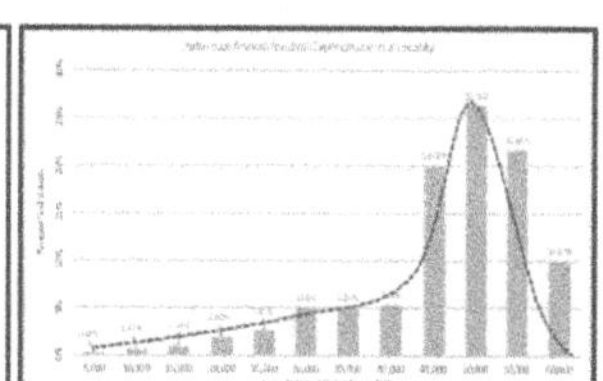

Positively skew
Longer tail
in +ve direction

Skewness ≈ 0
Equal tail
in each direction

Negatively skew
Longer tail
in -ve direction

Mean, Median, Mode, and Skewness

For the example here, the population pattern can be assessed using the measures of mean, variance, standard deviation, and skewness.

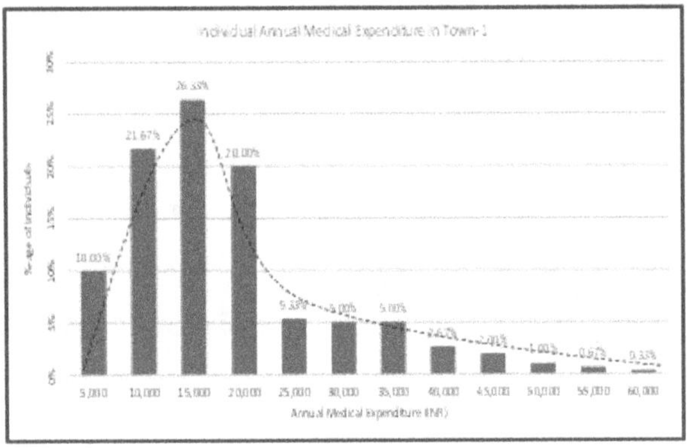

$$\mu = 18{,}233$$
$$\sigma^2 = 110{,}878{,}889$$
$$\sigma = 10{,}530$$
$$\text{Skewness}=1.31$$

KEY TERMS

- **Central tendency**: A dataset tends to cluster around a central point. This property of the dataset is known as a central tendency.
- **Dispersion**: The spread of the dataset is referred to as its dispersion. It is "some kind of an average" of distances of all values from its mean.
- **Outliers**: They are very large or very small data values which are far away from the central values.
- **Skewness:** The spread of the dataset may be symmetric or asymmetric around the central point. The Data Science jargon for this is *skewness*.

Issue Brief III: Software Applications

Software applications are sets of instructions or programs that facilitate the performance of designated operations with computers. This section introduces specific software packages used for data analysis and presentation.

A variety of these applications are available for data analysis today. The choice of software depends on the requirement of the analyst. Typically, the primary considerations for choosing the right application are as follows:

(1) **Size of data to be analyzed:** Some applications (e.g., MS-Excel) have limited data handling capacity.
(2) **Security:** Security of data is crucial. Generally, open-source applications may not guarantee data security.
(3) **Cost:** All applications are not free. Open-source software like R, RStudio, and Tableau Public are free to use, whereas MS-Excel, commercial versions of Tableau, Stata, and SPSS are proprietary software applications and require single payment or annual subscription as a license fee.
(4) **User-friendliness:** Some software are easy to use like MS-Excel. Others like R, SPSS, or Stata can be intricate to some and might require specialized training to make effective use of these applications.
(5) **Analysis and presentation:** Each application contains unique features. MS-Excel can produce graphical presentations which however cannot be as customized as in other applications like R or Tableau.

MS-Excel

MS-Excel is a widely used spreadsheet software (see Figure 1). Developed by Microsoft, it is a part of the Microsoft Office package, requiring a license fee to use. Initially, this was developed for Windows but is now available for macOS, Android, and iOS too.

Essential features of MS-Excel spreadsheet include the following:

1. **Ease of calculation using formulas:** MS-Excel offers approximately 500 formulas, and every new version release of MS-Excel adds more to the list. The calculations with these formulas range from simple

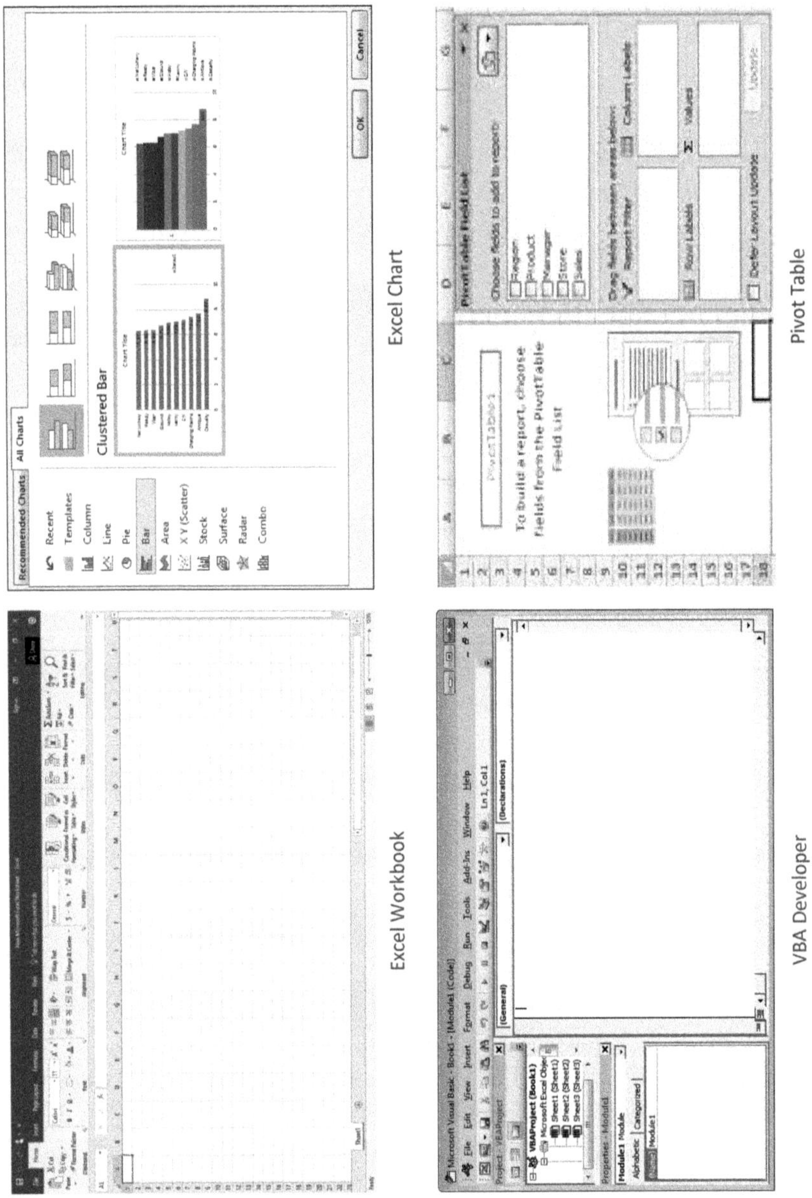

Figure 1 MS-Excel

arithmetic to complex calculations which are crucial to the field of mathematics, finances, engineering, or statistics.

2. **Graphing tools:** Data can be presented graphically as line graphs, bar graphs, pie chart, histogram, area graph, scatter diagram, box and whisker plot, etc.
3. **Pivot tables:** A unique feature available in MS-Excel, pivot tables allow users to easily cross-tab large amounts of raw data.
4. **Macro Recording (auto code builder):** Another interesting feature of MS-Excel, Macro recorder is a tool which allows users to record the tasks performed in MS-Excel spreadsheets as a visual basic for application (VBA) programming algorithm and store the algorithm for later repeat execution.
5. **Programming language:** This provides extended options for programmers to develop algorithms beyond the macro record can do. Also, programmers can build their own customized formulas using VBA.

MS-Excel supports add-in data installations. These add-ins provide additional functionalities to MS-Excel like other calculations than those using formulas. One of the most commonly used add-ins is data analysis pack that helps users to perform regression analysis, inferential testing, random number generation, etc.

The newer "Office 365" Microsoft Office package requires a monthly or annual subscription, includes regular product updates, and has online storage capacity. This is different from their conventional upfront one-time payment product.[11]

R

R is a popular programming language, compiler, and software environment for a data analyst. Its open-source environment and capacity to compute complex statistical and mathematical problems make it one of the most used software environments. R has a tremendous scope to produce a variety of graphical presentations, i.e., maps, charts, graphs, etc.

[11] Available at https://products.office.com/en-in/excel (accessed 17 February 2018).

R can very well compute statistical models like linear and nonlinear modeling, classical statistical tests, time series analysis, classification, clustering, and others.

Following are the popular R software:

- R Packages

R Packages are a collection of R functions, data, and set of compiled codes. There are some packages which come with R by default, but more

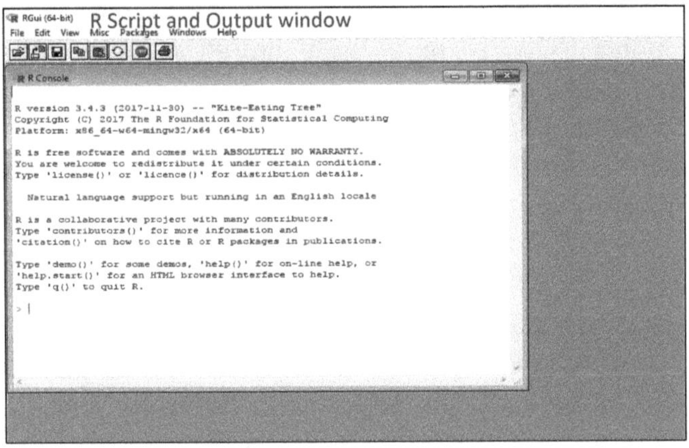

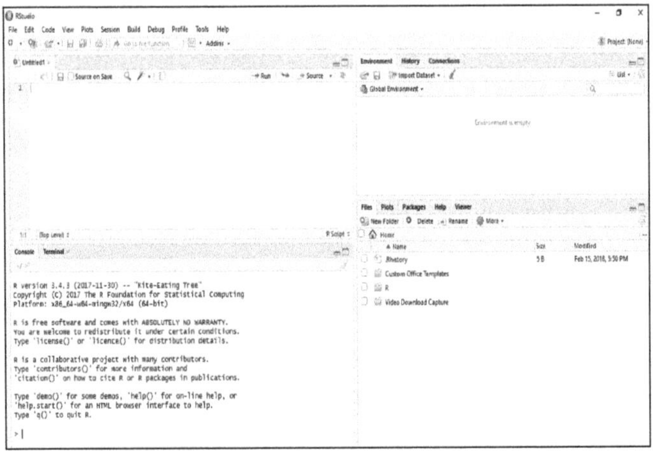

RStudio Script, Output, Data View and Graphic Viewer.

Figure 2 R and RStudio

can be added to extend the capability of R. There are thousands of packages published and available for use on popular R public repository named as "The Comprehensive R Archive Network (CRAN)." Some of the commonly used R packages are data.table, ggplot2, dplyr, plot3D, etc.

- RStudio

This provides an easy-to-use platform for R. With this platform, the user can utilize visual screen to write an R code in the code editor, produce output in console or viewer, and look at workspace or history at the same time (see Figure 2).

- Shiny

It is a unique package that helps build interactive web applications straight from R. This can also host standalone applications on a webpage or create dashboards (an information tool helps analysis and presents a set of indicators for monitoring). Shiny applications can be extended with CSS themes, HTML widgets, and JavaScript actions.[12]

- RStudio commercial, RStudio server pro, and R connect

These are paid professional software products by RStudio which hand over enterprise-grade security, priority support, and commercial product license for the subscribed period.[13]

SPSS

As the name suggests, Statistical Package for Social Sciences (SPSS) is a highly preferred software for people involved in research, social sciences, and epidemiology (see Figure 3).

SPSS is used for descriptive statistics (i.e., central tendency, dispersion, skewness, and kurtosis), cross-tabulation, frequencies and other descriptive statistics, numerical prediction using different regression models like linear regression, multiple and logistics regressions, etc. Also, the

[12]Available at http://shiny.rstudio.com/ (17 February 2018).

[13]Available at https://www.rstudio.com/ (17 February 2018).

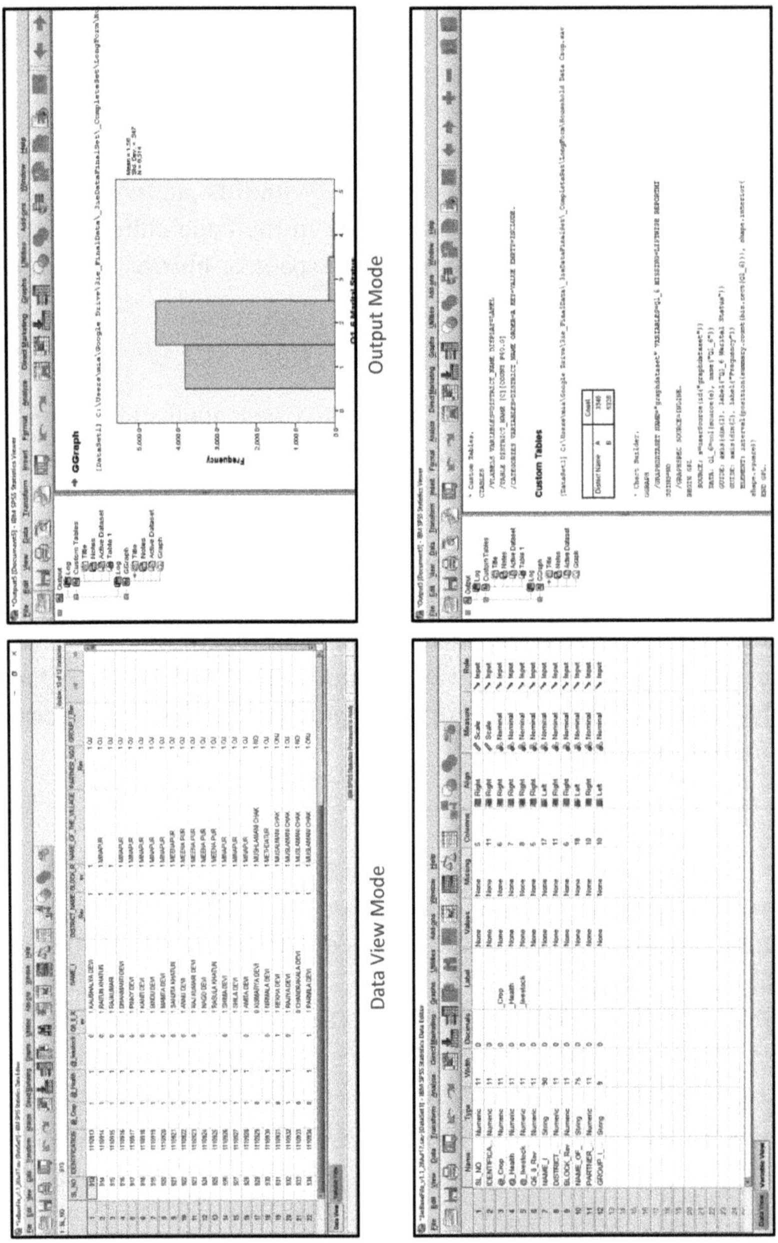

Figure 3 SPSS Statistics

prediction for different categorical groups using factor analysis, cluster analysis (two-step, K-means, hierarchical), etc.

SPSS Statistics can perform the computation of basic to advanced statistical analysis. IBM also provides advanced software called SPSS Modeler and SPSS Analytics server. SPSS Modeler can further deal with machine learning algorithms and text analysis, whereas SPSS Analytics Server can handle enormous amounts of data and is very suitable for integration and analysis of big data (large volume of data, generated out of social media, machines, and electronic transactions; the extent of data available in 2016 was around 16 zettabytes, and this is expected to increase 10-fold by 2025[14]).

Stata

Stata is also one of the widely used statistical software package, used by researchers and data analysts (see Figure 4). It provides high-end statistical analysis and graphical presentation. It is not open-source software.

This package is capable of producing several statistical and mathematical computations using in-build commands and dropdown menus and through extensive coding. This software can deal with standard data analysis methods like basic tabulations and summary statistics, case–control analysis, time series analysis (analysis includes pattern recognition over the period), regression analysis, generalized linear models (GLMs), cluster analysis, power analysis, choice modeling, sample selection, and more.

Also, Stata can take care of advanced analysis like multilevel models, survival models, panel data regressions, structural equation modeling (SEM), Bayesian analysis, etc.

Tableau

The uniqueness of this software application is that it provides a solution in the form of visual presentation rather than conventional tabular numerical solutions (see Figure 5). Tableau provides high-end graphics which are

[14]International Data Corporation (IDC) report published in April 2017.

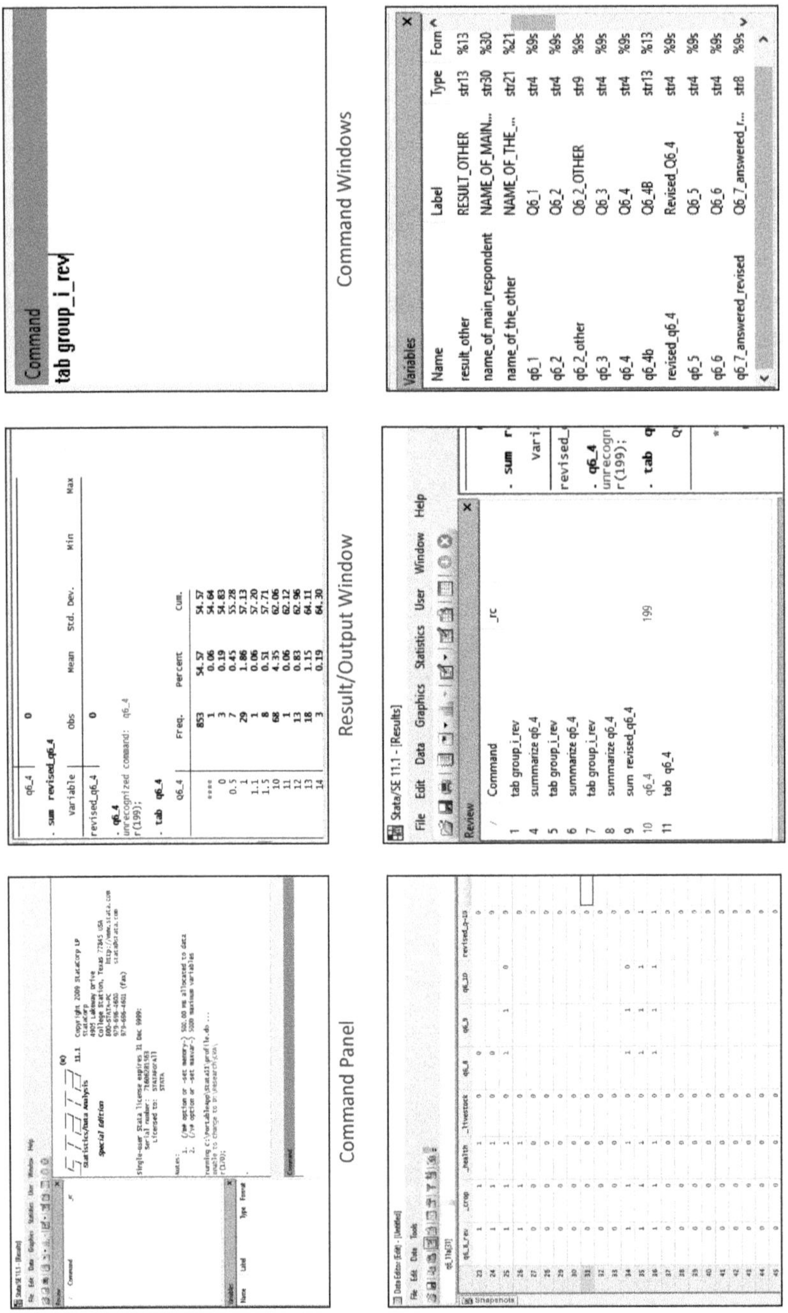

Figure 4 Stata

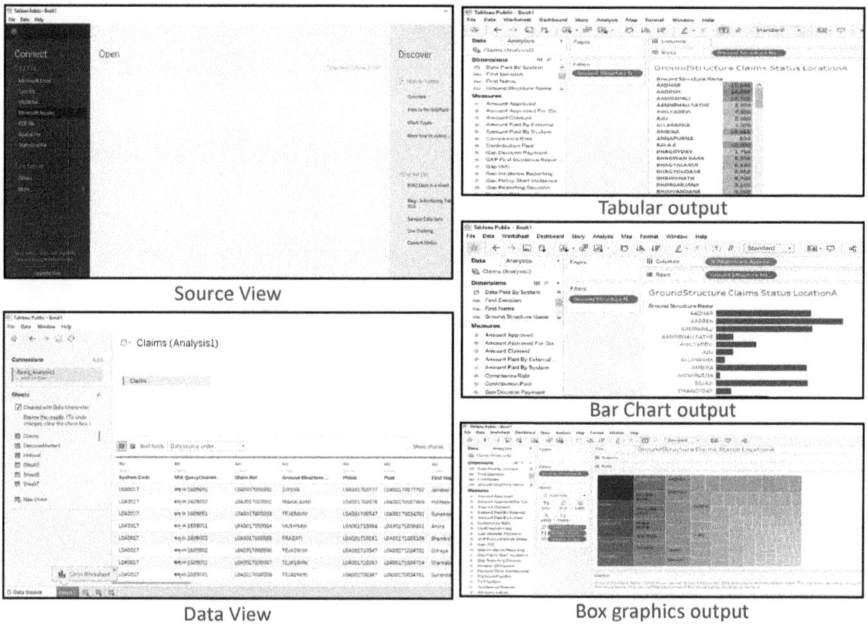

Figure 5 Tableau

not readily available in other applications. This application is useful in handling big data, business dashboards, map presentations, survey analysis, time series analysis, etc.

Chapter 14

MIS in Microinsurance

LEARNING OBJECTIVES

Upon completion of this chapter, the reader should be able to:

- Describe the role of MIS in the activities of microinsurance
- Understand how MIS can help overcome the challenges of managing CBHI information
- Enumerate the information that can be stored in MIS and its source
- Discuss ways of improving database efficiency
- Describe the data structure for records of premium collected and for claims processing
- Explain the stages of claims processing and the role played by MIS in this process

Abstract

When a microinsurance scheme is up and running, it generates both financial and non-financial data which help to perform analysis. Thus, data are not merely a by-product but have an intrinsic value. The way to capitalize on such data is to record and process them continuously, generate reports on demand, and assist the scheme managers in making informed decisions based on specific indicators. Such data processing requires a Management Information System (MIS). In this chapter, we understand the functioning of MIS in a microinsurance setup.

Chapter Outline

What is Management Information System?

MIS is an acronym for *Management Information System.*

The stage is set for implementation of the scheme once the benefits package is finalized. Chapter 12 (and the *Microinsurance Business Processes Handbook* by Dror and Jambhekar (2016)) provides a detailed discussion of the business processes for implementation of such schemes. An operational scheme generates records for all financial and non-financial transactions. These data need to be stored and analyzed for operational efficiency, monitoring, decision-making, and research purposes. The function of the MIS is to store and analyze the data.

MIS is a frequently used management jargon. The large variety of sources from which data are obtained render the task of managing information as a resource of the organization complicated. Another complication is that it is difficult to distinguish at a glance which bits of information may be relevant or irrelevant. Therefore, it is necessary to define both the information that an organization should collect and the structure in which such information would be recorded and retained for future reference. Stated simply, only when there is an *orderly continuous repetitive process, which is not random*, which is accessible to office bearers, can the source of information be useful. The MIS is the set of interconnected components for collection, processing, storage, and communication of information needed to carry out managerial functions.

Simply put, *it is a system of collecting data continuously and translating them into functional tools* to assist the four essential managerial functions of *planning, organizing, leading, and controlling.*[1]

Developing an MIS requires knowledge of the following four key areas:

(1) **Managerial tasks:** It helps the management to make timely strategic decisions for efficient use of limited resources.

[1]Those interested in reading more about organizations and management may refer to standard management textbooks.

(2) **Data needs:** Decisions cannot be based on voluminous data with minimal relevance to the organization's activities (see Chapter 13, Data in Microinsurance). Designing or managing a comprehensive MIS starts with discussions on the data that are relevant for decision-making.
(3) **Source of data:** Then comes determination of sources for collection of data in a timely, accurate, and acceptable manner and form (see the section on Data Sources in Chapter 13, Data in Microinsurance). Many software packages are designed to process data.
(4) **Key Performance Indicators:** The KPIs inform the efficiency of management functions and success of the organization's operations. These can be represented graphically and can be in the form of reports, presentations, and memos in printed format or as soft copies (more about KPIs is discussed in Chapter 15).

The role of MIS in insurance

Before we discuss MIS in microinsurance, let us look at the role of MIS in the insurance industry. Insurance companies provide risk coverage for specified risks within certain limitations and qualifying conditions, in return for a price, commonly called premium. The insurer indemnifies the insured (usually the person who paid the premium) when loss-generating events occur that are predefined as reimbursable.

The main activities of an insurance company are as follows:

(1) **Underwriting** — The process of raising investment capital to cover the total amount of risk that each risk-taker is willing to accept at a specified premium. The origin of the term is from the practice of each risk-taker to write his/her name under the risk he/she agreed to take. Before accepting a risk, each underwriter evaluates the potential clients risk exposure and then decides whether "to accept the risk, and under which limitations and conditions and for what premium."
(2) **Client acquisition** — "Acquiring" means obtaining offers for insurance from potential clients, usually by engaging third parties as intermediaries (e.g., agents, brokers). As there is a cost to developing a

client base (e.g., payment of commissions to intermediaries), this function is often described as "acquisition."

(3) **Product servicing (aka after-sale service)** — It is the process of receiving, adjudicating, and settling claims, in cases that the insured submit claims on the occurrence of an insured adverse event.

(4) **Fund management** — It means managing investments and liquidity requirements of the fund to comply with regulations and is in line with the objectives of the organization (e.g., a for-profit insurer would seek profit maximization, a mutual fund would seek to enhance welfare gains of the members).

(5) **Reinsurance** — It is the function of deciding which part of the insurer's underwritten risks should be ceded to other companies (insurance of insurers is called reinsurance).

For underwriting, it is necessary to have historical information about risk exposure by risk category. The books of accounts and membership lists must reflect the name of the insured person and the premiums received. For claims settlement, it is necessary to have the details of the insurance coverage, validity of the coverage, and applicable terms and conditions that apply to each client. Fund managers require updated financials for decisions on investments and liquidity required. The design of the MIS must be such that the required information would be available on demand.

The data sources chosen determine the reliability and accuracy of the information. For example, the details filled in by the applicant on the application form determine the correctness of the client database and help in hassle-free claim settlement. When a new MIS is started, it may not have any historical data, but a client database that is maintained for several years can provide the information required to improve existing products or design new ones.

Here we discuss the requirements of the MIS for the core business of the insurance company, i.e., providing insurance cover to those who solicit it. MIS would also be required for the management of human resources (HR), accounts, and other activities of the company. These would form a part of the overall MIS for the organization.

Role of MIS in microinsurance

We define microinsurance as voluntary, contributory, and group-based insurance schemes in which the prospective members participate in package designing and setting of the premiums, and/or in the governance of the scheme (participation in governance may entail roles in client acquisition, claims settlement, underwriting (e.g., when risks are mutualized in part or in full) and dispute resolution (Dror and Jambhekar, 2016, p. xxii). A mutual model, called Community-Based Mutual Aid Scheme (CBMAS) has been discussed in detail in the handbook (Dror and Jambhekar, 2016, p. xxii) and manual (Dror and Jambhekar, 2017, p. xviii). The discussion of microinsurance MIS is based on this model.

Microinsurance operations are like those of an insurance company, with the notable difference that the objective is creating welfare gains (aka profit-sharing) for the members rather than profit taking by shareholders. The management tasks in microinsurance operations can be simplified as follows:

- package design (in the first year) and package revisions in subsequent years;
- managing policies (enrollment of new policies, renewals, and closing the records of members who are no longer eligible for coverage);
- claims processing: adjudication, decisions, payment of claims, and dispute resolution;
- monitoring and evaluation.

Developing MIS for microinsurance is more challenging because microinsurance serves the population in the informal sector, where even basic information (like documentary proof of birth, marriage, death, etc.) may be hard to obtain. This lack of documentary infrastructure is aggravated further by the lack of trained human resource to manage the MIS. The requirement of computerized MIS cannot be over-emphasized. While theoretically it is possible to maintain manual MIS, such system is prone to more human errors, inconsistencies, lack of audit trails and internal validations at the time of data entry, and higher risk of physical destruction due to loss, fire, etc., and difficult to manage as the operations expand. Therefore, it is necessary to develop a simple MIS that can be easily managed by the local talent and skills available within the community. To illustrate this point, we discuss examples from MIA-MIS[2] in the following chapters.

SELF-TEST QUESTIONS

1. Discuss the role of MIS in the various activities of an insurance company. Does its role change in a CBHI setup? Why/Why not?
2. What kind of challenges do an organization face in managing information? How can an MIS help in the management tasks of microinsurance?
3. To develop an MIS, which four key areas should be well understood?

MIA-MIS — Collection, Storage, and Processing of Data

Applying the systems approach to understand MIS, we have the following (Figure 14.1):

- **Input** — which in case of microinsurance are the forms, receipts, and claim papers;

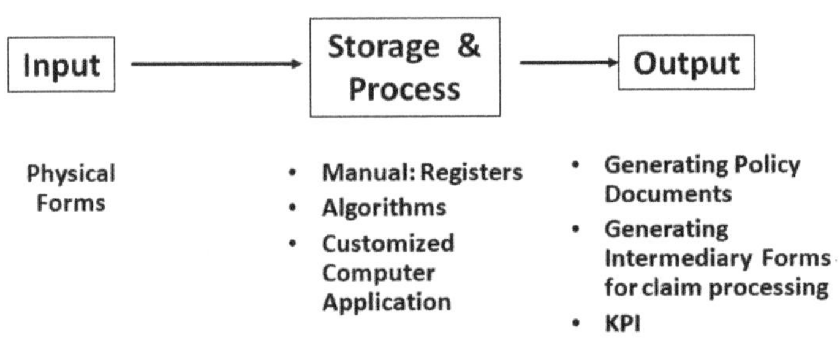

Figure 14.1 Systems Approach to MIS

[2]A database application designed and developed by Micro Insurance Academy for management of CBHI.

- **Storage and process** — which can be physical registers or a specialized software;
- **Output** — the documents generated on demand, reports, and KPI calculations.

For enrollment in health microinsurance, the data collected using the enrollment form includes the following:

- policyholder and details of his/her household;
- details of the insured people/items;
- details of the nominee;
- particular benefits package;
- location = address;
- religion;
- caste;
- socioeconomic status (APL/BPL);
- income;
- name;
- sex;
- age;
- education status;
- marital status;
- occupation;
- income;
- health status — pre-existing diseases;
- habits (smoking, alcohol);
- whether renewal or new policy.

For claims processing, the following data are collected:

- details about the ailing person;
- details of the event;
- evidence/proof documents;
- name;
- sex;
- age;

- policy reference;
- household Id number;
- individual Id number;
- ailment or condition;
- period (dates);
- details about the provider;
- name, address, type of provider (private/public);
- procedures taken;
- OPD/IPD;
- medication/operation/ imaging/ lab test;
- expenditure;
- benefit types;
- bills;
- proofs of procedures;
- discharge certificate;
- lab reports;
- imaging reports;
- doctor's prescriptions, etc.

The output from the enrollment data is the participatory note.

The data are stored in a structured format — each called "a field" and together "data fields." An example helps to recollect the earlier discussion about structured data.

Policyholder's name is Manoj Pandey. He has two dependents; Gita (his spouse) and Ravi (his son). This is an example of unstructured data.

The same data can be converted into the following format:

Structured Data

Surname	First name	Relation with policyholder
Pandey	Manoj	Self
Pandey	Gita	Wife
Pandey	Ravi	Son

In a computerized system, similar data thus will look like the following:

Household-level data

HHIDPSL	PHHID	DateOfEntry	DateFirst	GroundStructureName	Country	District	GeoLevel	Address	Phone	...	...	...	...	...
1	LOA001100001	03-07-2013	14-Jun-13	SURYA	NEPAL	BANKE	SONPUR	SINDURI-9		...	...	...	...	...
2	LOA001100002	24-05-2013	14-Jun-13	SURYA	NEPAL	BANKE	BAGESWO	BAGESWORI-2		...	...	...	...	...
3	LOA001100003	24-05-2013	14-Jun-13	SURYA	NEPAL	BANKE	BAGESWO	B-GAUN-1	9848030911	...	...	...	...	...
4	LOA001100004	22-04-2013	14-Jun-13	SURYA	NEPAL	BANKE	BAGESHW	B GAUN-2	9848012855	...	...	...	...	...
5	LOA001100005	16-05-2013	14-Jun-13	SURYA	NEPAL	BANKE	BAGESWO	B-GAUN-2	9848202205	...	...	...	...	...
6	LOA001100006	06-06-2013	14-Jun-13	SURYA	NEPAL	BANKE	BAGESWO	SRIJANA TC	9848057503	...	...	...	...	...
7	LOA001100007	03-05-2013	14-Jun-13	SURYA	NEPAL	BANKE	BAGESWO	B-GAUN-9	9848244305	...	...	...	...	...
8	LOA001100008	15-06-2011	14-Jun-11	SURYA	NEPAL	BANKE				...	...	...	...	...
9	LOA001100009	23-04-2013	14-Jun-13	SURYA	NEPAL	BANKE	BAGESHW	B GAUN-3	9848181222	...	...	...	...	...
10	LOA001100010	16-05-2013	14-Jun-13	SURYA	NEPAL	BANKE	BAGESWO	B-GAUN-3		...	...	...	...	...

Individual-level data

PHHID	PUID	DateAdded	Slno	FirstName	MiddleName	LastName	Sex	AgeInYears	AgeInMonths	DOB	MaritalStatus	...	...	...	...	...
LOA001100001	LOA00110000101	14-06-2013	1	RUKMA		JAISI	FEMALE	26		15-06-1987	2=MARRIED	...	...	...	...	...
LOA001100001	LOA00110000102	14-06-2011	2	Nandakala		Jaise	FEMALE	61		15-06-1950	1	...	...	...	...	...
LOA001100001	LOA00110000103	14-06-2012	3	BHARAT		JAISE	MALE	26		15-06-1986	2=MARRIED	...	...	...	...	...
LOA001100001	LOA00110000104	14-06-2013	4	SANSKAR/RUPSON		JAISI	MALE	3		15-06-2010	1=UNMARRIED	...	...	...	...	...
LOA001100001	LOA00110000105	14-06-2013	5	DHAN	BAHADUR	JAISI	MALE	65		15-06-1948	2=MARRIED	...	...	...	...	...
LOA001100001	LOA00110000106	14-06-2013	6	NANDAKALA		JAISI	FEMALE	60		15-06-1953	2=MARRIED	...	...	...	...	...
LOA001100001	LOA00110000107	14-06-2013	7	Chandra	Bahadur	Jaisi	Male	65		15-06-1948	2=MARRIED	...	...	...	...	...
LOA001100002	LOA00110000201	14-06-2013	1	BIMALA		KAUCHA	FEMALE	30		15-06-1983	2=MARRIED	...	...	...	...	...
LOA001100002	LOA00110000202	14-06-2011	2	Payel		Kaucha	FEMALE	6		15-06-2005	8	...	...	...	...	...

The process consists of an algorithm or rules or steps for computing.

Example — To answer the question of *how many people have joined the scheme from Meenapur village in Muzaffarpur District of Bihar who are 60 years and above.*

We follow the steps given subsequently:

Step 1
GOTO the table for individual records (open the corresponding register).

Step 2
COUNT the number of records who live in Village = "Vaishali" AND District = "Muzaffarpur" AND State = "Bihar" AND Age>= 60.

Step 3
Report the number.

The algorithm should be well defined so that the answer is independent of the individual using the system.

Data from MIS can also be represented graphically as shown in Figure 14.2.

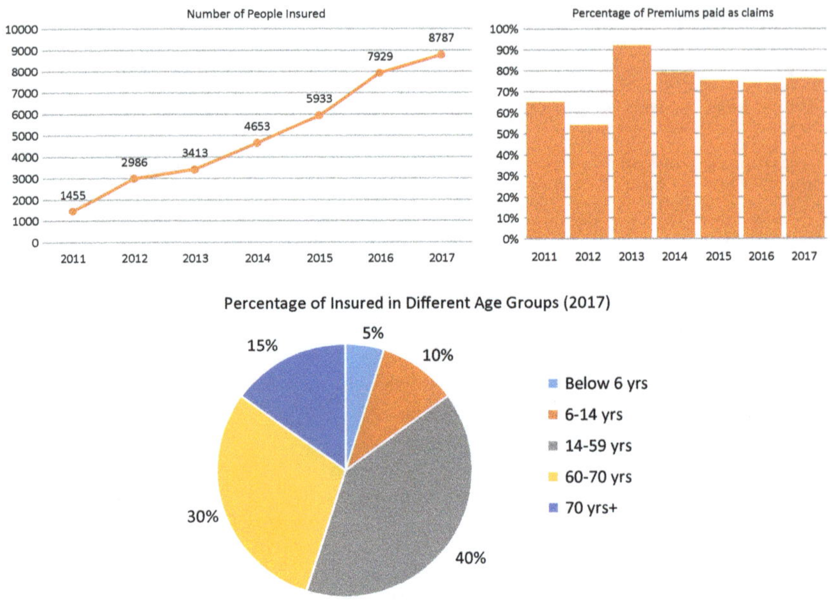

Figure 14.2 Graphical Representation of Data from MIS

SELF-TEST QUESTION

1. Describe MIS in microinsurance using the systems approach. What kind of information would the MIS store and what is the source of this information?

Database — Enrollments and Premiums

Enrollment

The Composition of Members Database

The members' database in the MIS is a repository of data about members of the scheme. It captures details of the policyholder and his/her household and details of all insured members of the household, including socioeconomic indicators and health indicators. This information is collected at the time of enrollment and renewal of the policy.

This chapter seeks to demonstrate the process of designing a template for members' database and explain the management of this database to take into account membership renewals, inactive memberships, deletions (or archiving), and package entitlement.

We begin by developing a template with a crude database (spreadsheet), and then take this discussion to more complex relational databases (RDBs, these act as the basis for data management in high-end offline and online applications) (see Figures 14.4 and 14.5).

Individual level Data

Name
Sex
Age
Education status
Marital Status
Occupation
Income
Health Status-Pre Existing Diseases
Habits (smoking, alcohol)
Whether Renewal or New Policy

Designing a Template for a Spreadsheet Database

At the time of enrollment/renewal, member data such as those shown in Figure 14.3 are collected.

These data are then entered in a spreadsheet template and captured under various fields (see Figure 14.4).

The spreadsheet database is now ready and comprises all the members' data that were collected (see Figure 14.5).

To make these data less erroneous (duplication or typing errors) and processable (ease of accessibility), this list of members should be linked to unique identifiers (UIDs). In Figure 14.6, we see a graphical presentation of tables and the assigned identifiers.

UIDs for Different Risk Groups

UIDs are needed in a database to avoid system duplicity. For instance, in the absence of UIDs, it is hard to distinguish between two different persons with the same name, or between two different households in the same village with the same household number.

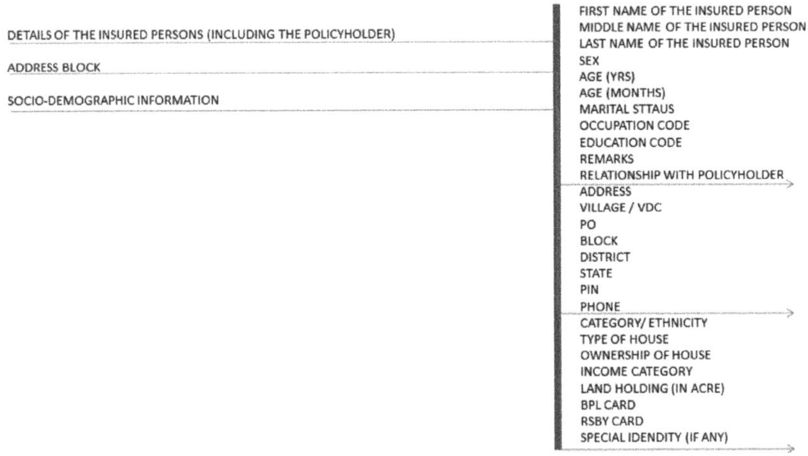

Figure 14.3 Member Data

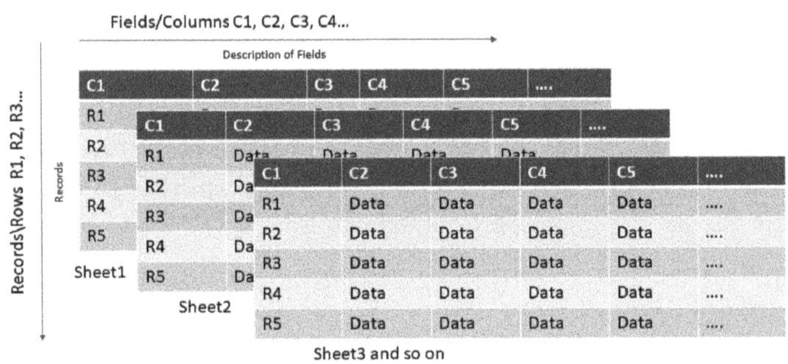

Figure 14.4 Spreadsheets

	A	B	O	P	Q	R	S	T	U	V	W	X	Y
1	ORIGINAL SLNO	DATE OF ENTRY	DETAILS OF THE INSURED PERSONS (INCLUDING THE POLICYHOLDER)										
2			FIRST NAME OF THE INSURED PERSON	MIDDLE NAME OF THE INSURED PERSON	LAST NAME OF THE INSURED PERSON	SEX	AGE (YRS)	AGE (MONTHS)	MARITAL STTAUS	OCCUPATION CODE	EDUCATION CODE	REMARKS	RELATIONSHIP WITH POLICYHOLDER
4	1	20-May-13	JOYTI	KUMARI	CHAND	FEMALE	26		2-MARRIED	1-Self-employed in	9-Class-IX		POLICYHOLDER
5	2	20-May-13	SAMRAT		SINGH	MALE	2		1-UNAMRRIED	8-Pre-school child	16 - Never been to school		4-Unmarried child
6	3	20-May-13	ALINA		RAMJALI	FEMALE	24		2-MARRIED	11-Housewife	10-Class-x		POLICYHOLDER
7	4	20-May-13	NAMITA		RAMJALI	FEMALE	3		1-UNAMRRIED	8-Pre-school child	1-Class-I		4-Unmarried child
8	5	20-May-13	GITA		ADHIKARI	FEMALE	39		2-MARRIED	11-Housewife	5-Class-V		POLICYHOLDER
9	6	20-May-13	SHARMILA		KC	FEMALE	35		2-MARRIED	11-Housewife	5-Class-V		POLICYHOLDER
10	7	20-May-13	RAJ	LAXMI	RAYAMAGHI	FEMALE	58		2-MARRIED	11-Housewife	8-Class-VIII		POLICYHOLDER
11	8	20-May-13	DIYA		CHAUDHARY	FEMALE	2		1-UNAMRRIED	8-Pre-school child	1-Class-I		5-Grandchild
12	9	20-May-13	LATA		GURUNG	FEMALE	27		2-MARRIED	2-Self-employed in	9-Class-IX		POLICYHOLDER
13	10	20-May-13	SITA	MAYA	THAPA	FEMALE	48		2-MARRIED	2-Self-employed in	16 - Never been to school		POLICYHOLDER
14	11	20-May-13	SURYA	BAHADUR	THAPA	MALE	50		2-MARRIED	3-Regular salaried e	8-Class-VIII		1-Husband
15	12	20-May-13	RAJ	KUMARI	SHAHA	FEMALE	45		2-MARRIED	2-Self-employed in	3-Class-III		POLICYHOLDER

Figure 14.5 Members' Database

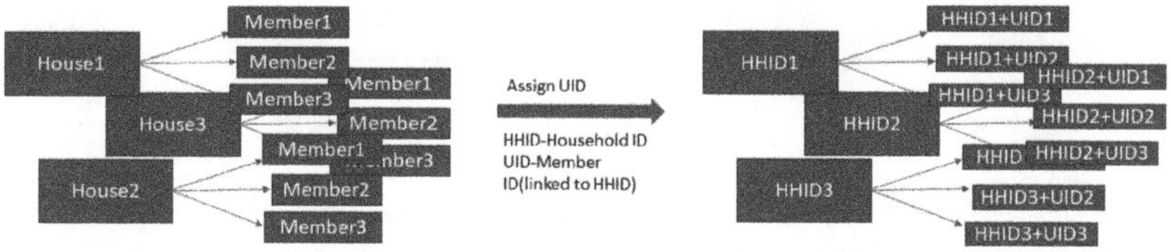

Figure 14.6 Assigning UIDs

	A	B	M	N	O	P	Q	R	S	T	U	V
1			Unique Identifiers		DETAILS OF THE INSURED PERSONS (INCLUDING THE POLICYHOLDER)							
2	ORIGINAL SLNO	DATE OF ENTRY	HOUSEHOLD ID	UNIQUE MEMBER ID	FIRST NAME OF THE INSURED PERSON	MIDDLE NAME OF THE INSURED PERSON	LAST NAME OF THE INSURED PERSON	SEX	AGE (YRS)	AGE (MONTHS)	MARITAL STTAUS	OCCUPATION CODE
4	1	20-May-13	RAN-13060001	RAN-1306000101	JOYTI	KUMARI	CHAND	FEMALE	26		2-MARRIED	1-Self-employed in agric
5	2	20-May-13	RAN-13060001	RAN-1306000102	SAMRAT		SINGH	MALE	2		1-UNAMRRIED	8-Pre-school child
6	3	20-May-13	RAN-13060003	RAN-1306000301	ALINA		RAMJALI	FEMALE	24		2-MARRIED	11-Housewife
7	4	20-May-13	RAN-13060003	RAN-1306000302	NAMITA		RAMJALI	FEMALE	3		1-UNAMRRIED	8-Pre-school child
8	5	20-May-13	RAN-13060005	RAN-1306000501	SITA		ADHIKARI	FEMALE	39		2-MARRIED	11-Housewife
9	6	20-May-13	RAN-13060006	RAN-1306000601	SHARMILA		KC	FEMALE	35		2-MARRIED	11-Housewife
10	7	20-May-13	RAN-13060007	RAN-1306000701	RAJ	LAXMI	RAYAMAGHI	FEMALE	58		2-MARRIED	11-Housewife
11	8	20-May-13	RAN-13060007	RAN-1306000702	DIYA		CHAUDHARY	FEMALE	2		1-UNAMRRIED	8-Pre-school child
12	9	20-May-13	RAN-13060009	RAN-1306000901	LATA		GURUNG	FEMALE	27		2-MARRIED	2-Self-employed in busin
13	10	20-May-13	RAN-13060010	RAN-1306001001	SITA	MAYA	THAPA	FEMALE	48		2-MARRIED	2-Self-employed in busin
14	11	20-May-13	RAN-13060010	RAN-1306001002	SURYA	BAHADUR	THAPA	MALE	50		2-MARRIED	3-Regular salaried emplo
15	12	20-May-13	RAN-13060012	RAN-1306001201	RAJ	KUMARI	SHAHA	FEMALE	45		2-MARRIED	2-Self-employed in busin
16	13	20-May-13	RAN-13060012	RAN-1306001202	SHIVA	DHOJ	SHAHA	MALE	46		2-MARRIED	3-Regular salaried emplo
17	14	20-May-13	RAN-13060012	RAN-1306001203	ANUSHA		SHAHA	FEMALE	19		1-UNAMRRIED	7-Attend educational ins
18	15	20-May-13	RAN-13060012	RAN-1306001204	AMISHA		SHAHA	FEMALE	15		1-UNAMRRIED	7-Attend educational ins

Figure 14.7 Spreadsheet Database with UIDs

The following are UIDs which can be used:

- Household Unique Identification.
- Individual Unique Identification.
- Package Unique Identification.
- Policy Unique Identification.

Spreadsheet Database with UIDs

UIDs can be introduced in the spreadsheet database, as shown in Figure 14.7.

In this database, Household ID represents an identifier of the household, whereas Unique Member ID represents individual characteristics.

Let us consider one of the records RAN-1306000101. The database gives us information that this person is a member of household RAN-13060001. The member JOYTI KUMARI CHAND is a 26-year-old FEMALE. She is MARRIED and is Self-employed in agriculture. She studied until Class-IX. She is a POLICYHOLDER and lives in SHANTINAGAR-5, KARKADO,

	A	B	C	D	E	F	M	N	O	P	Q	R	S	T	U
1	ORIGINAL SLNO	DATE OF ENTRY	REFERENCE TO POLICY				Unique Identifiers								
2			PACKAGE IDENTIFIER	POLICY START DATE	POLICY EXPIRY DATE	POLICY PERIOD (IN MONTHS)	HOUSEHOLD ID	UNIQUE MEMBER ID	FIRST NAME OF THE INSURED PERSON	MIDDLE NAME OF THE INSURED PERSON	LAST NAME OF THE INSURED PERSON	SEX	AGE (YRS)	AGE (MONTHS)	MARITAL STATUS
4	1	20-May-13	1306	15-Jun-13	14-Jun-14	12	RAN-13060001	RAN-1306000101	JOYTI	KUMARI	CHAND	FEMALE	24		2-MARRIED
5	2	20-May-13	1306	15-Jun-13	14-Jun-14	12	RAN-13060001	RAN-1306000102	SAMRAT		SINGH	MALE	2		1-UNAMRRIED
6	3	20-May-13	1306	15-Jun-13	14-Jun-14	12	RAN-13060003	RAN-1306000301	ALINA		RAMJALI	FEMALE	24		2-MARRIED
7	4	20-May-13	1306	15-Jun-13	14-Jun-14	12	RAN-13060003	RAN-1306000302	NAMITA		RAMJALI	FEMALE	3		1-UNAMRRIED
8	5	20-May-13	1306	15-Jun-13	14-Jun-14	12	RAN-13060005	RAN-1306000501	GITA		ADHIKARI	FEMALE	34		2-MARRIED
9	6	20-May-13	1306	15-Jun-13	14-Jun-14	12	RAN-13060006	RAN-1306000601	SHARMILA		KC	FEMALE	35		2-MARRIED
10	7	20-May-13	1306	15-Jun-13	14-Jun-14	12	RAN-13060007	RAN-1306000701	RAJ	LAXMI	RAYAMAGHI	FEMALE	56		2-MARRIED
11	8	20-May-13	1306	15-Jun-13	14-Jun-14	12	RAN-13060007	RAN-1306000702	DIYA		CHAUDHARY	FEMALE	2		1-UNAMRRIED
12	9	20-May-13	1306	15-Jun-13	14-Jun-14	12	RAN-13060009	RAN-1306000901	LATA		GURUNG	FEMALE	27		2-MARRIED
13	10	20-May-13	1306	15-Jun-13	14-Jun-14	12	RAN-13060010	RAN-1306001001	SITA	MAYA	THAPA	FEMALE	48		2-MARRIED

Figure 14.8 Spreadsheet Database with the Package Identifier

BANKE, NEPAL. She is a Brahman/Chhetri by religion. She lives in a Pucca house, which is her owned property. She earns over ₹90,000 per annum. She also owns 1 KATTHA of agriculture land.

Spreadsheet Database with Package Identification

Another identifier that is linked to the member database is the insurance package identifier. This identification represents members' entitlement to insurance package (Figure 14.8).

Relational Database

While spreadsheets offer an easy way of data storing, processing (retrieval, sorting, filtering, searching, or performing calculations), and presenting, they have limited data-holding capacity. Also, spreadsheets offer limited functionality for amending the database through data insertion, or deletion, or appending of two datasets. This is where RDBs have an advantage over spreadsheet databases.

An RDB is a common set of multiple datasets organized by tables, records, and columns. RDBs establish a well-defined relationship between database tables. Tables communicate and share information, which facilitates data searchability, organization, and reporting.[3]

In an RDB, we have two or more tables linked with UIDs.

UIDs are the criteria for creating relationships between data points of one table with another table(s). Relations between tables can be defined as one to one, one to many, or many to one.

Another advantage of RDBs is that it offers data normalization, which means optimized storage, faster processing, and quick presentation. RDBs

[3] https://www.techopedia.com/definition/1234/relational-database-rdb (accessed 12 April 2019).

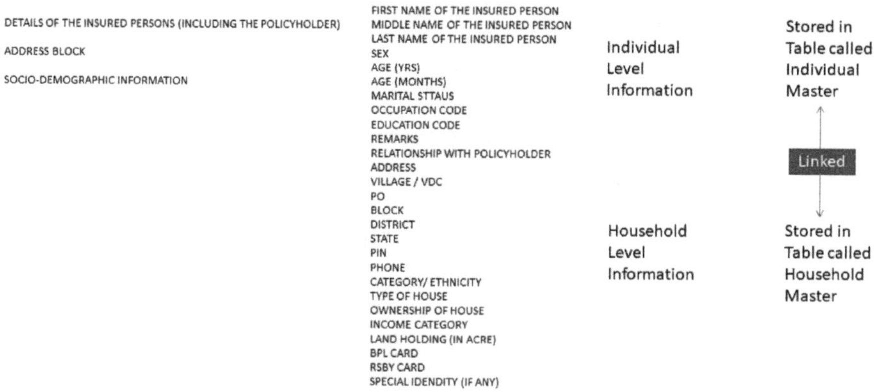

Figure 14.9 Enrollment Data in an RDB

provide ample scope for normalization using data segmentation into multiple tables with optimized linkage. This increases the processing capacity and performance of the application. The relational convenience allows for a single data point to be stored in multiple tables using a unique linkage key. This helps in avoiding repetitive entries of address and socio-demographic information for each.

In Figure 14.9, the enrollment data is saved at two levels — the individual level (Table — Individual Master) and at the household level (Table — Household Master). A link is established between these two tables so that details of address and socio-demographic indicators are not repeated.

SELF-TEST QUESTIONS

1. What do we mean by UIDs? Enumerate some UIDs which can be used in spreadsheet databases holding microinsurance members' information.
2. What are RDBs? What advantages do they have over spreadsheet databases?

Understanding Normalized

Table Structure To understand the benefits of a normalized table structure, let us look at the example given in Figure 14.10.

The data in the spreadsheet here have a repetition of address details and socioeconomic status for some individuals. This can be avoided

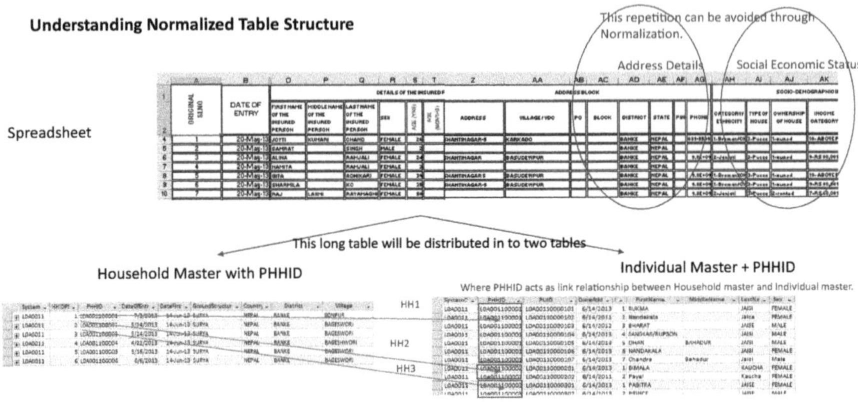

Figure 14.10 Understanding Normalized Table Structure

through normalization, where one large spreadsheet table is split into two tables: Household Master with PHHID, and Individual Master + PHHID. Since PHHID acts as a link between these two tables, the number of fields required in individual tables is reduced.

Improving Database Efficiency

Identifying Permanent Data It is essential to identify data which are permanent, which are unlikely to change in the short term. This distinction avoids data repetition and enhances the efficiency of the database. It also helps developers by providing some separate storage space for data retrieval in case of later use.

(1) Household and individual master tables are permanent and so are the identifications allotted to each household and individual.
(2) Household location parameters remain permanent unless migrated (which is less probable).
(3) Members residing in the households remain the same unless some of them shift to other households (marriage) or die or migrate (which is also rare).
(4) Member characteristics can also be permanent (like name, gender, age at joining, date of birth, etc.) or variable (source of earning, income, age, education, habits, marital status, etc.).

Package Entitlement in an RDB: In microinsurance, the benefits package defines the benefits, price, and terms and conditions for risk cover. The scheme agrees to cover the underlying risks for a predefined term. To be able to access the package entitlement details for each, the member's database needs to be linked with package details and coverage term (usually one year in health and livestock insurance). This linkage requires a set of tables with package details, price, terms and conditions, etc.

In MIA-MIS, the package entitlements/premiums are shown in the subsequent tables.

Package Details Master Table: It holds details of the package like the term of coverage, the name of the package, type of package, description, etc.

Package Renewal Master Table: This table includes details of linking packages of previous years, e.g., enrollment in package "X" in the first year but renewed with package "Y" in a later year. This table helps the system to identify the renewal linkage in such cases.

Premium Rate Master Table: This table includes the premium payable amount.

Premium Installment Master Table: This table retains information on premium payment in several installments (accommodating the practice of many providers to allow monthly, quarterly, half-yearly, or other options for premium payment).

In Figure 14.11, we can see how the data from the member's database and the package database provide the information for the policy database. The policy database helps us to understand package entitlements for each member.

SELF-TEST QUESTIONS

1. Explain how database efficiency can be improved by identifying permanent data.
2. Using a figure, describe how data from the member's database and the package database provide the information about members' package entitlement.

Database Modification: We have seen that the Member database constitutes data relating to households and individuals with characteristics. This data gets accumulated on a year-to-year basis. Four significant

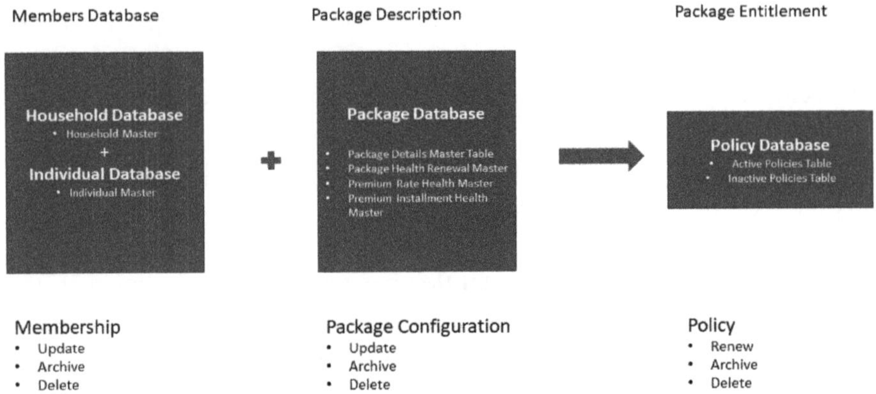

Figure 14.11 Package Entitlement in an RDB

modifications can be done to member's database, i.e., updating, archiving, deletion, and renewal.

(1) **Updating:** Members database is a listing of members who have joined the scheme at least once. This database can be updated at any point in time. This listing may include inactive and prospective members as well. Updating the members' database does not mean the policy is generated against the same and risks are covered.
(2) **Archiving:** Archiving database is another way of achieving an efficient database. This can be seen as shifting of data of inactive members to another database with an option of retrieval at the time of need. This helps the active database to work in an optimized manner. Data need to be archived within a set duration or in situations where there is a dearth of storage space.
(3) **Deletion:** Data should be deleted only if they become redundant for future use. Deletion of any data should be considered cautiously. Data deletion can lead to data discrepancy. For instance, deletion of a member from members' database in the case of death may lead to discrepancy counts, in case the member had claimed in previous years when he/she was an active member of the scheme.
(4) **Renewal:** Continuation of risk cover for two or more consecutive coverage periods needs a change in policy term of an assigned package linked to members' database.

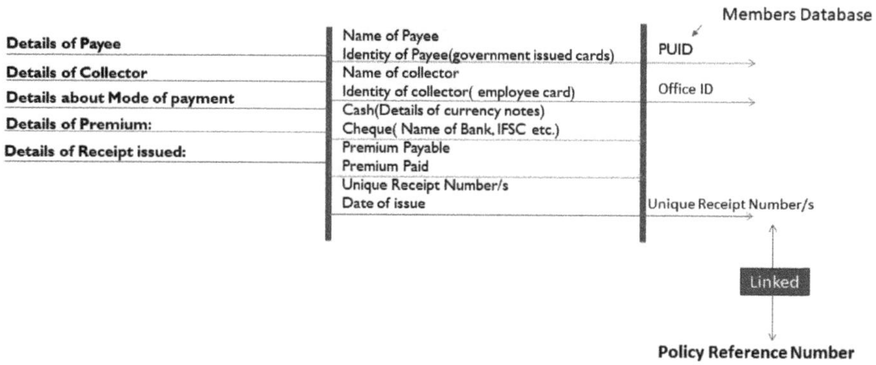

Figure 14.12 Records of Premium

Premiums

At the time of collection of premium, the information gathered from members is saved in a database template in MIA-MIS.

The data collected include the following (Figure 14.12):

- details of payee;
- details of collector;
- details about the mode of payment;
- details of premium;
- details of the receipt issued.

A unique receipt number is issued for each transaction. This ensures that the premiums are paid for the defined policy. In the MIA-MIS, this is reflected by creating relational linkages between the receipt number and the policy reference number.

Difference between policy database and member's database

The policy database represents members who have paid the premium in full and are covered under the policy. The member database, on the contrary, represents members who may or may not be covered under the policy.

A policy reference number is issued only to members who have paid the premium in full. Thus, members appearing in the policy database have a

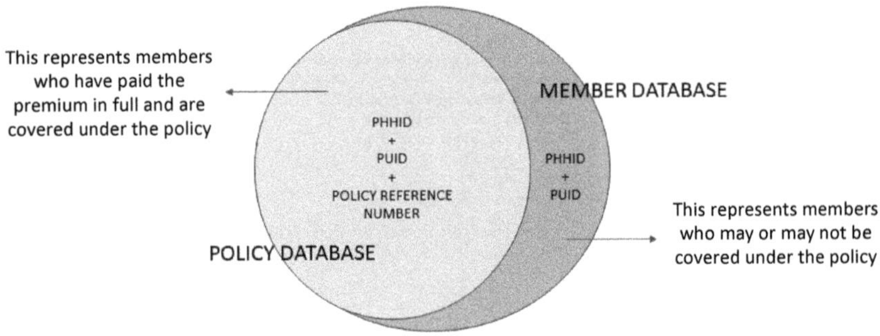

Figure 14.13 Policy Database

policy reference number, and they are called policyholders. As shown in Figure 14.13, the member's database is a superset of the policy database.

A policy reference number can be allotted to individuals or to the household (same for each member) depending on the policy type that covers the household as a unit or each person as a separate unit. The policy reference number is not permanent for the household or individual, as this number varies with the policy term.

Data structure for records of premium

The data structure for records of premium collected uses three sets of tables as follows:

(1) **Policy Master:** This is a household-level database where each household is allotted a policy reference (a UID).
(2) **Policy Master 1:** This is an individual-level database holding information at the member level and is linked to the household policy database by the field PolicyRef (which is the same for each member in case of family coverage and differs in case of individual type policies).
(3) **Policy Master 2:** This is the premium payment database at a household level. Premium payment is made at a household level. The table "Policy Master 2" reflects the premium payment status of a policy, whereas "Policy Master" represents premium payable. These two tables in Figure 14.14 are also linked with policy reference, and the policy can be printed only if payment payable and paid show compliance of 100%.

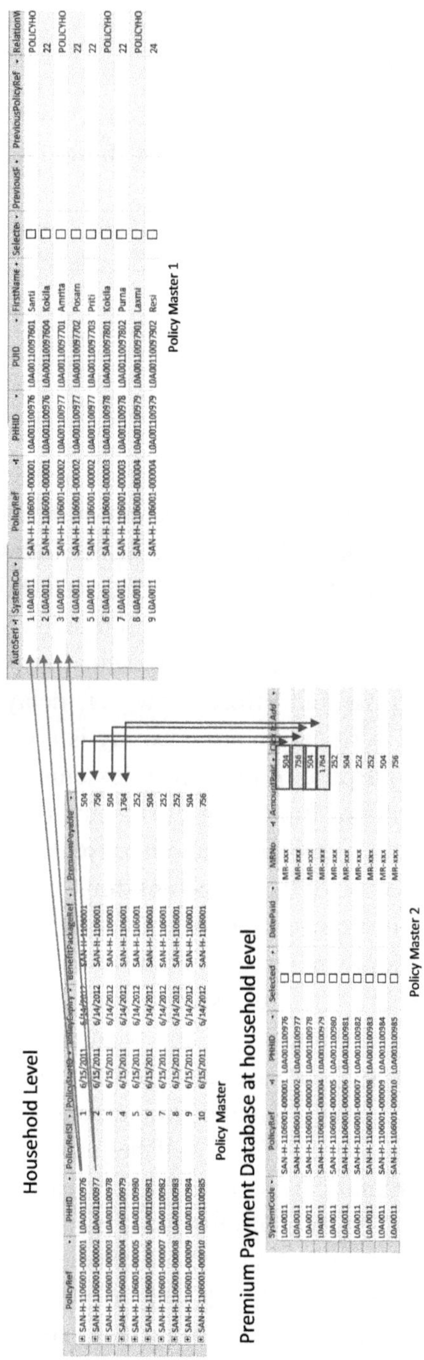

Figure 14.14 Policy Master

SELF-TEST QUESTIONS

1. Differentiate between the policy database and member's database. At any point in time, which of these databases has more records. Why?
2. Describe the data structure for records of premium collected.

Claims Database

Claims processing

Claims processing is the, if not the, most critical activity of any insurance scheme — be it microinsurance or commercial insurance. It entails a certain degree of principles and ethics, which, if not followed, may severely jeopardize the reputation of the scheme. First, no valid claims should be rejected or disapproved. At the same time, no fraudulent claims should be passed. Hence, scrutinizing the claim documents forms the central part of the activity. It takes time and effort. However, delay in approving the claims for the sake of verification and scrutiny is not acceptable because it defeats the primary purpose of insurance: lessening the burden of hardship financing. Incidents of fraudulent claims and other forms of forgery that are quite routine in commercial insurance are extremely low in microinsurance schemes because of their inherent thrust on community involvement. An ideal microinsurance scheme addresses the issue starting from benefit package development. In a microinsurance benefit package, the benefits are kept simple so that, unlike commercial insurance, everybody understands what the entitlements are and what are not. Hence, technical knowledge (medical) is not essential for processing microinsurance claims. In the microinsurance schemes implemented by Micro Insurance Academy, it is the members of the self-help groups who process the claims of their community. Last but not the least, the whole process should be accomplished in an environment of transparency so that nobody bears any grudge against the scheme. If a claimant is dissatisfied with the decision on his/her claim, he/she should be allowed to appeal to the ombudsman seeking a further review of his/her claim.

While processing claims, a scheme accesses and generates a large amount of administrative data. However, if stored and analyzed systemically, the dataset provides lots of insights into the implementation of the scheme. There are two types of claim settlement processes in insurance. In the first type of claim settlement, the claim is directly paid to the provider instead of the claimants. Hence, the insured person gets free service from the providers. This is called a CASHLESS facility. The second type of claim settlement is a method of reimbursement. Under this method, the insured is expected to bear the cost at the time of treatment and later seek reimbursement of his/her bills. From a scheme's point of view, both are the same. It has to process a claim. The claimant may be an insured person or a provider.

Steps in claims processing

Claim Intimation: Some scheme requires prior intimation about (or prior approval of) a forthcoming claim. The claimant or some other member of his/her household may intimate the scheme about the cost-generating health event that has occurred to an insured person of the household. It may not be mandatory for some schemes.

Claim Submission: The claimant must submit details of his/her illness, treatment records, and proofs of payment made to various providers in a prescribed form along with all evidence (doctor's prescription, discharge certificates, lab and imaging reports, medical bills, proof of payments, etc.).

Claims Decision (Approval, Rejection, or Query): The claim committee of the scheme scrutinizes and verifies the documents and takes a claim decision. A claim decision is also recorded in a prescribed template and with justifications.

Claim Payment: A payment advice is made based on the claim decision.

Claims processing and MIS

A claim is registered in the system when it is intimated or submitted. A claim remains open until it is paid. A claim already paid may reopen if the claimant chooses to appeal for a review to the ombudsman. The first set of information comes to the scheme when the claim is submitted. During the process, much new information is generated and stored for action that immediately follows (for example, claim decision is followed by claim payment) and making management decisions for the smooth running of the schemes. The MIS used by the scheme must have provisions to capture and analyze this information.

Data structure for claims processing

The forms and documents submitted by the claimant and generated in the process have very different templates, and hence, information collected through them cannot fit into one structure. Otherwise, the structure is too big, not normalized, and with many blanks making the system inefficient and ineffective. At least four different structures are needed to accommodate all data types. All types of claim documents together, at least four different structures are needed to accommodate all data elements relevant to claim to process (Figure 14.15).

ClaimHealthMainMaster: This table holds the complete brief of information about a particular claim.

In this table, each claim and all associated information (name of the claimant, date of claim submission, amount claimed, date of approval, claim amount approved, amount paid, etc.) will appear once referred with a UID called Claim Reference Number (ClaimRef.).

ClaimHealthHospitalMaster: This table can hold multiple entries of hospital details of a single claim (ClaimRef.), i.e., name of the hospital, type of hospital, admission date, discharge date, name of the referred hospital, admission date, etc.

ClaimHealthHospitalMaster: This table can hold multiple entries of hospital details of a single claim (ClaimRef.), i.e., name of the hospital, type of hospital, admission date, discharge date, and name of the referred hospital.

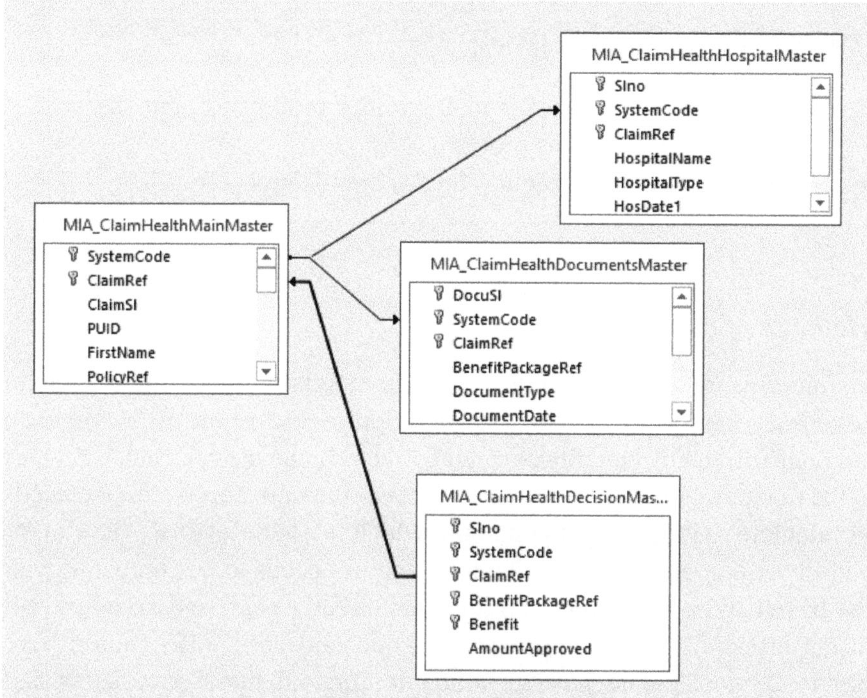

Figure 14.15 Claims Data Structure

MIA_ClaimHealthDocumentsMaster: This table is placed to have all sets of bills and documents submitted along with a claim. This table can have multiple entries of bills and documents (bills of treatment, consultation, medication, or surgery, etc.) linked to a single claim reference number.

ClaimHealthDecisionMaster: This table includes details of the calculation that underlies a final decision about the total amount that can be approved. In this table, each claim and all associated information (name of the claimant, date of claim submission, amount claimed, date of approval claim amount approved, and amount paid, etc.) appear once referred with a UID called Claim Reference Number (ClaimRef.).

All the tables mentioned above have one common field named ClaimReference. We can combine any two or more tables using this standard field. This field is called the primary key.

SELF-TEST QUESTIONS

1. Explain the steps involved in claims processing and the role played by MIS in this process.
2. Describe the data structure for the claims processing.

Methods of claim calculation

In microinsurance (also in general commercial insurance), the claim committee first decides on the bill-wise approved amount. Bills which do not conform to any benefits covered by the scheme are rejected. This part is the manual. However, once bill-wise amounts are approved, one needs to calculate the total payable amount which is not necessarily the sum of all bill-wise approved units. The total amount needs to be compared with the benefit-wise threshold, cap amounts already paid, and amounts still in the process (already approved, but not paid yet.). MIS should have provision to calculate payable amounts after all these parameters and restrictions are taken into consideration. The following is the flowchart (See Figure 14.16) of the claim-processing module of MIA-MIS (the MIS developed by Micro Insurance Academy for the implementation of its microinsurance schemes):

Utilization of claim data

(1) Claim data of the scheme provides historical trends of incidence and severity. One can do modeling with the claim data to examine whether there is a trend in the dataset indicating review of premium.
(2) Claim data is essential for computation of claim ratio which is a key performance indicator of any scheme.
(3) Claim data may produce results which are of epidemiological interest — whether any particular population segment (age–sex

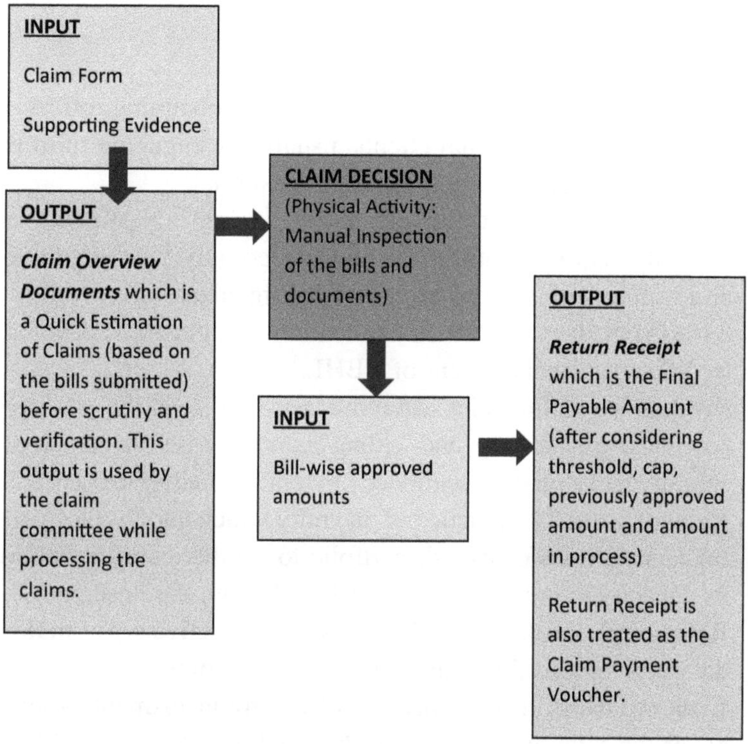

Figure 14.16 Claim Process Overview

combination, caste, geographical locations) is more vulnerable to any particular morbidity type.

(4) The gap between the date of claim payment and claim submission indicates the efficiency of the scheme concerning timely payment.

SELF-TEST QUESTION

1. With the help of a flowchart, explain the claim-processing module of MIA-MIS.

KEY TERMS

- **Client acquisition:** "Acquiring" means obtaining offers for insurance from potential clients, usually by engaging third parties as intermediaries (e.g., agents, brokers).
- **Fund management:** It means managing investments and liquidity requirements of the fund to comply with regulations and in line with the objectives of the organization.
- **MIA-MIS:** It is a database application, designed and developed by MIA, for management of CBHI.
- **Product servicing (aka after-sale service):** It is the process of receiving, adjudicating, and settling claims, in cases that the insured submit claims on the occurrence of an insured adverse event.
- **Reinsurance:** The practice of an entity which underwrites risk to transfer portions of its risk portfolio to another entity to increase its capacity to meet substantial risks is known as reinsurance.
- **Relational database (RDB):** This is a collective set of multiple datasets organized by tables, records, and column.
- **Underwriting:** It is the process of raising investment capital to cover the total amount of risk that each risk-taker is willing to accept at a specified premium.
- **UDIs:** These are key fields that are used in a database to avoid system duplicity.

Bibliography

Dror, DM and Jambhekar, S (eds.) (2016) *Microinsurance Business Processes Handbook*. New Delhi: Social Re Consultancy (Pvt) Ltd and Micro Insurance Academy.

Dror, DM and Jambhekar, S (eds.) (2017) *Microinsurance Implementation — A Training Manual*. New Delhi: Social Re Consultancy (Pvt) Ltd and Micro Insurance Academy.

Selected Websites

The following website pertain to the content of this chapter:

- For more information on RDBs, go to https://www.techopedia.com/definition/1234/relational-database-rdb (accessed 12 April 2019).

Part 5

Monitoring, Evaluation, and Sustainability

Chapter 15

Key Performance Indicators

LEARNING OBJECTIVES

Upon completion of this chapter, the reader should be able to:

- Understand the purpose of having Key Performance Indicators (KPI) for CBHI
- Explain the calculation involved in arriving at various KPIs
- Elaborate on the implications of the KPIs and their contribution to decision-making

Abstract

Monitoring a CBHI scheme is an essential task as it highlights the achievements and challenges of the scheme. This information is essential both for existing members and for prospective participants. We have developed several KPIs to monitor the performance of the CBHI schemes, and we discuss their implications in this chapter.

Chapter Outline

A variety of indicators measure the performance of any organization, department, process, or activity. Indicators are numerical values, calculated using mathematical or statistical formulas. These values are regularly calculated to monitor the progress in achieving the defined goals and objectives of insurance operations. Likewise, in microinsurance, the performance of a scheme is assessed using various KPIs. The chapter contains a review of the following 23 KPIs that make it possible to monitor the effectiveness of any microinsurance scheme:

(1) Incurred Claims Ratio
(2) Promptness of Claims Settlement
(3) Renewal Rate
(4) Household Renewal Rate
(5) Claims Rejection Ratio
(6) Growth Rate (Participation)
(7) Coverage Ratio
(8) Liquidity Ratio
(9) Average Compliance Rate
(10) Average Gap between Decision and Payment
(11) Average Gap between First Incidence Date and Reporting
(12) Average Gap between Submission and Decision
(13) Average Gap between Submission and Payment
(14) Average Number of Insured per Policy/Average Enrollment per Household
(15) Average Reimbursement Percentage
(16) Average Gap between the Last Date of Incidence and Reporting
(17) Average Gap between Policy Start Date and Incidence
(18) Average Gap between Submission to IA and IC
(19) Expense Ratios (Trend)
(20) Actual Incidence Rate
(21) Utilization Ratio/Claimant to Participation Ratio (Trend)
(22) Quick Claims Ratio
(23) Utilization Ratio (Trend)

KPI No. 1: Incurred Claims Ratio

This KPI is also known as Loss Ratio.

Definition: The Loss Ratio is the percentage of the income from premiums that is paid as claims.

Implication: Too high a claims ratio implies that the business is not profitable. When the claims ratio is too low, the premium is excessive. In the short term, this could generate high profits. However, once the community realizes it has been over-charged, the members are unlikely to agree to renew their coverage. Ideally, the loss ratio should be in the range of 70–80%.

In any particular year, the claims ratio may be very high or very low, and this is considered normal in the insurance business. For example, in a drought year, many insured farmers are expected to get payouts resulting in a very high claims ratio. Similarly, in a good monsoon year, none of the insured farmers get a payout, resulting in 0% claims ratio. Hence, the management should pay attention to the following:

(i) cumulative claims ratio;
(ii) the trend in the claims ratio.

When the trend in the claims ratio is either increasing significantly or decreasing substantially, the scheme management must review the premiums.

The claims ratio is calculated as follows:

$$\frac{\begin{array}{c}\text{Total claims approved} + \text{Claims in process}\\ + \text{Claims incurred but not reported}\end{array}}{\text{Total earned premium}}.$$

Total claims approved are the sum of the following:

(i) claims approved and paid;
(ii) claims approved but not yet paid.

This information is readily available from the books of accounts and Claims Register.

A Claims Register is the record of all claims, which are registered as soon as they are received. The Claims Register must be updated about the status of each claim throughout the process of claims processing, approval, and payment.

Claims in Process, as implied by the name, are all the claims that have been received but not yet decided (neither approved nor rejected). The Claims Register should provide this information for every claim.

In addition, the scheme has some financial obligations in respect of claims *Incurred But Not Reported* (IBNR). It is well known that insured members take some time to submit claims. This delay means that the information on the number of IBNR claims, or their monetary value, cannot be established based on the books of accounts or the Claims Register. Hence, it is prudent for the scheme to estimate its IBNR obligations based on historical claims data. Many insurance companies fix a limited time for submission of claims, to reduce the carry over of IBNR obligations from one year to the next.

The practice of many CBHI schemes is to collect the annual premium up front. Therefore, at any time during the year, the scheme would hold some portion of the premium income for a lapsed period (called "earned premium"), and some premium that has not yet been earned. The earned premium at the end of eight months is estimated as follows:

$$\frac{\text{Total premium received} \times 8}{12}.$$

The denominator represents 12 months (the annual premium paid up front).

When the premium is collected in some other intervals, the multiplying factor must be changed accordingly.

The management may wish to calculate the earned premiums for the purpose of comparing it to the claims ratio. Doing so every month enables the management to obtain information about claims distribution across the months of the year. Such information is instrumental for financial and operational planning.

The above formula of the claims ratio can be simplified when the calculation should only reflect the total annual ratio. At the end of each policy year ("policy year" means the 12 months from the date that the policy started), the entire premium is earned Premium, and in principle, all claims should have been submitted and settled. When there are zero claims in the process, zero IBNR claims, and total earned premium is the same as the total premium received, the formula for calculation of the claims ratio is simplified as follows:

$$\frac{\text{Total claims paid}}{\text{Total premium received}}.$$

Illustration

The following illustration shows how to calculate the incurred claims ratio at different points of time. Assume that Scheme X covers health risks for 1 year, starting from 15 June 2015.

This scheme enrolled 13,703 individual members, paying a premium of ₹502 per person per year.

The information about incurred claims and earned premiums is available from the Management Information System (MIS) of the scheme. The management requests to know the claims ratio on 15 February 2016.

On 15 February 2016, the total amount of claims paid is ₹3,500,000; claims in progress amount to ₹270,000; and IBNR claims are estimated at ₹150,000. Also claims paid till 14 June 2016 is ₹5,200,000 with no outstanding claims or unreported claims.

Using this information and the formula shown earlier:

Incurred claims amount till 15 February 2016 amounts to ₹3,920,000 (= ₹3,500,000 claims paid + ₹150,000 IBNR + ₹270,000 claims in progress).

The earned premium till 15 February 2016 (precisely eight months from the inception of coverage) is ₹6,878,906 (total premium) × 6/12, i.e., ₹4,585,937.

Incurred claims ratio as on 15 February 2016 = 3,920,000/4,585,937, i.e., 85.47%.

Also, incurred claims ratio as on 15 June 2016 = 5,200,000/6,878,906, i.e., 75.59%.

Data Needs and Sources of Data	
Data needed	Source of data
1. Claims: received, approved, and paid for a particular scheme (historical claims data) 2. Premium data	1. Claims Register/Books of Accounts 2. Policy Registers/Books of Accounts

KPI No. 2: Promptness of Claims Settlement

Definition: This indicator provides information on how quickly claims are settled within the scheme.

Implication: The earlier, the better.

The meanings of promptness and settlement may vary from one scheme to another. Ideally, it should be the difference between the "date of incurring the claim" and the "date of claim payment." Many schemes conveniently use the difference between the date of receiving the claims and the date of claims decision. This difference, however, does not reflect delayed submission of the claims or delayed payment of the claims even when decisions are made early.

This KPI is represented as a simple frequency distribution (and percentage distribution) of the number of days between the date of incurring the claim and the date of claim payment for all claims settled during a specified period. Promptness of claims settlement can be represented as shown in Table 15.1.

Table 15.1 shows that whereas most of the claims were settled within 8–30 days, it took more than 90 days to process 7.5% of the claims.

SELF-TEST QUESTION

1. When the claims ratio is too high, it means that the scheme is not profitable. Does this imply that a very low claims ratio is ideal for a CBHI scheme? Explain.

Table 15.1 Claim settlement duration

Interval (days)	Number of claims	% of claims
0–7	200	10
8–30	1,200	60
31–90	450	22.5
More than 90	150	7.5
Total of claims	2,000	100

KPI No. 3: Renewal Rate

Individual Renewal Rate

Definition: This ratio gives the percentage of individuals who renew their policy as against those individuals who are eligible to renew their policy.

Implication: A higher renewal rate implies greater satisfaction of the members toward the insurance product and services received. This shows their willingness to continue their membership with the scheme. On the contrary, a low renewal rate is reflective of dissatisfaction with the product and/or services.

The individual renewal rate is calculated as follows:

$$\frac{\text{Total number of individuals renewing their policy}}{\text{Total number of individuals eligible to renew their policy}}.$$

Data Needs and Sources of Data	
Data needed	Source of data
Number of individuals renewing their policy	Current Enrollment Register
Number of individuals eligible to renew their policy	Last coverage period's Enrollment Register

KPI No. 4: Household Renewal Rate

Definition: Proportion of enrolled households (with at least one member) that renew their coverage, out of the total number of households that are eligible for renewal.

Implication: A higher renewal rate implies greater satisfaction toward the insurance product and the services received. This shows a willingness to continue with the existing product and services. On the contrary, a low renewal rate indicates dissatisfaction with the product and services, and consequently a lack of interest toward the offer.

The household renewal rate is calculated as follows:

$$\frac{\text{Total number of households renewing their policy}}{\text{Total number of households eligible to renew their policy}}.$$

Illustration

A health insurance scheme has a coverage term of one year commencing on 15 June 2015.

Enrollments for 2015–2016: Individuals — 13,703, Households — 3,826;

Enrollments for 2016–2017: Individual — 15,000, Households — 4,000, Individual Renewals — 8,000, Household Renewal — 2,500.

Using the aforementioned formulas:

Individual renewal rate: 8,000/13,703, i.e., 58.38%;

Household renewal rate: 2,500/3,826, i.e., 65.34%.

By monitoring the trends in both the household and individual renewal rates, it is possible to track the intentional enrollment by high-risk individuals in microinsurance schemes. A downward trend in the individual renewal rate along with a consistent or higher household renewal rate may result in higher incidence rates of risks covered by the microinsurance scheme.

KPI No. 5: Claims Rejection Ratio

Definition: This ratio indicates the percentage of claims which are rejected or disqualified in claims processing out of the total number of reported/submitted claims.

Implication: A low claims rejection ratio seems good for enrolled members and indicates a good understanding and awareness about claims processing, terms and conditions of the scheme, and required documents for claims submission. However, critics point out that a low claims rejection ratio could indicate that the claims processors and verifying authorities are lenient toward processing the claims. A high claims rejection ratio is unfavorable for enrolled members and could negatively affect future enrollments. It also reflects a lack of understating toward claims processing. This indicator should also be given critical importance as, "if the ratio is higher than 5%, it could mean that the scheme is too restrained with regards to its coverage policy, and therefore the program could lose appeal to its clients."[1]

The claims rejection ratio is calculated as follows:

$$\frac{\text{Total number of rejected claims}}{\text{Total number of reported claims}}.$$

Data Needs and Sources of Data	
Data needed	Source of data
1. Total number of rejected claims 2. Total numbers of reported claims	1. Claims Register 2. Claims Register

SELF-TEST QUESTIONS

1. How are the individual and household renewal rates of a scheme calculated? How does monitoring these two indicators help the sustainability of the scheme?
2. How is a scheme's "promptness of claims settlement" represented? In your opinion, how would this influence the decision of a person to enroll in a scheme?

KPI No. 6: Growth Rate (Participation)

Definition: This indicator represents the rate of change in participation from one year to another.

[1] Performance Indicators for microinsurance practitioners, workshop report Luxembourg, 16–17 October 2006. Available at http://www.findevgateway.org/sites/default/files/mfg-en-paper-performance-indicators-for-microinsurance-practitioners-2006_0.pdf.

Implication: The growth rate of participation is one of the essential indicators used to monitor the acceptance of the scheme by the community members. An increasing growth rate implies increasing participation, acceptance of the insurance product, and willingness to continue. On the contrary, a falling growth rate reflects dissatisfaction toward the microinsurance scheme.

The growth rate is calculated as follows:

$$\frac{\text{Number of participants in the current coverage period} \\ - \text{Number of participants in the last coverage period}}{\text{Number of participants in the last coverage period}}.$$

Illustration

Table 15.2 shows the number of participants enrolled in scheme X from the year 2011 to 2016.

Scheme X began in 2011 with 4,173 participants, and the number of participants grew at a rate of 89% in 2012. After that, the yearly growth rate has been falling, with a negative growth rate in 2016 (Figure 15.1).

Using the above-mentioned formulas:

Growth rate for 2012 = 89%, i.e., (7,880 – 4,173)/4,173.

Growth rate for 2013 = 51%, i.e., (11,870 – 7,880)/7,880, and so on.

Table 15.2 Participants enrolled in Scheme X (2011–16)

Year	Participation	% Growth
2011	4,173	—
2012	7,880	89
2013	11,870	51
2014	12,232	3
2015	13,703	12
2016	12,582	–8

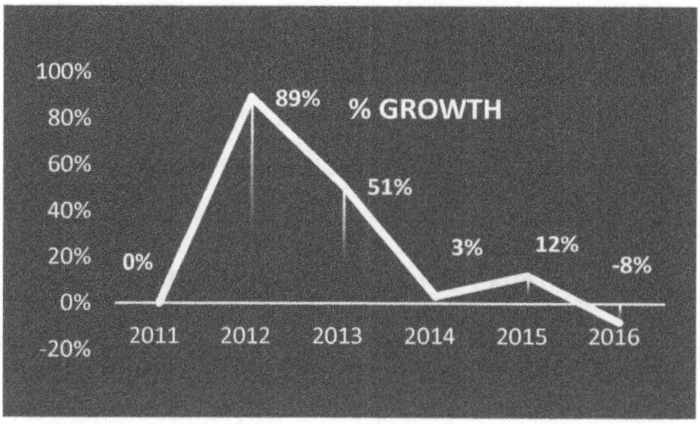

Figure 15.1 Graphical Presentation of the Yearly Participation Growth Rate of Scheme X since 2011

Data Needs and Sources of Data	
Data needed	Source of data
1. Number of participants in the current coverage period 2. Number of participants in the last coverage period	1. Current Enrollment Register 2. Previous Enrollment Register

SELF-TEST QUESTIONS

1. Of the various KPIs available for assessing program acceptance, which is the most suitable in your opinion? Why?
2. How would you interpret the claims rejection ratio?
3. In Figure 15.1, there is a marked fall in the growth rate after 2012. What could be the reasons behind this fall?

KPI No. 7: Coverage Ratio

Definition: The coverage ratio is the achieved enrollment as a percentage of the targeted population in a microinsurance scheme.

Implication: This indicator reflects the actual outreach of the scheme in comparison to the expected target. The higher the ratio, the more successful is the scheme's outreach.

The coverage ratio is calculated as follows:

$$\frac{\text{Number of enrolled persons}}{\text{Number of targeted participants}}.$$

Data Needs and Sources of Data	
Data needed	Source of data
1. Number of enrolled persons 2. Number of targeted participants	1. Enrollment Register 2. Qualitative (calculated)

The penetration rate or participation ratio serves the same purpose as the coverage ratio. However, these indicators are used for a broader target, where the targeted population size is the entire population of the area.

KPI No. 8: Liquidity Ratio

Definition: This ratio measures the capability of a microinsurance scheme to pay claims and all recurring expenses incurred at least for three months.

Implication: This ratio should be at least equal to 1 at any point of time for an ongoing microinsurance scheme, to ensure the smooth delivery of the scheme's short-term outflows. A value lower than 1 implies that the scheme cannot pay its short-term obligations. At the same time, a very high liquidity ratio could mean that the scheme is losing out on the opportunity for investment returns.

The liquidity ratio is calculated as follows:

$$\frac{\text{Cash or cash equivalents}\begin{pmatrix}\text{investments easily convertible}\\ \text{to cash in a short span}\end{pmatrix}}{\text{Short-term outflows}}.$$

Illustration

Scheme X has the following information:

Cash and cash equivalent	
Cash in hand	1,719,727
Cash at bank	300,000
Cash equivalent (short-term bonds, marketable securities, treasury bills, etc.)	200,000
Total cash and cash equivalent	2,219,737

Short-term Outflow

Average claims amount for at least three months	1,300,000
Administration cost for three months	300,000
Total short-term outflows	1,600,000

Using the aforementioned formula:

Liquidity ratio = 2,219,737/1,600,000, i.e., 1.39.

Data Needs and Sources of Data

Data needed	Source of data
Cash or cash equivalents	Books of Accounts
Short-term outflows	Forecasted expenses and claims (calculated)

KPI No. 9: Average Compliance Rate

Definition: The premium compliance rate is the amount of premium paid as a percentage of premium payable per household. Usually, in a rural setup, participants pay premiums in installments as per the availability of money. The microinsurance scheme representatives collect all the installments within the defined time duration. Averaging the compliance rate across all households gives the average premium compliance rate.

Implication: The average compliance rate should be 100%. When the value is lower than 100%, it means that some household/did not pay the full premium. This calls for further investigation of all listed household/s that have not paid the premium in full. These households can be identified by reviewing the household-level compliance rate.

The average compliance rate is calculated as follows:

$$\frac{\sum_{k=1}^{n} \text{premium paid by } k\text{th household}}{\sum_{k=1}^{n} \text{The premium payable by } k\text{th household}}.$$

Data Needs and Sources of Data	
Data needed	Source of data
1. Premium paid by the *k*th household 2. Premium payable by the *k*th household 3. Number of households enrolled (n) 4. Number of members per household	1. Enrollment registers and Books of Accounts 2. Premium per person-year or coverage period (PPPY) 3. Enrollment Register 4. Enrollment Register

KPI No. 10: Average Gap between Decision and Payment

Definition: This indicator provides information about the promptness of claims dissemination at the scheme activists' end after the claims' decision (either at claims committee or coordination committee level).

Implication: This average gap should ideally not exceed seven days. This implies all claims are disseminated within seven days on an average after the claims' decision. An average gap which is higher than seven days reflects inefficiency on the part of the scheme activists in claims dissemination.

This average gap is calculated as follows:

$$\frac{\sum_{k=1}^{n} \text{Number of day}(\text{s})\text{taken to pay } k\text{th claim after the decision}}{n}.$$

Data Needs and Sources of Data	
Data needed	Source of data
1. Date of decision of the *k*th claim 2. Date of payment of the *k*th claim 3. Number of claims paid (*n*)	1. Claims Register 2. Claims Register 3. Claims Register

SELF-TEST QUESTIONS

1. What is the ideal liquidity ratio for a CBHI scheme? What are the implications of a ratio higher or lower than this?
2. What information does the indicator "Average Gap between Decision and Payment" provide? Give its implications.
3. What does the coverage ratio measure? How is this calculated?
4. How is the average compliance rate of a scheme measured? In case this value is low, what measures can be taken to improve the rate?

KPI No. 11: Average Gap between First Incidence Date and Reporting

Definition: This indicator provides information about the promptness of enrolled members in reporting their claims. Numerically, this indicates an average number of days taken by a member in claims reporting.

Implication: The lower the value of the gap, the more efficient the scheme is. The lesser the number of days, the stronger the likelihood that members understand about the claims processing. It suggests that members are aware of how to submit a claim.

This average gap is calculated as follows:

$$\frac{\sum_{k=1}^{n} \text{Number of day}(\text{s})\,\text{taken to report the } k\text{th claim after the first incidence}}{n}.$$

Data Needs and Sources of Data	
Data needed	Source of data
1. Date of the first incidence of the *k*th claim 2. Reporting date of the *k*th claim 3. Number of claims reported (n)	1. Claims Register 2. Claims Register 3. Claims Register

KPI No. 12: Average Gap between Submission and Decision

Definition: This indicator reflects the timeliness of claims processing. Once claims are submitted, the claims committees and coordination committees must verify the eligibility and validity of the claims and decide on them as soon as possible.

Implication: A scheme with a low average gap indicates that claims are decided at the earliest. Such quick decision-making helps to build trust toward the scheme's claims and coordination committees and helps in retaining members and encouraging prospective enrollment in the scheme.

This average gap is calculated as follows:

$$\frac{\sum_{k=1}^{n} \begin{matrix}\text{Number of day(s) taken to decide the} \\ k\text{th claim after successful submission}\end{matrix}}{n}.$$

Data Needs and Sources of Data	
Data needed	Source of data
1. Date of submission of the *k*th claim 2. Date of the decision of the *k*th claim 3. Number of claims decided (n)	1. Claims Register 2. Claims Register 3. Claims Register

KPI No. 13: Average Gap between Submission and Payment

Definition: This indicator gives information about the total time taken by the scheme in claims processing and dissemination. It is the average turnaround time (TAT) from the time of submission of the claim to payment.

Implication: The TAT needs to be minimal. Any unnecessary delay in claims processing and dissemination may lead to a loss of trust in the microinsurance scheme.

This average gap is calculated as follows:

$$\frac{\sum_{k=1}^{n} \begin{array}{c}\text{Number of day}(\text{s})\text{ taken to make payment of} \\ \text{the } k\text{th claimafter successful submission}\end{array}}{n}.$$

Data Needs and Sources of Data	
Data needed	Source of data
1. Date of submission of the *k*th claim 2. Date of payment of the *k*th claim 3. Number of claims paid (*n*)	1. Claims Register 2. Claims Register 3. Claims Register

KPI No. 14: Average Number of Insured per Policy/ Average Enrollment per Household

Definition: This indicator provides information about the significance of the scheme to the enrolled households. Numerically, this indicates average memberships in the scheme per household.

Implication: The average number of insured per active policy should be uniform with the average household size for a particular microinsurance scheme. Equivalence in these two averages confirms *en bloc* affiliation.

This ratio is calculated as follows:

$$\frac{\sum_{k=1}^{n} \text{Number of individual(s) enrolled from } k\text{th household}}{n}.$$

Illustration

Scheme X has the following information

Year	Individual	Household	Average Enrollment/Household
2011	4,173	1,670	2.50
2012	7,880	3,270	2.41
2013	11,870	4,180	2.84
2014	12,232	3,612	3.39
2015	13,703	3,826	3.58
2016	12,582	3,560	3.53

Graphical presentation (Figure 15.2).
Using the above-mentioned formulas:

Average enrollment/household for 2011 = 2.50, i.e., 4,173/1,670;

Average enrollment/household for 2012 = 2.41, i.e., 7,880/3,270;

Average enrollment/household for 2013 = 2.84, i.e., 11,870/4,180.

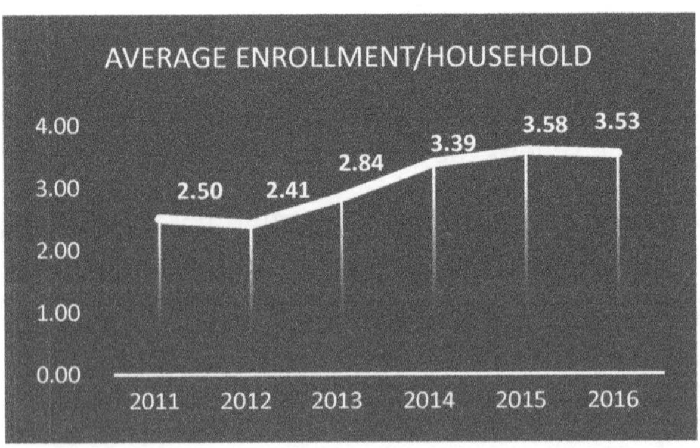

Figure 15.2 Average Enrollment per Household

Data Needs and Sources of Data	
Data needed	Source of data
1. Number of enrolled members per household 2. Number of households enrolled	1. Enrollment Register 2. Enrollment Register

KPI No. 15: Average Reimbursement Percentage

Definition: This indicator is the average reimbursement paid as a percentage of the amount claimed from a microinsurance scheme.

Implication: This percent should be 100% if there are no deductions and maximum capping involved.

This ratio is calculated as follows:

$$\frac{\text{Total claims amount reimbursed}}{\text{Total amount claimed}}.$$

Illustration

Scheme X has the following information:

Year	Number of Claims	Amount Claimed	Amount Paid (as Claims)
2011	813	600,379	461,830
2012	2,544	2,548,379	1,820,271
2013	4,007	4,525,733	3,017,155
2014	5,178	5,987,830	4,606,023
2015	5,081	6,846,755	4,721,900

Using the above-mentioned formulas:

Claims amount reimbursed/amount claimed for 2011 = 77%, i.e., 461,830/600,379;

Claims amount reimbursed/amount claimed for 2012 = 71%, i.e., 1,820,271/2,548,379;

Claims amount reimbursed/amount claimed for 2013 = 67%, i.e., 3,017,155/4,525,733 as shown Table 15.3.

Table 15.3 Average reimbursement paid (2011–15)

Year	Number of claims	Amount claimed	Amount paid (as claims)	Average reimbursement (%)
2011	813	600,379	461,830	77
2012	2,544	2,548,379	1,820,271	71
2013	4,007	4,525,733	3,017,155	67
2014	5,178	5,987,830	4,606,023	77
2015	5,081	6,846,755	4,721,900	69

Data Needs and Sources of Data

Data needed	Source of data
1. Amount reimbursed	1. Claims Register/Books of Accounts
2. Amount claimed	2. Claims Register/bills and documents submitted

SELF-TEST QUESTIONS

1. When the indicator "Average Number of Insured per Policy/Average Enrollment per Household" is equal to 1, it implies *en bloc* affiliation. Discuss.
2. Explain the relationship between the indicator "Average Gap between Submission and Decision" and the decision to enroll in the scheme. Do you think the "Average Gap between Submission and Payment" is a more useful indicator? Why/Why not?
3. How is the Average Reimbursement Percentage measured? What could be the reasons behind this indicator being less than 100%?
4. Why is it useful to measure the "Average Gap between First Incidence Date and Reporting"?

KPI No. 16: Average Gap between the Last Date of Incidence and Reporting

Definition: This indicator is used to assess the claimants' knowledge about claims processing and their promptness in reporting claims.

It measures the effectiveness of insurance education and awareness programs conducted by the CBHI.

Implication: When the average gap between the last date of incidence and reporting is less than the average gap between the first date of incidence and reporting, it implies an increase in the knowledge base of the enrolled members as regards claims processing.

This ratio is calculated as follows:

$$\frac{\sum_{k=1}^{n} \text{Number of day(s) taken to report the } k\text{th claim after the last incidence}}{n}.$$

Data Needs and Sources of Data	
Data needed	Source of data
1. Date of the last incidence of the *k*th claim 2. Reporting Date of *k*th claim 3. Number of claims reported (n)	1. Claims Register 2. Claims Register 3. Claims Register

KPI No. 17: Average Gap between Policy Start Date and Incidence

Definition: This indicator is the average of the differences of all claims' incidence dates and the coverage start date. It assesses the tendency of bad risks to join the scheme. For instance, people who expect to be hospitalized for a short period prefer to enroll in a scheme that covers health risks with hospitalization, to avail benefits from the scheme.

Implication: There should be a sufficient average gap between these two dates. It calls for investigation if the value of this indicator is small and continues to grow smaller in the subsequent years. This could imply that the scheme runs the risk of adverse selection, which could lead to high claims ratios and subsequently insolvency of the scheme. We are assuming that the start date is the same for each member of the particular scheme.

This ratio is calculated as follows:

$$\frac{\sum_{k=1}^{n} \text{Number of day(s) between incidence date of } k\text{th claim and coverage start date}}{n}.$$

Data Needs and Sources of Data	
Data needed	Source of data
1. Scheme coverage start date 2. Incidence date of the *k*th claim 3. Number of claims reported (*n*)	1. Enrollment Register 2. Claims Register/bills and documents submitted 3. Claims Register

KPI No. 18: Average Gap between Submission to IA and IC

Definition: This indicator helps to measure the time that the scheme activists take to deliver the claims that they receive from claimants for submission to the claims committee office/Scheme Coordinator.

Implication: This average should be three days or less (the lower, the better).

This ratio is calculated as follows:

$$\frac{\sum_{k=1}^{n} \text{Number of days taken by scheme activist to deliver the } k\text{th claim to scheme coordinator}}{n}.$$

Data Needs and Sources of Data	
Data needed	Source of data
1. Date of the *k*th claim submission to SA 2. Date of the *k*th claim submission to SC 3. Number of claims delivered to SC (*n*)	1. Claims Register 2. Claims Register 3. Claims Register

The average gap indicators discussed earlier (b/w decision and payment, b/w submission and payment, or b/w policy start date and incidence) and the average claims reimbursement indicator are always considered as good indicators to evaluate the effectiveness of a scheme. However, at the same time, considering indicators like minimum and maximum gap, and reimbursement highlight both the extremes of distributions. This also helps in calculating the range (the gap between maximum and minimum values) and average (estimate) for cases where the actual average is hard to find.

The range and average are calculated as

$$\text{Range: Maximum}\left(\bigcup_{i=1}^{n} \mathbf{X}_{\mathrm{i}}\right) - \text{Minimum}\left(\bigcup_{i=1}^{n} \mathbf{Y}_{\mathrm{i}}\right).$$

$$\text{Average (Estimate): } \left\{\text{Maximum}\left(\bigcup_{1}^{n} \mathbf{X}_{\mathrm{i}}\right) + \text{Minimum}\left(\bigcup_{1}^{n} \mathbf{Y}_{\mathrm{i}}\right)\right\} \Big/ 2.$$

SELF-TEST QUESTIONS

1. Give an indicator that can help in identifying adverse selection behavior among the participants. What solution would you suggest minimizing this risk?
2. Define the KPI "Average Gap between Submission to IA and IC." What is an ideal value for this indicator?
3. What are the implications of the indicator "Average Gap between the Last Date of Incidence and Reporting"?

KPI No. 19: Expense Ratio (Trend)

Definition: This is the amount spent on scheme expenses expressed as a percentage of the contribution collected during the coverage period. Usually, these expenses are calculated per person per year as an expense load.

Implication: The lower the expense ratio, the more beneficial it is for the scheme. During the scheme's initial years, the expenses are quite high, but they show a declining trend over time. A failure to reduce expenses in subsequent years could challenge the scheme's sustainability.

The expense ratio is calculated as follows:

$$\frac{E_i\left(\text{Expenses paid in } i\text{th coverage period}\right)}{Y_i\left(\text{Contribution collected for "}i\text{th" coverage period}\right)},$$

where i (coverage period) = 1st, 2nd, 3rd ....

Data Needs and Sources of Data	
Data needed	Source of data
1. Expenses paid in the ith coverage period 2. Contribution collected in the ith coverage period	1. Books of Accounts 2. Enrollment Register/Books of Accounts

KPI No. 20: Actual Incidence Rate

Definition: Incidence rate is an essential parameter in premium calculations. At the time of inception of the scheme, the expected incidence rate is generally used for rate making. The expected incidence rate tells us about the expected frequency of occurrence of an event, whereas the actual incidence rate is a record of the scheme's experience, i.e., how often events have happened since the inception of the scheme. For instance, microinsurance schemes covering health risks measure the actual incidence rate of hospitalization over the years as it helps in tracking any variation in the actual and expected incidence rates.

Implication: The actual incidence rate should be as close as possible to the expected rate to validate the pricing basis. Over- or underestimation of incidence rate leads to over- or underestimation of premium. Overestimation makes the scheme incompetent, whereas underestimation makes the scheme vulnerable to insolvency.

This ratio is calculated as follows:

$$\frac{\text{Number of hazardous events in the } i\text{th}}{n_i},$$

where i (coverage period) = 1st, 2nd, 3rd ...

Data Needs and Sources of Data	
Data needed	Source of data
1. Number of hazardous events (say hospitalizations, deaths, accidents) in the ith coverage period 2. Number of individuals enrolled in the ith coverage period (n_i)	1. Claims Register 2. Enrollment Register

KPI No. 21: Utilization Ratio/Claimant to Participation Ratio (Trend)

Definition: This ratio defines the fraction of enrolled individuals, who have claimed during the coverage period.

Implication: This ratio indicates familiarity with the scheme (claims processing, package benefits). Although it is good to see an increased utilization ratio in the initial years, this ratio should converge to a number after a few years. A consistent increase in this ratio shows the overutilization of the microinsurance scheme. An increasing trend also reflects an increasing incidence rate.

This ratio is calculated as follows:

$$\frac{\text{Number of individuals claiming in the } i\text{th coverage period}\left(X_i\right)}{\text{Number of individual enrolled in the } i\text{th coverage period}\left(Y_i\right)},$$

where i (coverage period) = 1st, 2nd, 3rd...

Data Needs and Sources of Data	
Data needed	Source of data
1. Individuals claiming in the ith coverage period 2. Individuals enrolled in the ith coverage period	1. Claims Register 2. Enrollment Register

KPI No. 22: Quick Claims Ratio

Definition: This ratio indicates the financial outflow of the scheme in the form of claims, as a proportion of earned pure risk premium. This ratio is a close proxy to the incurred claims ratio. The quick claims ratio evades the complicated calculations involved in measuring the incurred claims ratio. It does so by way of avoiding outstanding claims, and IBNR claims reserving, and instead using an assumption of truncated claims period, i.e., all claims are assumed to be paid 60 days before the present date.

Implication: This ratio should not exceed the 100% benchmark. If the ratio goes beyond this benchmark in any coverage period, it means that the premium collected to pay the claims is not sufficient, and the basis of premium calculations needs to be revised to avoid such a situation in the future.

This ratio is calculated as follows:

$$\frac{\text{Total claims paid}\left(\text{prior 60 days}\right)}{\text{Earned pure risk premium excluding buffer of 60 days}}.$$

Data Needs and Sources of Data	
Data needed	Source of data
1. Total claims paid (prior 60 days) 2. Earned pure risk premium excluding 60 days buffer	1. Claims Register 2. Enrollment Register/Books of Accounts

KPI No. 23: Utilization Ratio (Trend)

Definition: This indicator represents the utilization of pooled contributions accumulated over the years, for the payment of claims at the end of every coverage year. The cumulative trend in claims and contribution show the financial stability of the microinsurance scheme. This stability needs to be monitored to achieve scheme sustainability.

Implication: This ratio should not exceed the cumulative pooled contribution (excluding administration expense load).

The utilization ratio is calculated as follows:

$$\frac{\sum_{i=1}^{\infty} X_i (\text{Cumulative claims paid at the end of } i\text{th coverage year})}{\sum_{i=1}^{\infty} Y_i \left(\text{Cumulative pure risk premium at the end of } i\text{th coverage year}\right)}.$$

The pure risk premium is the contribution collected excluding any administrative or profit margins.

Data Needs and Sources of Data	
Data needed	Source of data
1. Claims paid at the end of the *i*th coverage year 2. Pure risk premium at the end of the *i*th coverage year	1. Claims Register/Books of Accounts 2. Enrollment Register/Book of Accounts

SELF-TEST QUESTIONS

1. How does actual incidence rate help in rate-making decisions?
2. Differentiate between the quick claims ratio and the incurred claims ratio.
3. How is the claimant to participation ratio calculated? What are its implications?
4. Identify an indicator that can help in assessing the sustainability of a scheme. How is it calculated?
5. How is the expense ratio calculated? Why is it expected to be high in the initial years?

KEY TERMS

- **Claims in Process:** This is the total amount of claims that have been received but not decided yet (neither approved nor rejected).
- **Loss ratio or incurred claims ratio:** It is the percentage of the premium paid as claims.
- **Premium compliance rate:** This is the amount of premium paid as a percentage of premium payable per household.
- **Pure risk premium:** The contribution collected excluding any administration and profit (if any) margins is pure risk premium.

Chapter 16

Impact Assessment of Microinsurance

LEARNING OBJECTIVES

Upon completion of this chapter, the reader should be able to:

- Define impact and explain the benefits of assessing the impact
- Distinguish between the *ex post* assessments and *ex ante* assessments of impact
- Discuss the need to distinguish between the *ex post* assessments and *ex ante* assessments of impact
- Explain the benefits of assessing the impact
- Discuss evidence related to CBHI schemes improving health service utilization
- Describe how CBHI provides financial protection for members
- Explain the positive impact of CBHI on the quality of care and social inclusion
- Discuss impact investments and the role of ESG investing and CSR investing

Abstract

The impact of microinsurance has two distinct orientations — *ex post* assessments and *ex ante* assessments. This distinction is helpful for donors/investors/lenders who are interested in the indicators and evidence of results that their financial commitments affect. Along with a growing interest in the impact of community-based health insurance (CBHI), there has been a surge in the detailed guidelines on the metrics, data elements, and methods to show the impact. We discuss here the evidence relating to the CBHI schemes improving health service utilization, providing financial protection for members, and improving the quality of care and social inclusion. The relevance of impact investments and the significance of environmental, social, and governance (ESG) investing and corporate social responsibility (CSR) investing is also discussed.

Chapter Outline

This chapter offers replies to two questions: What is impact? And what benefit is there in assessing it?

There are two quite distinct orientations to this topic: *ex post* assessments and *ex ante* assessments of impact. The *ex post* assessments refer to assessing the impact of projects/programs after those interventions have occurred. The *ex ante* assessments refer to the definition of the expected impact before the funds are allocated to align with investors' *desiderata.*

This distinction needs to be qualified, as of course, donors/investors/lenders are interested in the indicators and evidence of results that their financial commitments affect. However, they accept the reasoning that the investment must first be made before its resulting impact can be measured. The logical framework of development work has accommodated the *ex post* orientation. A different orientation is typical among managers of investment funds, whose traditional logical framework has been to ensure the financial return, which in recent years has broadened to include, in addition to the focus on yield, an interest in other impacts as well. Therefore, this chapter attempts to cover the answers to these critical questions from both viewpoints.

The distinction of the orientations has been absent in the publications on impact assessment in microinsurance published in 2012 (Radermacher *et al.*, 2012) (as a chapter in the Microinsurance Compendium II) and in 2014 (Radermacher and Roth, 2014) (as a manual for practitioners). The earlier publications offered a framework (theory of change, guidelines about indicators, etc.). The implication was that everybody wants to know whether their time, money, and efforts are making a difference, and what that difference is. The years since then have shown that goodwill (let us try hard and hope for the best) was not enough, as both the target population and the funders of projects demand strong evidence of the impact, and how much impact is happening.

Moreover, today, there are very detailed guidelines on the metrics, data elements, and methods to show the impact. Such guidelines were unavailable just a few years ago, and they change constantly. Also, the availability of data is continuously increasing, and the cost associated with collecting and analyzing the data is decreasing with the growth of digital financial services in the informal sector and at the base of the economic pyramid. Hence, it stands to reason that the impact assessment of microinsurance shall become more prevalent and sophisticated.

What is impact?

Funders talk of "impact investing," social change actors talk about "collective impact" and "social impact," and academics talk about their "research impact." The dictionary definition for impact in the social sector is *to have a substantial effect on someone or something*. In microinsurance, that *someone* or *something* could be a single community/CBHI, or it could be much broader when the action reaches entire population sub-groups. A local project in one location cannot be expected to deliver results at the level of the population of an entire country. Or funding of a single activity, e.g., insurance education about health microinsurance, can expect a strong effect only on the consequences of awareness-raising activities, but not strong effects on the delivery of health services across the entire population. The distinction of the scope is useful mainly for the assessment of responsibility for actions.

As for measuring impact, the standards and methods that are nowadays considered robust and valid require considerable data collection and analysis. Microinsurance practitioners may be challenged to collect and analyze all the data; in justifying a more limited scope, they might even cite Albert Einstein's statement that "Not everything that counts can be counted, and not everything that can be counted, counts." However, a more practical approach is to accommodate the need to collect both quantitative and qualitative data that are required for evidence-based measurement of impact. Indicators are very helpful in identifying the data requirements for impact assessment.

Ex post assessments

Our interest in assessing the impact of health microinsurance stems from the premise that under settings of voluntary and contributory enrollment, the population must be convinced that being insured is preferable to remaining uninsured. However, the preliminary question is what measurement of impact might contribute to catalyzing demand for health insurance among the potential customers.

SELF-TEST QUESTIONS

1. Define the term "impact." In the microinsurance context, what is the scope of assessing impact?
2. Distinguish between the *ex post* assessments and *ex ante* assessments of impact. Identify the end users of these assessments.

As we deal with health insurance, there is a temptation to consider whether health insurance improves health. An extensive systematic review of this question was carried out in the USA in 2004 (Levy and Meltzer, 2004, 2008); it reported that hundreds of studies stated that insured persons tend to have better health outcomes than uninsured persons. The authors of that report conceded that some studies provided convincing evidence that health insurance improves some health measures of some population sub-groups. However, the partial evidence falls short of establishing a systematic causal relationship between health insurance and health for entire populations because other, unobservable factors may influence the observed correlation between insurance and good health in many of the studies. We conclude that in the context of demonstrating the impact of CBHI, this line of inquiry is probably unsuitable, notably because the population may be too small to achieve statistical strength and because benefits packages are too partial to cover all health needs.

Other researchers were more interested in examining the impact of health insurance on financial and social results. For instance, a systematic review of the literature published in 2012 (Spaan *et al.*, 2012) chose to examine the impact of health insurance on no less than six parameters. These include the following: (i) resource generation to finance health services; (ii) financial protection of insured persons against catastrophic health expenditures; (iii) improved utilization of health care services; (iv) improved healthcare quality; (v) improved social inclusion; and (vi) improved involvement of the community in the organization of health services. This review looked at the impact literature relating to various forms of health insurance provision (CBHI, social health insurance, and private health insurance). We can thus recall their conclusions, especially as regards CBHI, which is our focus. Regarding CBHI, the study concludes the following, among other things:

(a) **There is strong evidence that CBHIs improve resource mobilization for health:** An analysis published a decade earlier (Preker *et al.*, 2001) claimed that one of the main weaknesses of the CBHI schemes is the low volume of revenues that they can mobilize from poor communities. The two findings are not contradictory, as they simply state that since the CBHI membership is contributory, the schemes can collect resources that were previously not paid for health insurance, but the overall volume is low, reflecting very low premiums.
(b) **CBHI schemes improve health service utilization:** Several studies echoed this finding with the caveat that the improvement was explainable by context-specific variables, which are not generalizable. For example, a study from Kenya dating back to 2012 concluded that "Insured members reported higher use of hospitalization care than the non-insured," … "this could be attributed to the fact JBHI has no per capita financial capping and does not require any copayments to access health care." Another study, published in 2018 on the situation in a location in Uganda regarding a small sub-group of the population, concluded that "voluntary CBHI increased health care utilization and reduced mortality for children under-5. However, the scheme required appreciable outside subsidy, which limits its wider application and replicability" (Haven *et al.*, 2018). Another study from Ethiopia

(Atnafu *et al.*, 2018) concluded that the insured reported a significantly higher rate of healthcare utilization than uninsured households.

The authors added an important caveat: "significant variations of enrollment status in community-based health insurance (CBHI) were observed in the following variables: educational status, family size, occupation, marital status, travel time to the nearest health institution, perceived quality of care, first choice of place for treatment during illness and expected healthcare cost of a recent treatment." Beyond the socioeconomic differences that might explain the higher utilization, the authors linked the high uptake with two distinct features. "First, the Ethiopian scheme is embedded within existing government administrative structures and … scheme performance and uptake are used as a yardstick to measure the success of the administration. Second, an existing social protection scheme was used to spread information, raise scheme awareness, and encourage uptake of health insurance" (Mebratie *et al.*, 2019). This information broadens the argument from "does health insurance lead to higher utilization of healthcare" to "does my CBHI gain the support of government to ensure that the members could access all health services provided by the government?" The study from Ethiopia offers evidence that corroborates an analysis published in 2016 (Dror *et al.*, 2016), which concluded that clarity about the legal or policy framework of operating the CBHI schemes encourages enrollments. The evidence from Ethiopia confirms that the government has effectively broadened outreach to grassroots groups even if it cannot fund the health insurance, by formulating supportive regulatory and policy provisions that leverage people's willingness to enroll in voluntary and contributory CBHI.

In summary, active and prospective customers of CBHI are interested in improving the utilization of healthcare. Proof of the nexus between being insured and higher utilization is evidence of a positive impact. Furthermore, the studies mentioned point that informal-sector populations view improved utilization as the result not merely of insurance but of successful use by the CBHI of symbiosis with the government (as a regulator and as a provider of services) that adds value over and beyond what their contributions could provide. People who agree to contribute want their money to deliver more services, rather than simply crowd out the government.

(c) **CBHI provides financial protection for members (measured by lower out-of-pocket expenditure):** Several more recent studies have echoed this finding. We mention here three examples. The first is a systematic review of the literature conducted in 2016 (Habib *et al.*, 2016) that concluded (based on 22 papers) that "micro health insurance, in the majority of cases, has been found to contribute to the financial protection of its beneficiaries, by reducing out-of-pocket health expenditure, catastrophic health expenditure, total health expenditure, household borrowings, and poverty." The second is from Rwanda, where CBHI is implemented nationwide as government policy. It found that being insured by the scheme significantly reduced annual per capita out-of-pocket spending, by about 83% of average per capita healthcare expenditure, compared to the baseline level in 2000. The impact, however, was more favorable to the rich than to the poor. The program also reduced the incidence of catastrophic healthcare spending significantly (Woldemichael *et al.*, 2019). The third example (Dror *et al.*, 2016) evaluated the financial protection that CBHIs extend by showing that after two years of being insured, the insured were less exposed to hardship financing (Binnendijk *et al.*, 2012) (i.e., borrowing with interest to fund healthcare costs). Hardship financing is often ignored because it is not counted as out-of-pocket expenditure on healthcare, yet it represents a considerable cost to the household. The other novel measurement of financial protection has been to measure the households' place in the income distribution (by quintiles) of their reference community. Movement from one quintile to another is called "economic mobility." The study found that the probability of an insured HH to benefit from quintile upgrade increased, and the risk of quintile downgrade decreased after being insured for two years. The study explains this finding, recognizing that more research could better expound the reasons for economic mobility.

As a side issue, we mention that some analysts, in the capacity of developing countries, to achieve health-related financial risk protection claim that low-income countries (let alone small CBHIs) cannot deliver the targets of the Sustainable Development Goals (SDGs) on this point in the next 20 years. First among those analysts is Verguet *et al.* (2017). In their paper, they argued that the projected achievements suggest that elimination of medical impoverishment will not be achieved by 2040 and that countries must urgently enact dramatic changes in policy to ensure financial risk protection to their populations.

(d) **There was only weak evidence of a positive impact of CBHI on the quality of care and social inclusion:** Quality of care is, of course, a rather vague concept. In the context of CBHIs that do not operate healthcare facilities, the real issue is what can CBHIs do to improve the quality of care. We mention here two studies about rather uncommon aspects of positive impact on the quality of care. The first study (conducted in rural India) looks at the reduction in self-medication as an indicator of improved healthcare seeking. *The* consumption of unprescribed medicines is recognized globally as a significant health risk that can lead to misdiagnosis, excessive or prolonged use of medicines, unsuitable dosage, drug interactions, and polypharmacy. The assumption tested was that *easier/more affordable access to healthcare for insured persons rendered self-medication less necessary*. The study of self-medication is, of course, independent of a uniform benefits package, which renders it relevant for impact analysis of CBHIs in multiple locations. The evidence in the cited study showed that post-intervention (i.e., when insurance was in operation for two years), self-medication was less practiced by insured HHs (Dror *et al.*, 2016). This reduction was conjured to be a positive change in health seeking/quality of care.

The second aspect has been to measure utilization by insured vs. uninsured persons of healthcare services provided by medically trained personnel. The implied assumption is that *health insurance enhances better quality of care when people access suitably trained professionals rather than untrained practitioners*. The insured group (composed of informal-sector workers in Bangladesh) reported significantly higher utilization of services by professionally trained staff than the uninsured group (Ahmed *et al.*, 2018). However, this study did not mention possible confounders (e.g., that may be because the investigated CBHI only reimbursed invoices of the medically trained providers or obtained a preferential pricing agreement). Thus, the doubt lingers whether the changed health-seeking pattern was inherent to insurance coverage, or may be due to other reasons.

The same difficulty of reporting an association (between being insured and an improvement) without proving the causality plagues another recent study from Ethiopia that aimed to measure the impact of CBHI on health-related quality-of-life (Gebru and Lentiro, 2018).

In summary, the demand-driven impact assessment of microinsurance is developing from a basic measurement of out-of-pocket expenditure to more nuanced interpretations of financial protection that include context-specific improvements of health-seeking practices. Considering that potential customers are interested in the local impact of their local CBHI, the expansion of studies to examine local improvements seems to be relevant and useful.

SELF-TEST QUESTIONS

1. Give evidence, cited in this chapter, to show that the CBHI schemes improve health service utilization.
2. With the support of evidence from the chapter, describe how CBHI provides financial protection for members.
3. Explain the findings of the two studies that demonstrated some uncommon aspects of the positive impact of CBHI on the quality of care.

Ex ante assessments

The second major reason to engage in impact assessment is the need to attract funding.

Gone are the days when projects were funded according to their input costs. Gone are also the days when there was a clear separation of the criteria and priorities of the public sector from the private for-profit sector. Today, funds for development labeled as "impact investments" are rapidly replacing traditional philanthropic granting. Impact investments are investments made to generate positive, measurable social, environmental, and governance impact alongside a financial return. The buzz words "Double Bottom Line" and "Triple Bottom Line" have created a different framework for the evaluation of investments, which led to the development of an ever-growing set of criteria to appraise companies and countries on how far advanced they are in respecting ESG factors. Environmental topics that are often considered relevant include climate change, natural resources, renewable energy, pollution and waste, environmental opportunities, and water. Social topics that are often considered relevant include human capital, product liability, stakeholder opposition, and social opportunities. Governance topics that are often considered relevant include corporate governance and corporate behavior.

The practice of ESG investing began in the 1960s at the impetus of certain investors (e.g., large pension funds of trade unions) that sought "socially responsible investing." The initial ESG practice led investors to create "negative lists," i.e., exclude from their portfolios stocks of business activities such as tobacco, weapons, highly polluting industries, or those that uphold undesirable political choices (e.g., the apartheid regime in South Africa). Today, the need to go beyond negative lists has led some companies to incorporate ESG factors into the investment process alongside traditional financial analysis.

Another supply driven action is to allocate corporate resources to make a positive impact on the environment under CSR. Originally, CSR started in the 1960s as a voluntary company-specific decision based on corporate ethic strategy. As such, it had to align with the business model. Examples of such alignment are the use of CSR to improve social services in catchment areas where the company draws its workforce or the protection of water in places where the company relies on natural water sources for its production activities. Today, the practice of CSR has become mandatory in a growing number of countries, governed by laws. With the transition to mandatory CSR came a widening of the interpretation of *improvements to the environment* to include the natural environment, the surrounding environment, and the social environment. The latter includes CSR policies to improve positive public relations and ethical standards to reduce business and legal risk by taking responsibility for corporate actions with consumers, employees, investors, communities, and others. Shareholders have questioned whether CSR activities contribute to shareholder value. One study of this question claimed that CSR activities create shareholder value if managers are appropriately monitored by long-term investors not to increase cash flow but to lower cash flow risk (Nguyen *et al.*, 2017).

The scope of topics of impact investing in general, including CSR activities, has become increasingly aligned to the 17 SDGs.[1] Some large companies have developed their framework for the evaluation of their impact portfolio.[2] Many other investors rely on consulting companies to guide their impact investment portfolio.

Moreover, recently, the Rockefeller Foundation teamed with others to create the Global Impact Investing Network (GIIN),[3] a non-profit organization dedicated to increasing the scale and effectiveness of impact investing around the world. The GIIN claims to be "the global champion of impact investing." At this stage, it builds critical infrastructure to make it easier for investors to translate their intentions into real impact results (notably its IRIS+ system[4]). IRIS+ encourages companies to adhere to the metrics GIIN has developed, which are designed to measure the Social Impact Objectives,[5] Environmental Impact Objectives,[6] and Sectors to Influence,[7] as well as financial performance metrics.

In conclusion, both the assessment and the impact of microinsurance are still in their infancy in terms of adapting to the rapid formalization of the *ex ante* assessment framework. Twenty years of promotion of microinsurance have led to the adoption of this form of social protection in many places, but mainly as stand-alone, often small projects. Stand-alone CBHI schemes are now challenged to prepare proposals and prospectuses for investors that respond to the complex framework that did not exist

---

[1] https://www.un.org/sustainabledevelopment/sustainable-development-goals/.

[2] For example, Zurich Insurance Group (Zurich) announced in March 2019 that it has for the first time successfully measured the environmental and resilience effects of its impact investment portfolio https://www.zurich.com/en/media/news-releases/2019/2019-0312-01.

[3] https://thegiin.org/about/.

[4] https://iris.thegiin.org/about/.

[5] https://iris.thegiin.org/metric/4.0/OD6247.

[6] https://iris.thegiin.org/metric/4.0/OD4108.

[7] https://iris.thegiin.org/metric/4.0/PD8808.

until recently. It is remarkable that philanthropic foundations have teamed with other stakeholders to create a support system to attract investors' capital toward impact investments. Development projects can perhaps seek inspiration from the metrics and logical framework. Ultimately, the success of impact investments depends on achieving impact at scale on the ground, where the development problems and opportunities are found.

SELF-TEST QUESTION

1. What do we mean by impact investments? Identify the ESG topics that are often considered for impact investments.

KEY TERMS

- **Economic mobility:** Taking the income distribution (by quintiles) of a reference community as the basis, movement from one quintile to another is called "economic mobility."
- ***Ex ante* assessments:** It is the expected impact before the funds are allocated to align with investors' *desiderata.*
- ***Ex post* assessments:** It means assessing the impact of projects/ programs after those interventions have occurred.
- **Hardship financing:** It means borrowing with interest to fund healthcare costs.
- **Impact:** Is means to have a substantial effect on someone or something.
- **Impact investments:** Investments made to generate positive, measurable social, environmental, and governance impact alongside a financial return are called impact investments.

Bibliography

Ahmed, S, Sarker, AR, Sultana, M, Chakrovorty, S, Ahmed, MW, Dorin, F, and Khan, J (2018) The Impact of Community-Based Health Insurance on the Utilization of Medically Trained Healthcare Providers among Informal Workers in Bangladesh. *PloS One*, 13(7), e0200265.

Atnafu, DD, Tilahun, H, and Alemu, YM (2018) Community-Based Health Insurance and Healthcare Service Utilization, North-West, Ethiopia: A Comparative, Cross-sectional Study. *BMJ Open*, 8, e019613.

Binnendijk, E, Koren, R, and Dror, DM (2012) Hardship Financing of Healthcare among Rural Poor in Orissa, India. *BMC Health Services Research*, 12(1), 23.

Dror, DM, Chakraborty, A, Majumdar, A, Panda, P, and Koren, R (2016) Impact of Community-Based Health Insurance in Rural India on Self-Medication & Financial Protection of the Insured. *The Indian Journal of Medical Research*, 143(6), 809–820.

Dror, DM, Hossain, SAS, Majumdar, A, Koehlmoos, TL, John, D, and Panda, PK (2016) What Factors Affect Voluntary Uptake of Community-Based Health Insurance Schemes in Low- and Middle-Income Countries? A Systematic Review and Meta-Analysis. *PLoS One*, 11(8), e0160479.

Spaan, E, Mathijssen, J, Tromp, N, McBain, F, Have, A ten, and Baltussen, R (2012) The Impact of Health Insurance in Africa and Asia: A Systematic Review. Geneva, WHO. *Bulletin of the World Health Organization*, 90, 685–692.

Habib, SS, Perveen, S, and Khuwaja, HM (2016) The Role of Micro Health Insurance in Providing Financial Risk Protection in Developing Countries — A Systematic Review. *BMC Public Health*, 16, 281.

Haven, N, Dobson, AE, Yusuf, K, Kellermann, S, Mutahunga, B, Stewart, AG, and Wilkinson, E (2018) Community-Based Health Insurance Increased Health Care Utilization and Reduced Mortality in Children Under-5, Around Bwindi Community Hospital, Uganda between 2015 and 2017. *Frontiers in Public Health*, 6, 281.

Levy, H and Meltzer, D (2004) What Do We Really Know about Whether Health Insurance Affects Health? In *Health Policy and the Uninsured: Setting the Agenda*, ed. C McLaughlin, pp. 179–204. Washington, DC: Urban Inst. Press.

Levy, H and Meltzer, D (2008) The Impact of Health Insurance on Health. *Annual Review of Public Health*, 29(1), 399–409.

Mebratie, AD, Sparrow, R, and Yilma, Z, Abebaw, D, Alemu, G, and Bedi, AS (2019) The Impact of Ethiopia's Pilot Community-Based Health Insurance Scheme on Healthcare Utilization and Cost of Care. *Social Science & Medicine*, 220(C), 112–119.

Nguyen, P-A, Kecskes, A, and Mansi, S (2017) Does Corporate Social Responsibility Create Shareholder Value? The Importance of Long-Term Investors

(November 25, 2017). Available at https://ssrn.com/abstract=2257846 (accessed 21 Aug 2019).

Preker, AS, Carrin, G, Dror, DM, Jakab, M, Hsiao, W, and Tenkorang, DA (2001) Role of Communities in Resource Mobilization and Risk Sharing: A Synthesis Report. Available from https://www.researchgate.net/publication/237254875_Role_of_Communities_in_Resource_Mobilization_and_Risk_Sharing_A_Synthesis_Report (accessed 8 May 2019).

Radermacher, R, McGowan, H, and Dercon, S (2012) What is the Impact of Microinsurance? In *Protecting the Poor: A Microinsurance Compendium.* Vol. II, ed. C Churchill and M Matul, pp. 59–82. Geneva: International Labour Organization.

Radermacher, R and Roth, K (Eds.) (2014) A Practical Guide to Impact Assessments in Microinsurance. A Joint Publication of the Microinsurance Network and the Micro Insurance Academy. Available at http://microinsurancenetwork.org/groups/practical-guide-impact-assessments-microinsurance (accessed 9 May 2019).

Gebru, T and Lentiro, K (2018) The Impact of Community-Based Health Insurance on Health-related Quality of Life and Associated factors in Ethiopia: A Comparative Cross-sectional Study. *Health and Quality of Life Outcomes*, 16, 110.

Verguet, S, Woldemariam, AT, Durrett, WN *et al.* (2017) Is the Sustainable Development Goal Target for Financial Risk Protection in Health Realistic? *BMJ Global Health*, 2, e000216.

Woldemichael, A, Gurara, D, and Shimeles, A (2019) The Impact of Community Based Health Insurance Schemes on Out-of-Pocket Healthcare Spending: Evidence from Rwanda. February 2019, IMF Working Paper Strategy, Policy and Review Department Doc. WP/19/38.

Selected Websites

The following websites pertain to the content of this chapter:

- For more information on defining and measuring Impact, go to https://clearimpact.com/how-to-define-impact/.

Index

I

K

Lightning Source UK Ltd.
Milton Keynes UK
UKHW020706060220
358268UK00001B/22